TWENTIETH-CENTURY INDONESIA

WILFRED T. NEILL

# TWENTIETH-CENTURY INDONESIA

COLUMBIA
University Press
New York
and London

Wilfred T. Neill is the author of *The Geography of Life* and *The Last of the Ruling Reptiles*.

Copyright © 1973 Columbia University Press
Printed in the United States of America

*Library of Congress Cataloging in Publication Data*
Neill, Wilfred T
   Twentieth-Century Indonesia.
   Bibliography: p. 391
   1. Indonesia—History. 2. Indonesia—Civilization.
3. Natural history—Indonesia. I. Title.
DS634.N45   1973     915.98'03'3     72-11718
ISBN 0-231-03547-0
ISBN 0-231-08316-5 (pbk)

*The decorative illustration appearing on chapter opening pages is a sketch by the author of a Balinese wood-carving on a rice-beater.*

9 8 7 6 5 4 3 2

*To the people of Indonesia,*
*with much affection*

# INTRODUCTION

From almost any standpoint—geological, biological, historical, cultural—the Republic of Indonesia is complex. Even the country's official motto, *Bhinneka Tunggal Ika,* emphasizes ethnic heterogeneity, the courtly Javanese phrase being translatable as "Unity in Diversity." This book is intended to unravel some of the complexities; to make Indonesia clearer in the mind's eye, and more intelligible to Westerners. There is urgent need to explain Asian attitudes and their environmental, cultural, and historical justification. For three centuries or more, many peoples in southern and eastern Asia had the problem of responding as best they could to stimuli from the West; but this tide began to turn when Japan launched her military might against the Allies in World War II. Ever since then, the West has found itself responding to military, economic, or political stimuli from such Asian nations as Communist China, Taiwan, Japan, Korea, Viet Nam, Laos, Cambodia, Malaysia, Indonesia, India, Pakistan, Bangladesh, Jordan, and others. This new tide of history is just getting under way; it has not even begun to near its peak, and Westerners will find an increasing need to ponder Eastern events. Specialists in Asian studies are constantly appalled by the way in which Western nations, trying to cope with such events, take little heed of Asian attitudes and rationales, and so flounder or else leap at expedients of the moment.

This book begins with the Indonesian land, its position on the face of the globe, its fragmentation into 10,000 islands, its soils and mineral productions. Description of the land leads naturally to that of the climate, which reflects geographic position and topography; and accordingly I have ended Chapter I with remarks on Indonesian temperatures and rainfall. Topography, soils, and climates interact to determine the vegetation, and so Chapter II describes the rainforest, the monsoon forest, and other vegetation types. Chapter II also deals with the plant species, III with the wild beasts, IV with the life of the waters. In this opening material I have looked on the land, along with its climate, vegetation, flora, and fauna, as the backdrop for man's drama. Thus, I have emphasized topics of obvious human concern: the arable soils and the processes that affect them, the volcanic eruptions that prove a mixed blessing, the gold and silver that lured the early adventurers, the tin and oil that attract modern investors, the monsoons and their meaning, the occasional catastrophes of nature, the impact of man on the tropical vegetation, the way Indonesians regard or utilize the wild and domestic plants and animals about them. The length of Chapter III does not reflect my special concern with zoology; Indonesians are in contact with a spectacular fauna which commands not only their attention but also that of scientists, conservationists, and educated people in many parts of the world. But having found no natural history work that covers this fauna, I have tried at least to mention virtually all the mammal, bird, reptile, amphibian, and fish families that live on the land or in the fresh waters of Indonesia.

The remaining and major portion of the book deals directly with the Indonesian people and their story. In telling this story I have tried very hard to counteract the chauvinism that pervades so much of Western writing. Of course chauvinism is only human, but it flourishes most rankly in the absence of facts. Much of the Western world heard little of Indonesia until World War II, a time when passions were high and all the warring nations were propagandizing their own people in a way intended to whip up patriotic emotions. A good many mistaken Western notions about the East have been inherited from that unfortunate day. Also, the less creditable activities of the Dutch colonial regime, and of several Western nations during Indonesia's Revolutionary War and Civil

War, have been glossed over in much of the previous literature. But these activities are precisely the ones that determined subsequent Indonesian attitudes toward the Netherlands, Britain, the United States, and the United Nations; they should not be elided in an objective work. With Asian countries becoming progressively more important on the international scene, the basis of their views, responses, and challenges should be made known. My account of Indonesia's history may reveal her modern attitudes to have been reasonable in the light of her experiences.

Chapter V is much simplified in its treatment of the peopling of Indonesia, but rather than specify the archeological problems that still exist in the islands, I preferred to develop the point that Indonesian ethnic diversity results from the differential spread of physical types, languages, and cultures. Present-day Indonesia has a continuum of cultures from Stone Age to modern, and thinking the modern to need minimal explanation, I have devoted a good part of this chapter to the life of certain less advanced peoples, inhabitants of Irian Barat. I wanted to show that these islanders' basic needs are much like those of everyone else, and their culture, however unfamiliar in some of its details, is highly organized and adapted to local conditions. Comparable life-ways once existed widely over Indonesia, providing a base to which more advanced culture traits were added selectively. Chapter VI describes the effect of Indians, Arabs, and Portuguese on Indonesia, to which they were lured by a traffic in natural products and an opportunity to missionize. As it happened, Christianity made headway in the islands only among less advanced tribes, but Indian and Arab religious thought profoundly affected the outlook of the dominant Indonesian ethnic groups, and so I have tried to explain certain Hindu, Buddhist, and Muslim tenets. Perhaps the reader will be surprised to learn what the Hindu, Buddhist, Judaeo-Christian, and Muslim mythologies have in common, and borrowed from one another. Hostilities have often been provoked over the fable component of the major faiths, and it is time now to emphasize instead the ethical and moralistic component, as well as common origin within a broad Eurasian zone where metaphysical and other thinking first advanced beyond the Neolithic level.

Chapter VII is long, for it deals with the lengthy period of Dutch hegemony over the islands. This chapter and the succeeding one bring the story up through the end of the Sukarno regime, becoming more detailed as they do so. I have interwoven Sukarno's biography with certain episodes of the twentieth century, partly because he was involved with many of these happenings, but also because I wanted to suggest that Asian leaders, like other people, cannot be expected always to act out of wholly dispassionate objectivity. The reader may find unexpected observations in the account of Sukarno, who often received skimpy or slanted press coverage in the West. For example, how many readers know that he had a hard-earned master's degree in engineering, could converse in two Asian and three European languages, and was a talented playwright? Or that he had already spent almost twelve years in prison or exile, merely for daring to speak and write against Dutch colonialism, at the time he was released by the Japanese, who promised independence? Or that he was personally humiliated in Washington and fêted royally in Peking at a time when he was casting about for encouragement in the staggering task of holding his young republic together?

Chapters VII and VIII may in fact hold several surprises. How many readers know that when Indonesia declared her independence two days after Japanese surrender in World War II, the first major battle of her Revolutionary War had to be fought not against the Dutch but against British troops who were well supplied with American equipment? Or that when the young Republic of Indonesia was torn by a civil war, the United States armed the rebel government against the established one? Or that when Sukarno announced confrontation of Malaya over a British-proposed five-state Federation of Malaysia, one of the five states had sought Indonesian aid in a struggle for full autonomy, another was involved with the Philippines in a dispute over a boundary not far from Indonesian Borneo, and Sukarno had expressed willingness to accept the federation if a United Nations referendum proved it acceptable to the two Bornean states that adjoined Indonesian territory?

Many Americans have lately been disturbed by the length and the death toll of the Viet Nam conflict, but how many have heard of the Atjeh War which lasted over thirty years, and which cost a quarter of a million lives before the Atjehnese of northern Sumatra were reduced to colonial subservience? There has lately been furor over the My Lai incident in which an American sergeant was accused of killing 102 Vietnamese during the course of a war; but how many Westerners recall (as Indonesians can) the Westerling Affair, in which a Dutch captain was accused of butchering, beheading, and executing 40,000 inhabitants of the island of Sulawesi during the course of a "Pacification Exercise"?

In Chapter IX I have offered only a brief account of General Suharto's new order in Indonesia, for the simple reason that it is new, just getting under way. For all her misfortunes, Indonesia was twice blessed. In the first half of the present century the winds of freedom were blowing ever more strongly through the world, but the Indonesian masses could take advantage of them only if they found a charismatic man behind whom they could rally, a man who wanted to be the very distillation of their attitudes and who would suffer imprisonment and exile in their behalf. Such a man emerged in the person of Sukarno. Yet, regardless of how a revolutionary may be venerated, there is no historical need for him when his revolution is won, for he is not psychologically constituted to grapple with the social, political, and economic problems that beset a new nation. And so Indonesians then came to need a man who could control affairs not through any cult of personality but through a well-established organization, a man whose sturdiness and honesty would command international respect, and who would buckle down to difficult tasks that had gone neglected. After several years' time and deep trauma, such a man emerged in the person of General Suharto.

Several of my favorite subjects have been omitted from this introductory book. It was tempting to review the old Indonesian literature: the regional writings in Javanese, Madurese, Balinese, Makasarese, Atjehnese, Sundanese, Minangkabau, and Malayan; the Arab-influenced *hikajat*, adventurous biographies; the *sedjarah* with their emphasis on genealogy; the free-verse *gurindam* and the short love poems called *sjair*. Even more tempting to review the twentieth-century novels and poems of social protest, and the works of the Indonesian modernists; but literature is better read than discussed, and there was no room for lengthy translations. I was at least able to fill Chapter X with *pantun*, the very revealing quatrains so popular with the Malayan-speaking peoples. I would also have been glad to pen a chapter on traditional Indonesian music and theater: the *wajang kulit* of Central Java, in which flat leather puppets are brought to shadowy life by the *dalang* who is much more than a puppeteer; the *wajang gedog*, in which the accompanying *gamelan*, orchestra, is tuned to the seven-toned *pelog* system; the Balinese *gender wajang*, accompanied by two or four instruments tuned to the five-toned *slendro* system; the Sundanese *wajang golek*, in which three-dimensional puppets are manipulated; the long *matjapat* solos; the *wajang orang* dances with their stylized postures. But from the modern Balinese *gamelan gong kebiar* to the age-old chants of Irian Barat tribesmen, Indonesian music should be heard, the performers seen. The book's bibliography will guide the interested reader to studies on many topics that I did not discuss, and to some commercial recordings of Indonesian vocal and instrumental performances.

My three periods of residence in Indonesia chanced to fall in as many different subdivisions of the country's modern history; that is to say, times before, during, and after World War II. At each period my principal concerns were different; and at one time or another during the years of residence, I came to know Sumatra, Java, Bali, Halmahera, Morotai, Biak, Supiori, the Padaidoris, and Irian Barat, as well as such nearby lands as the Philippines, Papua, and North-East New Guinea. But whatever the concerns of the moment, I have maintained an especial interest in the Malayo-Polynesian languages, which were carried to Indonesia, Melanesia, Polynesia, Micronesia, Madagascar, and other regions from a homeland in what is now Viet Nam and Cambodia. I have particularly enjoyed the study of Malayan, which in modernized version is Bahasa Indonesia, the official language of the republic; but I discovered that if a Westerner like myself really wanted to understand Malayan, with its many figures of speech, he would do well also to study the history, culture, environment, and day-to-day experiences of the native-born speakers. This study, as much as residence in and travel through the islands, emboldened me to attempt a broad treatment of Indonesia, even though most previous authors have preferred to unfold only their own particular specialties.

Bahasa Indonesia was developed out of Malayan by a commission of scholars at a time when there was a pressing need for an Indonesian national language and for widespread literacy in it. Accordingly, the spelling of a good many Malayan words was simplified by fiat. Since this book is about Indonesia, I have felt constrained to follow the commission's recommendations, but in some instances have done so only with reluctance. For, contrary to the recommendations, I would retain the "rough breathing" sign (') in certain Malayan words borrowed from the Arabic, and keep the apostrophe that serves as a glottal check and as a substitute for the Arabic *alif*. Almost anyone familiar with literary Malayan is likely to be perturbed by some Bahasa Indonesia simplifications of spelling, for in most cases, the arbitrarily simplified words are of much historical and etymological interest; many of the irregular spellings in Malayan are those of words borrowed from the Sanskrit in the days of Indianization, or from the Arabic in later days when Islam was spreading through the islands. The commission acknowledged that the Indonesian variant of Malayan might undergo further alteration in the future, especially since a language is changed not by decree but by usage. Taking this statement as an invitation to comment on possible future trends in Bahasa Indonesia, I suggest that in any written language, the literary style need not be wholly abandoned simply to cater to the limitations of the would-be or barely literate. In being rather conservative where the commission was liberal, I do not merely indulge a personal attitude toward linguistic changes; Malayan is the property not only of Indonesia but also of Singapore and Malaysia, where the older and more scholarly usages prevail. These usages are likewise common in a worldwide body of literature relating to the Malayan-speaking world.

I have gladly accepted the commission's replacement of the awkward Dutch *oe* by its English phonetic equivalent *u*. However, such replacement creates problems in the treatment of certain personal names, for some Indonesians extended it even to their own appellations. After spelling reform, Indonesia's greatest revolutionary continued to sign his name "Soekarno," but said that "Sukarno" might be used by others in references to him. I have referred to him throughout as Sukarno, except in circumstances (for instance, in quotations) where the original spelling is called for. Since Indonesia's present leader, General Suharto, came to international attention only after the promulgation of Bahasa Indonesia, I have used only the modern version of his name.

In the text, I have cited some Malayan words as having been borrowed from the Sanskrit, Arabic, Portuguese, or Persian. All such loan-words became altered in pronunciation and orthography; I give only the derived form, which may depart markedly from the original. I have not added an English plural ending, "s", to Malayan root-words, since these can be regarded as already plural. I have used "Hindu" as a religious designation only, without reference to nationality or ethnic group.

Finally, I have not troubled anyone to answer questions or to read any part of the manuscript prior to its submission, so my interpretation of Indonesian affairs should not be held against anyone else.

Wilfred T. Neill
New Port Richey, Florida

# CONTENTS

North

95    100    105°    110°    115

Bangkok

BURMA

THAILAND

CAMBODIA

SOUTH VIET NAM

Mekong R.

Saigon

10°

GULF OF SIAM

SOUTH CHINA SEA

SABANG

Banda Atjeh

5°

George Town

MALAYSIA (WEST)

Medan

Lake Toba

Prapat

Kuala Lumpur

Singapore

Selat Melaka

SIMEULUE

KEP. NATUNA

KEP. ANAMBAS

BRUNEI

SABAH

MALAYSIA (EAST)

SARAWAK

NIAS

0° Equator

KEP. RIAU

KEP. LINGGA

Pontianak

KALIMANTAN

Balikpapan

Padang

Djambi

BANGKA

GREATER

SUNDA

KEP. MENTAWAI

Pegunungan Barisan

Palembang

Selat Karimata

BELITUNG

SUMATRA

Bengkulu

Bandjarmasin

INDIAN

5°

ENGGANO

Telukbetung

Selat Sunda

JAVA

KEP. KARIMUNDJAWA

SEA

BAWEAN

KEP. KANGEAN

RAKATA

Djakarta

Bogor

Semarang

MADURA

Surabaja

Bandung

JAVA

Madiun

Djokjakarta

Surakarta

Kediri

Malang

BALI

Singaradja

Denpasar

PENIDA

LOMBOK

SUMBAWA

GEOGRAPHICAL EQUIVALENTS

KEP. (Kepulauan)........Archipelago

Peg. (Pegunungan)......Mountain Range

Puntjak .................Mountain Peak

Selat.....................Strait

BARAT..................West

Teluk.....................Bay

10°

CHRISTMAS I. (Aust.)

OCEAN

95°    100°    105°    110°    115°

Manila

125                130°                135°                140

P A C I F I C

PHILIPPINES

SULU
SEA

THE REPUBLIC OF

**INDONESIA**

Scale of Miles
100        0        100        200        300

O C E A N

CELEBES
SEA                KEP. TALAUD

KEP.
SANGIHE

Morotai

Manado                KEP.                Equator                0°

Gorontalo        Ternate    HALMAHERA

Teluk Tomini    TIDORE    WAIGEO

KEP.
TOGIAN        BATJAN                NUMFOOR    SUPIORI

KEP.                                            BIAK
BANGGAI        SALAWATI    Sorong

SULAWESI        KEP. SULA    KEP. OBI    MISOOL        JAPEN    Djajapura

Teluk Berau                Teluk    Tariku-Taritatu Plain    NORTH-
BURU        CERAM    Fakfak    Sarera                        EAST
WOWONI        AMBON    CERAM        Kaimana    Puntjak    Peg.    NEW
                        KEP.            Sukarno    Djajawidjaja    GUINEA
akasar        BUTUNG        WATUBELA    Teluk        Peg.
KABAENA                            Kamrau    Sudirman    IRIAN
MUNA    KEP.                Mimika                BARAT
SELAJAR    TUKANGBESI    KEP. KAI                    NEW
                        (EWAB)        KEP.            GUINEA    PAPUA
LORES    SEA    BANDA    SEA            ARU
SER    SUNDAS            KEP.    KEP.            DOLAK
FLORES    WETAR    KEP.    BABAR    TANIMBAR        Merauke
    KEP.    LETI
    SOLOR    ATAURO    KEP.
    KEP. ALOR    (Port.)    SERMATA
OCUSSI-AMBENO    Dili    A R A F U R A    S E A
PADAR    (Port.)    TIMOR    PORTUGUESE
SULU  SEA        TIMOR                            10°
UMBA            Kupang
SAWU    ROTI

TIMOR                                            CORAL

SEA            Port Darwin                        SEA

A U S T R A L I A

120°        125°            130°            135°            140°

# CHAPTER I

# INDONESIA: THE PHYSICAL

# SETTING

WHERE the Indian Ocean merges with the tropical Pacific, some 3,000 inhabited islands are strung out in a broad belt across the equator. Most of these islands, along with perhaps 7,000 tiny islets and the near-by waters, make up the *Republik Indonesia,* by population the fifth largest of nations, and by area the sixth.

When the Venetian traveler Marco Polo sailed the South China Sea in the thirteenth century, the first harbinger of European irruption into the fabled Indies, he was rather disturbed to hear that the island now called Sumatra "lies so far to the southward as to render the North Star invisible." In fact, the greater part of Indonesia lies in the southern hemisphere, where the mariner's beacon is not Polaris but the Southern Cross. The equator, passing through southern Halmahera, northern Sulawesi, central Borneo, and central Sumatra, roughly bisects this tropical land; for the Republic extends to about 6 degrees to the north of the equator and to about 11 degrees south of it. In the Riau Archipelago of northern Indonesia, there are places no more than a dozen miles from the Asian mainland; while to the southeast, in the mangrove swamps of Irian Barat, there are places no more than 150 miles from Australia. During the years of the Indonesian Revolution, 1945 to 1961, a Malayan phrase meaning "from Sabang to Merauke" was popularly used to describe the expanse of territory that hopefully would be freed from colonial exploitation. The port of Merauke in the southeastern part of the country is more than 3,000 miles farther east and more than 1,000 miles farther south than the island of Sabang in the extreme northwestern part. And so Indonesia, with its islands and seas together, is almost as large as the United States; but, of course, much Indonesian territory is water. The Republic's actual land area, about 735,865 square miles, is a little less than half the land area of Europe, and less than a quarter that of the United States. Still, nations with more land than Indonesia include only Canada, Communist China, the Soviet Union, the United States, Brazil, Australia, India, Argentina, and Mexico; and of these nine giants, only the Soviet Union and the United States are generally regarded as richer in natural resources—at least in those kinds that can presently be utilized.

Four centuries after Marco Polo, the literate pirate William Dampier was amused to see that in the East Indies there was confusion about the days of the week. When the Portuguese, Dutch, and English traders held the day to be Friday, it was only Thursday by Dampier's reckoning, and by that of some Spaniards. The matter was of considerable interest to the Muslim inhabitants of the coastal cities, for Friday was (as Dampier put it) "the Day of their Sultans' going to their Mosques." Local residents agreed with the Portuguese, Dutch, and English; *hari djumat,* the day of assembly, was the European Friday. The reason for the confusion is easy to see. Dampier and some of the Spaniards had reached the East Indies by sailing west from the New World, while the European traders had sailed east around the Cape of Good Hope; and in those days, of course, the International Date Line and the time zones had not yet been established. Today, Indonesia overlaps three of these zones. As in other parts of the world, the zonal boundaries are irregular, fixed in a way that places commercially linked areas in the same zone. The Indonesian capital of Djakarta, in western Java, is six hours ahead of London and twelve hours ahead of New York City. All of Sumatra and Java, along with some nearby smaller islands, are on Djakarta time. Borneo and Sulawesi, as well as various smaller islands south of Sulawesi, are one hour ahead of Djakarta, while the Moluccas and Irian Barat are two hours ahead.

For convenience, the archipelagos of Indonesia are often divided into four geographic groups: the Greater Sundas, the Lesser Sundas, the Moluccas, and Irian Barat (western New Guinea) with its nearby islands. The Greater Sundas group includes Sumatra, Java, and Sulawesi, as well as Borneo, which is predominantly Indonesian. Most Indonesians would use the spellings Sumatera and Djawa for the first two of these islands, and might refer to all Borneo as Kalimantan. When the Indonesians finally became a free people after long-continued colonial status and a revolt against it, they rejected many place-names that had been imposed on them by Europeans, returning in most cases to older names of local origin. The name Kalimantan is an old and poetic one, referring originally to a fabled isle in a legendary sea. In Malayan, of which the official Indonesian language is a modernized version, *kalimantang* means "appearing as a shining streak," a splendid designation for an island in a tropical sea. A broad strip of northern Borneo is not Indonesian (independent little Brunei and East Malaysia, which includes Sarawak and Sabah); and so to avoid confusion, the name Borneo may be used for the entire island, leaving Kalimantan for the Indonesian portion alone.

Sulawesi is the currently preferred designation for the curiously sprawling island that was long known as Celebes. Sulawesians say that early Portuguese explorers, asking about the island's name, kept their eyes on iron knives carried by the inhabitants. These inhabitants, mistaking the question, replied "*Sele besi*," iron knives; and so the island was improperly dubbed Celebes. Of course, the story may be only a legend, an effort to rationalize what was originally nothing more than a mispronunciation of Sulawesi; for the early European explorers were casual in their approach to indigenous place-names, some of which were rendered in several versions or even assigned to the wrong areas. "Borneo," for example, is but a European rendition of Brunei; while to Marco Polo, the present Borneo was "Java Major" and Sumatra was "Java Minor." Polo's "Sundur" was described as being an uninhabited island, but Sunda was an old designation for West Java. Because Sunda once guarded a maritime bottleneck through which much shipping passed, its name became widely known; hence the reference to western and parts of central Indonesia as the Sundas, Greater and Lesser.

The Lesser Sundas group includes the double chain of islands from Bali eastward through Timor. Only part of Timor is Indonesian; its eastern half is Portuguese, as is the nearby island of Ataúro and islets such as Jaco. There is also a Portuguese enclave, Okusi Ambeno (Ocussi-Ambeno), in western Timor. Holdings in or near Timor and the island of Macao off the coast of China are all that remains of Portugal's formerly vast empire in the South Pacific. *Timor* is simply Malayan for "east." Indonesians apply the name Nusa Tenggara to the Lesser Sundas. *Nusa* is a Javanese word adopted into Malayan, and meaning "islands"; *tenggara* is Malayan for "southeast." A third Indonesian island group, the Moluccas, was once ruled by a man called Maluche or Maluku, and the early Portuguese explorers referred to "King Maluku's Islands," a usage later corrupted to "Moluccas." At least, so goes the tradition. Indonesians now refer to the Moluccas as Maluku, but the two names are so similar that the more familiar one need not be abandoned. The Moluccas group includes islands lying east of Sulawesi and north of the Lesser Sundas: the Arus, the Tanimbars, Buru, Ceram, the Sulas, Obi, Batjan, Halmahera, Morotai, and the Talauds, to name the most important. These comparatively small islands are not often remarked on today, and it is strange to realize that they once played a major role in the world's history. For the Moluccas were called the Spice Islands in the days when a more valuable cargo than spices could scarcely be loaded. To the Spice Islands came the merchant ships of Portugal, Spain, England, and the Netherlands—European nations which would oust the Chinese and Arab traders, squabble with each other over the South Pacific, and try to stake out colonial empires there. Today, old forts and churches, mostly fallen into ruins, are tangible Moluccan reminders of the early spice trade.

The fourth and last group, as noted, includes the western half of New Guinea. This was formerly known as Netherlands New Guinea, but has been Indonesian since 1963, and has been dubbed Irian Barat. *Irian* is one Indonesian name for the island of New Guinea. Its derivation is uncertain; *irian* could mean "spitefulness," perhaps in reference to the New Guinea tribesmen who have been notably hostile toward intruders. *Barat* is a Malayan word meaning "west." By people in the Moluccas, New Guinea was called *Papua*, a word meaning "woolly hair," and referring to a distinguishing characteristic of most New Guineans. The usage was picked up by spice traders in the Moluccas and carried back to Europe. Today, of course, the name Papua is restricted to the southeastern quarter of New Guinea, outside Indonesian territory. Salawati, Misoöl, and the former Schouten Eilanden (Biak, Numfoor, and Japen) lie close to Irian Barat and might be grouped with it. The eastern half of New Guinea, made up of Papua to the south and North-East New Guinea to the north, is administered by Australia as a Territory.

This four-part grouping of the Indonesian islands is often seen and is sometimes very useful, but its usefulness depends on the subject under discussion. For example, if one is concerned with the Indonesian distribution of certain wildlife—say the mammals— then a Greater Sundas group is recognizable; for the four principal islands of that group, all of them large and environmentally diverse, received their mammal life chiefly from the tropics of continental Asia. But if one is concerned with the distribution of people, it is immediately obvious that a Greater Sundas group has little homogeneity. Java is the most densely populated region on earth, while Borneo is one of the most sparsely populated. As another example, the islands of the Lesser Sundas might have various physical features in common, but when it comes to human affairs, Bali must be set apart from the others; for the Balinese differ from most nearby islanders in religion, art styles, and many customs. In fact, when human affairs are directly involved, many of the islands of Indonesia are better treated individually.

During Dutch colonial times, the present Indonesia—then the Netherlands East Indies and Netherlands New Guinea—was subdivided into provinces which functioned as administrative districts.

With some modification the subdivision was carried over into post-colonial times, and the province names are worth nothing, for they often appear in the historical and sociological literature. Atjeh Province includes northern Sumatra, Simeulue, and the Banjak Islands. Just south of Atjeh is the North Sumatra Province, extending from Nias and the Batu Islands eastward across Sumatra. West Sumatra Province includes the Mentawais and a broad strip along the western slope of Sumatra, while Riau Province reaches from the eastern lowlands of central Sumatra eastward through the Riaus, Linggas, Anambas, Tambilans, and Natunas. South of Riau, and restricted to the eastern versant of Sumatra, is the small province of Djambi. The rest of Sumatra, along with Bangka and Belitung, makes up South Sumatra Province. West Java Province occupies the western part of Java; Central Java Province includes central Java and the Karimundjawa Islands; and East Java Province is made up of eastern Java, with Madura, Bawean, and the Kangeans. Kalimantan is divided into West, Central, South, and East Kalimantan Provinces. North Sulawesi Province extends from northern Sulawesi northward through the Talauds, South Sulawesi Province from southern Sulawesi southward through the Tukangbesis, Bone Rate, and Madu. Maluku Province does not correspond very well to the geographic Moluccas, stretching as it does from Morotai and western Halmahera westward through the Sulas and southward through Wetar, the Letis, the Tanimbars, and the Arus. Some provinces—for example, Atjeh—correspond fairly well to the distribution of an ethnic group, but most do not; and Maluku Province is ethnically so very heterogeneous that there have been proposals to quarter it. West Irian Province includes not only Irian Barat, Salawati, Waigeo, and the Biak-Numfoor-Japen group but also a section of east-central Halmahera. Bali Province is small, encompassing only Bali and nearby Penida. West Nusa Tenggara Province is made up of Lombok and Sumbawa, and East Nusa Tenggara Province of the islands from Sumba and Flores eastward through Alor and Indonesian Timor. Thus, West and East Nusa Tenggara together do not equal the expanse of the geographic Lesser Sundas.

Each province has its peculiarities. Atjeh calls to mind the Atjeh-

6

nese, orthodox Muslims who fought Dutch colonialism for so long. North Sumatra is the home of the Nias Islanders with their ceremonial armor and megalithic shrines; the home also of the Batak, who passed from cannibalism to Christianity in a few generations, and in whose land is one of the world's most scenic lakes, Toba. West Sumatra is the home of the Minangkabau, heterodox Muslims who contributed greatly to the genesis of modern Indonesian literature, and from whom came such political leaders as Mohammad Hatta, Soetan Sjahrir, and the Hadji Agus Salim, as well as many poets and novelists. (Anthropologists may think of the Minangkabau in connection with gabled long-houses, and a social system emphasizing descent and inheritance from the female line.) Riau Province calls to mind a swampland with oil wells, and, particularly in the Riau and Lingga archipelagos, a populace who speak exceptionally pure Malayan. Djambi Province recalls an ancient day when its principal town, also known as Djambi, was a cultural and commercial center of the Malays, and Westerners had not yet arrived to exploit the island's mineral resources. South Sumatra Province is now linked with oil shipment through the river port of Palembang, and with tin mining on Bangka and Belitung; but Palembang, too, was anciently the capital of an independent state. West Java Province is the land of the Sundanese, but it also includes Djakarta, the nation's capital, with a heterogeneous population of around 3,000,000. In the comparatively rainy, forested, westerly part of this province, some ethnic groups keep to the old ways, and the Darul Islam rebels, Muslim fanatics, hid out there until the 1960s. In Central Java, inhabited mostly by Javanese, and in East Java where Javanese and Madurese intermingle, the old Javanese-Hindu culture held on longest, and in the southern parts of these provinces are many ruins and restorations dating from Hindu and Buddhist times; but on the north coast of the two subdivisions are seaport cities, including the naval base of Surabaja. Bali Province, famous out of all proportion to its size, is the home of the Balinese, who are Hindu-animist in belief, and whose charm lies in their combination of a simple peasant economy with a rich cultural heritage—a rare combination indeed. (But Bali's Denpasar is a modern city whose general appearance is familiar to Westerners.)

7

And so on through the list of provinces: each has its capital city, its peculiar history, and its characteristic ethnic groups—about 350 such groups, with 250 mutually unintelligible languages, just in the islands west of Irian Barat. But Indonesian cultures and history afford material for later chapters. First, the islands themselves should be described, especially in terms of what they offer man.

It is interesting that of the ten largest islands in the world, five belong wholly or in part to Indonesia: New Guinea is the second largest and Borneo the third, while Sumatra, Sulawesi, and Java hold fifth, eighth, and tenth places, respectively.

A complex arrangement of land and sea attests to mighty geologic forces at work in this part of the world during past ages. The more easterly of the islands—Waigeo, Salawati, Misoöl, the Arus, the Biak-Japen-Numfoor group, and New Guinea—are the exposed portions of an otherwise submerged platform called the Sahul Shelf, a part of the Australian continental shelf. Some islands of northwestern Indonesia—the Mentawai Archipelago, Sumatra, Bangka and Belitung, Java with nearby Madura and Bali, the Riau and Lingga archipelagos, and Borneo—are the exposed portions of another platform, the Sunda Shelf, which is part of the Asian continental shelf. Between the two platforms is a deep-sea area in which marine sediments have accumulated to great thickness, and into which volcanic ash has been carried by submarine sliding and the slow but powerful currents of the deep. Sailing toward Bintan in northern Indonesia, Marco Polo noted that "the sea, for the space of sixty miles, is not more than four fathoms in depth, which obliges those who navigate it to lift the rudders of their ships, in order that they might not touch the bottom." He was over the Sunda Shelf, much of which is but shallowly submerged. Polo would have been surprised if he had learned the depth of the water beyond the shelf. The Sulu Sea, the Celebes Sea, the Banda Sea, and the Flores Sea are all more than three miles deep. Mountain ranges, vast but submerged, rise from the sea bottom to the east and west of Indonesia and in the gap between the Sunda and Sahul shelves.

Beginning possibly around the end of the Cretaceous period, perhaps 63 million years ago, the deep-sea area and parts of the

Sunda Shelf were compressed and folded, thrown up into two parallel ridges, which here and there appear above water as islands. This folding extends northwest beyond Indonesia. Its northward course is marked by the Nicobar and the Andaman Islands, the Arakan Range of western Burma, and finally by the Himalayas, which swing westward. Each of the two Indonesian ridges has the shape of a great arc with a northwardly turning hook at its eastern end. The more westerly of these two ridges is marked by small islands that parallel the west coast of Sumatra, as well as by Sumba, Timor, and the Tanimbar (Timor Laut) group, with Ceram and Buru forming the hook. The eastern ridge is marked principally by Sumatra, Java, and a single line of islands from Bali to Wetar, with the Bandas at the tip of this arc's hook. The two ridges are different in certain geologic features, notably in the degree of volcanic activity. On the islands of the westerly arc, such activity has nearly or quite ceased, and ominous volcanic peaks are not a prominent feature of the landscape. In contrast, the islands of the easterly arc are dotted with volcanos. Indeed, from almost any point in this arc at least one volcanic cone is likely to be visible, perhaps slumbering blue-gray on the distant horizon, or perhaps actively trailing a plume of smoke by day, and reddening the sky by night. A majority of Indonesians spend their lives in sight of a volcanic crater.

Indonesian volcanos are not confined to the easterly ridge, for they are also present on Sulawesi and in the northern Moluccas. In the stretch of islands from Sumatra and Java eastward through the Bali-Wetar chain, and thence northward through Sulawesi and the Moluccas, more than 400 volcanos exist, and more than 100 of these have been active in historic times. About 77 of them are regarded as still active, but the figure is tentative, for a crater will occasionally come to life after decades or even centuries of quiescence. For example, in the year 1646 the little volcanic island of Makian, west of Halmahera, was rent by a violent eruption, which opened a chasm into the heart of the crater. In 1860, when the English naturalist-explorer Alfred Russel Wallace visited Makian, he found it clothed to the summit in vegetation, and with a dozen populous villages on its flanks. But in 1862, after 215 quiet years, Makian exploded again, killing most of the inhabitants, showering

9

nearby islands with ash, and darkening the air with dust at Ternate 35 miles away.

As another example, in 1883 the volcanic island of Krakatau (more accurately Rakata), west of Java, blew up with inconceivable violence, a blast in the 10,000-megaton range. Six cubic miles of earth, rock, forest, farms, people, livestock, and wildlife were blown into the upper atmosphere to drift as dust for years, providing the world with unusually colorful sunsets. One might suppose this explosion to have liberated whatever pressures existed in the earth beneath Krakatau; yet in 1927 it became evident that something was going on beneath the lagoon that now covered the crater remnant. In 1928 a small, new volcano appeared above the water, and continued to build its cone for years thereafter. Indonesians dubbed it *Anak Krakatau*—"Krakatau's baby." Gunung Agung ("prominent mountain") on Bali, quiet for more than a century, erupted three times in 1963, taking 1,700 lives and leaving 87,000 people homeless; and then nearby Batur, quiet since the 1920s, exploded and forced 1,200 people to flee their villages.

Indonesian volcanos differ considerably among themselves in size, details of shape, and degree of activity. Some of them rise from plains as isolated, symmetric cones; but others are clustered, or perhaps stand aligned on mountain ridges. Composite volcanos, after long periods of dormancy, are likely to explode with exceptional violence. Single or composite, a volcano may be quickly altered by an eruption, or slowly altered during dormancy by erosion and other natural processes. Papandajang in Java is now about 8,600 feet high, but it was once much higher; in the year 1772 it blew its summit away, destroying 40 villages. Tengger, also in Java, is a huge crater with a sandy plain inside it; from the plain arise several lesser volcanic cones, which are usually steaming and smoking. Near Bandung in western Java, tourists may descend into the crater of a volcano whose unusual shape is suggested by its name of Tangkuban Perahu, "overturned boat." Gama Gama, a volcano making up most of Ternate, has a triple crater. On Sumatra, a cone rises to form the island of Samosir in huge Lake Toba, while nearby Pusuk Bukit (more appropriately Bukit Busuk, "hill of stinks") is noteworthy for sulfur springs and encrustations of sulfurous chemicals. On Bali, some of the craters hold enormous bodies of water. Mutu, a mountain in eastern Flores, is remarkable in holding three closely grouped crater lakes, each a different color; for dissolved chemicals stain one lake a deep Burgundy red, a second jade green, a third milky blue. (During his years of exile on Flores, Indonesia's late president Sukarno was much impressed by this strange mountain, and applied its name to the dramatic club he had organized to pass the time.) A volcano cannot be dismissed as dead simply because its crater now holds a lake. When Kelut in eastern Java erupted in 1922, the water of its crater lake, mixed with ash to form mud, swept down upon a hundred villages, taking 5,500 lives; Dutch engineers subsequently bored a tunnel through the crater wall to keep the lake drained and so perhaps avoid another such disaster. And Gunung Salak, visible from Bogor in western Java, is the quiet, truncated remnant of a volcano that belched mud over an enormous area in 1699.

Irian Barat is nonvolcanic even though mountainous. In the New Guinea region, live volcanos are concentrated in the northern part of the Territory of North-East New Guinea, along with some nearby islands, and toward the eastern extremity of Papua. These craters are part of a volcanic belt that stretches to the Bismarck Archipelago, the Solomons, the New Hebrides, and New Zealand. A recent, violent eruption within this belt was that of Mount Lamington in Papua; it killed 3,000 people in 1951.

Subterranean pressures are finally relieved by eruptions, and volcanos eventually die. With time, activity may cease over large expanses of volcanic country, leaving only dead craters. This has happened in much of Sulawesi, whose active volcanos are now confined to the northern part of the island. A peak near the center of Timor reportedly erupted in the year 1638, but that island today is considered essentially nonvolcanic. South of Viqueque in Portuguese Timor, an old crater is in the so-called solfatara stage, no longer likely to erupt but still emitting a little gas, and building mud cones a few feet high. Many hot springs in Timor also provide evidence of dying vulcanism there. On Borneo, the last eruption took place about 50,000 years ago, to judge from the geologic studies so far made. In several presently nonvolcanic parts of Indone-

11

sia, there are scattered large tracts where the vegetation is poorer and scrubbier than would be expected, and it is surmised that these tracts were repeatedly burned over as a result of volcanic activity that has since come to an end.

Excluding Irian Barat, the highest elevations of Indonesia are provided by volcanos, active or otherwise. On Sumatra, Kerintji is 12,484 feet high. Almost as high, at 12,224 feet, is Rindjani on Lombok, just east of Bali. Rindjani is often called simply Lombok Peak, for its towering presence dominates the comparatively small island. Semeru, in eastern Java, reaches 12,060 feet. Rantekombola, at 11,335 feet, was long regarded as the highest mountain on Sulawesi, but an ever higher one, of 11,500 feet, has been reported in the great ridges that lie just inland of Todjo. Other well-known volcanos of Indonesia include Leuser (11,371 feet), Utjap Mulu (10,259), Abong Abong (9,892), and Merapi (9,488) on Sumatra; along with Slamet (11,427), Raung (10,932), Lawu (10,712), and Merapi (9,551) on Java. It is not surprising that two volcanos have been given the same name, Merapi. In many parts of Indonesia, a volcanic peak may be referred to locally as Gunung Merapi. *Api* means "fire" in Malayan and several other Indonesian languages, while the prefix *mer-* imparts a sense of action to the word it accompanies. *Merapi* therefore means blazing, ablaze. *Gunung* is the word for "mountain," and so Gunung Merapi signifies an active volcano. Java's Merapi, near Djokjakarta, erupted in 1954.

The list of large Indonesian volcanos has not been exhausted, for peaks more than 9,000 feet high are scattered over the Greater Sundas, along with many others not so high. Elsewhere in the volcanic parts of the country, most of the peaks are under 9,000 feet, although there are a few notable exceptions. The presently nonvolcanic islands often have high mountains also, Borneo rising to more than 9,000 feet in Kalimantan and to 13,455 feet atop Mount Kinabalu in Sabah. Even the smaller nonvolcanic islands are comparatively high in most cases, with a maximum elevation of 1,860 feet on Semeulue, 2,907 on Nias, 1,332 in the Mentawai Archipelago, 4,019 on Sumba, 5,820 in Indonesian Timor, and 9,712 in Portuguese Timor. Thus, the familiar story-book description of a south sea island—a low-lying expanse of coral rock and tropical greenery encircling a palm-fringed lagoon—is not particularly applicable to Indonesia. It does have its lagoons and verdant lowlands, as well as coral reefs both submerged and elevated; but its islands, at least its 3,000 inhabitable ones, were mostly produced by volcanic action and the uplifting of sedimentary rock, and their landscape is characteristically dominated by highlands.

In Indonesia, rugged areas exceeding 2,000 feet in height might conveniently be described as mountains, those between 500 and 2,000 feet as hills, and flatter areas below 500 feet as plains. By this definition, the mountainous portions of Indonesia include western Sumatra, east-central Irian Barat, most of inland Java, a large part of inland Kalimantan, and practically all of Sulawesi. Extensive plains exist in eastern Sumatra, southern Kalimantan, and southeastern Irian Barat, those of Sumatra and Kalimantan being low and swampy in many places. The rest of Indonesia is hilly for the most part. In addition to mountain, hill, and plain, a fourth landform is recognized by physiographers: the plateau, an area above 500 feet in height, steep-sided but comparatively flat on top. Indonesia has many scattered plateaus, usually produced by uplifting; but most of them are small, and need not be listed.

New Guinea warrants separate mention, for among islands it is second in size only to Greenland, and is almost continent-like in its topography. Vast mountain ranges, trending roughly northwest-southeast, run almost the full length of the island, reaching their greatest height in Irian Barat, interposing a formidable barrier between the northern and the southern coasts. From the western end of the Nassau Range eastward to the Papuan border, a distance of over 300 miles, there is probably no pass through the highlands at an elevation under 13,000 feet. Outstanding peaks in this non-volcanic region are Idenburg (15,748 feet), Wilhelmina (15,585), Juliana (15,420), and Wilhelm (15,400); but greater than these, at 16,500 feet, is the highest of the Carstensz Summits in the Nassau Range. There have been rumors of even greater peaks in this part of the world, including a fabled "Mount Hercules" which supposedly towers higher than Everest; but it is now certain that a maximum elevation is reached on the Carstensz Summits. Still, it is no wonder that even during modern times, there were rumors of marvels hidden in Irian Barat, for the interior of that land was poorly known and only partly mapped as late as World War II. In early 1959 a Dutch expedition got under way toward the Star Mountains east of Juliana Summit, where it set about filling in the last sizable blank on the map of Irian Barat.

In the year 1623, Jan Carstensz sailed from Ambon (Amboina) to the Ewab (Kai) and Aru archipelagos and then skirted the southern coast of Irian Barat. This coast is usually cloudy, but Carstensz happened to find it clear. "Some ten miles, as I should judge it, inland there lay very high mountains which were in many places white with snow," Carstensz wrote. And he continued, "It was surely somewhat strange so near to the equinoctial line to find snow lying upon the mountains." The idea was, in fact, too strange to be accepted by Carstensz' contemporaries or by several later explorers whose view was blocked by clouds; and over two centuries went by before Carstensz' observation was verified. The mountains he had seen were more like 50 miles away than ten, but he had correctly identified the distant glitter of snowfields and glaciers. Four peaks of Irian Barat—Carstensz, Idenburg, Wilhelmina, and Juliana—are permanently capped with snow and ice, while reports suggest that snow has also fallen on several other peaks but did not remain permanently. The great ridge between Carstensz and Juliana is bordered both to the north and to the south by precipices, some of them as much as 80 miles long and with a maximum drop of 10,000 feet. Atop the ridge are vast glaciers which show vertical faces of clear ice where they reach the edges of the chasms —"antarctic" scenery just four degrees below the equator.

It has seemed desirable to introduce Irian Barat's peaks and ranges by their names of long standing in the geological and other literature; but actually, these names have lately been replaced. The Dutch had called the central uplift Sneeuw Gebergte, "Snow Range," and its principal divisions the Oranje Gebergte and the Nassau Gebergte. After western New Guinea passed into Indonesian hands, the uplift was renamed Pegunungan Maoka, the Oranje Gebergte became Pegunungan Djajawidjaja, and Juliana Summit became Puntjak Mandala. (*Pegunungan* is a mountain range, *puntjak* a peak.) The Nassau Gebergte was renamed Pegunungan

14

Sudirman, thus honoring General Sudirman who was a commander-in-chief of the army during Indonesia's war for independence. The greatest peak of Pegunungan Sudirman, the highest prominence of the former Carstensz Toppen, was renamed Puntjak Sukarno. Further renaming is anticipated.

Less spectacular than mountain ranges but still of much geological interest are coralline and other limestones, uplifted from the sea bottom in many parts of Indonesia. Along the coasts of various islands, from the Mentawai Archipelago and southern Java eastward to the Ewab and Aru groups and northward through Waigeo into the Moluccas, coral reefs have been elevated and now appear well above sea level. When Alfred Russel Wallace traveled through Indonesia, he was impressed by the strange sight of reefs well above the water. "In many places I have observed the unaltered surfaces of the elevated reefs, with great masses of coral standing up in their natural position," he wrote, "and hundreds of shells so fresh-looking that it was hard to believe that they had been more than a few years out of the water." In elevated reefs of greater age, the actual shells are occasionally replaced in faithful detail by some mineral; and the casts thus formed, harder than their limy matrix, weather out of the rock and lie free. When Europeans began to explore Indonesia, they found that the local people were gathering these casts, which were in demand by Chinese traders whose ships were cruising among the islands. In far-distant China, the mineralized shells would be converted into nostrums.

A reef-building coral organism is a primitive form of animal life, soft and gelatinous like its jellyfish kin but capable of forming a rock-hard wall about itself. Countless millions of these coral polyps, living colonially, will eventually build an enormous mass of rock, the so-called reef. On the reef live other organisms—other kinds of coral, mollusks, certain worms, microscopic foraminiferans, some algae—similarly able to form a kind of rock from the chemicals that are dissolved in sea water. From a geological standpoint, the significant feature of a reef is the depth at which it will form. The reef organisms can stand no more than a few hours exposure to air, and so will not live much above the low-tide mark. Yet, the reef-building corals need sunlight, and they grow in warm,

15

clear seas, down to about 200 feet. There could be no better evidence of the geologic forces that lift up the land and the sea bottom than is found in Indonesia, where some old reefs now stand 3,900 feet above sea level. Many uplifted reefs are tilted, one end still beneath the water, the opposite end perhaps 300 feet above sea level; some are broken and displaced by faults. On the other hand, deep-sea dredging has brought up reef fragments from great depths, showing that in some places the Indonesian sea bottom has been depressed rather than elevated.

Many Indonesian areas of uplifted limestone have become riddled with caves, not just shallow grottos but also long tunnels, rooms, and vertical shafts connecting caverns of different levels. Man has always made use of such caves. On Borneo, cave deposits dating back many thousands of years are rich with the tools and weapons of ancient hunters, and the bones of the beasts on which they fed. On Java and Sumatra, caves have yielded ceramic vessels and stone figurines, relics of Indonesia's Buddhist and Hindu period. On Biak, caverns are littered with cans, bottles, and cartridge cases, the melancholy debris of World War II.

So-called karst areas are widely scattered over Indonesia. These areas (which resemble and take their name from the Karst Plateau in Yugoslavia) are underlain by limestone, and are characterized by sinkholes, caverns, and underground pools or watercourses. Over sizable expanses of karst terrain, the drainage is mostly subterranean, and streams are therefore few. But in most parts of Indonesia the rainfall is heavy and streams are numerous; thus, a karst expanse is likely to be bordered by a river. Irian Barat offers the world's most impressive karst scenery; on a part of the Vogelkop Peninsula, sinks more than 1,000 feet across are clustered so densely that only knife-like ridges separate them.

The southwestern quarter of Sumatra is noteworthy for rocks that are not sedimentary but igneous: glassy or ashy rocks produced by volcanic activity. Rocks are diverse in the great mountainous uplifts of Kalimantan and Irian Barat, the latter region probably having a greater variety of rocks, soils, and minerals than any other part of Indonesia. The mountains of Irian Barat were formed in part by up-welling magma, molten material from deep in the earth; and from the solidified magma have come igneous rocks such as granite and diorite. Sedimentary rocks such as limestone and dolomite were uplifted, while heat of molten magma altered the structure of various rocks, for example converting limestone into marble. Thus Irian Barat has the three main types of rocks: igneous, sedimentary, and metamorphic.

There are many rivers in Indonesia, especially on Sumatra, Kalimantan, and Irian Barat, but most of them are no more than fair-sized; for of course an island could not produce the huge rivers that arise from continental drainage, nor would long streams be expected where mountains rise not far from the sea. In some years the Indonesian rainfall is exceptionally heavy, particularly in the Greater Sundas, and the streams may flood. The rampaging rivers do much damage; yet they have one beneficial effect in depositing mineral-rich silt over the bottomlands, often in quantities rarely approached by streams of temperate lands.

The Mamberamo of Irian Barat is Indonesia's largest river. Arising from the northern flanks of the central highlands, it is navigable for almost 100 miles by steamers of 12-foot draft. In the southern flanks, a little east of Irian Barat, a much greater river has its origin. This, the Fly, swings westward as though to enter Irian Barat; but the eastern boundary of that country, otherwise following the 141st meridian, likewise swings westward along the west bank of the Fly, and so leaves that river in the Territory of Papua and North-East New Guinea. Many rivers flow southward out of the central highlands of Irian Barat, the largest and best known of them being the Digul. Of course, the importance of a river is not entirely a matter of its size and length, for much depends on the location of the stream and its mouth. On Sumatra, the Hari is the most important river. About 250 miles long and navigable upstream for 55 miles, it flows through oilfield country, and has a river port, Djambi, at the head of navigation. South of the Hari is the Musi, 325 miles long and likewise with a river port, Palembang. The Musi is remarkable for its huge delta, 240 miles across. The most important river in Java is the Solo, 335 miles long and noted for its rich burden of silt. Kalimantan has the largest Indonesian rivers outside Irian Barat, the best known of them being the

Barito. Rising near the Sarawak frontier and flowing about 550 miles to the Java Sea, the Barito is navigable upstream to Bandjarmasin, another very old center of Indonesian trade. Longer and larger, although not as well known, is the Kapuas, which traverses 710 miles in its flow from the Sarawak frontier to the South China Sea, and which is navigable for 560 miles. Outside Sumatra, Java, Irian Barat, and Kalimantan, the Indonesian rivers are all short, and need not be mentioned individually. But even the smaller rivers are sometimes important for irrigation, and they could be used in the development of hydroelectric power. Such development has gotten under way in Sumatra and Java, and will doubtless be extended.

Strangely, large Indonesian lakes are comparatively few. Best known of them is Toba in northern Sumatra, a body of water measuring 55 by 18 miles. Volcanic activity produced an island in Toba, and then connected the island to the mainland by a narrow isthmus. Sumatra has five other large lakes. Kalimantan has two: Luar with its marshy valley, and Kenohan Djempang on the lower Mahakam River. Sulawesi has four sizable lakes, called Poso, Limboto, Tuwuti, and Tempe. There is a scattering of both upland and lowland lakes in Irian Barat, but New Guinea's most famous lake country lies just across the border in Papua. In the anthropological literature, reference is often made to a "central lake plain" of Irian Barat, walled in by mountains and drained by rivers that unite to form the Mamberamo. This area has numerous bottomland and floodplain lakes, none of any great size. Crater lakes are fairly common in volcanic parts of Indonesia, but they tend to be rather impermanent, blown into steam at unpredictable intervals.

The Indonesian population is strongly concentrated in regions of recent or continuing volcanic activity. To a Westerner this situation would at first appear surprising, but it is easily explained. Young volcanic soils are by far the most productive ones, indeed the only ones that could support a large population of farmers. The rural inhabitants of Indonesia feel that any given volcano is likely to erupt only at long intervals. Also, these people are fatalistic in outlook. Life is full of hazards, but perhaps one survives them; *insja Allah*, it is as God wills. In the meantime, why starve on poor land? So the farmers are lured to some volcano by the promise of richer soil there.

An erupting volcano often throws out an enormous quantity of mineral matter. Tambora, on Sumbawa, set a record in this regard, ejecting an estimated 36 cubic miles of material when it exploded in 1815. The blast reduced the mountain's height by 4,100 feet, and left a crater seven miles wide. Ash, lava, and shattered rock fell to earth in a zone 400 miles across. (New England experienced its terrifying "year without a summer" because Tambora's dust, drifting in the upper air, blocked off the sun's warmth.) Such explosions, repeated from place to place over the centuries, have enriched the soils of the volcanic parts of Indonesia. Of course, with time the minerals may be leached out, dissolved and washed away; and so the younger volcanic soils are the best for farming. When Krakatau blew up in 1883, much ejected ash and dust fell on the Lampung district of southern Sumatra, where the agricultural yield rapidly improved on the previously leached-out soils of that area. On crater slopes, one function of man-made terraces is the holding back of volcanic minerals until they can be worked thoroughly into the ground. When streams flow through a volcanic area, they may pick up a rich burden of minerals; and in parts of Indonesia, such streams have been used for irrigation, to good effect. The generally high temperatures of Indonesia hasten the weathering of the parent rock into soil, but rainwater run-off will leach out various soil constituents; and the leaching proceeds more rapidly in parts of the country where precipitation is heavy. In such places the soil may become quite poor unless it is periodically revitalized by volcanic ash and dust. Areas with a well-marked dry season are less rapidly affected by leaching, for during the drier months this process is checked, and there may be some upward movement of water and dissolved nutrients through the soil.

As mentioned, the uplifting of sea bottoms has provided Indonesia with an abundance of sedimentary rocks, such as sandstone, shale, and particularly limestone. In many areas where volcanic activity has come to an end, the weathering of sedimentary rock is virtually the only source of new soil. If, as is often the case, the parent rock is sedimentary and the rainfall is heavy, the leached-

19

out soils are too poor ever to support a large population if farming is to be the principal means of subsistence. Poor, thin soils, derived from sedimentary rock, are also likely to be very permeable, and so not amenable to irrigation. Studies on Java have revealed the striking relationship of soil type to population density and standard of living. For example, south of Malang in eastern Java there was an expanse of young alluvial soil, irrigated by mineral-rich waters from nearby areas of recent or continuing volcanic activity; and there was also an expanse of thin, permeable soil overlying limestone. The former area had four times the population density of the latter. Or take the situation near Djokjakarta, also in eastern Java. The notably active and unpredictable crater of Merapi, about 20 miles away, had provided some of the Djokjakarta area with young volcanic soils. In the Kotagedeh district, just southeast of Djokjakarta, the population density was found to exceed 2,300 per square mile, and rice cultivation was the principal means of subsistence. But just east of Kotagedeh, and separated from it by an escarpment, was a limestone plateau called Gunung Sewu. The thin, permeable soil of the plateau was planted mostly with cassava, not a highly valuable crop but one that can be grown without irrigation. The population density on Sewu was less than a quarter that of Kotagedeh, and the cassava growers were poverty stricken as compared with their rice-growing neighbors. The above studies and population figures date back to the 1940s and 1950s, but they typify the situation in much of Indonesia, where soil productivity has been a major factor governing population density, and where volcanic soils are the only ones that will support a great number of farming people. It is no coincidence that Java has, for its size, more people and more active volcanos than any other area in the world.

This is not to say, however, that the presence of young volcanic soils automatically results in a high population density; rather, it permits such density if the local people know and care to use the agricultural techniques that exploit these soils most effectively. No other crop in the world will produce as much food per acre as rice grown in irrigated fields of Java's volcanic regions. But for centuries in parts of North Java and Madura there existed trading king-

doms with an economy based not on agriculture but on the shipping of cloves, nutmeg, mace, and other tropical produce; and after
Europeans monopolized the trade of the Indies, the people of these
areas took mostly to diversified gardening in permanent plots, not
to the wet-rice cultivation that is so richly rewarding in starchy
grain. And there are Indonesian ethnic groups who, having remained somewhat isolated from the cultural mainstream, carry on
a simple, Neolithic-level agriculture which does not take full advantage of the soil's potential.

In southern Irian Barat, a port on the Digul River is called
Tanah Merah. A detailed map of Indonesia will reveal many scattered localities with this same name. *Tanah* in this case means
"earth," and *merah* means "red." A place called Tanah Merah received its name from the local exposure of a reddish, clay-like soil.
This kind of soil develops through a natural process of weathering
and chemical change called laterization, and in recent years it has
become obvious that the process could threaten agriculture in Indonesia and other tropical lands. Where temperatures are consistently high and rainfall abundant, as is the case in many parts of
Indonesia, leaching of the soil is hastened. It is further hastened by
the work of bacteria, earthworms, insects, and other living things,
which break down organic materials and aerate the soil. Most of
the organic material, the silica, and the basic (i.e., alkaline) chemical compounds can be leached out, along with most of the potassium, calcium, phosphorus, and other substances necessary to plant
growth. About all that might remain are relatively insoluble substances, notably oxides of iron, aluminum, nickel, and manganese.
The oxides of iron or aluminum impart to the soil its characteristic
reddish or yellowish coloration. In extreme cases, leaching can
convert the soil to the mineral laterite, which hardens to brick-like
consistency when exposed to sun and air. Laterization has been
going on for ages. The process is much slowed if the soil supports
rainforest, a type of vegetation widespread in Indonesia; and even
savanna, a kind of tropical grassland, helps protect the soil. But of
course the natural vegetation is cleared away when an area is to
be planted in some commercial crop, and then, exposed to air and
rain and tropical sun, the soil declines rapidly in its productivity.

21

Laterization, and some other processes affecting tropical soils, have only recently come to be understood. When Europeans first began to take an interest in Indonesia, they were impressed by the extensive forests of giant trees. Reasonably enough, they assumed that the local soil, being capable of supporting magnificent rainforest, should likewise be capable of supporting crops. Many an unsuccessful agricultural venture proved the assumption to be poorly founded. Plants do need certain elements such as nitrogen, phosphorus, and potassium, which they obtain from the soil; but most plant growth is accomplished through the process of photosynthesis, whereby water and carbon dioxide, in the presence of sunlight and the green pigment called chlorophyll, combine chemically to form a sugar and liberate oxygen. Plant sugars, including the complex one known as cellulose, are derived through this process, and so are plant starches after further chemical reaction. The tropical sun and heavy rainfall have much to do with the growth of rainforest in Indonesia, and in parts of the country where the rainfall is comparatively scanty or highly seasonal, this kind of vegetation will not develop regardless of the nature of the local soils. The giant trees of the rainforest send their roots deep into the ground, bringing up at least a small quantity of minerals from the level where the parent rock is being converted into soil. The rainforest continually recycles the soil nutrients, building up little or no humus. If undisturbed, it does shield the soil from laterization; but when the trees are felled and hauled away, with them goes a major percentage of the nutrients. Laterization is accelerated, and the denuded patch may yield a commercial crop for only a few years before becoming practically sterile.

Scientists distinguish between the red soils that are already highly laterized and the reddish to yellowish soils that have so far been saved from extreme laterization. Fortunately, brick-like laterite has not developed at many places in Indonesia, where most soils retain at least a small quantity of plant nutrients, and might still profit from fertilization and irrigation. But over much of the country, laterization is a potentiality that must be considered, especially in connection with large-scale agricultural development, and with flood control projects which halt the deposition of revitalizing silts by flood waters. Only in two parts of Indonesia are the soils not particularly susceptible to laterization: the two great mountainous regions on Kalimantan and Irian Barat respectively. In such regions of massive uplift, with a diversity of environments and parent rocks, the soils are complex.

Here and there in Indonesia, laterization has converted soil to iron ores such as hematite and limonite, or to bauxite, an aluminum ore. The country has extensive reserves of low-grade lateritic iron ore on Kalimantan and Sulawesi, with a few deposits of high-grade hematite. In the Star Mountains of Irian Barat, magnetite exists in the river beds and in the ground, often in sufficient concentration to deflect a compass needle markedly. However, the iron ores of Indonesia have been little exploited. Bauxite was first mined in Indonesia in 1935 on the island of Bintan in the Riaus, just southeast of Singapore. In the latter 1930s, Japan was buying nickel from mines in southeastern Sulawesi, and since 1959, cooperation of Japanese companies with Indonesian State Enterprise has considerably increased nickel production on that island. Nickel and cobalt have been discovered on Irian Barat.

Coal, called *arang batu,* "stone charcoal," has been mined for well over a century in Kalimantan. This mineral also exists on Java and Sumatra, the latter island having the finest coalfields of the country; and there is an abandoned coal mine in Nusa Laut, south of Ceram. Manganese, phosphate, sulfur, and iodine have been mined in Java, while Sumatra and Kalimantan have yielded industrial diamonds. But more valuable than any of these, from a standpoint of the Indonesian economy, is tin, which comes from Singkep in the Lingga Archipelago, Bangka, and Belitung, as well as from central and eastern Java. (Here and elsewhere in the book, "Bangka" refers to the island lying off the southeastern coast of Sumatra, not the islet of Bangka off the northern tip of Sulawesi.) The most important mineral production of Indonesia is crude oil together with less important natural gas. In past decades, the more productive oilfields have been those of eastern Sumatra, northern Java, and eastern Kalimantan; but oil has also been found on Ceram and western Irian Barat. Very recently, several productive oil wells, in addition to oil-and-gas wells, have been drilled off

Java's northern shore, and there has also been an oil strike off the coast of northern Sumatra. Favorable foreign investment laws having been enacted in 1967, by 1970 at least 30 oil companies had signed production-sharing contracts with *Pertamani*, the Indonesian government company. By the end of 1970, Indonesia was producing about a million barrels of oil a day. (A "barrel" in the oil business is 42 U.S. gallons.)

Writing of Borneo, Marco Polo exclaimed, "The quantity of gold collected there exceeds all calculation and belief. From thence it is that the merchants of Zai-tun [now Communist China's Kwangtung Province] and of Manji in general [southern China] have imported, and to this day import, that metal to a great amount." And writing of "Lochak," an unidentifiable province in or near Indonesia, he declared, "Gold is abundant to a degree scarcely credible." It is true that around Polo's time, golden ornaments and *objets d'art* were being produced in Indonesia, finding their way as trade or tribute into the coffers of distant khans or local sultans. Some fine old examples of Indonesian gold work have reached museum collections; many such are displayed in the Golden Room of the Djakarta Museum: ornaments, knives, crowns, even a golden throne. But long before Polo focused Western attention on the gold of the Indies, there were extensive trade routes through the islands, and one need not suppose that gold was always mined in the same places where golden ornaments were seen. It has been mined on Borneo, although more in Sarawak than in Kalimantan; also on Sulawesi. There have been vague reports of the metal in the Star Mountains of Irian Barat, but such rumors are to be expected from almost any region that has been inadequately explored. (Gold has indeed been found in New Guinea's central highlands east of Irian Barat.) Both gold and silver are mined in the uplands of Sumatra and western Java. Modern silver work of several kinds can be bought at Djokjakarta's shopping center, Malioboro. Filigree gold or silver work, although coming from Sumatra, is offered in the shops of Djakarta and Bandung; and in the latter city, items of Javan silver are also marketed. Javan gold and silver are worked and put on sale at Tjeluk in Bali.

But all this is not to imply that mining or working of precious metals is highly important to the Indonesian economy. With reference to financial value, crude oil has appropriately been nicknamed "black gold," and one might extend the metaphor by applying the name "white gold" to the milky sap of the Pará rubber tree (See Chapter II), which has done so well on Indonesian soils. In modern Indonesia, oil and rubber are the principal sources of revenue, not the gold and silver that captured the imagination of European explorers and that still fascinate modern tourists.

Compared with gold, ordinary salt seems prosaic, but in historical perspective it has been the more important in human affairs. Where man eats a good bit of meat or fish, he receives enough salt for his physiological needs, but where for ecological or cultural reasons he subsists mostly on plants, he must deliberately add salt to his diet, two to five additional grams per person per day. Thus, in many parts of the premodern world, dense settlement of agricultural peoples was possible only if the requisite amount of salt could be traded for, or somehow extracted from the environment. In premodern Indonesia, this mineral was available from soil compounds or saline springs in an extensive area of northeastern Java, roughly from Semarang to Surabaja. At coastal localities of Simeulue, the Mentawais, southwestern Java, Madura, northeastern and southwestern Sulawesi, and eastern Timor, salt was extracted from seawater. Neither anthropologists nor historians have paid sufficient attention to salt, but it may be supposed that in Indonesia, as in other parts of the world, trading centers developed wherever a surplus of the mineral was produced, and that political power accrued to those who controlled the salt trade. In later times, the salt-rich countries of western Europe found a ready market for this mineral in India and Indonesia. *Garam* is an Indonesian name for salt, *pegaraman* a salt-pan in which saline water is evaporated. *Asin*, another Indonesian name for salt, is a word that can be traced all the way to the northern Philippines, where Pangasinan Province received its name from its coastal saltworks.

So much for mineral productions. Several references have already been made to ecological effects of temperature and rainfall, and the chapter may close with a cursory review of Indonesian climate. Since the country lies entirely between the Tropic of Cancer

25

and the Tropic of Capricorn, it is a "tropical" land in the strict sense of the word. But to people in temperate regions, such as most of the United States and Europe, the word "tropical" usually has climatic implications, and tropical countries are popularly supposed to be very hot. The facts of the matter may therefore be surprising. So-called temperate climates really are intemperate, in that they swing seasonally between extremes of hot and cold. In contrast, seasonal swings of temperature are not marked in the tropics. In the lowlands of Indonesia, regardless of the time of year, the temperature will usually go no higher than about 88 degrees Fahrenheit during the day, and no lower than about 73 during the night. At the capital city of Djakarta, over a period of 55 years the highest temperature recorded was 96, the lowest 66; and during this period, the mean temperature for January (78.7 degrees) was not very different from that for April (80.4) or July (79.4) or October (80.6). The following chart gives a good idea of Djakarta's equable temperatures (to the nearest degree):

| MONTH | AVERAGE DAILY HIGH | AVERAGE NIGHTLY LOW | MONTH | AVERAGE DAILY HIGH | AVERAGE NIGHTLY LOW |
|---|---|---|---|---|---|
| January | 84° F. | 74° F. | July | 87° F. | 73° F. |
| February | 84 | 74 | August | 87 | 73 |
| March | 86 | 74 | September | 88 | 74 |
| April | 87 | 75 | October | 87 | 74 |
| May | 87 | 75 | November | 86 | 74 |
| June | 87 | 74 | December | 85 | 75 |

Data closely comparable to the Djakartan figures are available for many scattered localities in the Indonesian lowlands.

When winter comes to the northern hemisphere, summer comes to the southern one. South of the equator, higher temperatures are usually to be expected in January than in July. It might therefore be asked why this is not true for Djakarta, which lies about 6 degrees below the equator. The answer is that January happens to be near the peak of Djakarta's rainy season, and the mean temperature of that month is lowered by the numerous rainy or cloudy days.

Record temperatures for Indonesian lowlands are established in

26

the extreme southern part of the country, along those coasts nearest to Australia. At Kupang in southwestern Timor, a maximum temperature of 101 has been reported officially, and a minimum of 60; but such readings are unusual. Kupang's mean temperature for January is about 81 degrees, for April also 81, for July 78, and for October 82. Each year the temperature is far more likely to reach 100 at, say, Chicago or Detroit or St. Louis than at any spot in Indonesia.

The account has so far been concerned with temperatures in the lowlands of Indonesia. But other factors being equal, temperature decreases with altitude. Since much of the country is mountainous, there usually are cool highlands not far from any lowland community. At an elevation of 1,500 feet, the temperature will rise to about 80 degrees in the day, and fall to 65 at night. During Dutch colonial times, the Dutch officials and their families often spent the weekend at some cool resort in the foothills. From the colonial capital, the Javan coastal city then called Batavia, the Djalan Pasar Minggu (Sunday Market Road) led south toward the uplands; and a 40-mile drive or a train ride brought the Dutch to a resort town so pleasing that it was named Buitenzorg, carefree. The residency of the governor-general was there, an official-looking palace situated among botanical gardens. In the distance was the jagged volcanic peak of Gunung Salak, which had been quiet since 1699. From Buitenzorg, not far from the Bandung road, at a locality called Tjibodas on the slopes of the twin volcanos Gedeh and Pangrango, the climate was so cool that a branch of the botanical gardens was established there in order to grow plants that would not thrive in the hot plains. Beyond the Tjibodas turnoff, a road led southeast toward Bandung. Some 27 miles out of Buitenzorg, the road climbed through terraced fields, and through plantations of tea and Cinchona, to reach Puntjak Pass. Here, at 4,800 feet, the temperature sometimes dropped into the 40s, and the local inns provided blankets for overnight guests.

Much has changed in Indonesia. Batavia is now called Djakarta. Buitenzorg is now Bogor, and its palace for a time became Sukarno's summer residence. But the gardens remain, and plantations, and terraced fields on the volcano slopes. The road still climbs past cool Tjibodas and to cooler Puntjak with its bungalows, chalets, restaurants, and golf course. Of course, temperature decreases with elevation anywhere in Indonesia, the mean annual temperature falling one degree Fahrenheit for roughly every 310 feet of ascent. The Djakarta-Puntjak road has been singled out for mention only because it was so well known in past times, and will probably become even more widely known in the future, what with the recent economic improvement and the increase of tourism in Indonesia.

It is not intended to imply that the cool Indonesian highlands have served only as resort areas. It is true that many of the larger communities developed as coastal ports, or else as river ports situated not far inland. (Principal port cities include Djakarta, Surabaja, Semarang, and Tjirebon on Java; Medan, Tandjungbalai, Rengat, Djambi, Palembang, and Menggala on Sumatra; Balikpapan, Tarakan, Bandjarmasin, and Pontianak on Kalimantan; Kupang on Timor; and Makasar and Manado on Sulawesi.) However, the technique of terracing has permitted the cultivation of volcanic slopes at remarkably high altitudes, and the fertility of volcanic soils has allowed the development of a sizable population in various mountainous areas. Towns have grown up in the highlands of Indonesia as well as along the coast. Bandung, established by the Dutch and now with a population exceeding 1,000,000, is located at an elevation of about 2,000 feet on a plateau surrounded by mountains. It is the third largest city of the Republic. The setting out of tea and Cinchona plantations has also fostered settlement in the uplands, for most such plantings are at elevations of 4,500 to 6,500 feet. In general, the really high mountains of Indonesia are too cold and precipitous to encourage much settlement along their upper slopes, but there are some surprising exceptions. The little-known highland tribes of Irian Barat, so often called a "Stone Age" people, are able to terrace and cultivate the mountain slopes that lie at an angle of 45 or even 50 degrees. And through reliance on the sweet potato rather than on the more usual tropical crops, the New Guineans have been able to carry their agriculture far above the frost line, up to 8,500 feet and in a few places up to 9,000.

The relative humidity—the amount of water vapor actually contained in the air, as compared with the maximum amount it could

28

contain at the time—is usually high in Indonesia, seldom falling below 78 percent. The country is not exceedingly windy; the seasonal winds that blow across it are rarely gusty, and even hard rains often fall straight down. On smaller islands, and along the coasts of the larger ones, a light breeze may blow from the sea in the evening and from the land later on during the night; but usually the air is fairly still. Of course, the Pacific, like the Atlantic, spawns great storms that move for hundreds or thousands of miles across the water, perhaps eventually smashing into the land and devastating it. Pacific storms, called typhoons, are in fact more numerous than their Atlantic counterparts, the hurricanes. The South China Sea has an average of 22 severe typhoons per year, but they usually move northward to menace the Philippines, southeastern China, or Japan. The tropical waters just north of Australia spawn an average of 13 typhoons annually, but only a minority of these strike Indonesian land. Beset by floods and volcanic eruptions, at least the Indonesian landsmen do not have to undergo yearly typhoons.

Needless to say, the mariners know and fear the great storms. One of their names for a typhoon, *badai,* is probably indigenous, but another, *topan,* is a borrowing of much interest. Cyclonic storms were given a similar name from the Mediterranean through the Indian Ocean to the South China Sea. The Greeks called them *typhon,* the Arabs *tufan,* the Chinese *tai-fung* (Cantonese) or *ta-feng* (Pekingese). The Chinese names, with the literal meaning of "great wind," are sometimes said to have only accidental similarity to the Greek, but the matter is debatable, since the Chinese converted borrowed words into meaningful phrases that could be written ideographically. Indonesian *topan* is probably borrowed from the Arabic, reinforced by the Chinese version and by Portuguese *tufão,* which was taken from the Arabic. Thus, a few short words conjure up a picture of those early days when Indonesia was involved with a maritime traffic extending from China to Arabia and the Mediterranean world.

Typhoons and earthquakes, similarly destructive to life and property, are often discussed together even though quakes are not a climatic factor in the usual sense of the phrase. Indonesia has many quakes, but fortunately, few are of high intensity. Djakarta has suffered one damaging quake in modern times, and in 1957 Djokjakarta experienced strong tremors under unusual circumstances. A *wajang kulit*, shadow-play, was being staged, a major performance depicting the final destruction of the gods and heroes of the Hindu epic *Mahabharata*. The story is regarded as sacred, and many Indonesians feared that to present it in its entirety was to endanger man's survival; but from all over Java they flocked to Djokjakarta to see it, nevertheless. At the precise moment the death of a favorite hero, Abimanju, was enacted, an earthquake shook all of central Java, and in Djokjakarta panic was averted only because the *dalang*, the priestly puppeteer, continued serenely with the drama. In 1971, Irian Barat felt tremors. Except in cities, earthquake damage is slight because so much construction is of flexible bamboo. But a quake, even if it does little harm, is a disturbing experience, and in almost any part of the country there will be at least a few oldsters who recall vividly a *gempa bumi*, "shaking of the earth." Perhaps they also recall *gelora*, the seaquake that makes the ocean churn and sends *bena*, the tidal wave, crashing onto the land.

Now to the important subject of rainfall. All of southeastern Asia, both continental and insular, has a so-called monsoon type of climate. That part of the world is often in the news, and so therefore is the word "monsoon"; yet the precise meaning of the word is rarely discoverable from the context in which it is used. A monsoon is not a kind of wind or of rainstorm; it need not even be a rainy period. "Monsoon" is from the Arabic *mausim*, season. Indonesians borrowed the word as *musim*. Italians in northern Africa borrowed it as *monsone*, and then the English picked it up as "monsoon." In temperate lands, there is a definite and fairly predictable change of temperature during the year; and this change, more than anything else, permits the division of the year into seasons. But in Indonesia and certain other tropical lands, the temperature at any one locality is not likely to change much throughout the year, and so some other climatic factor must serve to demarcate the seasons. This factor is the wind, which changes its prevailing direction at fairly predictable intervals. And so a monsoon is simply a season of the year, characterized climatologically not by its temperature but by its wind direction.

Indonesia lies between the continents of Eurasia and Australia, the first of these in the northern hemisphere, the second in the southern. Part of the year, the northern hemisphere is tilted toward the sun, and at that time the great land mass of mainland Asia becomes very warm, heating the air above it. The heated air rises, exerts less pressure. In the terminology of the weather reports, a "low-pressure area" has formed over Asia, in this case a huge low into which air keeps moving from areas of higher pressure. This movement of air is perceived as wind. In other words, when the northern hemisphere is having its summer, there is a low-pressure area over Asia but high-pressure areas over Australia and the Indian Ocean; and so the wind blows from Australia and the Indian Ocean toward Asia. But as the months go by, the situation changes. Winter comes to the northern hemisphere, while the southern hemisphere is tilted toward the sun. Continental Asia becomes cold, and the air above it is at high pressure. Australia, in contrast, is at its hottest, and so a low develops over it. Accordingly, movement of the air is now from the Asiatic high toward the Australian low. But this seasonal change of wind direction is complicated by two conditions. First, when summer comes to the southern hemisphere, the high over the Indian Ocean merely weakens, and does not become a low as does the one over Australia at that time. Second, the wind currents cannot flow directly from a high to a low, for their courses are twisted by the spin of the earth.

It might be asked why a seasonal difference in wind direction should occasion so much interest. Consider the situation in, say, the month of January. Winter has come to continental Asia, and a high has developed over it. Cold, dry winds flow out of Asia, toward the Australian low. Near the equator they meet winds flowing northward from the high that remains permanently over the Indian Ocean. Having converged, the winds rise into the upper atmosphere; and as they do so, they begin to cool. They have picked up much moisture in their passage across the ocean, but this begins to condense as the result of cooling; and so heavy rains fall upon most parts of Indonesia. Now consider the situation in, say, the month of July. Winter has come to Australia. A weak high has developed over that continent, and a stronger one over the Indian Ocean. Winds flow from these highs toward the Asiatic low, picking up moisture from the ocean, but in general not dropping this moisture until they reach continental Asia. Thus, when the winds are blowing from Australia toward Asia, rainfall decreases over most parts of Indonesia.

In short, when the north temperate lands, such as most of the United States and Europe, are having their winter, Indonesia is having its rainy season; and when the north-temperate lands are having their summer, Indonesia is having its dry season—at least a comparatively dry one. The seasonal winds will not strike all parts of the country from precisely the same direction, for, as noted, the air flow across Indonesia's great expanse is deflected by the earth's rotation. In many areas, the wind is more westerly (i. e., out of the west) than easterly during the rainier part of the year, while the reverse is true during the drier part. Therefore, reference is often made to the west monsoon and the east monsoon, the former bringing rain to southern Sumatra, Java, and the Lesser Sundas, the latter bringing drier air from Australia to these same islands. But a local resident might call each monsoon by a term that refers accurately to its prevailing wind direction in his area. Or the expressions *musim hudjan* and *musim kemarau*, rainy season and dry season, might be used where there is a pronounced seasonal variation in the amount of rainfall.

Before each shift of prevailing wind direction, there is a brief period of unsettled weather, with thunderclouds, lightning, and fitful breezes. In many areas this period is designated by some word meaning a sign or indication. It is also called *pantjaroba*, a word that may likewise be used for the changing of the tides. Locally, the amount of rainfall can be affected by the topography; for winds must rise to pass over mountainous regions, and in rising they cool. Then they may drop their moisture as rain—drop it especially on the mountain slopes that face the wind, leaving the lee slopes dry.

A seasonal change in wind direction is important because there is a concomitant change in the amount of precipitation. What does this mean in terms of actual rainfall as measured at weather stations? At Djakarta about 12 or 13 inches of rain may fall in January, and a comparable or even greater amount in February. But soon afterward, precipitation begins to decline, with about 8 inches in March, 5 or 6 in April, 4 in May, 3 in June, and perhaps a little less than 3 in July. August is the driest month, and may have less than 2 inches of rainfall. Thereafter, precipitation begins to increase again, with 3 inches in September, 4 or 5 in October, close to 6 in November, and close to 8 in December. These figures (based on a 44-year average) are generalizations, however. For unknown reasons, some years are unusually dry and the crops are parched; other years are unusually rainy, and the crops are attacked by fungi and insects if not washed away by floods.

The rainfall figures for Djakarta are approximated in many other parts of Indonesia, but not all. Toward eastern Java, and even more toward the Lesser Sundas, there is a decrease in annual precipitation, and a sharper contrast between a wet season and a dry. For example, at Kupang on Indonesian Timor, the rainfall in January may be about 15 or 16 inches, and scarcely less in February. The March rainfall is substantially less, about 8 or 9 inches, and then the dry season arrives. April may have only 2 or 3 inches, May perhaps less than 2. June may bring less than a half-inch, July less than a quarter-inch. The countryside becomes sere and dusty, but relief is not in sight; for August may have only a tenth-inch of rain, and the same is true of September. In October the precipitation begins to increase very slightly, to perhaps three-quarters of an inch. November brings 3 or 4 inches, December 10. Thus Kupang's annual rainfall, about 59 inches on the average, is decidedly less than Djakarta's 72 inches. Of course, even 59 inches of annual rainfall is not considered scanty precipitation; but as it happens, the rainfall is most strongly seasonal in those parts of Indonesia where it is the scantiest. For many kinds of wild plants and animals, as well as of commercial crops, five or six dry months are intolerable regardless of how the rains pour during the rest of the year.

In general, the average annual rainfall is 80 inches or more in

Sumatra (except its northern tip), Kalimantan, eastern and southern Sulawesi, the Moluccas, and Irian Barat. Within this high-rainfall area, the annual precipitation may reach 150 inches at scattered localities, especially where mountains force the moist air to rise. It reaches more than 200 inches in parts of western Sumatra, where Mount Singgalang near Bukittinggi has a downpour 320 days of the year. A little north of Indonesian territory, in Sabah, Mount Kinabalu has a downpour every day, and a yearly total of more than 400 inches—about 36 feet of rain in some years. Indonesian areas with 60 to 80 inches include northern and eastern Java, Madura, and northern Sulawesi. The Lesser Sundas have 40 to 60 inches at most localities. The minimum for any part of the Lesser Sundas, and so for any part of Indonesia, is 38 inches. Curiously, even in the rainy portions of Indonesia it is not often raining. That is to say, the rain usually arrives as a hard but brief shower, leaving the rest of the day overcast or clear. During the rainy season in many areas, the morning is clear or a little cloudy; a hard rain arrives in the afternoon, and then the sun comes out brightly for an hour or two before evening. Once in a while, the expected afternoon downpour is delayed until after dark. Djakarta's mean annual rainfall, 72 inches, represents an average of only 357 hours of rain during the year. The following chart of long-term averages reveals that in Djakarta even the rainiest months can have many days that are fair or merely cloudy:

| MONTH | NUMBER DAYS WITH RAIN | MONTH | NUMBER DAYS WITH RAIN |
|---|---|---|---|
| January | 18 | July | 5 |
| February | 17 | August | 4 |
| March | 15 | September | 5 |
| April | 11 | October | 8 |
| May | 9 | November | 12 |
| June | 7 | December | 14 |

In temperate lands, the name of a season has connotations beyond the climatic. A mention of spring, for example, calls to mind not just the returning warmth after winter's cold but also the leafing out of trees, the flowering of many plants, spring plowing and the sowing of many crops, the return of migratory birds, and a re-awakening or reappearance of much small wildlife. Similarly, Indonesians see many natural phenomena correlated with the monsoons. Nearly half the people are supported by wet-rice cultivation, and the arrival of the wet season presages the flooding of the *sawah*, the irrigable fields. Many crops grow in response to the rain, whose coming therefore sets off a cycle of agricultural activities. Some wild plants (although not all, by any means) send forth their new leaves or their blossoms at the start of the rainy season, and some fruits (again not all) ripen at the peak of this season. Numerous migratory birds, leaving continental Asia at the beginning of winter, predictably arrive in Indonesia just before or during the start of the wet monsoon. In areas where there is a marked seasonal difference in rainfall, there are small organisms—for example, certain frogs, lizards, snakes, and insects—characteristic of the wet season, others just as characteristic of the dry. Keen-eyed peasants and uncivilized tribesmen note the seasonal changes in the fauna, perhaps attaching mystical significance to the appearance and disappearance of various animal species at about the same time each year.

And as a later chapter will show, the discovery of the monsoonal winds and their reliability had considerable effect on Indonesian history; for once the courses of these winds had been charted, sailing vessels could follow them eastward across the Indian Ocean without the need for slow, dangerous coastal cruising.

# CHAPTER II

# PLANT LIFE AND MAN
# IN INDONESIA

THE PRECEDING chapter, dealing mostly with the physical factors of the Indonesian environment, is logically followed immediately by an account of the country's vegetation, whose nature is determined by the interaction of climate with soils and topography. It is well to distinguish at the outset between flora and vegetation. A floral study emphasizes the kinds of plants that grow in any given area, and deals mostly with the local species or higher taxonomic groups (genera, families) into which species are arranged by botanists. Vegetational studies, however, are carried on mostly by ecologists who emphasize the structure of the plant community: whether forest, open woodland, grassland, or some other consistently recognizable type.

Of Indonesia's vegetation types, the most impressive is tropical rainforest. The trees of this forest are of great height, their trunks rising perhaps 100 feet or more before the first branching, the tremendous boles often supported by wide-flaring buttresses. High overhead, the leafy crown of one tree is interwoven with that of the next, forming a closed canopy beneath which the light is dim even at midday. At scattered intervals, trees of exceptional size tower even above the canopy. Because the light is so dim beneath the canopy of the undisturbed rainforest, there is no dense growth of shrubs or herbs on the forest floor, which instead is fairly open. The dimness, the stillness, the tree trunks rising like great columns to the canopy overhead—these features of the rainforest impart to it a cathedral-like solemnity. In temperate lands, a forest usually is dominated by just a few species of trees, and the total number of arborescent species will not be great at any particular locality; but in tropical rainforest, hundreds of species of trees may grow in one fairly small area. (Well over 3,000 kinds of trees are known from the rainforest in Sumatra and Kalimantan alone.) The identification of all these species is a frustrating problem for the botanist who wanders through the rainforest, for the leaves, flowers, and fruits—the taxonomically distinctive structures—grow a hundred feet above his head. There is not much truth to the idea that a tropical forest is ablaze with gaudy blooms; the flowers are there, but most of them are borne in the sunlit upper branches and are visible only from some vantage point higher than the treetops. Because tropical rainforest develops where the climate is equable, there is no well-marked season during which most plants come into bloom. Nor is there a distinct season during which most trees drop their leaves; with a few exceptions, the trees of the rainforest are green all year.

Also characteristic of the tropical rainforest are lianas and epiphytes. Lianas are large vines; they are of many kinds but all of them grow over the treetops and pile up, cable-like, on the ground or among the branches. Epiphytes are plants that grow on the trunks or branches of other plants, not parasitically but merely for support. The best known tropical epiphytes are various orchids and ferns, but many other Indonesian plants are epiphytic.

The climatic requirements of tropical rainforest are suggested by the name of that vegetation type. Tropical temperatures are necessary—not extremely high temperatures but consistently warm ones, with little seasonal variation. Most Indonesian rainforest grows in areas where the mean temperature of almost any month is about 78 degrees Fahrenheit, and the mean temperature of the coolest month not below 77—an equable regimen indeed.

If rainforest is to grow, the rainfall must be heavy, 80 inches or more as a rule, and with no strongly marked dry season. As mentioned previously, rainfall decreases and becomes more seasonal toward eastern Java and the Lesser Sundas. In this region and in parts of Sulawesi, there develops a different vegetation type, monsoon forest. Like tropical rainforest, the monsoon forest in its undisturbed state will include many fine trees, decked with lianas and epiphytes; but in the monsoon forest, many of the trees will be of kinds that drop their leaves as the dry season gets under way. Thus, the advent of the rainy season will soon be followed by leafing forth, as well as by flowering and fruiting. Some trees and shrubs of the monsoon forest may retain their leaves all year, but if so, the leaves are apt to be of a coarse texture, resistant to desiccation. The monsoon forest is also noteworthy for an abundance of bamboos, which may form large clumps or thickets.

Both tropical rainforest and monsoon forest develop on soils that are susceptible to laterization. In both, the tree roots penetrate deeply into the ground, and so the soil may be darkened by organic material to a depth of many feet. But not much surplus of organic material will develop, even at the surface, which first receives the fallen leaves and the toppled trunks of dead trees. Both kinds of forest exert some control over the immediate environment. Beneath the canopy, humidity is kept at a high and constant level, wind currents are slowed, temperature vagaries ameliorated, and light-loving plants excluded in favor of the shade-loving seedlings of the forest trees. Of course, the rainforest, with no seasonal fall of leaves, is more effective in keeping the humidity, air currents, temperature, and illumination at a constant level. In either forest type, the physical factors of the environment will be more nearly constant near the ground, for the treetops must receive the full impact of sun and wind. Thus, a forest offers a series of different environments at different heights, from the soil to the upper branches. This stratification is important to animal life, for there are animals that burrow in the soil, others that inhabit the thin layer of surface debris and fallen logs, still others that live somewhere between the ground and the canopy. Many are confined to the canopy, some of them frequenting the sunlit upper stratum thereof.

In Indonesia, various names are applied to forest vegetation. One of them, the word *hutan* (sometimes rendered *utan*) is familiar to Westerners in the combination "orangutan" "man of the forest," now an English name for an Indonesian ape. But *hutan* really means the wilds, as opposed to settled areas. Another name for forest is *rimba*, or in some areas *rimbu*. *Rimba* is the primeval or virgin forest. When the *rimba* is opened up in any way that permits the sunlight to reach the ground, a thick growth of herbs, vines, shrubs, and small trees will fill the clearing. In some areas this tangled growth is known as *semak*. With time, the larger trees seed in and grow, and the former clearing becomes second-growth forest, or *belukar* as it is called. Scientifically minded writers usually avoid the word "jungle," whose connotations are derived more from fiction than fact; if the word has any usefulness here, it is as an English equivalent of *belukar*, especially *belukar* with a great deal of *semak*.

Indonesia has a few large expanses of what is called swamp peat forest. This vegetation type develops on low-lying coastal plains, where the ground is so waterlogged that soil bacteria cannot convert fallen plant material into humus. Within large areas of swamp peat forest, there are rivers and scattered tracts of somewhat higher ground; such areas may be occupied by villages. As swamp peat forest approaches the coast, it gives way to yet another vegetation type, mangrove swamp. "Mangrove" is a general name for a number of trees, not necessarily kin to one another but all salt-tolerant to some degree. Some of the mangroves are concentrated toward the seaward edge of the swamp and grow well below high tide mark. But others are concentrated toward the landward edge of the swamp and are not exposed to inundation except perhaps during exceptionally high tides. The trunks and roots of the mangroves hold back the silt and plant debris, gradually building land; and so over the centuries the mangrove swamp creeps seaward, with some other vegetation type following behind it. Indonesian mangrove swamp is best developed just seaward of large expanses of swamp peat forest, but it also occurs along other coasts where the land slopes gradually into a shallow sea.

Several vegetation types, developing only at higher elevations, are of much ecological interest, but they are of limited geographic extent and will be mentioned just briefly. Vegetation changes rather predictably with altitude, and in the mountains one can recognize certain vegetation zones arranged one above another. In general, and with local exceptions, tropical rainforest of typical aspect will grow about as high as 1,950 feet in Indonesia. From this elevation up to about 3,300 feet there exists what may be called a submontane forest, and from 3,300 up to nearly 8,000 feet a montane forest. At these elevations, a good many of the trees and lesser plants are of kinds with relatives in temperate lands. Parts of the montane forest are sometimes called cloud forest, for they are kept humid, in fact dripping, by cloud banks which drift into them. Along the cloud-misted upper border of the montane forest, the trees may be stunted, their trunks and branches coated thickly with mosses, the rocks and ground likewise moss-covered. Such vegetation is sometimes called moss forest, or more romantically, elfin forest—a cold, dank zone without trace of man, without bird song or the chirp of insect, the silence broken only by the incessant drip of icy water from the dwarfed and twisted trees. Above the moss forest, from about 8,000 up to 13,000 feet (if the mountain is high enough), there exists a subalpine forest. Finally a timberline is reached, and above it is a so-called alpine scrub of "Arctic" aspect. Above the alpine scrub there is only rocky fell-field, and then snow and ice.

Tropical rainforest, monsoon forest, and swamp peat forest are the three most important vegetation types of Indonesia, not only from the standpoint of geographic extent but also from that of economic significance. Climate, topography, and soils would permit these three to cover most of Indonesia. But nature only proposes; man disposes. Today, Indonesia is far from being one great expanse of forest, for over the centuries the activities of man have altered the country's landscape. Most Indonesian ethnic groups have been agricultural, and have made their impact upon the forest. Especially important in this connection has been the ancient and

41

widespread technique of *ladang* agriculture. A forest patch is cut and the fallen timber burned to produce *ladang*, a field that will not be irrigated. (*Huma* is a Javanese word equivalent to Malayan *ladang*.) For a few years a *ladang*, enriched by ashes, will be very productive; but then the yield declines rapidly, and the tribesman or peasant cuts and burns another patch of forest. The first patch might eventually grow up in trees again, but this will take quite a few years. Therefore the cultivator may need a dozen or more clearings, one under cultivation and the others in various stages of regrowth. The cutting, burning, planting, and harvesting of a patch, repeated many times over the centuries, has an adverse effect on the lateritic soils. In some areas the *ladang* cultivator is seminomadic, moving on through the forest to clear a new patch every few years, perhaps never returning to the old ones.

The regrowth of forest in the *ladang* is often hampered by the presence of a coarse, fast-growing grass known scientifically as Imperata. (Actually, there are several species of this widespread genus, but it is not necessary to distinguish among them here.) Imperata is called *alang-alang* in Java, *kusu-kusu* in the Moluccas, *lalang* in many parts of Indonesia, *lalang Djawa* in the Malay Peninsula, *cogon* in the Philippines, *kunai* in Papua. When a clearing is abandoned, Imperata may quickly invade it, forming a dense cover. During the drier part of the year, this grass is highly inflammable; a patch of it is likely to be burned over accidentally, or perhaps intentionally in a fire-drive for game. The fire kills most of the herbs, shrubs, or small trees that may have gotten started in the clearing; the Imperata blades are burned, but in an amazingly few weeks this hardy grass has sprouted tall and green again from buried rootstocks. Cattle also hamper the regrowth of forest. In much of Indonesia the *kerbau*, the domestic water buffalo, is permitted to graze in the clearings; and when it does so, it eats the tender herbs, shrubs, and tree seedlings without making comparably great inroads on the grass. Also, the grass may be deliberately burned to produce new, green shoots for the *kerbau*, or for the *sapi*, ordinary cattle. In the absence of fires and livestock, Imperata probably would be replaced eventually in many areas by *semak*, and then by *belukar*. Several grasses other than Imperata are similarly capable of taking over extensive tracts.

*Ladang* cultivation has been widespread in Indonesia certainly for 2,000 years, and probably for a much greater time. It is still the predominant method of agriculture in east-central and most of southern Sumatra; parts of northern Sumatra; most of Kalimantan; eastern, west-central, and most of northern Sulawesi; all of the Moluccas; most of the Lesser Sundas from Sumbawa eastward; and most of Irian Barat.

Sometime before the first century A.D., India made contact with Indonesia, and as the centuries went by, Indianized states were formed in Sumatra, Kalimantan, Java, and other islands. The Indians popularized the technique of *sawah* agriculture. *Sawah* is a field that is meant to be flooded; it is surrounded by a small dike, and if it is on the mountainside, the slopes must be terraced. Sometimes the flooding is left to the rains, but the result of this procedure is unpredictable, for rainfall might be too much, too little, or poorly timed. Usually, ditches or bamboo pipes lead water to the *sawah* from a nearby stream. Wet-field cultivation is now the predominant method of agriculture in parts of northern, west-central, and extreme southern Sumatra; much of Java; parts of southeastern and extreme western Kalimantan; most of southern and parts of central and northern Sulawesi; almost all of Madura, Bali, and Lombok; and scattered parts of Sumbawa, Flores, Sumba, and Timor. Both *ladang* and *sawah* agriculture are carried on together in north-central Sumatra, extreme western Java, and east-central Sulawesi.

A third type of cultivation was introduced by the Dutch in colonial times: the so-called estate agriculture, characterized by large plantations. One valuable crop plant, the oil palm, is profitably raised only on such plantations; several other plants, although grown by individuals or, more often, village collective enterprise, also make profitable estate crops. The principal crops of the plantations are rubber, oil palm, sugarcane, tobacco, fibers such as abaca and sisal, coffee, tea, and Cinchona; less important are coconuts, various spices, and a few others. The details and economics of estate agriculture need not be of concern at this point. Suffice it to say that estate crops are fairly diverse, and accordingly, plantations have been established in both the lowlands and the mountains, the choice of locality depending on the requirements of the

43

plant that is to be grown. The principal estate areas include the uplands of western Java, the uplands and the north coastal lowlands of central Java, some Javan lowlands around the Straits of Madura, and the uplands of eastern Java; as well as northeastern and west-central Sumatra. There are scattered plantations in several other parts of the country, also.

Still other kinds of agriculture are practiced in Indonesia. Largely confined to Java and Madura are *pekarangan,* mixed garden land, and *tegalan,* land not irrigated but continuously cropped. (In some areas, the word *pekarangan* simply means an open yard.) Widespread are small garden plots in connection with individual homesteads; village gardens tended communally; fields produced through the drainage of swampland; small-holdings of coconuts, coffee, or some other crop; and small plantings of Pará rubber trees in *ladang.* In Indonesia, about four people out of five are supported by some kind of cultivation. With this figure in mind, it is easy to see how agricultural practices could have altered or removed much of the country's forest.

Today, Indonesia's greatest continuous expanses of tropical rainforest are found in eastern and central Kalimantan, where *ladang* agriculture has been limited chiefly to the river borders, and where between 80 and 90 percent of the land is still forested. On the divides between the rivers, there are vast tracts where one could walk for days and never catch a glimpse of the sky through the unbroken canopy. But in western Kalimantan, with a denser population and more extensive *ladang* agriculture, only 50 to 60 percent of the land is forested. There is a large area of swamp peat forest in southern Kalimantan, and two others near the western tip of the island. Mangrove swamp borders the southern and eastern coastlines in many places. About 70 to 80 percent of Irian Barat is in rainforest. There is, however, a long east-west strip of deforested uplands where the tribesmen have much land under cultivation, and where they burn the Imperata or other grasses repeatedly to drive out wild game and enemy warriors. Here, many grassy valleys are quite treeless, the activities of man having helped produce a vegetation type called savanna. At higher altitudes, stands of evergreen oaks occupy abandoned village sites. Irian Barat is the only part of Indonesia where the mountains are high enough to permit the development of all the altitudinally zoned vegetation types of the country, from tropical rainforest in the lowlands to alpine scrub on the peaks. Near the southeastern corner of Irian Barat there is swamp peat forest, passing into mangrove swamp at the coast. Mangrove swamp is also conspicuous around Teluk Barau (the former McCluer Gulf) and Teluk Kamrau.

In northern and northeastern Sumatra, about 70 to 80 percent of the land is in forest, much of it rainforest. In extreme northern Sumatra, however, decreased rainfall and the activities of man have militated against the growth of forest; the predominant vegetation in savanna woodland, a kind of grassland with scattered trees. The southern tip of Sumatra, and a broad band across the island's middle, are about 60 to 70 percent forest, while for the remainder of the island the figures are about 40 to 50 percent. Indonesia's greatest expanse of swamp peat forest occupies the Sumatran lowlands east of the uplift called Pegunungan Barisan ("series of ranges"). This expanse reaches from about Tanah Puteh southward almost to the southern tip of the island. Sumatra's formerly or currently producing oilfields, such as Duri, Sebanga, Bekasap, Minas, Lirik Ukul, Tempino, Kenali Assam, Betung, Benakat, Limau Djerigi, Selara Ladangpait, Gresik, Kluang, Talang Akar, Suban, and Talang Djimar, lie mostly in this swampy belt or just outside it. As usual, the swamp peat forest passes coastally into *hutan bakau* ("mangrove wilderness"), the mangrove swamp. There is also a good bit of mangrove swamp along the northeastern coast, considerably less along the western. The small islands west of Sumatra, as well as Bangka and Belitung to the east, have been extensively deforested. A few scattered expanses of rainforest remain on the extreme western end of Java; but for the most part Java has been cleared, only 20 to 30 percent of the land being still in forest. Much of this island has been given over to *sawah*, irrigable fields. Of the forest that remains, a greater part has been saved for the cutting of *kaju djati*, the timber Westerners call teak. Madura is largely under cultivation. On Sulawesi, the amount of forested land is about 60 to 70 percent in the north and northeast, 40 to 50 percent elsewhere. Of the Lesser Sundas, only Wetar is still well forested. On other islands of this group, from Bali through Timor, somewhere between 10 and 20 percent of the land is forested. The deforestation of Bali is not surprising, for the island has a very large population, and one that relies heavily on *sawah* agriculture for subsistence. But it is remarkable that such islands as Sumbawa, Flores, and Timor, in spite of a comparatively low population density, have been deforested to a greater degree than even such heavily settled islands as Java and Madura. This circumstance is thought to reflect the inflammability of the vegetation during the dry season of the Lesser Sundas; the frequent fires militate against the return of forest to areas that have been cleared. On Timor are stretches of country covered not with forest but with grassland in which trees are scattered, expanses resembling the savanna woodland that stretches across northern Australia. It is believed that activities of man, such as timbering, grazing, and burning, have limited the effectiveness of Timor's somewhat reduced and seasonal rainfall, permitting the local development of a vegetation type more characteristic of the drier lands that lie south of Indonesia.

From the foregoing remarks, it would seem that Indonesia still has quite a bit of forest. This is true, but much of the timber is *belukar,* second growth. Less than a fifth of the land supports *rimba,* the virgin or primeval forest. Since the country attained independence, the government has done what it could to encourage emigration from overcrowded Java and Madura to the thinly settled, and therefore still forested, lands of Sumatra and Kalimantan. Indonesians usually have strong emotional ties to the *kampung* and *tanah air,* the village and native land; and so there has been no great wave of migration toward the outer islands. Nevertheless, Sumatra and Kalimantan are frontiers that are becoming somewhat more attractive to settlers, and the further deforestation of the country is to be expected. Indeed, in 1971 some Indonesians began protesting the activities of foreign firms which had been logging out the Kalimantan forests with no effort to replant.

Now to review the Indonesian flora. It is rich, made up of a great number of species. Exactly how many, no one can say, for botanical exploration of the country is not complete. In Borneo alone there are twice as many kinds of plants as in all of Africa. A list of known Indonesian plants would probably run to 35,000 species, perhaps more. Several factors combine to bring about this richness. For one thing, plant species are always numerous in wet tropics, and therefore in most of Indonesia. Also, the country offers a variety of environmental situations, from coastal lowlands to high mountains, and so is ecologically suitable for a diversity of plants. The subdivision of the country into many islands likewise has some bearing on floral richness. Plants, even the higher or seed-bearing kinds, are very ancient, and through the millennia many plant stocks have diversified, evolved into different species on different islands of Indonesia. Finally, the country has been in a geographic position to receive plant migrants from both Asia and Australia. This last consideration is, however, less important than might at first be suspected, for Australian plant life in general has not been very successful in pushing northward, not even into nearby New Guinea. Students of plant distribution recognize a florally distinctive area, the Malaysian Province, extending from the Philippines and the southern half of the Malay Peninsula southward through New Guinea. The Malaysian Province is bordered to the north by the Continental Southeast Asiatic Province, while to the northwest is the Indian Province. These three Provinces together make up the Indo-Malaysian Subkingdom. To the west of this subkingdom is the African Subkingdom, and to the east the Polynesian Subkingdom. The three subkingdoms together make up the Palaeotropical Kingdom. This geographic classification implies, among other things, that many plant species, or groups of related species (genera or families), are restricted to the Malaysian Province, giving it distinctiveness. Some may range widely through it, while others are confined to one portion of it. Of course, man has carried many plants far beyond their natural ranges, but at this point we are concerned with original distribution. Various plant species or groups naturally extend from the Malaysian Province far into continental Asia, Africa, Polynesia, or elsewhere; but not many are shared between Indonesia and Australia, the latter forming a Kingdom of its own. In the discussion that follows, the plants mentioned

47

need not be confined to Indonesia or the Malaysian Province, for in any region some of the most conspicuous, interesting, or useful native plants may also range to quite distant lands.

Ferns are abundant in Indonesia, some of them delicate and graceful, others tree-sized. In Java a tree fern, Alsophila, reaches a height of 50 feet. It is common on the slopes of Gedeh and Pangrango, the twin volcanos mentioned previously. The wool-covered rhizome of Dicksonia, another Javan tree-fern, gave rise to the European legend of the "Scythian lamb," supposedly part animal and part plant. On Kalimantan and Irian Barat, steep hillsides often become saturated with rainwater, break loose, and slide down into the valley, leaving raw scars that are rapidly invaded by a thick growth of ferns large and small. These thickets persist for decades before the scar is reclaimed by forest. A fern of the genus Adiantum, known to florists as walking fern, comes from Indonesia and other tropical lands. Many Indonesian ferns are epiphytic, growing on tree trunks or branches. One such is a nest fern, Asplenium. Plant debris accumulates in its leaf clusters, providing a medium in which small animals can burrow. On Java, a nest fern sometimes harbors an earthworm two feet long. A staghorn fern, Platycerium, often grown in conservatories, also comes from Indonesia. It its native land, it sometimes harbors frogs, lizards, and small snakes beneath its flattened leaves. From Java to New Guinea, a gigantic fern called Aglaomorpha grows high among the branches. A cycad, superficially palm-like in appearance but actually representative of a more ancient plant group, often grows near rocky shores of Indonesia; nurserymen in the United States know it as sago palm, queen sago, or fern palm. The conifers, cone-bearing trees, are poorly represented in the tropics, but it is interesting to note that true pines, species of the genus Pinus, grow in the highlands of northern Indonesia, Podocarpus and Araucaria in Irian Barat uplands. An incense cedar, Libocedrus, is found at high altitudes of Irian Barat. Another conifer, a Dammara known as Amboina pine, is widespread in Indonesia; its resin is one source of gum-dammar, used in varnishes.

Passing to the flowering plants, the palm family is diverse in Indonesia. The coconut palm, Cocos, called *pohon kelapa* or *pohon*

*njiur,* is conspicuous on many shores and is also grown on plantations although it is not particularly an estate crop. *Kelapa muda,*
green coconuts, yield an edible soft pulp quite different from the
firm meat of the ripe nuts; and *air kelapa,* watery juice of the
young nuts, is different from *santan kelapa,* the milk that can be
pressed from the ripe meat. Copra, the semidried meat of the coconut, is exported. Coconut oil, extracted from copra and with a high
glycerine content, has been used in baking and candy-making, the
manufacture of soap and other cosmetics, candle-making, and the
production of synthetic rubber, airplane brake fluid, and safety
glass. *Sabut kelapa,* the fiber of the coconut husk, has been used
for cordage, fish nets, door mats, mattress stuffing, brushes, insula-
tion, and packing material. The flower of the coconut palm can be
tapped for a juice from which sugar is extracted, or the juice may
be fermented and distilled to produce an alcoholic beverage. Obviously, the coconut palm is an important plant in Indonesia.

The Areca palm is also important, but for different reasons. It resembles a small coconut palm, and the nut looks much like a diminutive coconut. The meat of the Areca nut, mixed with lime and
rolled in a pepper leaf, is chewed as a mild narcotic and stimulant.
Among uncivilized or isolated ethnic groups, the lime (*kapur*) is
obtained by burning mollusk shells. It liberates an alkaloid from
the nut meat, and the pepper leaf renders the mixture "hot," mask-
ing the nut's astringency. The tree and its nut are often called betel-nut, although betel was originally a Portuguese name for the
climbing pepper whose heart-shaped, leathery leaf enfolds the
quid. *Pinang* is the Malayan name for the Areca palm (*penang* in
the Malay Peninsula), *sireh* for the pepper, *sireh makan* for the
quid. There are many names for the betel-box, the container in
which the mixture is kept; it may be a simple gourd, or it may be
an elaborately decorated metal box. A special pouch is made to
carry betel-nuts, and special nutcrackers to open them. For at least
2,400 years, betel-nut has been used in Indonesia. There was a
time when *sireh* was proffered by Indonesian courtiers in the same
way that their European counterparts proffered snuff from fancy
boxes. Today *sireh* is used especially, although not exclusively, by
peasants and uncivilized tribesmen. (But not all tribesmen; for the

49

custom of taking *sireh*, introduced into New Guinea from the eastern part of the island, has not reached some upland peoples of western Irian Barat.) The chewing of betel-nut, like any other practice that makes life more tolerable, has had its fanatical opponents. When a quid is being chewed, the saliva becomes bright red, and the chewer's crimson mouth is a surprising sight to anyone unfamiliar with betel-nut. In parts of New Guinea, the nearby presence of a village is often revealed by numerous red splatters of expectoration on the forest floor. After years of chewing *sireh*, the teeth turn coal-black.

Several kinds of Indonesian palms, mostly belonging to the genera Metroxylon and Arenga, yield *sagu*, a starch called sago in English. When sago is to be prepared, the palm is felled, the thick trunk split, the starchy pith removed, grated, and washed. When the water is drawn off, the residue is edible as a thick broth, or can be baked into biscuits. When the residue is made into a paste and forced through a sieve, the resulting product is the "pearl sago" of commerce, *sagu rendang* of the local people. The West formerly imported a great deal of sago for use in puddings, cocoa, and cattle feed; but the real importance of sago is as a starchy food for several million people in and near Indonesia. Sago is especially valued toward eastern Indonesia, in other words outside the main rice-growing region. In most areas, the sago palm (called *pohon rumbia*) is cut from the wilds; but a few ethnic groups, such as the Toradja of Sulawesi, cultivate the plant. If left undisturbed, the sago palm trunk sends up a number of sprouts from its base; these are nourished by the starch of the parent trunk, which soon dies. Thus, the cutting of the sago palm, properly timed, does not reduce the local abundance of the species. The principal sago-yielding palm, a species of Metroxylon, is confined to the Malaysian Province. Quite a few kinds of palm, and even cycads and tree ferns, yield sago, but it is usually of an inferior grade. One Arenga palm, called *aren*, yields not only sago but also sugar and cordage, as well as roof thatching that lasts for decades even in a tropical climate. Balinese temples are often thatched with *aren* leaves.

The fishtail palms of the genus Caryota yield sago, sugar, wine, and fiber, as well as a hard wood used by uncivilized tribes in the

manufacture of bows. In New Guinea, most bows are made of Caryota wood, and the long cane arrows are tipped with this same
wood, which is called black palm. Leaves of the lontar palm, a
species of Borassus, were used in early times as a sort of paper on
which written characters were scratched, and lontar leaves were
even bound together as books. It is said that the curlicue nature of
several early Asian scripts reflected the difficulty of drawing
straight lines on the ribbed palm leaf without splitting it. Today,
lontar leaves are made into fans, mats, buckets, hats, and thatching. Most parts of the lontar palm—leaves, stems, pith, juice, and
fruits—are somehow useful; fiber, timber, musical instruments,
starch, sugar, wine, edible seed sprouts, and fruit pulp all come
from this plant. The sugar is made from the lontar sap, which is
collected by tapping the flower stalks; the wine, or toddy, is produced by fermentation of this sap. Palm wines are various, but in
general they combine a slightly musty odor like that of Chianti
with a delicate, faintly sweet flavor that has no counterpart in the
familiar wines of the West. The leaf stems of the buri palm, Cory-
pha species, are so thick and woody that they can be made into
fence rails and furniture, and the buri flower stalk may weigh half
a ton. Strips of buri leaves are woven into hats, and into a matting
which in the past has been used for sails around Makasar. The lin-
dung, a palm of the genus Pinanga, is noteworthy for its thousands
of black fruit borne on red stems. It and some Indonesian fan
palms of the genus Licuala are grown both locally and in foreign
lands as ornamentals.

Not all palms have the familiar "feather duster" shape of the
ornamental kind. The name *rotan* (in English, rattan) is applied
to a number of Indonesian palms, mostly of the genera Calamus
and Daemonorops, that twist and climb upon other trees, held in
place by steelhard spines on the leaf tips. Great lengths of rattan lianas are pulled down by villagers to be made into cordage,
baskets, chair bottoms, furniture, whips, and suspension bridges of
a rude sort. "Malacca" walking canes are also of rattan. One species
of Calamus, confined to the Malaysian Province, yields a resin
known as dragon's blood. Another important palm throughtout Indonesia and in some nearby lands is the nipa (from the Malayan

*nipah*). Salt-tolerant, nipa grows on coasts and along river mouths, sometimes in pure stands, at other times in company with mangroves. If any plant association merits the term "impassable," it is a certain kind of nipa swamp, where the great, spiny leaves of one palm overlap those of the next. Like the mangroves, the nipa builds coastal land. Its sap yields sugar and wine; but its really useful part is the leaf, often 20 feet long and a main source of thatching material. It would be interesting to know how many people are sheltered by a roof of nipa thatching—millions, no doubt

The orchid family is represented by 2,500 species in New Guinea alone, with hundreds more farther north in Indonesia. Most of the species are epiphytic, but some grow upon rocks, and others are rooted in the ground. Contrary to what might be expected, epiphytic orchids are not confined to rainforest. Numerous members of this family are adapted for life where there is an alternation of wet and dry seasons, and so monsoon forest also has epiphytic orchids. Indeed, some species exist where rainfall is inadequate to support forest; they grow in savanna woodland, or even upon the scattered trees of the savanna. The gaudiest cultivated orchids are produced by artificial selection or hybridization, but many of the wild species are extremely showy when in bloom. Indonesia yields species of such genera as Bulbophyllum, Coelogyne, Cymbidium, Habenaria (which is terrestrial), Paphiopedilum, Phalaenopsis (moth orchids), Spathoglottis, Spiranthes, and Vanda, all popular with orchid fanciers. In the New Guinea green-hood orchid, Pterostylis, the flower has a trap-door lip that closes behind a visiting gnat or mosquito; there is an escape tunnel, but in passing through it the insect picks up masses of pollen, which it will later carry to another blossom. Anoectochilus, a dwarfed and terrestrial jewel orchid from Java, is grown for its colorful leaves rather than its flowers: and a Bornean Malaxis is likewise raised as a foliage plant. A Macodes grows on rocks in caves of Borneo and Java; its leaves are mottled with green, gold, and bronze. A species of Grammatophyllum, found from Java northward, is sometimes called the queen of orchids, for its stemlike pseudobulbs are 15 feet or more in height, and the flower stalk, itself about 6 feet long, may bear 100 or more blooms. The flower, yellow with reddish-brown spots, is about 6 inches across.

The terrestrial bamboo orchid, Arundina, has tall sprouts and can be grown as a hedge. A small epiphytic Polystachya, with greenish-yellow flowers, is not particularly attractive, but is remarkable in ranging through the tropics of both Asia and the New World. How did it manage to attain such a distribution? A scorpion orchid of the genus Arachnis is widespread in Indonesia; the common name derives from the grotesque shape of the yellow and brown flower. A giant Arachnis from Borneo is known as the spider orchid. Indonesian species of Renanthera have been artificially crossed with those of Vanda in order to introduce into the latter genus the brilliant red color of the Renanthera flower, and species of Ascocentrum have been crossed with Vanda to make hybrids of compact form. *Anggrek* is a general name for epiphytic orchids in Indonesia, although a strikingly distinct kind may have a designation of its own.

Another interesting family is that of the bananas. More than 60 species of bananas are native to southeastern Asia. The familiar cultivated ones are practically seedless, and it is surprising to see Indonesian wild bananas with large, black seeds. Two wild species of Indonesia may have been involved in the ancestry of the New World's more familiar cultivated variety. Some Asian bananas are big, fat, and red-skinned, others yellow and almost a yard long, still others tiny and with edible skins. Certain bananas are not edible until cooked; but these, called plantains or cooking bananas, are often prized more than the immediately edible kinds. Plantain slices are used to season meats, stews, and other dishes, while thinner slices, deep-fried and salted, are served as an appetizer. *Pisang* is the Indonesian name for banana or plantain. Both are consumed locally, but neither is important as an export crop. Abaca is a banana whose fiber, called "Manila hemp," makes exceptionally fine rope. In Dutch colonial times, abaca plantations were established here and there in western Indonesia, but the Philippines remained the leading producer of "Manila hemp." In Indonesia the fibers of the abaca and of the Sumatran banana have been used in the weaving of textiles. Patterned in reddish-brown, natural, and dark blue, these banana-fiber textiles have the rich look of tapestry. The dwarf Sumatran banana is also cultivated for its leaves, which are beautifully variegated with green and red, and the larger Bornean blood banana is similarly prized for colorful foliage.

The Pandanus family is a small one, but its members, called screw-pines, attract the attention of any visitor to Indonesia. The Pandanus trunk, supported by a number of above-ground roots, appears to be on stilts. Trunk and exposed roots are studded with spines. The leaves, sword-shaped and edged with spines, grow in clusters at the end of otherwise bare branches. The juice of the clustered fruitlets has a sharp flavor like that of fresh pineapple, and the seeds are nutritious. The leaves are sometimes plaited into baskets, betel-nut bags, sleeping mats, ceremonial mats, and food covers. Pandanus is often conspicuous along rocky coasts, but it also grows high into the mountains. The generic name, Pandanus, is from the Malayan *pandan,* while the common name of screw-pine alludes to the spiral arrangement of the young leaves and the plant's similarity to the pineapple in leaf and fruit. In New Guinea, *aran* is one name given to a distinctive mountain Pandanus, whose bright red fruit cluster is prized by tribesmen. Its fruitlets are not eaten raw but are boiled, or else soaked and then roasted. Freycinetia, a climbing relative of Pandanus, grows on Java.

A much larger family is that of the aroids, the arum-like plants. Indonesian species of Pothos and Raphidophyllum are climbing aroids of the forest; they are popular outside the country as house plants. A species of Aglaonema is another house plant that comes from Indonesia. But to people of that country, the most important aroid is taro (Colocasia and related genera). Cultivated from ancient times and distributed from Africa through tropical Asia into Polynesia, taro exists in several hundred varieties. The leaves make edible greens after boiling to remove acridity, but the plant has been cultivated principally for its rootstock, which becomes palatable after heating or boiling. Or the ground-up rootstock may be boiled and allowed to ferment, producing a sort of mush best known in the United States by its Hawaiian name of poi. Taro is an important crop in Indonesia, where it may be grown in a ditch, beside an otherwise unproductive swamp, or around the edge of the *sawah.* Taro is not an export crop, but for many a family it is a source of food and occasionally a little revenue. Several Indonesian plants related to taro have variegated or otherwise decorative leaves, and so are widely grown as ornamentals in the gardens of the West. Among them are a Javan Caladium with green and white leaves, and several varieties of Alocasia. A famous aroid is the Sumatran plant known botanically as Amorphophallus. Its leaves are small and unimpressive, but its flower, which pushes up from an underground rootstock, develops into a giant vase-like structure, 8 feet tall and equally wide. Above the purple and yellow vase there arises the spadix, a tubular column of bright yellow; the entire flower may be 15 feet high. The grotesque bloom has an odor of rotting meat, and is pollinated by carrion beetles. Smaller but still impressive species of Amorphophallus grow in other parts of Indonesia.

Of the grass family, the species of Imperata have been mentioned. The bamboos (*bambu* in Malayan) are also grasses. Giant bamboos, such as Dendrocalamus, reach a height of 100 feet, and these large species are important to tribesmen and peasant farmers. The externally visible joints of the bamboo are represented internally by partitions, one of which serves as a bottom when a short length of bamboo is used as a pail or cooking utensil. A longer length, strong yet light, can be used as a house piling or joist. With the partitions removed, long lengths make excellent water pipes, bringing irrigation water to the *sawah*. Near Merauke in Irian Barat, tribal hunters and warriors use a wide strip of giant bamboo for a bow. In Java, the *betong* and the *tali*, bamboos of the genus Gigantochloa, supply almost everything that is needed to build a house; not just the framing but also a flooring of flattened canes, along with walls and partitions of *bilik*, woven bamboo strips. Narrower strips, cut and tied while green, lash the framework together and bind it rigidly when they dry. In many parts of New Guinea, a bamboo tube is crammed with tobacco, and so becomes a tobacco pipe. Life-preservers, arrows, quivers, jars, bridges, knife sheaths, betel-boxes, fishing rods, walking canes, flutes, animal cages—there seems no end to the variety of things that are made from bamboo in some part of Indonesia. Split bamboo can be made into nets, hats, wickerwork, mats, and umbrella frames. Contrary to what might be expected, extensive use of bamboos and lianas is not characteristic of the Irian Barat tribes. Bamboos are hard, lianas tough, and both are difficult to gather and work without iron axes, hatchets, machetes, small knives, and planes. Thus, bamboo craftsmanship became best developed in western Indonesia. In many parts of the country, the seeds and young sprouts of certain bamboos are gathered for food. A Javan bamboo develops mineral masses in some of the joints, an opalescent, phosphorescent substance chemically much like opal, and prized in the Orient as a medicine. The common bamboo of Indonesia has been imported into many lands as an ornamental.

Sugarcane, Saccharum, is another famous grass. Perhaps it originated in India, but it reached Indonesia centuries ago. In the 1920s and early 1930s, sugar was Indonesia's most valuable export, ranking ahead of even rubber and oil. Partly as a result of the Great Depression, sugar dropped to third place by the latter 1930s. In later years there was a further decline in sugar exports, partly because peasant cultivators were turning away from sugarcane in favor of other crops, but also because internal consumption of sugar increased. Sugarcane is most profitable as an estate crop. It needs a fairly constant supply of water, and since it takes more than a year to mature, in some areas the canefields must be irrigated during the dry season. This plant is called *tebu* in Idonesia, where it is still grown extensively.

But of course the most important grass of Indonesia is rice, a cereal on which about half the world's population is dependent. The wild ancestor of rice, a semiaquatic Oryza, may have ranged from Indonesia to the Asian mainland, and may first have been cultivated in India or Indochina. Early European explorers found many strains of cultivated rice in Indonesia, but the grain never did spread to all parts of the country. Most New Guinean peoples failed to take up its cultivation; and in the Moluccas, rice never displaced sago as the principal starchy food. Rice grows best in the *sawah*, the fields that can be flooded; and no other grain, not even wheat or maize, will produce as much food per acre as *sawah*-grown rice. There is also a strain of rice that can be grown without irrigation, providing the rainfall is plenteous. Dry-rice cultivation is less profitable than wet-rice, but at least it permits the raising of this grain by ethnic groups who practice only *ladang* agriculture.

Rice is not an export crop; it is consumed locally, by millions of Indonesians at every meal. Indeed, the expression *makan nasi,* meaning to take a meal, literally means to eat rice. Most *sawah* is given over to this grain, at least during part of the year.

The many names for rice attest to its importance in Indonesian agriculture and diet. *Padi* is the rice plant, rice in the husk, or a head of rice (hence the English phrase "paddy fields"). *Beras* is husked rice, *bertih* is unhusked rice roasted in a pan, *nasi* is cooked rice, *nasi goreng* fried rice, *nasi kuning* rice flavored and colored yellow by saffron or turmeric. *Beras pulut* (Malayan) or *ketan* (Javanese) is glutinous rice, while *nasi guri* is rice cooked in an earthen pot with meat, shrimp, vegetables, and seasonings. *Nasi ulam* is rice with an uncooked side dish, *nasi kebuli* rice with eggs and half a dozen spices, *lontong* rice cooked in banana leaves, *bubur santan* rice porridge made with coconut milk. Asjura, the tenth day of the first month, is a Muslim holiday on which it is appropriate to serve *bubur asjura,* a rice porridge with peanuts, eggs, and several kinds of beans. The Dutch spread the fame of what they called *rijsttafel,* "rice-table," an Indonesian meal that combines rice with meat, fish, vegetable, relish, and fritter side dishes. Of course the peasant cultivator finds the elaborate, restaurant-style *rijsttafel* beyond his means, but he is familiar with many ways in which rice can be cooked and garnished. To him, *sawah* is a rice-field; *lumpang* (mortar) is a rice-block; *penuaian* (reapings) and *panenan* (harvest) mean the rice crop.

The ginger family is conspicuous in Indonesia. The common ginger, Zinziber, is valued for its spicy rootstock, as is its relative the bitter ginger. *Bandrek* is a gingery drink popular in Indonesia, especially in the uplands where it is served piping hot. It is made by steeping thin slices of fresh gingerroot in water to which brown sugar has been added. Other members of the ginger family are prized as ornamentals. Red ginger, Alpinia, comes from the Moluccas. Tapeinocheilus, widespread in Indonesia, has cone-shaped flower clusters of bright orange; and similarly widespread is the gigantic torch ginger, Phaeomeris, with scarlet flowers. Likewise in the ginger family is a Javan Ammomum known as cardamom. (More accurately, it is one of several different plants called by this name.) Cardamom seed was one of the plant products loaded by European trading ships long ago in Indonesia, the peppery seeds being used as a carminative and digestant, as well as to mask the taste of other medicines.

The dogbane family has a famous member in Indonesia: a species of Rauwolfia, ranging from Java northward into continental Asia. It is a source of reserpine, a tranquilizing drug whose use was ancient in India, although not until the 1950s did Western physicians also begin to employ Rauwolfia extracts in the treatment of mental disturbances and hypertension. Similarly ranging from Java northward is a species of the dogbane genus, Strophanthus, noteworthy because some of its members yield cortisone, a drug that reduces swelling.

The mulberry family has several valuable representatives in Indonesia, among them the figs. The fig of commerce is not native to Indonesia, but the country has other species of its genus, Ficus. Some of these have edible fruit, others woody and inedible. The Java, ivory, and cluster figs are Indonesian, and so is the India-rubber tree, a very familiar ornamental but one whose identity as a fig will come as a surprise to many. As a potted, indoor plant, the India-rubber tree does not reach above shrub size; but in its native homeland, from Indonesia to continental Asia, it is a huge tree of the forest. Some tropical members of Ficus are called strangler figs, for they wrap around and kill other trees. The famous banyan, with its multiple trunks, is a fig perhaps originally confined to India although now seen in Indonesia. Artocarpus, the breadfruit, is related to the figs and similarly belongs to the mulberry family. Widespread in Indonesia and Polynesia, it is an important tree, for the fruit is edible, the wood is easily worked, the inner bark is a source of fiber, and the milky juice can be mixed with coconut oil to make caulking. Tapa cloth, once used in Polynesia for clothing, mats, and tapestries, and admired today for its artistic quality, was sometimes made from the inner bark fiber of the breadfruit; but another member of the mulberry family, Broussonetia or paper mulberry, yields tapa of a better grade. Species of Broussonetia are scattered from Japan to Indonesia. Anciently, tapa cloth was widely manufactured in Indonesia, but in many parts of the country it was supplanted by other textiles. However, some ethnic groups have continued to make tapa cloth, which is in some demand for its decorative possibility.

The pepper family warrants comment. The betel-pepper has been mentioned. A species of Piper, it may have originated in Indonesia but was subsequently carried well beyond the confines of the Malaysian Province. Another species of this genus is the common black pepper, a plant originally Indonesian, and the basis of a great pepper trade in Sumatra before the arrival of the Europeans. White pepper is a specially processed form of the black pepper. Raised mostly by smallholders, pepper is still an important crop in Indonesia. Another genus of the pepper family, Peperomia, is concentrated in the New World tropics; but there is a Javan species that is grown as a climbing ornamental. In recent times, various genera of the gesneriad family have also come to be prized as house plants. The best known gesneriads, Gloxinia and the "African violet," are not from Indonesia, but Java has produced an Aeschynanthus called lipstick plant, and a miniature creeping gesneriad known as Agalmyla. The cultivated Monophyllaea is a gesneriad from Sumatra. Indonesia has also supplied some ornamental members of the spurge family: a tree-sized Bischofia, an Acalypha with bright leaves, and a Codiaeum (generally miscalled Croton) with strikingly variegated foliage.

Now to depart from family listing to focus attention on a miscellany of noteworthy plants from Indonesia. Other ornamentals deriving from that country include a widespread amaranth called Joseph's-coat; two Ardisias; a wax-gourd, Benincasa, grown mostly as a curiosity although its fruit can be pickled; a Dillenia; and two red-flowered Clerodendrons. Also familiar to horticulturists are a colorful Coleus from Java; huge Crinums, members of the Amaryllis family, from Sumatra; the air-potato, Dioscorea, a member of the yam family; and several kinds of Hoya. Aquatic plants include the East Indian lotus, with a pink blossom, and several Cryptocoryne grown in aquaria. Even the horticulturist would be surprised by some Indonesian species of Rhododendron. Their restriction to uplands is not unexpected, since in various other parts of the world the genus is best represented at high altitudes; but it is astonishing that some Indonesian species are epiphytes, flourishing high above the ground on the branches of large trees. Indonesia also has terrestrial Rhododendrons. A Brassaia, often sold as a "Schefflera," and grown in the ground when under cultivation, commonly becomes epiphytic in Indonesia. Oroxylum is a tree whose botanical name means "mountain-wood," although it is common on the Atjeh coast of Sumatra. Its flowers open after dark, from about 10:00 P.M. to midnight, giving off a pungent odor that has often been described as "foxy." The flowers, which are pollinated by bats, are later replaced by gigantic, sword-shaped seed pods which reach a full yard in length. When ripe, the pods split open to liberate winged seeds that drift away like moths on the coastal breezes.

Other floral oddities of Indonesia are the tropical pitcher-plants, various species of Nepenthes, a genus that is placed in a family of its own. At least one Nepenthes does not climb, but others do. The "pitcher" is an insect trap, and the plant is carnivorous, digesting its small prey. Pitcher-plants are found on trees not only of the forest but also of the savanna woodland. Concentrated toward New Guinea are the curious ant-plants, several aberrant genera of the madder family growing epiphytically on the branches of trees. They are not confined to trees of the rainforest, but often adorn those of the more open situations, and even those of the mangrove swamp. The leaves and stems of an ant-plant are not remarkable in appearance, but they dangle from what resembles a huge potato, a lumpy mass honeycombed with tunnels and cavities which more often than not are inhabited by fiercely stinging ants. Sometimes water accumulates in the cavities, and the damper ant-plants are inhabited not by ants but by treefrogs. In New Guinea, a little treefrog of the genus Hyla is found in ant-plants during dry spells; and a lizard, the snake-eyed skink, lays its eggs in the plants. Neither the frog nor the lizard is absolutely dependent on these plants, but some of the ants are thought to be. An Indonesian Dischidia, of the milkweed family, is even more remarkable than the ant-plants. Many of its leaves are of ordinary appearance, but others have the shape of pitchers. Certain of these pitchers hang down, holding water and nutrients, and the plant is nourished by sending a root down into its own pitcher; but some of the pitchers grow upside down, stay dry, and provide a home for ants. Dischidia ranges beyond the boundaries of the Malaysian Province.

Not so the genus Rafflesia, one species of which is something of a botanical classic. The sticky Rafflesia seeds adhere to the feet of elephants and to the beaks of seed-eating birds. Somewhere in the Sumatran or Bornean rainforest, a Rafflesia seed chances to be rubbed off against the partially exposed root of a large vine, Tetrastigma. The seed germinates and forms a parasitic union with the vine, the Rafflesia tissues penetrating and permeating those of the host plant. Nourished by the vine, the parasite develops only a small, formless vegetative body—until the time comes for blossoming. Then the Rafflesia sprouts a fantastic bloom a yard across and up to 15 pounds in weight. The thick, fleshy petals are scarlet with white spots, and surround a white bowl. The odor is putrid, attracting flies and carrion beetles, which serve as pollinators. Scattered in occurrence and unpredictable in blooming, Rafflesia has been seen in the wild by few botanists. One species flowers rather frequently on Nusa Kambangan near Tjilatjap, Java.

Several trees are noteworthy. One of these, a Koompassia commonly known as tapang, is the tallest tree of the Indonesian rainforest, and one of the tallest in the world. Reaching a height of 250 feet, it rivals the redwoods of the United States. Like so many trees of the rainforest, the tapang is supported by enormous, wall-like buttresses that flare outward from the trunk. Many oriental timbers —ballow, bilian, bintangor, chingai, damar laut, daru, ebony, ironwood, kamuning, kranji, mangrove, meranti, mirabau, russock, sandalwood, sapan wood, selangan batu, selangan kacha, seraya, tampinis, tembusu—are cut in Indonesia, but this does not mean that all of them are particularly characteristic of the country. Of the ones listed, all but ebony, ironwood, mangrove, and sandalwood bear names derived from, or more accurately corrupted from, the Malayan. It was in the Malay Peninsula, not Indonesia, that these names entered the English language.

An especially important timber is teak, Tectona. Native to Indonesia and mainland areas farther north, it has been planted at many localities both inside and outside its natural range. Although the tree itself does well in the rainforest, its wood is of inferior quality there, the most productive plantings being in areas with a marked dry season.

Much Indonesian lumber comes from the tall trees of the dipterocarp family. Although widespread in the Old World tropics, the dipterocarps are especially numerous in Indonesia, where they yield not only timber but also gums, fragrant resins, varnishes, and pitch. Gurjun balsam, used in medicine and varnish-making, is extracted from several Indonesian dipterocarps. In some areas, the rainforest is made up principally of trees belonging to this family.

No account of Indonesia would be complete without mention of *pohon durian*, the tree that yields the durian fruit. *Durian* means spinosity, the reference being to short, heavy spines that cover the skin of the fruit. Indonesian cuisine is noted for the deliberate combination of contrasting flavors or textures, and this may be why Indonesians so relish the durian, whose flesh combines the texture of a smooth custard, the flavor of butter-almond ice cream, and the scent of rotting onions. The large seeds, a dozen or so in number, are chestnut-like and edible after roasting. The durian tree, a member of the Bombax family, is widespread in the Malaysian Province, where it is sometimes cultivated, the fruit of the cultivated variety being larger than that of the wild. When wild durians ripen and fall to the ground, they are sought out by many kinds of wildlife; and the orangutan does not wait for them to fall. To the gratification of local residents, a durian tree, whether wild or cultivated, will bear twice a year, producing as many as a hundred fruits at a bearing. Alfred Russel Wallace said that it was worth a trip to the Orient just to eat a durian, but a good many Western visitors never come to share the Indonesian fondness for this remarkable fruit.

The country's vast flora could be reviewed from many standpoints. Attention might first be drawn to some of the comparatively few species or groups that range into Indonesia from an Australian homeland. Here one could mention a Casuarina, called beefwood or Australian "pine." Capable of rooting on coastal dunes and along rivers, it has spread widely through the islands, and is also planted by man as an ornamental and a windbreak. The genus Eucalyptus is highly characteristic of Australia, and mention should therefore be made of a lone species that has managed to invade the rainforest of the Malaysian Province. A fine tree, it takes root mostly in abandoned clearings, and so activities of man may have encouraged its spread into Indonesia and the Philippines. Eucalyptus trees of another species predominate in Timor, where they form a part of the savanna woodland. Silk oaks, Grevillea, range into Indonesia from an Australian center.

A few strange patterns of plant distribution involve the islands. For example, New Guinea has about 20 species of southern beech, Nothofagus; other species of the genus live in New Caledonia, Australia and Tasmania, New Zealand, and southern South America. Or consider Lagenaria, the bottle gourd. Its fruit is made into bottles, dippers, and various containers, not just in and near the Malaysian Province, but also in Africa and again in the New World tropics. It is of demonstrably great antiquity in both hemispheres, and this circumstance has led some archeologists to suspect that primitive man took it across the Pacific. Many plant groups are interesting because they abound in north-temperate regions, and appear again at scattered localities in Indonesia, where they are usually restricted to cool highlands. Examples include oaks, horse-sugars (Symplocos), skullcaps, chinquapins (Castanopsis), primroses, buttercups, cinquefoils, roses, gentians, rabbit-tobaccos, hollies, buckthorns, and blackberries. In parts of the moss forest, blueberries make up much of the woody vegetation.

Rather than distribution, utility might command attention, and in this connection note should be taken of Derris, belonging to the pea family. It is called "New Guinea dynamite," for its root contains a substance that stuns fishes as though an explosive charge had been set off underwater. The drugged fishes are edible, and so Derris is used as a fish poison, not just in New Guinea but over a large part of the Old World tropics. Another Indonesian fish poison is the fruit of Barringtonia, a common tree of the strand. At least 18 other kinds of plants have been used as fish poisons in one or another part of Indonesia, and studies on their effectiveness have led to the commercial production of rotenone. This chemical, in addition to being an insecticide, is used when fishes are to be removed from managed waters, or to be collected for scientific study. During Operation Crossroads, in 1946, a great quantity of rotenone was used to collect marine fishes at Bikini Atoll where atom bombs were tested, and at other atolls not exposed to atomic explosions. It sometimes happens that a fish poison is also given in small doses as a vermifuge, narcotic, or medication. Thus, seeds of Hydnocarpus have been employed from India to Java as a fish poison, but are valued by oriental physicians as a vermifuge and a medication for some skin diseases. A species of Hydnocarpus is a source (not the only one) of chaulmoogra oil, for several thousand years the principal medication for leprosy.

Southeastern Asia is a part of the world in which extensive use has been made of plant toxins—not just chemicals that stun fishes, but others that are poisonous when ingested or when introduced directly into the blood stream. Investigation into a supposed arrow poison of Java was the first step in experimental physiology. In 1809 a French physiologist, François Magendie, used wooden barbs to inject small quantities of the substance into dogs, which quickly died. Obviously, the efficacy of the arrow poison was not a figment of Javanese imagination, as had been suspected. Today we know that the lethal ingredient of the concoction was strychnine, an alkaloid produced by several plants of the genus Strychnos. The Javanese made their arrow poison by boiling the bark of a local Strychnos, but the strychnine of commerce is derived from the satiny, button-like seeds of the nux-vomica tree, another tropical Asian species of Strychnos. A febrifuge, a vermifuge, "bitters," and a supposed snakebite antidote have all been extracted from Strychnos plants in Indonesia. The genus is a member of the Logania family, to which also belongs Buddleia, an Asian ornamental called butterfly bush.

Less sensational than Strychnos, but far more important to man, is the genus Gossypium of the mallow family; its species yield cotton. Several species of wild cotton are scattered over Africa, Asia, and the New World. In the Old World, the plants may have been prized for their oily seeds long before their fiber was used, but as much as 5,000 years ago cotton cloth was turned out in India. Asian native cottons, including the Indonesian, are short-staple. Today, of course, cotton cloth can be imported into Indonesia along with

64

raw cotton, reducing the importance of the native species; and the finest examples of Indonesian cotton work, made from native fiber and tastefully colored with plant dyes, are to be found mostly in museum collections or among family heirlooms. The *kain sarung* or "sarong," the *selendang* or shawl, the *ikat kepala* or headcloth, the *selimut* or blanket-like shoulder cloth, and various items of ceremonial apparel—these traditional garments are commonly although not invariably made of cotton. Traditional styles of cotton cloth decoration include *batik* or resist-dyeing, *ikat* or tie-dyeing, embroidering with gold or silver thread, and spangling with gold, mica, or mirror glass.

In considering Indonesian plants from the standpoint of utility, the account is far from exhausting the list of ones that provide an edible fruit, nut, seed, rootstock, or leaf. For example, there is the mango, whose genus, Mangifera, has many species in southeastern Asia. The common mango probably was first cultivated in India, but it is often seen in Indonesia where it is called *mangga*. (There are, however, other names such as *kuini*, *mempelam*, and *ruminja*, applied to different varieties.) Several kinds of native wild mango are called *pauh*, and are valued both for timber and fruit. Around villages, the coolest spot is likely to be beneath the deep shade of a mango tree, and so various fruits or other produce may be hung from the lower branches of a mango tree as a simple method of refrigeration. The mango, a member of the sumac family, is not related to the mangosteen, a Garcinia of the gamboge family. The mangosteen may once have been confined to the Moluccas, but it was spread widely by man. Its fruit, called *manggis*, is apple-sized and has a hard, reddish-purple skin. Although one of the most delicious tropical fruits, the mangosteen is enjoyed only by people who live where it grows, for it does not ship well. The rambutan is yet another well-known Indonesian fruit. A Nephelium of the soapberry family, it is closely related to the Chinese litchi. *Rambutan* means hairiness, in allusion to the fruit's woolly shell, which resembles a chestnut bur. The *pulasan* is related to the rambutan but has a pinkish, pebbly skin. Visitors to the gardens at Bogor may recall an avenue of tall, buttressed Canarium trees; these yield the Java almond. Then there are the Malay-apple with its apple-flavored berries, the galip or nungi nut, the New Guinea okari whose red, pulpy rind conceals a nut of exceptional size and savor, several kinds of yams, a palm-lily yielding starch, wild passionfruit, various palm buds that can be sliced as salad, the palm fruit called *buah salak*. The present list of noteworthy plants may seem long, but any knowledgeable oldster from a rainforest village could easily quadruple it. He might tell of *kuntji* ("lock"), whose root is antidiarrhetic; *bajam duri* ("spiny spinach"), useful for treating burns; *raweh*, which will blister men and dogs; *padas*, also blistering; *katjubung*, which causes drowsiness and relieves asthma, but is also used by robbers to put prospective victims into deep sleep; and so on through an impressive roster of plants that yield food, drink, seasonings, incense, intoxicants, perfumes, rubber, dyes, glues and varnishes, soaps, fiber, cordage, medicines, insecticides, abortifacients, reputed aphrodisiacs, and contraceptives.

This cursory review of the native Indonesian flora may appropriately close with the spices, perhaps the best-known plants of the islands. It is strange that obscure chemicals, secreted by tropical plants as a protection against insects and other enemies, should have profoundly affected the history of the world. Yet, this was the case. In the rainforest and the monsoon forest, there is an abundance of fungi, bacteria, and insects, against whose inroads the higher plants are sometimes protected by chemicals that infuse the leaves, bark, flower buds, or seeds. As it happens, some of these chemicals will also protect meat and other foods against spoilage and can impart to foods a flavor that man soon learns to enjoy. The spices of the East were known in Europe long before the Portuguese found the sea route to the Indies. (In Old French, reference was so often made to the "four species"—cloves, nutmeg, and cinnamon from the Orient, along with saffron from southern Europe and western Asia—that through a misunderstanding of "species," the word "spices" came into being.) Before the Portuguese began to infringe on Arab trade monopolies around the early 1500s, spices were rare and expensive in Europe, too rare to be used very widely as a mere preservative; they were prized as medicines and supposed aphrodisiacs, and a carton of them was a status symbol. Each autumn in Europe, most cattle herds had to be reduced considerably for lack of winter feed, and the beef had to be salted or pickled if it were not to be wasted. Nutmeg and cloves proved to be especially effective both in preserving this meat and in improving its flavor. The nutmeg tree, Myristica, and the clove tree, Eugenia—respectively called *buah pala* and *buah tjengkih*— in those days were virtually confined to the Moluccas; and of course mace, *bunga pala*, had the same geographic origin as nut- meg, being derived from the covering of the nutmeg seed. Deter- mined to follow the spice trade back to its source, the Portuguese were led into the Moluccas. They were soon followed by other Eu- ropeans, who struggled among themselves and with Muslim mer- chant princes for control of this trade, which expanded to include not only cloves, nutmeg, and mace, but also black pepper and cin- namon. With time, spices of Indonesia were introduced into other tropical lands; new spices were found, and new techniques of pre- serving or seasoning foods. Yet the country has remained a major producer of black pepper, nutmeg, mace, and so-called cassia bark. The last comes not from any Cassia but from a Cinnamomum tree, *kaju manis*, and is valued chiefly for the oil of cinnamon that can be extracted from it.

So much for the native flora. In almost any region, some very common plants are not native but were introduced, and occasion- ally it is hard to decide the category in which an Asiatic plant be- longs. Coconut, banana, taro, Areca, betel-pepper, Lagenaria, and breadfruit were carried so widely by prehistoric man that the orig- inal ranges cannot be determined with certainty. A puzzle has been the origin of the sweet potato, principal crop of the New Guinea uplands. Cultivated sugarcane, rice, and mango probably came from India, but were discussed with the native flora of Indo- nesia because they seemed to have wild relatives or prototypes in that country. On the other hand, the cultivated citrus fruits will be considered introductions, although some of them probably have been in Indonesia for a very long while. Most citrus fruits, species of the genus Citrus, were first brought under cultivation some- where on the Asiatic mainland. Books often state that *limau* is the Malayan name for the lemon, and sometimes for citrus in general. Quite a few Malayan words were borrowed from Persian, and *limau* is probably from the Persian *limun,* as English "lemon" surely is (by way of the French in the latter case). But *limau* is a word used mostly in the Malay Peninsula; *djeruk,* a Javanese term, is the usual Indonesian name for citrus. In some parts of Indonesia, *djeruk* signifies an orange, in other parts a grapefruit. *Djeruk manis,* "sweet citrus," is sometimes the sweet orange, but more often the tangerine; occasionally it is the grapefruit, which is sweeter than the sour orange. *Djeruk djambu,* literally "pumpkin citrus," is surely the grapefruit; *djeruk nipis,* "elongate citrus," the lemon or lime. The pommelo may have grown in Indonesia among other places, but its better-known descendant, the familiar grapefruit, arose under cultivation in the West Indies and was then carried back to the Orient. In spite of popular belief in the West, most citrus fruits are not fully tropical; needing a touch of winter cold to develop full flavor and color, they do best on the periphery of the tropics. Thus, Indonesia has not developed an important citrus industry, although plantings of citrus are numerous.

Probably, early Chinese and Indian writings would throw light on the introduction of several tropical crops into Indonesia, but these sources are not readily available. Even for the time of beginning European expansion into southeastern Asia, sources are fewer than might be wished. The Portuguese period in Indonesia, roughly the sixteenth and early seventeenth centuries, saw the introduction of maize, cassava, tobacco, and red pepper, all from the New World tropics where they had been cultivated by the American Indians, but all doing well in an Asiatic setting. The red pepper, Capsicum, is not related to the black pepper but belongs to the nightshade family. Already prizing several "hot" seasonings, the Indonesians were ready to accept another; and red pepper is still commonly grown in the country. There it is called *tjili,* its Mexican Indian name having been borrowed into Malayan just as it was into English (chili). Tobacco is another member of the nightshade family, its generic name, Nicotiana, honoring Jean Nicot, who obtained tobacco plants from Portugal and introduced them into France. New Guinea tribesmen, like European courtiers, became enthusiastic over tobacco-smoking as soon as the plant was revealed to them. Tobacco spread into the fastnesses of New

Guinea far in advance of European exploration; even remote mountain tribes grew it or traded with their neighbors for it. As among the American Indians, so among the New Guineans: tobacco-smoking came to have mystical significance and was integrated into tribal rituals. In modern Indonesia, tobacco is widely raised. It is called *tembakau*, a word ultimately derived, like English "tobacco," from the West Indian name for a tobacco pipe.

The cassava of the New World, also known as manioc, resembled several native Indonesian plants in that its rootstock yielded starch. In one variety of cassava, the starch was available only after a poisonous substance had been removed from the rootstock, but this, too, was no novelty to Indonesians. Cassava came to be grown very widely in the country, where it is called *ubi kaju*. *Ubi* is a general name for a root crop, while *kaju* means woody; for in contrast with cassava, the native root crops such as taro and yam have fleshy stems. *Ubi pohon,* another name for cassava, means a tree-like root crop, again in allusion to the woody, branching structure of the plant. The word tapioca, a Brazilian Indian name for the cassava's starchy product, was spread by the Portuguese, but not to Indonesia, where there were already plenty of designations for plant starches. *Gaplek* and *koleh-koleh* are among the present Indonesian words for tapioca. With time, cassava became an important crop in the limestone regions of Java, where the native starch-yielding plants do not thrive very well.

But the most significant introduction of the Portuguese period was maize, or corn as it is called in the United States. Known scientifically as Zea, maize was developed thousands of years ago by American Indians from a wild grass. In the New World it held the same position that rice held in tropical Asia, or wheat in temperate Eurasia. In the American tropics, maize was raised by so-called *milpa* agriculture, which is simply another name for *ladang* agriculture; and so this grain had great potentialities for Indonesians who lived outside the wet-rice areas. Today, maize is the principal grain in Sulawesi, Timor, much of eastern Java, and Madura. Local names for this crop are revealing. Through contact with India, the Indonesians learned about wheat centuries before they learned of New World maize. Even though the wheat plant was not adapted

69

to thrive in the climate of Indonesia, its grain was known there. One Indonesian name for maize, *gandung* or *gandum,* evidently represents a transfer to this grain of an old Persian name for wheat. Another Indonesian term for maize, *djagung,* may similarly be borrowed, for it is also applied to Turkish wheat. *Terigu,* the present word for wheat, is of Portuguese derivation. In the uplands of Timor, the Portuguese were remarkably successful in establishing both wheat and the "Irish" potato, but neither crop aroused the enthusiasm of the Timorese.

The Dutch, having ousted the Portuguese from Indonesia during the seventeenth century, soon introduced many other crops. One of these was coffee, Coffea, a genus of the madder family. The coffee tree was native to northeastern Arica, but was spread by the Arabs, who enjoyed the drink that could be brewed from the coffee "bean." Europeans had learned of coffee by the latter 1500s; and soon thereafter, coffee houses sprang up through much of Europe. Near the end of the seventeenth century, an Amsterdam burgomaster carried coffee seeds from Mocha (Mukha) in Yemen to Batavia in Java. A coffee tree bears its first crop in its third year, and it did not take the Dutch long to discover that the plant would do well in Indonesia, where it became an estate crop of the highlands. It is called *kopi* or *kahwa,* both names stemming (like English "coffee") from the Arabic *gahwe.* It is now an important export crop.

Coffee was introduced in the days when Indonesia was being exploited by the Vereenigde Oost-Indische Compagnie, the United East-India Company. In 1798 this firm was dissolved, and a newly organized Dutch government assumed direct control of Indonesia. Early in the nineteenth century, the colonial government of Indonesia established an institute for tropical plant research at Buitenzorg, and began to develop the gardens there. During the nineteenth and early twentieth centuries, with tropical agriculture becoming progressively more scientific, and with the Dutch in a position to command the land and the human resources of Indonesia, a variety of estate crops were successfully introduced. Most important of these were Pará rubber, tea, Cinchona, oil palm, and sisal. The last is the fiber of an Agave, brought from Yucatán. The oil palm, an Elaeis, was brought from the rainforest of western Africa. The oil, used in lubricants and cosmetics, is extracted from the nut. Cinchona is the generic name of certain trees native to South America, especially to the Amazonian slopes of the Andes where South American Indians treated malaria with an infusion of Cinchona bark. The Inca word *quina,* meaning bark, gave rise to the English "quinine," and, through Dutch, to the Indonesian *kenini.* The quinine content of Cinchona bark was a boon to travelers and residents in the tropics, for malaria was everywhere a scourge. So great was the demand for the bark that the South American trees were almost all stripped, and Cinchona plantations were quickly established in other lands. Java received its first trees in 1860. The cultivation of Cinchona was urged and encouraged by the Dutch colonial government, and Java soon outranked all other areas in the quantity and quality of its bark. About 90 percent of the world's quinine supply was coming from Javan bark when the Japanese took over Indonesia in World War II. The tea tree, Thea, was mentioned in the sixteenth century by a Portuguese explorer who described its dried leaves as a product of China and Japan. The plant, a relative of the garden shrub Camellia, was perhaps native to India and first cultivated in China, but the drinking of tea was known from India to Korea. Early in the seventeenth century, Dutch ships loaded tea at Javan ports and carried it back to the Netherlands; but not until the nineteenth century did the Dutch colonial government urge the extensive planting of tea trees in the uplands of Java and Sumatra. Indonesia became a leading producer of *daun teh,* the processed leaves; while *air teh,* the beverage, became locally popular. The Indonesian word *teh,* like English "tea," is from the Chinese spoken at Amoy, a port much visited by Portuguese and Dutch ships in early days.

The most valuable introduction of Dutch colonial times, however, was Pará rubber. Rubber was another discovery of the American Indians, who used it to make a variety of things, from dolls and game balls to overshoes and enema bottles. For a long while in Europe, the substance was merely a curiosity, or at best something that rubbed out pencil marks more effectively than bread crumbs. European uses for rubber multiplied slowly, then very rapidly after the process of vulcanization was discovered around 1840. Many unrelated plants were eventually found to yield a latex that could be turned into rubber. An early industry was based on Castilla, a genus of the mulberry family, with species widespread in the New World tropics. Castilla rubber was extracted by cutting the tree down and then girdling it many times. With this treatment, Castilla trees soon became rare, and attention turned to Pará rubber. The latter is often called Hevea, but this generic name has been bandied about in the scientific literature to such an extent that the common name is preferable for clarity. Perhaps rightly to be called Siphonia, the Pará rubber tree is a member of the spurge family, and was Amazonian in distribution. Seeds of Pará rubber were taken to Kew Gardens near London, whence seedlings were later sent to British colonies in tropical Asia. The plant was not a success until the 1890s, when H. M. Ridley of the Singapore Botanical Gardens discovered that the living tree could be tapped repeatedly if the margin of the tap-wound were pared on each occasion. But as late as 1900, the Dutch in Java felt that the India-rubber tree, a Ficus, held more promise than the South American species. Eventually it became clear that the Pará rubber tree, coming from Amazonian areas of rainforest on lateritic soil, would do well in the similar environment of Sumatra and what was then Dutch Borneo; and Indonesia became a leading producer of rubber. Sticky gums, including the sap of the India-rubber tree, had long been used in Indonesia as birdlime; they were called *getah*, a name soon extended to the milky latex of the Pará rubber. The Javanese name for latex, *karet*, is also widely known.

Comparatively minor crop plants and ornamentals entered Indonesia by a variety of routes. For centuries there was a slow migration of people from southern China into Indonesia, a movement encouraged by the Dutch; and the incoming Chinese often brought their own vegetables. Chinese cabbage and Chinese mustard, species of Brassica, reached Indonesia in this fashion. Cucumber, eggplant, Indian mustard, and cowpeas arrived from India. As noted, the "Irish" potato was introduced into Timor by the Portuguese, but it reached other parts of Indonesia by a different route. One of its Indonesian names is *ubi Benggala*, a circumstance implying introduction from Bengal in eastern India. This plant is neither Irish nor Bengalian but was taken from a New World homeland to such far-flung lands as Ireland and India. Although the potato had an enormous impact on the economy of temperate Europe, it never became popular as a crop in tropical Indonesia. Peanut, avocado, pineapple, guava, papaya, tomato, various squashes and pumpkins, cacao, soybean, and other beans have been imported into the latter country at one time or another, with varying degrees of success. A distributional puzzle is offered by Ceiba, a giant tree of the rainforest. Earlier works regarded it as native to the West Indies, the East Indies, and parts of Africa, but such a distribution is likely to have come about through the activities of man. It is presently regarded as native to the New World tropics, where it is indeed widespread, yet it has been in Asia long enough to have developed a distinctive variety there, and local residents are often surprised to learn that it is regarded as an introduction. The English name for the Ceiba's valuable fiber, kapok, is not from any American Indian language; it is from the Malayan *kapuk*. This and another Indonesian name, *kabu-kabu*, liken the fiber to that of cotton. Within its Asiatic range (Indonesia northward to the Philippines, the Malay Peninsula, and Ceylon), the Ceiba has many close relatives that are assuredly native and that similarly yield a waterproof floss called *kapuk*. Another fiber plant warranting separate mention is ramie, a stingless nettle of the genus Boehmeria. Today it grows at scattered localities from Indonesia northward to India, China, and Japan, but a part of this distribution reflects dissemination by man, and the original range may have extended only from India to China. At any rate, before the twentieth century most ramie fiber was produced on the Asiatic mainland; later the plant was grown experimentally in several tropical and subtropical countries. World War II gave impetus to the ramie industry, for the fiber had many desirable qualities: great tensile strength, comparative immunity to shrinkage and weakening when soaked, resistance to mildew, rot, and smokestack gases. Ramie is still of interest. In Indonesia, where it is called *rami*, it is grown most frequently in Sumatra,

Finally, reference should be made to flowers that brighten the Indonesian landscape. While many are native, or were imported

73

from nearby lands, others originated in quite distant parts of the world. The spread of ornamentals has received less attention than that of crop plants, but one may be sure that the Dutch were responsible for bringing various flowers to Indonesia. The gardens at Buitenzorg, later Bogor, came to harbor about 10,000 varieties of plants, with another 6,000 at cooler Tjibodas; and in this vast assortment there were many imported ornamentals whose seeds, sprouts, or seedlings became available for distribution. Some Indonesian sultans also maintained fine gardens with both native and imported plants. Among the most frequently seen ornamentals of the country are a tall Canna with orange-red blossoms, a thorny Bougainvillea vine with scarlet bracts, and Delonix or royal poinciana; yet, the first of these is from the New World tropics, the second from southern Brazil, the last from Madagascar. The frangipani or Plumeria (rightly Plumiera) is called "temple flower of the East," and on several Indonesian islands the temple dancers or other performers crown themselves with garlands of frangipani. Almost anywhere on Indonesia the evening breeze may bring the pervasive scent of this flower, yet Plumeria was originally imported from Central America, as was the Poinsettia, which now grows wild on the hillsides of Bali. Long ago, Antigonon or coralvine was regarded as especially suitable for planting around Catholic missions and cemeteries, and so it was taken by the Spanish from its Mexican homeland to the Philippines, whence it spread into adjoining regions. Among the ornamentals that are commonly seen in but not native to Indonesia are a pink-flowered Dombeya, some Bauhinias or orchid trees, the Bombax tree, angel's-trumpet or Datura, the African tulip tree, purple-flowered Jacaranda, the potato tree, oleander, bottlebrush, Gloriosa or jungle lily, bleeding heart, Pandorea, and trumpet vine. To this list may also be added yellow Allamanda, some kinds of Hibiscus, an Aloe, crown of thorns, shrimp plant, "Singapore holly" (neither a holly nor from Singapore), devil's backbone or slipperflower, Plumbago, Cape honeysuckle, bird-of-paradise, flamingo flower (Anthurium), and night-blooming Cereus.

Today, at Bogor, the Indonesian General Agricultural Research Station continues to experiment with both native and introduced

74

crop plants and ornamentals, looking especially for varieties with greater economic potential. And over the centuries, a wide selection of plants—many orchids, the banana, plantain, taro, the common bamboo, rice, the India-rubber tree, teak, mango, cloves, nutmeg, cinnamon, and dozens more—have been carried from the Indonesian region to other parts of the world, where they have sometimes proved exceedingly valuable. But that, of course, is another story.

# CHAPTER III

# ANIMAL LIFE AND MAN
# IN INDONESIA

As NOTED, the Indonesian native flora is essentially Asian, and the whole country falls within a single floral province. The native vertebrate fauna—mammals, birds, reptiles, amphibians, fishes—is distributed in quite a different fashion, however. Ignoring the fishes for the present, the Indonesian vertebrates are of Asian affinity in and near Sumatra, Java, and Borneo, but often of Australian affinity in and near Irian Barat. Why should the higher animals of Indonesia be distributed so differently from the higher plants?

Studies at Krakatau throw light on this problem. When Krakatau erupted in 1883, the island remnant was left sterile except perhaps for microorganisms, and even some distant islands were similarly wiped free of life. Scientists kept a careful watch on the rate at which living things returned to Krakatau. Ferns, coconut palms, wild sugarcane, figs, and orchids soon reappeared, their seeds or other propagative parts being carried probably by wind or water; and a dozen years after the blast, most of the island was again covered with greenery. Lower animals, notably insects and spiders, also arrived in fair numbers; but not so the vertebrates, which for a long while were limited to a python, a monitor lizard, one or two rats, several bats, and a good many birds. Less than fifty years after the explosion, Krakatau supported a fine rainforest with a complex flora, but the scientists estimated that it might take two or three million years for the fauna to be restored, so rarely did vertebrates reach the island. Thus, studies at Krakatau revealed that, in general, the ferns and seed-bearing plants cross wide barriers far more readily than the vertebrates, and so can spread rapidly through an archipelago if the islands offer suitable climate and soils. Furthermore, many living plant families and genera are exceedingly ancient, and have had a great length of time in which to cross barriers—far more time than has been available to most living families and genera of vertebrates.

The Pleistocene period, often called the Ice Ages, saw repeated formation of vast ice sheets at high latitudes; and during peaks of glaciation, when so much water was bound up in glacial ice, the sea level was lowered over the entire world. The Sunda Shelf was largely exposed, and animals could move overland from continental Asia into what are now the Mentawais, Sumatra, Bangka, Belitung, Java, Madura, Bali, the Riaus, the Linggas, and Borneo. In a like fashion the Sahul Shelf was largely exposed, and Australian animals could move overland into what are now New Guinea, Waigeo, Salawati, Misoöl, and the Biak-Japen-Numfoor group. Not all Asian animals moved onto the Sunda Shelf, nor all Australian ones onto the Sahul; but each shelf area received far more animals than it would have if sea level had remained high. In contrast, the central islands of Indonesia never developed any continental connection, although sea barriers around and among them were doubtless narrowed at times of low sea level.

Students of vertebrate distribution now recognize what is called the Asian Tropical Subregion, extending from the tropics of India, extreme southern China, and the Philippines southward through those Indonesian islands that lie on the Sunda Shelf. This subregion is bracketed with the African Subregion to form an African-Asian Tropical Region. The latter in turn is bracketed with temperate and Arctic regions farther north to form the Eurasian–

78

African–North American Realm. This general arrangement implies, among other things, that there has been considerable faunal interchange among Eurasia, Africa, and North America. But New Guinea and nearby islands on the Sahul Shelf, along with the Pacific archipelagos from the Bismarcks to Samoa, make up the New Guinean Subregion, which is bracketed with an Australian Subregion to form the Australian Region, the only region of the Australian Realm. Thus, the land vertebrate fauna of Sumatra, Java, and Borneo has more affinities with that of Europe or the United States than with that of Irian Barat. Much effort has been expended to discover exactly where, why, and how an Asian fauna meets an Australian one in Indonesia. Alfred Russel Wallace, who explored that part of the world in the 1850s and 1860s, was especially concerned with these questions. He concluded that a line drawn through the Makassar Strait and the Lombok Strait marked the eastern limit of an essentially Asian fauna in Indonesia. His thinking focused attention on many problems of animal and plant distribution, geology, and evolution. Today, with far more data available, it seems well to recognize a broad Indonesian zone of transition standing apart from any subregion. This zone is designated the Celebesian Transition, after the former name of its largest island. Made up of Indonesian islands lying between the two great shelves, the Celebesian Transition has a sparse but interesting fauna in which Asian and Australian elements are commingled.

To view animal distribution from a standpoint not of biology but of immediate human concerns: only a small percentage of Indonesia is urbanized to a degree that excludes wildlife, and the people of the large western islands are in contact with a major segment of the world's richest fauna, that of tropical Asia. In this fauna are a few species that will attack man, more that destroy his crops or livestock, still more that are eaten or that can be hunted for sport, many that yield hides or other salable products, and some that can be domesticated for one purpose or another. Nor is man's attention to this fauna solely on a practical level. Traditional dances, music, and folktales reflect an abiding interest in wild beasts; and except where Islamic tenets discourage realistic representations, animal motifs are often discernible in painting, sculpture, wood carving, and related arts. Since animism is still firmly entrenched, many beasts are deemed to have supernatural powers that must be reckoned with; skillful hunters and animal trainers are thought to have mystical rapport with wildlife. Animal names in Malayan, the basis of Bahasa Indonesia, reveal that the people regard many wild species with whimsy, some with admiration, a few with dread, hardly any with indifference. The fauna of western Indonesia is also of great interest to scientists and intelligent laymen, whatever their nationality. In Sumatra and Borneo, especially, there are ecosystems of a complexity not approached in any temperate land; there are extraordinary vertebrates and lower animals whose study would yield many a scientific surprise.

A somewhat different situation exists in Irian Barat, where the people, except in a few coastal settlements, river ports, government posts, and mission stations, are just emerging from a Neolithic cultural level. These people are still in very close contact with the local wildlife. Of the continental vertebrate faunas, the Australian is by far the least useful to uncivilized man, and the insular New Guinean fauna is a depauperate version of the Australian. Except for the introduced pig and deer, New Guinea provides no mammal that is both large enough and abundant enough to be an important source of meat or hides. While no native marsupials attack man, many raid his gardens and fruit trees. Native placental mammals include only rats and bats, which are often damaging to crops. True vipers and pit vipers, present in western Indonesia, are lacking from New Guinea; but not so the elapid or cobra-like snakes, which abound. New Guinean amphibians are limited to frogs, mostly small ones; freshwater fishes are comparatively few. The uncivilized tribes of New Guinea have had to depend on animal groups that were of only minor significance to Neolithic-level peoples in most other parts of the world. Even where the pig and deer are present, the tribesmen derive a large part of their animal protein from the flesh of birds, rats, bats, possums, freshwater turtles, certain frogs and tadpoles, beetle larvae, bee and wasp grubs, a kind of large spider, and land snails, along with eggs of birds and reptiles. Daggers are made of cassowary limb bones, spear points of human limb bones, cassowary claws, or hornbill beaks. Rat jaws, dog teeth and ribs, flying-fox bones, and splinters of cassowary bone are worked into various small tools and ornaments, while drumheads are of python or monitor lizard skin. Costumes are decorated with feathers, beetle wings, and narrow strips of fur taken from bats and small marsupials. A hornbill's beak, a flying-fox skin, or a tuft of parrot feathers may be worn by a man to denote successful headhunting. Various marine shells, traded inland, have several uses to be discussed later.

In keeping with the need for small animals, New Guineans construct an exceptionally great variety of traps, some of them marvels of ingenuity. Of stone artifacts, the axe blade is by far the most important, partly because it is used when land is cleared, but also because it is used to chop away underbrush and build pole-ladders when small, arboreal game is pursued. The shortage of really useful large animals is reflected in more than the material culture of the tribesmen. Around the villages, children often show the malnutritional effects of a diet that is high in starch, low in animal protein. Tinned meats are accepted avidly when made available, and village dogs eaten as needed. Perhaps inadequacy of diet accounts for the rapidity with which the tribesmen accepted and spread new crop plants as soon as these were introduced. In settled areas, individual or tribal ownership is extended not just to villages and gardens but also to hunting grounds, stretches of river bank, Pandanus trees, wild nut trees, even cassowaries. Property rights are insisted upon, and armed clashes have occurred over their enforcement. While cultural and psychological factors are involved with insistence upon such rights, it is tempting to speculate that the remarkably strong emphasis on them in part reflects the scarcity of edible or otherwise useful large game. In like fashion, cannibalism has ritual or ceremonial aspects, but in some parts of New Guinea (more so east of than within Irian Barat), human flesh has been a prized addition to a diet that is otherwise lacking in meat. Although keen observers of animal life, the New Guineans credit various species with magical powers, and populate the forest with mythical beasts. Ceremonial songs, accompanying some particular activity, often make reference to a bird, mammal, or reptile thought to have connection with or supernatural influence upon that activity. Wood carvings and other forms of artistic expression often have mystical significance, and may portray a cassowary, crocodile, monitor lizard, or some other beast. Many languages are spoken in Irian Barat, but in any of them, a species of animal life is usually called by a name that stresses its real or fancied usefulness. Although the New Guinean fauna is of limited utility to uncivilized man, it is of surpassing interest to scientists. Many animal groups, rising to dominance in Eurasia, Africa, and the New World, never reached the long-isolated Australian Realm, which has continued to harbor more ancient groups that died out elsewhere. And within this realm and region, the New Guinean Subregion offers the only sizable expanse of wet tropics, faunally a good bit different from drier and mostly temperate Australia.

As mentioned, the comparatively remote islands of the Celebesian Transition have a very limited fauna. Furthermore, except for Sulawesi they are fairly small islands which under any circumstances could not harbor the variety of animals to be found on, say, New Guinea, Borneo, Java, or Sumatra. People of the Transitional islands are often oriented strongly toward the sea, from which they derive much of their day-to-day sustenance and a few salable commodities. Although the insular terrestrial fauna is sparse, it may well include one or a few animal species of exceptional interest to science. These may have evolved on the islands or may have persisted there as relict species after all their congeners had vanished from the mainland. But whatever their origin, insular species usually have a precarious hold on life, and so they make up a high percentage of the birds, mammals, and reptiles that have already been exterminated by the spread of civilized man and his technology. Several distinctive vertebrates of the Transitional islands are therefore in an especially hazardous position, and bid fair to vanish sooner than the rest of the world's fauna.

While the spice trade was particularly important in luring Chinese, Indians, Arabs, and finally Europeans to Indonesia, much earlier exploration of that country, and the spread thereto of cultural traits from mainland Asia, can be credited to Chinese or Indian demand for marine products, hornbill beaks, edible birds'-nests, plumes, sharks' fins, rhinoceros horns, and materia medica derived from the animal kingdom. Later on, Islam reached Indonesia from India. A mighty cultural force as well as a religion, Islam followed the trade routes, and even before modern times it had spread as far east as the Aru Islands, where the Arabs could trade for pearls, mother-of-pearl shells, trepang, tortoiseshell, and bird-of-paradise skins. As the old Asian traffic in bird skins and plumes was extended to Europe, there developed a network of trade routes linking remote Irian Barat with European capitals. When a bird-of-paradise was killed on Waigeo, its plumes might equally well come to adorn the head of a cannibal chief or a Paris dowager. English calico, American cotton cloth, muskets and gunpowder, crockery, brass gongs and cannons, salt, chewing and smoking tobacco, cutlery, arrack and other liquors, opium, trinkets—these flowed southeastward to the last ramifications of the Indonesian trade routes, along with nonmaterial concepts and outlooks.

In short, the fauna has assumed a variety of roles in the Indonesian story, and warrants review. In this chapter, description will be limited to certain land-dwelling mammals, birds, reptiles, and invertebrates. Since the emphasis will be on human concerns, there seems to be no need to follow taxonomic sequences rigidly, or to discuss animal groups that are scarcely known outside the zoological literature.

The account may begin with the mammals. Many families of them invade Indonesia from the Asian mainland, and are not represented east of Wallace's line (ignoring a few species that have been carried about by man). The Asian component of the Indonesian mammal fauna includes the cat, bear, dog, weasel, elephant, rhino, tapir, chevrotain, goat antelope, tree shrew, loris, leaf monkey, ape, hedgehog, flying lemur, pangolin, rabbit, bamboo rat, and mouse-tailed bat families. This component is concentrated on the large, ecologically diverse islands of western Indonesia: Sumatra, Java, and Borneo. The Asian component also includes the civet, cattle, deer, pig, tarsier, macaque, squirrel, Old World porcupine, shrew, and hollow-faced bat families; but these, while more diverse in the vicinity of Sumatra, Java, and Borneo, have one or more representatives that range east of Wallace's line, reaching the Celebesian Transition although not Irian Barat (again ignoring a few species that traveled with man). On the other hand, several families invaded Indonesia from the Australian mainland, ranging no farther west than New Guinea or nearby islands on the Sahul Shelf. In this category are the spiny anteater, kangaroo, bandicoot, and marsupial "cat" families. The Australian component of the Indonesian mammal fauna also includes the possum family, which ranges through New Guinea into the Celebesian Transition. A small percentage of the Australian vertebrate fauna has been able to move into the islands east of New Guinea, but the circumstance is not important here. The fruit bat, sheath-tailed bat, false vampire, horseshoe bat, common bat, free-tailed bat, and Old World rat families are present throughout Indonesia.

The cat family has several Indonesian representatives, most famous being the tiger, which ranges from the Asian mainland southward to Sumatra, Java, and Bali but strangely has never reached Borneo. Books often give its Malayan name as *rimau* or *harimau*, but these are usages principally of the Malay Peninsula and parts of extreme northern Indonesia. The tiger is more widely known by its Javanese name of *matjan,* or in some areas *matjang.* Like most other large carnivores, it is feared to a degree unjustified by its behavior; and it is further credited with magical powers. Villagers in tiger country may refer to the beast only by honorifics such as *nenek* ("grandparent") or *datuk* ("grandfather," "family head"), and may believe in *matjan kadangan,* the were-tiger who sometimes walks as a man. Feared or not, the tiger has been nearly or quite exterminated in most parts of its range, and conservationists regard it as an endangered species.

The leopard, a smaller animal, has a better chance for survival, for it can tolerate more ecological disturbance and is less inclined to avoid settled areas. Although ranging widely in Africa and continental Asia, in Indonesia the leopard is restricted to Java and the nearby Kangeans. It is called *matjan tutul,* a curious name reflecting a belief that the leopard will feed on the tiger's leavings. But usually the leopard pulls down its own prey: various wild birds and mammals, and sometimes domestic stock such as fowl, kids, and piglets. The so-called black panther, *matjan hitam,* is merely an abnormal leopard. Blackish leopards do not breed true, and in fact are of reduced fertility; but as they can be born of normal, spotted parents, they are common in some areas, including Java.

The lion does not reach Indonesia, yet it is known there by its Sanskrit-derived name of *singa*. This beast, once ranging into parts of southern Asia, was admired by those Sanskrit-speaking priests and merchants who first set up Indianized states in western Indonesia. That was long ago, but *singa* is still remembered, especially in parts of Java that were formerly Hinduized, and in Bali where Hinduism still prevails. The capital of Bali, Singaradja, bears a Sanskrit-derived name originally meaning "lion-king." Lion masks and effigies are often seen in Balinese ceremonies.

A little-known member of the cat family is the clouded leopard, found from southern China to Sumatra and Borneo. It is marked not with spots but with large, irregular blotches, and the odd pattern, in shades of black, brown, and yellowish-gray, camouflages the animal when it stretches out on a large branch. One of its names, *harimau dahan*, is appropriate, since *dahan* in this case means "of the large branches." This cat is said to feed on birds, a circumstance that does not explain why it has proportionately the largest canine teeth of any feline.

Several small members of the cat family range from the Asian mainland south to one or more islands of western Indonesia, among them being the marbled cat, golden cat, fishing cat, leopard cat, and flatheaded cat. The bay cat is restricted to Borneo. Scientists once thought that a wild relative of the domestic cat inhabited Timor, but Indonesians were correct in calling this animal *pus hutan*, "puss-of-the-woods," for it was nothing more than a house cat gone wild. Probably it was introduced by the Portuguese, who carried mousers on their ships.

The smallest member of the bear family, the sun bear, is found from the Asian mainland south to Sumatra and Borneo. It spends much of its time in the trees. The English name of sun bear draws attention to a large, light-colored spot or ring on the animal's chest. The Indonesian name for the animal is *beruang*—and much history is bound up in this vernacular usage. Centuries ago, metallic coins were introduced into the Malayan-speaking world by the Chinese, along with a designation the Malays rendered as *wang* or *uang*. Today, *uang* is any sort of money, but *beruang*, "has money," is still a name for a little bear with a dollar-spot on its chest.

Like the bear family, the dog family has but one wild representative in Indonesia. This is the dhole, a hardy beast ranging from Siberia to Java and Sumatra. It may have the build of an Irish terrier and the reddish coloration of a collie, but it is a formidable predator that hunts in packs. The dhole pack is said to attack even the buffalo, snapping at its flanks, chasing and harassing it into exhaustion, and finally pulling it down. The dhole's Indonesian name, *adjak*, means "urging on." (One recalls that a breed of hound has similarly earned the name of harrier.) The dhole did not figure in the ancestry of the domestic dog, to which it is not closely related. But of course the dog, the first animal domesticated by man, was brought to or through Indonesia a number of times even in the remote past; for the dingo, Australia's wild dog, accompanied the aborigines in their migration to that continent, and the New Guineans also kept dogs. Feral dogs of New Guinea represent a stock not closely related to the Australian dingo, and are probably decended from village animals gone wild. No doubt the dog likewise accompanied the Malayan-speaking peoples in their peregrinations, and from their language comes its Indonesian name, *andjing*. The dog, derived from wolf-like beasts of a colder clime, has proven of limited value as a hunting animal in the rainforest, and only in some temperate lands has it been bred into a house pet, a target of human emotional displays. Thus, in most parts of Indonesia, *andjing* is viewed objectively, as a village scavenger. Orthodox Muslims consider it unclean. In contrast, *kutjing*, the neat and mannerly house cat, is a pet the Indonesians often regard with affection.

Indonesian members of the weasel family resemble the martens, weasels, mink, badgers, and otters of other lands. Otters are known as *andjing air*, "water dogs." One of the badger-like species, which the Dutch called *stinkdas*, has the fearless attitude and mighty stench of a skunk. Its English name, teledu, is from a Malayan word meaning insouciance, indifference.

Whereas the cat, bear, dog, and weasel families have familiar representatives in temperate lands, the civet family is confined to warmer parts of the Old World. (The so-called civet of the United States is really a skunk.) The family is an important element in the Indonesian fauna. The name "civet" is from an Arabic designation for an oily substance secreted by these animals. The secretion, coming from glands near the anus, has been prized in the manufacture of perfumes that enhance the desirability of the human female. Several kinds of civets can be milked, so to speak, of their secretion at intervals of a few days. *Dedes* is a Javanese and Sundanese word adopted into Malayan, and meaning a civet, its valuable product, or any kind of musk. Of Indonesia's many civets, some resemble the house cat in tamability, and have been carried by man from island to island so often that original ranges are hard to determine. The best-known species is the musang. Ranging from southern China and the Philippines to Ceram, it lives in the tops of palm trees, but will transfer its residence to *atap*, a palm-thatched roof. Here it is welcomed, for it will feed upon insects, scorpions, and other unpopular inhabitants of the thatching. The English name is from the Malayan, although in some places only the female is called *musang*, the male warranting a separate name by virtue of its musk. The mongooses, which also belong to the civet family, are represented by several species in Indonesia, none east of Borneo and Java. They are called *garangan*, a word meaning bloodthirstiness or violence; like the weasels which they superficially resemble, they have acquired a reputation as killers of small game.

The Asian elephant, as a wild animal, ranged from the mainland southward only to Sumatra. Feral elephants of Borneo are believed to be descendants of domestic stock. *Biram* is one Indonesian name for the elephant, but this animal is more often called by its old Sanskrit-derived designation, *gadjah*. (In chess, the bishop is also *gadjah;* for in the Indonesian version of the game, the pieces are known as king, minister, elephant, horse, castle, and pawn. *Bermain gadjah*, literally to play elephants, is to play chess.) Today the elephant's services are most valuable in the teak forests of the Asian mainland, where the great beasts are taught the five basic tasks of pushing, pulling, picking up, kneeling, and deflecting branches. Only minor use has been made of the elephant as a work animal in Indonesia, but here as in other lands it is spectacular in pageantry. Just as many Christians carry a medallion or statuette of the mythical St. Christopher to protect them from the hazards of a journey, so do Balinese say a short prayer to Ganesa, the elephant-headed god, to confer success upon an undertaking; for Ganesa, like the elephant, is a remover of obstacles. *Gading*, the elephant's tusk or ivory, has been carved in Indonesia, but the wild elephants of that country have not figured prominently in the ivory trade, for they are smaller than their mainland kin, and even the adult males have small tusks or none at all. In the heyday of the plume traffic, tusks were swapped for marine products and bird-of-paradise skins with the Aru islanders, but the tusks were rarely those of Indonesian elephants.

Two species of rhinoceros inhabit Indonesia. Their story is a depressing one. The *badak* or Javan rhino was formerly known from the Asian mainland to Sumatra and Java, but was exterminated from most parts of its range. It requires forest vegetation and pools in which to wallow. In Java it once inhabited not only the swamp peat forest and rainforest of the lowlands, but also the mountains almost to the upper limit of the montane forest. Today, about two dozen *badak* survive, confined to Menandjung Udjung Kulon ("west-end peninsula") where a game preserve has been established on the western tip of Java. This preserve, about 65,000 acres in extent, is mostly *belukar*, broken by thickets, bamboo groves, and patches of *alang-alang* grass. Shortly after World War II, a notorious Chinese poacher thought he would take advantage of the political turmoil by slipping into the reservation and bagging all the rhinos there; but he was himself killed by a tiger. Fear of the big cat kept other poachers out until the newly organized Indonesian government could police the reserve. Conservationists the world over applaud the Republic of Indonesia in its effort to save the Javan rhino. Unlike the *badak* which is one-horned, the *badak kerbau* ("buffalo-like rhino") or Sumatran rhino carries two horns on the nose, one behind the other. Formerly the *badak kerbau* ranged from the mainland of southern Asia to Sumatra and Borneo, and was characteristic of thickly forested uplands with scattered pools. Perhaps 200 Sumatran rhinos remain, unfortunately not on

88

any reservation but widely scattered. The Javan and Sumatran rhinos, as well as the Indian rhino which never reached Indonesia, were extirpated from most areas by sport hunting and deforestation. All three had become rare by the beginning of the twentieth century, and preservation of the few remaining animals is surprisingly difficult. The Chinese, both in China and in other countries, believe that a bit of rhino horn will restore an old man's waning virility, and will pay incredible sums for it—as much as $2,000 for a single horn. Other parts of the rhino's carcass, especially the blood, bones, skin, and certain organs, are also salable, for they are thought to contain at least a bit of the mystical potency that is supposedly concentrated in the horn. The Chinese demand for the horn is so great that poachers risk being shot or imprisoned to kill the few rhinos that remain on game preserves; and in many a zoo, the keeper's morning inspection has revealed that the rhino's horn had been sawed off mysteriously during the night. In the Bogor Museum on Java, not only were the horns stolen from mounted specimens on display; plaster replacement horns were stolen three times within a single year. The rhino's so-called horn is not firmly attached to the skull, but grows from the skin in the fashion of hair or nails. Chinese faith in its potency stems from the "doctrine of signatures," a primitive belief whereby some physical characteristic of a natural object is held to denote its medicinal value; a yellow flower might remedy jaundice, or a lobed leaf prove valuable in treating liver complaints. Thus, some of the world's most remarkable animals are sacrificed to irrational symbolism. A leading conservationist has suggested that the only way to save Asian rhinoceroses would be to interest the Chinese in a synthetic rhino horn containing testosterone.

In Indonesia the name *badak* is sometimes transferred to the Malayan tapir, a bulky beast distributed from the Asian mainland to Sumatra. The baby tapir is marked with longitudinal blotches and spots of yellow on a brown background, but the adult is black with a sharply defined patch of white covering its hindquarters, and so may be called by a name meaning "patched" or "pied." The tapir's snout gives it a pig-like look, accounting for the name *babi gadjah*, "elephantine pig"; but the animal's flesh is beef-like. In

some places the tapir is called *kuda air,* "water-horse." The origi-
nators of this name certainly knew the habits of the tapir, which in
spite of appearance has some horse-like ways; for the aroused male
will gallop about enthusiastically, tossing its head and whinnying
in a fashion that immediately calls to mind a stallion. *Kuda,* the
domestic horse, has been introduced into Indonesia on several occasions. Herds of feral horses, accompanied by a few mules, were
noted in New Guinea during World War II, probably having been
liberated when settlers were evacuated. The feral ponies of Timor
are the progeny of stock brought to that island long ago by the
Portuguese. The Arabs took horses to Indonesia before the Portuguese did, but even before the arrival of Islam, knowledge of *kuda*
had reached the islands; for horses and horse-headed gods
abounded in the religious art and literature of Indonesia's Hindu
period.

Other domestic animals introduced into Indonesia include the
goat, called *kambing,* and the sheep, known as *domba* or *biri-biri.*
Once again, animal names throw entertaining sidelights on history.
*Domba* is a Persian name for sheep; it is one of many Persian
words borrowed into Malayan, probably from the speech of those
Parsees who became traders after their arrival in India. *Biri-biri* is
the name for sheep in several Indo-European languages of India
and Ceylon. It came into Malayan by way of Hindustani. In various regions of the world, but especially in parts of southeastern
Asia, people were subject to a disease whose symptoms included
swelling of the extremities, mental lassitude, and lack of muscular
coordination. In Malayan this affliction was called *penjakit biri-
biri,* "sheep's disease." Christiaan Eijkman, a Dutch physician in
Java, noted that pigeons developed comparable symptoms when
fed white rice left over by patients in a hospital at Batavia. During
a temporary shortage of white rice, patients were fed natural or
under-milled rice, and their leftovers quickly brought the pigeons
back to health. After laboratory experimentation, Eijkman concluded that "sheep's disease" could be brought on by a diet of
white rice or cured by a diet of natural rice. But his published find-
ings were ignored for years; and people continued to die of this
malady, especially in armies, prisons, labor camps, rubber planta-

tions, and some peasant villages—anywhere that a diet of white rice was not supplemented by other foods such as meat, beans, and leafy vegetables. Today it is known that "sheep's disease" results from a shortage of Vitamin B $_1$, present in the outer layer of the natural rice grain but milled away during the preparation of white rice; and this vitamin deficiency disease is called "beri-beri," an English version of an Indonesian and Indian name for sheep.

Ram fighting is a popular sport in Indonesia. The battlers, *biri-biri djantan*, are not fat, woolly sheep of the kind familiar in the West, but are leaner and more goat-like, short-haired, muscular about the neck and shoulders. The arena is no more than a convenient spot of open ground. Early in the morning, the handlers bring the animals to the arena, tethering each to a separate post. The combat is delayed until a crowd has gathered, bets have been laid, the combatants inspected knowingly, and peanuts vended. When the spectators' tension has risen to a peak, the handlers untie two of the rams. At this stage it is only necessary to point the animals at each other, and they charge forward to meet head-on with a crash of horns. Again and again they slam their heads together, while horn splinters fly. Eventually the tired battlers draw apart, eyeing one another. The handlers then tweak the rams' testicles, and the animals resume combat until one of them is downed or driven off. Although cockfighting is officially frowned upon, ram fighting is generally approved.

Indonesia has one native animal superficially resembling a sheep or goat: the Sumatran serow, known as *kambing hutan*, "wild goat." Its near relatives are other serows and the goral of southeastern Asia, the chamois of Europe, and the Rocky Mountain "goat" of western North America. The Sumatran serow, long-legged and short-horned, with pointed hoofs, is adapted for life high in the mountains. Other native hoofed animals include several species of wild cattle. The water buffalo, *kerbau*, may have reached one or more islands of western Indonesia as a wild animal; but if so, it has been nearly or quite replaced by the domestic breed. Undersized *kerbau* of northwestern Borneo may be the remnant of an indigenous race, but feral herds on Sumatra, Java, Timor, and Sulawesi are probably descendants of domestic stock, as is surely the case with those on New Guinea and Australia. The *kerbau* has been imported into such lands as Africa, China, and southern Europe; but since it needs to bathe and wallow at frequent intervals, it is most useful in rainy country where mucky fields must be plowed. Patient and plodding, it will also draw a wagon to market. Sulawesi is the only home of the anoa or *sapi hutan*, a distinctive animal and the smallest of wild cattle. About three feet high at the shoulder, it has short, straight horns quite unlike the majestic span of the *kerbau*. Yet another species of cattle, the banteng, ranges as a wild animal from the Asian mainland to Borneo and Java, and is domesticated on Bali. Its English name is from the Javanese, but a related Malayan word, *banting*, signifies thrashing or stamping about, in allusion to the animal's behavior when disturbed. Unlike the *kerbau* and the anoa, the banteng is very closely related to ordinary domestic cattle of the kind familiar in the West. Such cattle probably had a multiple origin from several wild species, the banteng among them. One Malayan name for domestic cattle is *lembu*, but most Indonesians use the word *sapi*. The Balinese, being Hindu, have a religious proscription against the killing of cattle; but the story of the "sacred cow"—at least as a completely inutile consumer of badly needed foodstuffs—is a myth of Western manufacture. In Bali as in India, Hindus raise cattle principally as draft animals, a pair of bullocks being ideal for plowing in a land where tractors are few. True, cattle are not eaten, but religious beliefs aside, there are practical reasons why they should not be. A butchered cow probably consumed 5,000 pounds of plant material for every pound of beef that it yields. If this material was grass, then the cow converted otherwise useless plants into food for man, beef. But only about 5 percent of Indonesia is grassland, and this is mostly concentrated toward Timor. Furthermore, Indonesian grasses are low in nutrients and make poor fodder. In general, arable land is planted with rice or some other crop, and only poor land can be given over to cattle, which under these conditions are most useful as a source of labor, milk products, and manure. Bali has also built up a sizable cattle export industry. Some Indonesian cattle, brown and with swept-back horns, resemble the wild species; but others, whitish and humped, were derived in part from

the Indian zebu. The Portuguese, reaching Indonesia in the six-
teenth century, soon brought additional strains of cattle and focused attention on them as a supplement to *kerbau*. On Timor, especially, cattle did well after introduction by the Portuguese. Bull
racing, bull grappling, and a humane sort of bullfighting in which
the animal is not killed are Indonesian sports possibly adopted from
the Portuguese, who did not share the Spaniards' enthusiasm for
the spilling of animal blood in an arena.

Turning now to the deer family, most islands of Indonesia are inhabited by the rusa. This animal, related to the European red deer
and the American wapiti, differs from both in that the antlers develop only three points each. The rusa varies in size and color
from one part of its range to another, and some mammalogists regard it as a group of closely related species. The group is also
widespread on the mainland of southern Asia, where its members
are often called sambar. Indonesian names include *rusa* (Malayan)
and *mendjangan* (Javanese). This deer is now found in scattered
areas of New Guinea, but was introduced there in fairly recent
times by man. Such introduction probably accounts for its presence
on many islands outside the original range.

Whereas rusa are hunted and eaten, hardly anyone in Indonesia
would molest the so-called mouse deer, which are not true deer
but chevrotains. Two mouse deer reach the country, both of them
diminutive but one especially so. The larger, ranging from the
Asian mainland to several islands of western Indonesia, is called
*napuh* or *pelanduk;* while the smaller, ranging only to Sumatra, is
known as *kantjil*. (There is, however, occasional inconsistency in
these usages, and other names exist.) Scarcely a foot high at the
shoulder, and given to scampering about in the underbrush, the
mouse deer seems more like a hare or a rodent than one of the
hoofed animals. On the Malay Peninsula and in Indonesia, the
mouse deer is the hero of many folktales, often being portrayed as
a clever little trickster who outwits his enemies. In these stories,
the animal is called *si-pelanduk* or *si-kantjil*, Mr. Mouse Deer; the
prefix *si-* in this case indicates humorous personification. (The
closely comparable Br'er Rabbit stories, even though ascribed by
Joel Chandler Harris to "Uncle Remus," actually originated with

the American Indians and may reflect Asian derivation in the remote past.)

Several members of the pig family inhabit Indonesia. The common wild pig ranges from the Asian mainland to Java, Sumatra,
and nearby smaller islands. As an adult it is uniformly dark, but
when a piglet it is longitudinally striped. The more localized Javan
pig is characterized by a cluster of three warts on each side of its
face, and a related wart-faced pig is found on Sulawesi. The
bearded pig, known from the Malay Peninsula to Borneo, Sumatra,
and a few smaller islands, has exaggerated sideburns. In Borneo
there is a giant pig that reaches a length of six feet; its head is
crested, and its tusks are hidden by a bristling moustache. The
wild boar, ancestor of the domestic hog, did not reach Indonesia,
but is closely related to the wild pigs of that country. All the native Indonesian pigs will interbreed with the domestic animal, and
the cross-mating becomes evident when a domestic sow produces
striped piglets in addition to the usual blotched or unicolor ones.
Pigs are abhorred in most parts of Indonesia, there being a Muslim
injunction against them—a taboo borrowed into Islam from Juda-
ism. However, the pig was carried about in Indonesia by man long
before the arrival of Islam. The Melanesians brought the pig with
them to New Guinea, where its arrival was a boon to Negritos and
Papuans already living there. The tribesmen eat the pig's flesh, use
the skulls and jawbones as longhouse decorations, and wear the
tusks as ornaments. Scrapers, gravers, spoons, and taro-scrapers are
made from the bones or teeth. Warriors rub their bodies with the
grease, blacken their faces with grease and charcoal, and hold ceremonies to propitiate the spirits of departed pigs. Ethnic groups
that resisted Islamization are scattered over Indonesia, and usually
they relish pork. The Balinese are noted for roast pig served
whole at feasts, and the Batak of Sumatra proudly dubbed themselves "pig-eaters." In non-Muslim areas of western and central Indonesia, village pigs are often swaybacked and potbellied to a degree suggesting deformity. The potbellied pig is a domestic breed
introduced by the Chinese, who especially prized the paunch meat.
In restaurants that cater to non-Muslim guests, meat dishes include
pork roll, pork with soy sauce or vegetables, sauté of pork with

dried squid, ham stewed with chestnuts, pork with noodles and vegetables, pork with salted fish and radishes, and many others. The Chinese influence in this cuisine is obviously strong.

Indonesian names for the pig include *tjeleng* and *babi*, the latter being widely used. *Babi hutan*, "wild pig," is a name for the common wild species, while the Javan pig is *babi tanah*, "earth pig." In Western lands, the pig symbolizes gluttony and physical uncleanliness because it is usually penned in mud and encouraged to overeat; but the animal is not so treated in Indonesia, where its actions give rise to different metaphors. To behave thoughtlessly or inconsiderately is *membabi buta*, literally "acting like a blind pig." Epilepsy is *gila babi*, "pig's madness," for a seizure is accompanied by gnashing of the teeth in the fashion of an enraged boar.

Although the common wild pig, wart-faced pigs, bearded pig, and giant pig are closely related to the domestic animal, not so the babirusa, an extraordinary pig confined to Sulawesi and Buru. It is a long-legged animal in which the upper and lower tusks of the male are prolonged into veritable horns. Both pairs of tusks point upward and then backward, one pair finally curving downward toward the eyes. The Sulawesian babirusa is exceptionally grotesque, for it is nearly hairless. The common name is from Malayan *babi rusa*, "deer-like pig."

Indonesian primates include some primitive ones: tree shrews called *tupai*, the slow loris, and tarsiers. The last are distributed over Sumatra, Java, Bangka, Belitung, Sulawesi, Borneo, and the southern Philippines. To the Dutch, a tarsier was *spookdiertje*, and it is indeed a "spooky" little beast of the night, its impish face dominated by enormous eyes. On greatly elongated hind limbs it leaps about among the branches and bamboos, searching for insects and lizards on which to feed. Not surprisingly, its eyeballs are locally regarded as useful in the treatment of human eye complaints. Better known primates are the monkeys, of which the macaque family is particularly important in Indonesia. The pig-tailed macaque, ranging from the Asian mainland to Sumatra, Borneo, Banka, and the Pagi Islands, is a husky monkey, rather baboonlike in stance and build. In fact, the Dutch often called it *baviaan*, baboon. This macaque is the famous "coconut monkey," the *beruk*, trained to climb coconut palms and throw down the nuts, selecting green or ripe nuts according to command. The training of the *beruk* is a specialized profession, and trainers are often badly scarred by this animal which can inflict a severe bite. A related species, the long-tailed or crab-eating macaque, often lives on beaches and will take to water; perhaps this is why it has been able to extend its range from the Asian mainland to Timor, although it has also been transported by man. Young long-tailed macaques make amusing pets, and were in demand by early European sailors on East Indian voyages. Local names include *monjet, kunjuk, ketek,* and *kera.* An extraordinary macaque is the so-called "black ape of the Celebes." Long-faced and nearly tailless, with a heavy brow-ridge, it is superficially ape-like in appearance. A gentle animal, it is not feared by local residents, and has been carried from its Sulawesian homeland to Batjan.

A second family of monkeys is that of the leaf monkeys and their kin. At least nine species of leaf monkeys are collectively distributed from the Asian mainland to Sumatra, Java, Bali, and Borneo. Often attractively patterned, they are slender, long-tailed monkeys, much given to dashing through the tree tops. (But a short-tailed, terrestrial species inhabits Sumatra.) They feed mostly on leaves, blossoms, and fruits, although catching an insect or raiding a bird's nest at times. Related to the leaf monkeys, and similarly vegetarian, is the proboscis monkey of Borneo. The adult male, potbellied and with a bulbous nose, looks like a grotesque parody of Western man; and Bornean villagers, who are usually slim and rather snub-nosed, often remarked on the similarity, although not in the presence of the Dutch.

Indonesian primates also include five species of long-armed apes, called gibbons. The largest of these, the siamang of Sumatra and the Malay Peninsula, stands about three feet tall. High in the tree tops, troops of siamang occasionally set up an incredibly loud howling. To amplify the call, the siamang has a throat pouch that can be distended like a balloon. Other gibbons are less vocal but do have a loud voice; the gray gibbon of Java and Borneo is called *wau-wau* or *uwau* in allusion to its raucous call. *Ungka* and *sarudung* are names given to the agile gibbon of the Malay Peninsula and Sumatra. It has several color phases, from dark brown to pale cream, almost white; and the light individuals, called *ungka putih,* "white gibbon," are prized as pets. The great apes are represented in Indonesia by the orangutan, which lives only on Sumatra and Borneo. As mentioned earlier, its common name is from Malayan *orang hutan,* "man of the wilds." Indonesians are familiar with this usage but prefer the names *mawas* (on Sumatra) or *mias* (on Borneo), for *orang hutan* could also mean the uncivilized tribes of the forest, and the phrase is so used in the Malay Peninsula. The orangutan shows racial differences, Bornean individuals being covered with rusty red hair, Sumatran ones with purplish-red; and Sumatran males grow a moustache. Even the adult male, weighing about 150 pounds, spends most of its time in the trees, moving slowly through the branches in search of fruit and edible leaves. The orangutan therefore needs large areas of continuous rainforest in which to live, and man's alteration or removal of the forest has brought this ape close to extinction. The surviving remnant is threatened by the demand for zoo specimens. Various governments, including the Indonesian, have prohibited the exportation of orangutans, but there exists a worldwide trade in protected animals of many kinds. Most orangutans are fatally injured while resisting capture, about one in ten surviving to reach a zoo. The survivor may sell for $4,000.

Flying lemurs, Asian gliding mammals without close relatives, reach Borneo and Java. To the Dutch, a flying lemur was *vliegende kat,* "flying cat." Indonesians do not distinguish flying lemurs from flying squirrels, but call both *kubung.* Rainforest is characterized by numerous animals that can glide from tree to tree, aided by some kind of extensible membrane that increases surface area without adding much weight. For example, western Indonesia harbors the flying lemur, flying squirrels large and small, the flying gecko, the flying frog, agamid lizards called flying-dragons, and even some aboreal snakes that flatten the body and sail off at an angle.

Another mammal group without close relatives is that of the scaly anteaters, with a few species in Asia and Africa. One of these, the pangolin, ranges from the Asian mainland to Sumatra, Java,

Bali, and Borneo. The upper parts of the body are protected by hard, overlapping scales, but the underside is not armored, and so the pangolin rolls itself up when disturbed. The name pangolin, although derived from a Malayan expression (*pengguling,* "one who rolls up"), is seldom heard in Indonesia, where the animal is most often called by the Javanese name *teringgiling.* On Java the visitor is assured that to hunt the *terringgiling* is to invite 40 days' bad luck.

In contrast with the geographically restricted flying lemurs and pangolins, the family of Old World rats is widespread over half the globe, and three of its members—the house mouse, the Norway rat, and the roof rat—have been carried by shipping to most parts of the world. The house mouse, *tikus piti,* was found throughout much of Indonesia even before the days of modern shipping, but the Norway rat, *tikus besar,* has turned up chiefly in port cities. The roof rat was probably native to the islands as far east as Sulawesi, while close relatives of it are distributed from the Asian mainland across Indonesia into Melanesia and Polynesia. These rats take up residence in thatching and bamboo pilings, an undesirable habit because rat fleas can transmit several diseases to man, bubonic plague among them. Many Old World rats, however, are inoffensive animals that live only in the wilds. This family has exceptional ability to cross water barriers, presumably on drifting trees and logs, and has spread through Indonesia to reach the Australian Realm, where it has produced terrestrial, arboreal, and semiaquatic species in both Australia and New Guinea. Among these species, the giant rats, some tree rats, rabbit rats, and water rats have invaded Indonesia from its eastern end.

A good many bat families have also spread through Indonesia, although by flying rather than rafting. Yet, some other bat families are quite restricted geographically, for these highly specialized animals may not find a home on every island they happen to reach. Huge colonies of mouse-tailed bats live in caves, ruins, and abandoned houses on Sumatra. A false vampire, ranging from the Asian mainland through Indonesia to Australia, is not related to the true vampires of the New World tropics, nor is it a bloodsucker; but it does have an unusual diet for a bat: fishes, frogs, rodents, and smaller bats, in addition to insects. The family of common bats, with well-known representatives in Europe and the United States, has members throughout Indonesia and beyond. Some of them, with orange and black wings, resemble great butterflies. In this family is the tiniest of bats, a flatheaded bat found from the Asian mainland to Sulawesi and Timor. It makes its home in the hollow stems of giant bamboos, finding ample room within the stem but having a problem of entry. In almost any bamboo thicket there are at least a few stalks that have been split, and this little animal can slip through the narrow aperture thus provided. Also in this family are the trumpet-eared bats, widespread in Indonesia and beyond. They are noteworthy not only for funnel-shaped ears but in some cases for bright colors; often the body is cinnamon and the wings black with yellow blotches. Another family, the free-tailed bats, includes perhaps the ugliest of mammals, the naked bat of Sumatra, Java, Borneo, and the Philippine island of Palawan. Pig-snouted and triple-chinned, with sparse hairs on its plump body, the naked bat is provided with a glandular throat pouch of uncertain function, and with wing pockets in which to carry its young.

All the foregoing families of bats and several others are interrelated; they are predators upon insects or, less frequently, upon small vertebrates. There exists, however, another group of bats whose members for the most part are vegetarians, feeding upon pollen, flowers, honey, fruit, or the juice that drips from ripe fruit. The short-nosed fruit bats, found from the Asian mainland east to Sulawesi, have a gutter that begins at the middle of the upper lip, passes between the nostrils, and extends to the top of the head. When one of these bats hangs upside down on or beside a fruit and begins to feed, the gutter keeps surplus juice out of its nostrils. The dog-faced fruit bats, widespread in the country, sometimes live in palm tops, and have been known to befuddle themselves by drinking from the container in which palm juice is being collected for toddy. The long-tongued fruit bats, similarly widespread, have an elongate snout and a protrusible tongue, equipment for nosing into flower blossoms and licking up the pollen. Like bees, some of these bats are pollinators of flowers. Tube-nosed fruit bats, found from Australia to Timor and Sulawesi, have a short muzzle, large eyes, and nostrils that are drawn out into long tubes. A common New Guinean species is marked with a clownish pattern of round spots, some of these markings green, others yellow or white. The pattern camouflages the bat when it hangs among leaves or on mossy bark. But the most impressive of the fruit bats are the flying foxes, several species of them, found throughout Indonesia and beyond. The largest has a wing span of five and a half feet. Whereas most smaller bats have gargoyle faces, pinpoint eyes, and exaggerated ears, the flying fox has a dog-like head with a long snout, bright eyes, and pricked-up ears of reasonable proportions. Often the head is covered with golden fur, in contrast with the dark-furred body. In some species, the genital region is covered only with black skin, and the genitalia of both sexes are rather human in appearance, a circumstance that accounts for several vernacular names in languages of Irian Barat and eastern New Guinea. Flying-foxes live in large colonies. During the day they hang motionless, presumably asleep, in the top of a rainforest tree, often the tallest tree for miles around. Each night at sunset they take wing, milling about in the air over the roosting tree, their Dracula shapes black against the red sky. But soon one bat streaks purposefully away, followed closely by another, then two or three more, until the cloud of bats has been drawn out into a column; and by the time the last one has joined the line, black night has fallen. A memorable sight to a Western visitor, although commonplace to Indonesians. For a visitor it is almost as memorable to be at the target end of the bats' nightly forays. He is awakened by chattering, squeaking, and squalling; he may think that monkeys are raiding the nearby fruit trees (unless he knows that Indonesian monkeys sleep by night and forage by day). The beam of a flashlight will reveal the troop of flying-foxes, stalking about among the branches, feeding, fighting, and copulating, biting into one fruit and then abandoning it to seize another. In the gardens of Indonesian sultans, each prized fruit was sometimes protected by a cage of split bamboo, to keep the bats off. Books often state that the Malayan name for the flying-fox is *keluang*, but in most parts of Indonesia the oft-spoken word has been contracted to *kalong*.

Some bats and rats, primitive marsupials, and even more primitive monotremes characterize the native mammal fauna of the Australian Realm. To anyone who knows Sumatra or Kalimantan, the rainforest of Irian Barat seems empty. The magnificent trees are there, the lianas and epiphytes. Yet no great cat slinks through the forest, no civet rustles the palm fronds, no squirrel frisks among the branches. There are no tapir tracks along the stream margins, no leaf monkeys to dash through the tree tops, no dim trails of rhino or elephant. Even the marsupials do not abound in Irian Barat, for these pouched mammals are in many cases adapted for life in the dry, temperate lands of Australia, and have not always moved into wet, tropical New Guinea.

Of the monotremes or egg-laying mammals, the platypus does not reach New Guinea, but the spiny anteaters do, one species being distributed from Australia into southern New Guinea, another confined to New Guinea and Salawati. In the latter species, the spines protrude above a coat of thick fur, and the animal can live in the cold uplands. The spiny anteater somewhat resembles a European hedgehog but is much larger. With cylindrical nose and heavy claws it roots and digs for soft-bodied insects. Unlike the platypus, which lays eggs in a nest, the spiny anteater carries its eggs in a pouch. The long spines protect the animal from the local small predators but not from man. Like some people in other lands, New Guinea mountain tribesmen often mutilate themselves to provide a hole or slit through which a bauble can be hung, and in some areas a spiny anteater's quill is used to keep the perforation open between ceremonial occasions when more elaborate earrings and septal ornaments are worn.

Of Irian Barat's marsupials, most familiar are the kangaroos. Really large species do not range to New Guinea; but smaller ones, the wallabies and pademelons, do so, some of them in fact reaching Waigeo, Salowati, Misoöl, the Arus, and the Kais. They are called *aha;* or in Malayan-speaking settlements the name *pelanduk* (mouse deer) may be transferred to them. Like the larger kangaroos, wallabies and pademelons hop about on enlarged hind legs; but the tree kangaroos, more diverse in New Guinea than in Australia, are excellent climbers. In the mountains of New Guinea, a big red tree kangaroo is usually encountered on the ground, but will leap up a tree when disturbed. Noisy and clumsy in its arboreal passage, it is followed and bagged by spearmen. Also hunted is the cuscus, a slow-moving arboreal marsupial of the possum family. There are several kinds of cuscus, collectively distributed from Australia through New Guinea to the Moluccas, Sulawesi, and Timor, as well as to islands east of New Guinea. A night prowler, the cuscus hangs motionless in the branches, camouflaged by a blotched pattern; but in New Guinea, keen-eyed tribesmen find the animal, bag it, and make its fur into a headband. Its flesh is edible, barely. The Indonesian name is *kuskus*. Also in the possum family are the flying phalangers, distributed from Australia to New Guinea and some nearby islands. One diminutive species, common in New Guinea, is among the most attractive of mammals. It has the conformation, size, silky pelage, enormous eyes, and gentle disposition of an American flying squirrel, but is striped with black on a background of bluish-gray. Australians call these little animals "sugar gliders," for they sail from tree to tree and feed upon nectar, flower petals, and the gum that exudes from various trees. Other flying phalangers, being fair sized, have been slaughtered for the Australian fur trade, and so have some luxuriantly furred possums that do not glide but merely climb.

It is often said that the marsupials of the Australian Realm, evolving in isolation, sometimes came to parallel the higher or placental mammals. For example, the "sugar glider" is a close parallel of the flying squirrels. Bandicoots are marsupials that somewhat parallel the rats and rabbits, although they lack chisel-like incisors. Small New Guinea bandicoots are reminiscent of overgrown shrews. ("Bandicoot" and "possum" are respectively Indian and American Indian names altered by English-speaking people and transferred to Australian marsupials. The American opossum is a marsupial, but the Indian pandikokku is a rat.) One group of pouched mammals, reaching New Guinea from Australia, has been likened to the cats. The marsupial "cat" is a small predator, beautifully marked with white spots on a reddish background. Although it feeds mostly upon rats, wild birds, and insects, it has been known to raid a hen-house. From both Queensland and New Guinea have come reports of a much larger marsupial "cat" patterned with stripes; but if such a beast exists, it has eluded scientific collectors. The marsupial "wolf," a striped animal the size of a collie, once inhabited New Guinea, as shown by a jawbone recovered from the debris of an ancient campsite in the mountains; but the "wolf" survives today only in the highlands of Tasmania, as far as is known.

So much for the mammals; now to consider the birds. Although mobile beyond most other vertebrates, many birds are exacting in their environmental requirements, and even if they fly or chance to be blown across a water barrier, they may not find suitable habitat upon arrival. Thus, the Indonesian bird fauna is not homogeneous but differs markedly from the western end of the country to the eastern. Pheasants, trogons, barbets, woodpeckers, bulbuls, leafbirds, finches, sun grebes, hoopoes, honey guides, broadbills, and nuthatches are confined chiefly to the more westerly islands, while cassowaries, Australian warblers, Australian magpies, magpie larks, bowerbirds, and birds-of-paradise are among the groups centered in the Australian Realm. In addition, many bird families have representatives in both western and eastern Indonesia; and here one might list grebes, cormorants, brush turkeys, ospreys, falcons, hawks and eagles, storks, ducks and geese, cuckoos, rails, button quails, jacanas, thick-knees, plovers and their kin, pigeons, parrots, owls, frogmouths, rollers, kingfishers, bee-eaters, hornbills, swifts, jewel thrushes, larks, swallows, cuckoo shrikes, flycatchers, babblers, Old World warblers, thrushes and their kin, wagtails, shrikes, sunbirds, honey-eaters, weaver finches, starlings, Old World orioles, drongos, and crows. But some of these widespread families have geographically restricted subgroups; for example, many pigeons and parrots are confined to the vicinity of New Guinea. The family of ibises and spoonbills is widespread in the tropics, including New Guinea, but it is strangely lacking from western Indonesia. The widespread stork family also avoids western Indonesia, although it reappears in New Guinea.

Pheasants, some of them splendidly colored, are numerous in western Indonesia. Finest of them is the great Argus pheasant, which reaches Borneo from the Malay Peninsula. Nearly seven feet long including the tail, it is patterned with bright eyespots; hence the reference to Argus, many-eyed being of Greek mythology. The courting male clears a patch of forest ground in which to display his plumage. He is rarely seen, but his call gives rise to the Indonesian name: *kuwau*. One member of the pheasant family, *ajam hutan* or wild chicken, is the ancestor of the familiar barnyard fowl. Among domestic breeds of chicken, the bantam game shows the closest approach to the wild bird, and no wonder; for Banten on western Java was often called Bantam, and chickens from there were not far removed from the ancestral stock. As a wild bird, the species may have ranged from the Asian mainland east to Sumba, but it has also been spread by man. Wild chickens on Sulawesi and the Moluccas are regarded as introductions. These birds live in small flocks, which burst from cover in the fashion of the American bobwhite. In second-growth forest of Morotai, a covey occasionally includes some white birds and some black ones in addition to the usual red; evidently there has been local admixture of wild and domestic stock. Cockfighting, *sabungan*, has been a popular pastime in Indonesia, as in several other Asian countries. *Ajam sabungan* is the name for a gamecock. Probably its comb, *balung*, has been trimmed to offer a smaller target to its opponent, and the feathers of its rump plucked away for the same reason. Its spurs, *djalu*, may be sawed off and the stumps fitted with steel blades, or perhaps only one spur is replaced by a blade. The handler blows into the bird's mouth, massages its bare behind with water, and goes through other antics which impress the spectators but perhaps not the gamecock. The two handlers swing their respective birds toward each other so that the beaks almost touch. By the third swing the birds are ready to fight, and they are permitted to do so, with heavy betting on the outcome of the battle. The Spaniards, learning the details of cockfighting in the Philippines, carried the art to the New World, where it has persisted. In several parts of the southern United States today, cockfighting is carried on in the oriental fashion—carried on clandestinely, for in most states the pastime is forbidden by law. And today Indonesian cockfighting is also mostly clandestine, for during the Sukarno regime the sport was forbidden, except in Bali, where it was permitted on holidays.

The peacock is another member of the pheasant family. The blue domestic peacock came from India and Ceylon, but a green one ranges from the Asian mainland to Java. *Merak* is the Indonesian name. *Ajam belanda*, "Dutch chicken," is the name for the turkey, a New World bird related to but not placed in the pheasant family.

Turning now to other bird families of western Indonesia, the barbets are colorful little birds related to woodpeckers although less given to pecking wood. Barbets are common from the Asian mainland to Java, Bali, and Borneo. Some of the species have earned the name "brain-fever bird," for at times they will repeat one clangorous note incessantly. Just as people in the backwoods of the southeastern United States believe that the nearby call of a ground dove presages a death, so may Indonesians consider the barbet a bird of ill omen, calling it *mati anak*, "child's death." Some barbets nest in tree hollows which they enlarge by chipping away the rotting wood, but the Indonesian species peck their way into clay-like nests of certain termites that live above ground. Bulbuls are songbirds widespread in the Old World tropics. Often living about yards or gardens, they are sometimes caged. Eastern poetry is full of references to the song of the bulbul, although in European translation (of the *Rubaiyat*, for example) the bird is changed into a nightingale. The best-known oriental species is the red-whiskered bulbul, a black and white bird with a scarlet cheek-spot and a scarlet rump, ranging from the Asian mainland to Java and Sumatra. Closely related to the bulbuls are the leafbirds, most of them marked with bright green or blue. The golden-fronted leafbird, common from the Asian mainland to the Sumatran highlands, both pollinates and spreads the oriental mistletoe, the sticky seeds of the mistletoe adhering to the bird's bill, and being wiped off on a branch where they remain and grow. The honey guides are principally African, but one species ranges from the Malay Peninsula to Sumatra and Borneo. Although they are drab little birds, they have remarkable habits. For one thing, they lay their eggs in the nests of other birds, leaving their young to be reared by foster parents. For another, they feed upon bees and wasps, breaking into bee hives, eating not only the grubs but also the wax, which they digest with the help of intestinal bacteria. Some African honey-guides will lead a man or a honey badger to a beehive, but a comparable habit has not been reported for the Indonesian species.

Among several essentially Australian or New Guinean bird groups, the cassowaries command attention. They are huge, flightless birds, with three species collectively distributed from northern Australia to New Guinea, the Arus, Ceram, Salawati, Japen, and New Britain. The largest stands more than five feet tall. A cassowary defends itself by striking out with the foot, one toe of which is provided with an enormous claw. Although books usually mention the cassowary's supposed ability to "disembowel a fullgrown man," in the wild the bird is shy, very reminiscent of the American wild turkey in its inclination to dash off at the first hint of disturbance. New Guinea tribesmen keep cassowaries as living "feather factories," and accidents happen about the villages as a result of human carelessness or aggression. The soft feathers are used in the manufacture of ceremonial bonnets, the wing quills become nose ornaments, and the leg bones are worked into daggers. Although principally vegetarian, cassowaries have been seen to scratch up burrowing lizards and devour them. Books often give the bird's vernacular name as *muruk*. This is the name in Melanesian pidgin, a lingua franca spoken mostly to the east of Irian Barat. The Indonesian designation, *suari*, is scarcely recognizable in its English derivative "cassowary." More remarkable than the cassowaries—although for different reasons—are the bowerbirds of Australia, New Guinea, and the Arus. They are crow-sized or smaller, the males often brightly colored and sometimes adorned with a small crest. In most of the bowerbirds, each male clears off a yard and builds some kind of structure therein. At its most elaborate, the bower includes a neatly cleared yard decorated with fern fronds, beetle wings, snail shells, and bits of resin; a surrounding curtain of ferns and bamboo sprouts hung with snail shells, berries, and scraps of bark; and a domed hut rising as high as nine feet, supported by growing saplings. New Guinea bowerbirds plant moss in the bower, and some of them also add an avenue of sticks painted on the inside with a greenish or bluish pigment that is mixed in the bird's mouth, and that is applied with a paintbrush of leaves or bark. At least one early naturalist, coming upon a bower in the mountains of New Guinea, refused to believe that it was not the work of man. Yet, the bowerbirds act not through intelligence but through automatic response to environmental and physiological stimuli. One might draw a comparison between the bowerbirds and the birds-of-paradise which occupy roughly the same region. In the birds-of-paradise, the males of each species have a distinctive and often spectacular plumage whose display attracts and arouses the females of the same species; but the bowerbirds have evolved an elaboration not of plumes but of innate behavior patterns, the males automatically building a bower whose physical characteristics predictably arouse the females.

Like bowerbirds, the birds-of-paradise characterize the New Guinean Subregion, the tropical portion of the Australian Region and Realm. But bowerbirds are concentrated in the cold, dripping cloud forest, whereas birds-of-paradise include species of the coastal swampland, the typical lowland rainforest, the atypical rainforest of somewhat higher elevations, the montane forest dominated by oaks or by southern beech, even the subalpine forest to the upper limit of tree growth. There are about 40 species of birds-of-paradise, all beautiful but only a few of them providing the filmy plumes that first brought the family to Western attention. Long before the arrival of the Europeans, bird-of-paradise skins and plumes were traded northwestward through Indonesia, reaching such faraway places as India and Nepal, where they were incorporated into royal headdresses and costumes. Sebastian del Caso, bringing Magellan's last ship back to Spain, stopped at Tidore, where he received bird-of-paradise skins from the *radja* of Batjan, dried skins prepared in the usual fashion, with the legs cut off. In Europe the legend soon grew that the skins were from footless creatures of the upper air, too ethereal to touch ground, the female laying her eggs and incubating them on the back of the volant male. The skins, it was said, came only from birds that died and fell to earth. The Portuguese, in the meanwhile, had encountered Indonesians who called the bird *manuk dewata*, "heavenly fowl," a name they took back to Europe as *manucodiata*. (Hence "manucode," still a designation for some birds-of-paradise.) How surprised the early Europeans would have been to learn that the

107

birds-of-paradise are not far removed from crows, which they often resemble in diet and raucous voice. When the Europeans began to trade in southeastern Asia, they acquired bird-of-paradise skins in India and the Moluccas, and thought the birds were native to these lands. It was many years before Westerners realized that the skins were actually coming from the Aru Islands, Waigeo, Batanta, and New Guinea. The traffic was eventually extended to other species which, although they lacked the filmy plumes, were very colorful and often provided with tail, breast, or head feathers of improbable length. Each year when the birds were in full plumage, Chinese, Arab, and Malay feather-buyers would set up camps on the New Guinea coast. Feather dealers thrived in Indonesia, Amsterdam, Paris, and London. In a peak year, as many as 50,000 skins reached Europe, and the ornithologists hunted for new species not in the wilds but in millinery shops. Trade skins afforded the basis for many a scientific description, and then came the problem of discovering the original homeland of each described species —a difficult task, for many of them were very restricted both geographically and altitudinally. In some cases the homeland could not be discovered at all, and no wonder; for certain of the "millinery shop species" were actually hybrids, produced unpredictably through the occasional crossing of two closely related species. In time, birds-of-paradise were given legal protection. Their skins are no longer exported, and comparatively few are smuggled. Women of the West can no longer wear bird-of-paradise plumes on their heads, but uncivilized tribesmen of New Guinea may continue to do so where the birds have not been exterminated. Indonesian names for the plume-bearing species include *burung sopan* ("dignified bird") and *tjendera wasit* ("demigods' intermediary"). But in the days of the plume trade, people in western Indonesia referred simply to *burung mati,* "dead birds," for no one ever saw live specimens.

Of bird groups widespread in Indonesia, the pigeon family is an important one. To a Westerner, familiar only with the street pigeon or perhaps a few drab little doves, the variety of Indonesian pigeons is astonishing. The fruit pigeons, which equal or exceed the street bird in size, are mostly metallic green in color, perhaps variegated with blue or bronze, and often patched with mulberry or pink. Almost anywhere in Indonesia, one or another species of fruit pigeon is likely to be common. Nearly invisible in foliage, these birds are conspicuous when they descend in pairs or small flocks upon the ricefields. Often they are called *burung padi*, rice birds. The Torres Strait pigeon, white with black markings, breeds on coastal islands from northern Australia to New Guinea and the Arus. It feeds upon wild nutmegs, persimmons, and berries. It is among the bird species that move south when spring comes to Australia; and in former times, huge flocks of Torres Strait pigeons would arrive in northern Australia around September or October, to be slaughtered by the settlers. The ways of this bird would strike a familiar note with American dove hunters, but those of the goura would seem outlandish. The goura (from Indonesian *gura*) is a stocky, turkey-sized pigeon that scratches about on the forest floor. It is delicate blue in color, with a mulberry back, and its head sports a crest of bluish feathers so lacy that they were once shipped to Europe along with plumes of the bird-of-paradise. There are three species of gouras, all New Guinean, and all endangered even though they reside in thickly vegetated places; for these giant pigeons take little alarm when one of their number is shot, and a hunter can bag a whole flock one by one. Interestingly, all the Indonesian pigeons, large or small, drab or colorful, resemble the American mourning dove in constructing a poor excuse for a nest, just enough twigs to cup the eggs.

Like the pigeons, the parrots have some exceptionally interesting species restricted to the eastern part of Indonesia. In fact, in the South Pacific region the parrot family is concentrated toward Australia, the species becoming fewer and fewer toward Asia; only three of them reach the Malay Peninsula. Conspicuous in and near New Guinea is a *burung kakatua* with a yellow crest: the sulfur-crested cockatoo, a bird often displayed in zoos. Although found in rainforest, it tolerates a good bit of clearing, and on comparatively barren limestone islands can exist in the heavier growth around waterholes. Even though in captivity this cockatoo will learn to imitate whistles and a few spoken words, it is not a mimic in the wild; like many other parrots, it utters a harsh cry, especially when it spots an intruder. Finest of all parrot-like birds is the great black cockatoo, a dusky, high-crested species nearly a yard long. Its bare cheeks change color from pale pink to bright red according to its emotion. The enormous, hooked beak is said to be used in cracking or cutting very hard palm nuts and Java almonds, and no doubt this is true; but in the rainforest it is not unusual to see a pair of great black cockatoos on a fallen log, ripping and shredding it in search of grubs. This species, which ranges from northern Australia to New Guinea and nearby islands, is called *kakatua radja*, royal cockatoo. In the red-sided eclectus parrot of New Guinea, the male is mostly green with a red beak, the female mostly red with a black beak; both sexes were popular as cage birds long before ornithologists realized that the two were not separate species. In spite of its fairly large size, the eclectus parrot is closely related to the diminutive lovebirds so often kept captive.

Lovebirds are Australian but have many relatives in New Guinea, oddest of them being the hanging parakeets which sleep hanging upside down in the fashion of bats. *Burung bajan* is the Indonesian name for parakeets generally. Gaudier than any of the caged parrots are some of the lories and lorikeets, trim little birds often marked with red, yellow, green, and blue. Flocks of them are a common sight in Indonesia, but not in aviaries, for they feed upon nectar which they crush from blossoms, and no one has found a substitute diet on which they will thrive for long in captivity. Although the word "lory" is often said to be from Malayan *luri*, the Indonesian name for these parrots is *nuri*. Long ago, in the days of the spice trade, more cage-hardy parrots were taken to Europe and sold as "newries."

Continuing the account of some widely distributed families, the brush-turkeys range collectively from northern Australia through Indonesia to the Malay Peninsula, the Philippines, and Micronesia. Once again, the activities of man are probably responsible for part of the distribution, brush-turkeys having been carried from island to island. These birds resemble a true turkey in size and in having a red, featherless head, but they are placed in a family of their own. The brush-turkey builds a huge mound of leafy debris in which to lay eggs. Decay of the nesting material keeps the mound's internal temperature up to about 95 or 96 degrees Fahrenheit. Mounds may be added to year after year until they reach an enormous size, and at certain localities they may be clustered in a communal nesting ground. From Australia through New Guinea to Micronesia, tribesmen visit these grounds to take some of the eggs, leaving others to hatch and never molesting the adult birds. The egg is larger and richer than that of a hen, and has a brick-red shell. The maleo, a brush-turkey of Sulawesi and the Sangihes, departs from family custom by burying its eggs in beach sand, a black sand that absorbs heat readily. On Lokon, a Sulawesian volcano, maleos were found to dig nesting holes into ground that was heated from beneath by volcanic steam.

Whereas the brush-turkey family is confined to Indonesia and nearby lands, the family of hawks and eagles is cosmopolitan. An impressive hawk of Indonesia is the Brahminy kite, cinnamon-colored with white head and underparts. It is often a bird of the seacoast, but in New Guinea it is seen far inland when tribal hunters burn off the grassland to drive out pigs and deer. The kites follow the advancing line of flame, diving into the smoke to seize flying grasshoppers which arise in swarms. Also impressive, although more restricted in range, is the serpent eagle, known from the Asian mainland to western Indonesia. The Dutch called it *slangenbuizard*, snake-hawk, and were pleased to see it swooping upon reptiles and rodents. In the mating season it sits upon a conspicuous perch, drumming its wings, waggling its tail, and making various calls. Indonesians liken it to a lecturer by calling it *batja*, a word meaning to recite or to read aloud. Another Indonesian name, *djambul*, draws attention to the bird's crest of enlarged feathers; *djambul* is the tassel of a fez, or the topknot into which a child's hair may be shaved.

The kingfisher family holds surprises for the Western visitor who knows only one or two minnow-catching species of north-temperate lands; for Indonesian kingfishers range from tiny, colorful insect-eaters to crow-sized predators upon reptiles. Alfred Russel Wallace would only call these birds "kinghunters." The blue-winged kookaburra, found from Australia to New Guinea, is a huge kingfisher that scans the more open forests and grassland for snakes and lizards. Around dawn, its explosive cackle is guaranteed to waken the soundest sleeper. It nests mostly in tree holes, while its smaller relatives dig burrows in the ground or into termitaria. The racket-tailed kingfisher of New Guinea and the Moluccas is blue above and white below, with a scarlet bill and greatly elongated tail feathers. It hunts in the forest for lizards and centipedes. The largest and most aberrant member of the family is the worm-eating kingfisher, a brown and black bird restricted to the New Guinea mountains, where it digs for earthworms with its shovel-shaped bill. Related to kingfishers are the bee-eaters, with several species in Indonesia and elsewhere. Slender of build, they are usually patterned in light green with accents of pink, tan, or blue. They fly out from their perches to catch insects in midair. The watcher can hardly believe his eyes when a bee-eater, so delicate of coloration, so characteristic of the air and the outer branches, suddenly flies straight into a ground burrow. In New Guinea, bee-eaters often dive into burrows dug by monitor lizards. Indonesians call these birds *sesapi laut*, a curious phrase implying that they drink seawater. Perhaps bee-eaters have been confused with their close relatives the kingfishers, some of which dive at saltwater fishes. Like the hawks, the kingfishers and bee-eaters are largely predaceous.

At the opposite extreme of avian dietary specialization is the family of Old World finches. While some of them take insects at times, most are seed-eaters. One very distinctive group of Old World finches, the waxbills, is of especial concern here, for several of its Indonesian members are popular cage birds. In this category are the red avadavat, the chestnut mannikin, some munias, and some parrot-finches. Most of these colorful, sparrow-sized birds are not confined to Indonesia, but enter the pet trade through scattered oriental cities. Several methods are employed in their capture. In parts of Indonesia, birdlime is made from the latex of fig trees, a substance gummy enough to hold a small bird that touches it. Oddly, the most appealing of the waxbills, the Java sparrow, is not very colorful, being soft gray above and smoky pink below. The tail is black, the head black with a white cheek patch, and the short bill bright red. Flocks of Java sparrows, kept in large cages of split bamboo, are offered for sale in many markets of the East. The bird's appeal is only to the pet fancier, however. The Dutch called it *rijstvogel,* rice bird, for it will descend in flocks upon the ricefields. The Javanese name, *gelatik,* draws attention to the bird's sparrow-like twittering. The original range may not have extended east of Java, but the species has been introduced in Papua and probably elsewhere. Indonesians often feel that small, softly cooing doves are more desirable cagebirds than any waxbill.

Bird's-nest soup is a culinary treat generally associated with the Chinese, but the nests are gathered in many parts of Indonesia as well as on the Asian mainland. The edible nests are the work of cave-swiftlets, members of the swift family. All swifts can produce copious saliva, which generally functions to glue nesting material together and to fasten the nest to a vertical surface. In some cave-swiftlets, the nests are of plant fibers in a saliva matrix. These nests are collected but are regarded as inferior, for they must be freed of the debris before the matrix can be used. Nests of highest grade are produced by two species of cave-swiftlet which build wholly with saliva. Since nests are often fastened to sea cliffs and cave walls, the gathering of them can be dangerous and is a specialized pursuit. The saliva has the consistency and translucency of hardened gelatin. Protein-rich, it will dissolve to make a consommé of delicate flavor. The Indonesian name for this consommé, *sop sarang burung,* has the literal meaning "birds'-nest soup." But in Asian, European, or American restaurants that offer Indonesian cuisine to Westerners, *sop sarang burung* is likely to contain only a small amount of the expensive saliva consommé along with a large amount of chicken stock, the delicate flavor of the consommé masked by such familiar Western ingredients as shredded chicken, minced ham, celery, salt, pepper, and onions.

The account of the Indonesian bird fauna may end with the hornbills, some of them larger than eagles, and all noteworthy for an enormous beak topped by a bony casque. From ancient times, the beak of the helmeted hornbill has been carved like ivory. At one time these beaks were traded northward through Indonesia to China. In other members of the hornbill family, the beak is not so hard, although adequate to hammer a lizard or snake to death, and to pluck fruit from the branches. Hornbills are noted for the habit of eating fruits of the strychnine and nux-vomica plants. The birds do not crush the seeds; so they do not liberate the toxins in their system. The hornbill is a symbol of marital fidelity, since the male walls the female into a hollow tree at nesting time. More accurately, the female fashions the barrier using droppings, regurgitated material, and mud brought by the male. A slit is left open through which the male feeds his mate. The wall hardens to brick-like consistency, protecting the female and her eggs or young; and the female will also guard the nest by stabbing through the slit with the tip of her beak. She and the young shoot excrement through the slit with remarkable accuracy, keeping the nest clean. Indonesian names for the hornbill usually involve some word meaning a cavity, in allusion to the nesting habits; and the word *gading*, "ivory," is added if the reference is to the helmeted hornbill. In the evening when hornbills come in to roost, usually in pairs but sometimes in small flocks, their wingbeats make a loud swishing, and the sound is a familiar one in forested parts of Indonesia.

In many terrestrial situations the lizards and snakes are as conspicuous as the mammals and birds, if not more so. The wall lizards (Lacertidae), glass lizards, pipe snakes (Aniliidae), xenopeltid snakes, colubrid snakes, true vipers, and pit vipers are among the families that entered Indonesia from the Asian mainland. Most species of these families do not range east of Sumatra, Java, or Borneo, although a few do. The flap-footed lizards characterize the New Guinean end of Indonesia; while the geckos, agamid lizards, skinks, dibamid lizards, monitors, pythons and boas, blind snakes, and cobra-like snakes are widespread in the country. But it should be noted that the skinks and cobra-like snakes, especially, include numerous species and genera that are restricted to New Guinea and vicinity.

Wall lizards, so conspicuous in Europe, are represented by only one genus in Indonesia: Takydromus, ranging from the Asian mainland to Sumatra, Java, Borneo, and the Natunas. It is very different from European lacertids, being elongate and vine-like, bright green with yellow lines. It is said to live in grass, but is very common along rocky shores in vines that grow over cycads. Not that it is particularly coastal; it is often seen in the gardens at Bogor. It is called *bengkarung ular,* "snake-like lizard." A glass lizard, Ophisaurus, found on Borneo, has close relatives in the United States, and like them it has a long tail that may break off and thrash about when the reptile is seized. Pipe snakes, Cylindrophis, are primitive, harmless snakes collectively distributed from the Asian mainland to Batjan and Wetar. One species, common around *sawah,* when disturbed will elevate its tail and disclose its red underside, while tucking its head under a coil of body. The display is thought to misdirect the attack of predators. Since the reptile superficially appears to have a head on each end of its body, it is called *ular kepala dua,* "two-headed snake."

The typical harmless snakes, family Colubridae, are diverse in Sumatra, Java, and Borneo, although much less so farther east. Only three colubrid genera have crossed Indonesia to reach Australia. One of these is Natrix, the watersnakes, which are excellent swimmers. People of western Indonesia are very familiar with *ular kadut* ("plaited snake"), a big, striped Natrix of the ricefields, and its congener *ular kisi* ("latticed snake"). As far as is known, Indonesian watersnakes are all egg-layers, like the European but not the American members of the genus. Some Indonesian species can spread a hood in the fashion of a cobra, mere bluff since all Natrix are harmless. A second genus ranging from Asia to Australia is Stegonotus, its members nocturnal, arboreal, brown in color with vague light marbling. A Stegonotus has angled ventral scales that enable the reptile to climb directly up a tree bole or buttress, the angulations holding the body to the bark. One New Guinean Stegonotus is given to creeping about over tree trunks by night, probably in search of treefrogs and geckos. The third far-ranging colubrid genus is Dendrophis, whose members are green and vine-like. *Ular tali,* "cord-like snake," is the appropriate name for a Dendrophis.

*Ular liar,* "wild snake," is the name given to the world's longest colubrid, a ten-foot Ptyas ranging from the Asian mainland to Java and Sumatra. It and its smaller congener, *ular korros,* are noted for extreme agility, for bluffing displays when cornered, and for predation on rats around villages.

Although colubrids are called typical harmless snakes, some of them have small, venom-conducting teeth in the rear of the upper jaw. One rear-fanged colubrid, a Boiga, is prized by reptile fanciers on account of its good disposition and its glittering, black-and-yellow coloration. The Bornean name, *ular tjintjin mas*, "gold-ringed snake," is more appropriate than the English designation of mangrove snake, for the reptile is found not only coastally but also interiorly from the Asian mainland east to the Moluccas. In snake-charming performances, the mangrove snake is often passed off as a deadly krait.

The flying snakes, mentioned previously, are rear-fanged colubrids, genus Chrysopelea, collectively distributed from the Asian mainland east to the Tanimbars. Their venom functions to overcome geckos, frogs, and bats which they capture among the branches. In one flying snake, the bright markings resemble flower blossoms, but no one knows whether this is an instance of camouflage. *Ular djelutong* is the name for flying snakes. *Djelutong* is a rainforest tree cut for timber, and tapped for an inferior latex called gutta percha (Malayan *getah pertja*, "tattered rubber"). The snake's vernacular name was probably derived from its ability to flatten and widen its body as though made of rubber, but some Indonesians regard the snake as a frequent inhabitant of *djelutong* trees. No Indonesian rear-fanged colubrid has been reported to inflict a severe bite on man, but the country has several other snake families with highly venomous members.

True vipers, with many species in Europe, are represented in tropical Asia only by Russell's viper, a dangerous, long-fanged snake. Its presence at a few spots on Sumatra, Java, and Komodo is puzzling, for the localities are well separated from each other and from the snake's mainland home (India to Thailand).

Pit vipers are related to true vipers, distinguished therefrom principally by a small pit on each side of the head between the eye and the nostril. The pit is a sense organ that detects heat and infrared radiation, permitting the snake to strike at an object that is hotter or colder than its background. Indonesian pit vipers include one moccasin, Agkistrodon, which reaches Sumatra and Java from the Asian mainland; and seven lanceheads, Trimeresurus, six of them also present on the Asian mainland, and only two of them ranging east of Wallace's line (to Sulawesi and Timor respectively). The moccasin, a relative of the American copperhead, is called *ular tanah,* "earth snake." Green, arboreal lanceheads are often called *ular bisa,* "venomous snake"; but one of the arboreal species, marked with green, yellow, black, white, and red, is regarded as a bringer of good fortune. This one is known as *ular tjintamani,* the latter word being the name of a mythical jewel to which many magical properties are ascribed. The snake will remain coiled for days on a pole or tree branch near a house, and so has been dubbed *ular nanti buluh,* "bamboo-remaining snake." Not knowing that snakes can go for months without food, local residents suppose that edible morsels are brought to the lancehead by a certain little bird of the forest. Tourists with oriental experience may recall the Snake Temple at Sungei Keluang, a village on Penang Island between George Town and the airport. Here, dozens of these lanceheads repose decoratively on twigs and branches arranged in vases; Westerners and some local residents suppose, albeit wrongly, that the reptiles are stupefied by the smoke of the burning joss-sticks.

Lizard and snake families of western Indonesia could be discussed at much greater length, but attention must be given to a few families that are known throughout the country. Of these, the geckos are found on every island. Most geckos are small, although some of these lizards are rat-sized. Many of them can scale a wall or run upside down along the bottom of a rafter, held in place by sharp claws and digital pads. In huts and houses they are tolerated for their predation on insects, and many a Western tourist will tell how a gecko, pouncing with undue enthusiasm on a fly, fell onto the table or into the bed. Some geckos call loudly, the small species with a clicking or chirping, the larger ones with a sort of two-syllable croak. Small ones are called *tjitjak,* larger ones *tokeh,* both names onomatopoetic. Certain *tjitjak* are respected because at dusk they come to the ground and vocalize as though performing an obeisance; but *tokeh* are greatly feared even though they are harmless. Also feared is the harmless little flying gecko, which has some ability to glide; it is called *ular papak,* "flattened snake." Sev-

117

eral of the smaller geckos have taken up residence with man, inhabiting houses and boats. House geckos, small stowaways, have been spread far and wide by ancient and modern shipping in the tropics and subtropics. The biologist is gratified when some nondescript little organism turns out to have extraordinary abilities, and in this connection a certain house gecko, common from the Asian mainland and Indonesia east to Hawaii, was lately discovered to be an all-female species; the female lays eggs which hatch without fertilization, and of course these produce only some more females.

Indonesian geckos prowl by night and hide by day, but the agamid lizards reverse this schedule and so are more frequently seen. Common throughout the country is a small agamid, Calotes, which somewhat resembles the American anole and is similarly capable of rapid color change. The usual color is green, changing sometimes to brown, yellow, or blackish. In the breeding season, the male develops a bright red suffusion of the lips, cheeks, and throat, earning it the name "bloodsucker." Local names include *lunduk* (Malayan) and *bunglon* (Javanese); Westerners often miscall the lizard "chameleon." Among agamids, the flying-dragons of the genus Draco are unique in being able to glide from tree to tree, aided by wing-like membranes which are supported by elongate ribs. Small, harmless, and often brightly colored, flying-dragons nevertheless are greatly feared; one myth has it that even their shadow brings death. Giant of the agamid lizards is the sailtail, Hydrosaurus, exceeding a yard in length, and found at scattered localities from New Guinea to Sulawesi and the Philippines. Given to sunning on branches overhanging the water, it dives when disturbed and swims away with the aid of a caudal crest.

The skink family is also noted for variety in Indonesia. In New Guinea alone, members of this family include little brown ones that hide beneath ground debris, tiny but muscular ones that burrow in the earth, big snake-like ones with reduced legs, striped ones that dash over the open ground, azure-tailed ones that frequent sea beaches. Then there are metallic green ones that run over fallen logs in the forest, bluish ones that leap from twig to twig, little ruby-tailed ones that hide under rocks. Particularly impressive is a big, emerald-green skink, Dasia, that lives on coconut palms along the beach. Even more impressive is a brown Tiliqua, nearly two feet long, given to prowling slowly and noisily through dead leaves around forest openings. Many of the Indonesian skinks are live-bearers, and the herpetologist often finds that they have given birth in the collecting bag. Skinks are called *ular berkaki,* "snakes with legs."

Monitors are medium-sized to very large lizards whose pointless English name reflects confusion of Arabic *waran,* "lizard," with English "warn" and German *warnen.* Several of the Indonesian species reach a length of five or six feet. They are most often seen dashing through the underbrush, or else clawing their way hastily up a tree trunk. Some of them dig long burrows in which to hide when alarmed. However, the very large and widespread water-monitor is usually seen on branches overhanging the water, and dives in when disturbed. The emerald tree-monitor, a brilliant green species of New Guinea, Salawati, and Misoöl, runs squirrel-like through the tree tops and vines, showering leaves behind it. At night it often sleeps clinging to the sword-like leaf of a Pandanus, and its weight may pull the leaf down so far that the herpetological collector, provided with a headlamp, can seize the reptile by the neck. Monitors have stout teeth but are slow to bite, and use their heavy claws more for digging, climbing, or grasping than for active defense. It is hard to believe the hair-raising stories told about the Komodo monitor of the Lesser Sundas, although it is the giant of the family and the longest lizard in the world, reaching ten feet in length. It has been billed as a predator on deer, hogs, water buffalo, horses, and man; but one suspects sensationalism and misinterpretation. The larger species of monitors are carrion-eaters, and should not be credited with having pulled down every animal whose rotting carcass they devour. Expeditions to Komodo found that the giant monitor could be lured with rotten meat but not with fresh, and two captive Komodo monitors in the London Zoo proved so gentle that a two-year-old child was allowed to play with them. Nor is there much merit to the oft-repeated statement that the giant monitor reached its present home (Komodo, Rintja, Padar, western Flores, and a few nearby islets) by swimming from Australia. Monitors, some very large, were widespread in the Old

119

World and the New before mammals of modern type had evolved, but fell back probably through inability to compete with a burgeoning horde of placental carnivores. A few monitors persist on mainland Asia and Africa, principally as scavengers and nest-robbers; but the living species are strongly concentrated in the region from the Lesser Sundas through New Guinea to Australia, the only part of the world not taken over by placental carnivores. On their remote little islands, Komodo monitors are not troubled with many predators or competitors. Komodo, Padar, and Rintja are set aside as game preserves, on which not only are the monitors protected but also the pigs and deer whose rotting carcasses feed the great lizards. The people of Komodo's lone village are fishermen, and only at intervals do deer poachers arrive from Sumbawa. Scientific collecting of the great reptile is carefully controlled by the Indonesian government. Goats, horses, *kerbau*, and long-tailed macaques, introduced by man, provide additional carrion for the Komodo monitor, whose chance for continued survival seems good. In early 1969, an eruption on Flores showered Komodo with volcanic ash, but the monitors seemingly were not affected. *Biawak* is the usual Indonesian name for any kind of monitor; but on Timor and Flores, rumors of the giant species led to the story of the *buaja darat*, "land crocodile." Komodo villagers call the giant *ora*, a cognate of Malayan *ular*, snake. Although quadrupedal, a monitor moves with rather serpentine undulations of body and tail; and the reptile's long tongue, forked and protrusible, is much like that of a snake.

Indonesia harbors not only the world's longest lizard, but also the longest snake, the reticulated python, which assuredly reaches 28 feet. This python's range is often given as the Asian mainland east to Timor, but the statement reflects failure to realize that Timor Laut, the reported eastern terminus of the range, is not Timor but the Tanimbars. The snake's presence so far east probably reflects an ability to swim or drift for days. Surely it can do so, for a reticulated python was the first snake to reappear on Krakatau after its eruption, having made its way there from either Java or Sumatra. The species feeds upon wild birds and mammals, including pheasants and small deer; but being able to survive on the outskirts of settlements, it also takes chickens, ducks, peacocks, pigs, cats, dogs, and rats. A common name, *ular sawah,* alludes to this snake's occurrence around *sawah,* the irrigable fields. (But in central Indonesia a python may be called *sawa, sava,* or *saa* simply because these words happen to mean "snake" in some languages of that region.) A shorter but stockier species is the Indian python, a 20-foot reptile at the maximum, known from the Asian mainland, Java, Sulawesi, and Sumbawa. Attractively patterned and rather docile for a python, this snake is popular with showmen of both the East and the West. In the wild it has been reported to feed upon deer, chevrotains, leopards, porcupines, monkeys, pigeons, peacocks, pheasants, ducks, and rats. A spectacular snake is the blood python, no more than nine feet long but very stout, elaborately patterned with shades of red, orange, yellow, and reddish-brown. Its name, *ular bakar,* means "fiery snake," in reference to the coloration. Found only in the Malay Peninsula, Singapore, Borneo, and Sumatra, it is rarely seen, little known, docile in captivity. In contrast, the green tree python is irascible, given to striking out when disturbed. This arboreal snake, seldom over six feet long, inhabits New Guinea, the Arus, and Mysore in the Schouten Islands near New Guinea. During the day, the green tree python coils in saddle-shaped position across a branch, camouflaged by its green color and by yellow or white scales which resemble flecks of sunlight. At night it stalks sleeping birds, its exceedingly long teeth being adapted for the penetration of thick plumage.

The rock snakes, genus Liasis, are a group of pythons centered in Australia and New Guinea. The largest of them, the amethystine python, allegedly reaches a length of 20 feet, although most large adults are about a yard shorter than this. The species ranges from Australia through New Guinea to the Tanimbars, Ceram, and Halmahera. The amethystine python is said to frequent mangrove swamps, live in trees, and eat possums. Perhaps it does all these things at times, but a good place to look for it is on the ground along a forest-grassland border, especially near rivers. In such places it eats bandicoots. For all its great length, it is a slender snake, and proportionately small-headed; one may doubt the assertion that it can swallow a 50-pound wallaby. Various smaller pythons inhabit Indonesia, as well as a few small boas.

Boas and pythons are nonvenomous, killing their prey by constriction, but members of the snake family Elapidae are provided with a pair of small, venom-conducting fangs in the front of the mouth. Most notorious elapids are the cobras. Although they inhabit Africa and Asia, their common name is from no African or Asian language, but from the Portuguese *cobra de capello*, "snake with a hood." The common or hooded cobra ranges from the Asian mainland to Sumatra, the Riaus, Bangka, Java, Borneo, Lombok, Flores, Sumbawa, and Alor. Although capable of dealing a fatal bite, when approached by man it is less likely to bite than to rear up and extend its hood. Snake-charmers who display this snake are in less danger than the spectators realize. Indonesian names include *ular senduk* ("spoon-shaped snake") and *ular hitam* ("black snake"). In western Borneo the hooded cobra is called *tedung naga*, a revealing name; *naga* was the Sanskrit designation of a race of mythical serpents or dragons. Like scientists who dubbed the cobra genus Naja, Borneans make use of a name that came from ancient India. The king cobra is placed in a separate genus, Ophiophagus. This name means "snake-eater," and is appropriate; for the king cobra, which reaches a length of 16 feet, preys upon lesser snakes. It has the habit, possibly unique among serpents, of building a nest from dead leaves and other vegetation. The nest is two-storied, the eggs being in the bottom part and the guardian female in the top. This impressive reptile ranges from the Asian mainland to Sumatra, Java, Simeulue, Nias, Borneo, and Sulawesi. Also in the Elapidae are four species of kraits, medium-sized snakes collectively distributed from the Asian mainland to Sumatra, Java, Borneo, and Sulawesi. They are called *ular belang*, "banded snake."

There are several other elapid genera of Asian affinity, and many of Australian. Australia and New Guinea are the only lands in which venomous species of snakes considerably outnumber the nonvenomous, a situation existing because few of the typical harmless snakes, family Colubridae, ever reached that part of the world, where the available ecological niches were taken over by elapids. Fortunately, many of the New Guinean elapids are small, secretive, and not dangerous to man. However, Australia and New Guinea harbor one gigantic elapid, the taipan, that rivals the king cobra in size, and that has an exceedingly potent venom. Furthermore, the venom load is large and the fangs very long for an elapid. Belligerent when disturbed, the taipan is the most dangerous snake in the world. New Guinea locality records are mostly for Papua, but the snake is known to tribesmen near Merauke in Irian Barat, and probably ranges more widely than records indicate. Also dreaded is the death adder, an elapid with the chunky build of a viper, found from Australia through New Guinea to the Moluccas. The elapid black snakes and brown snakes, of medium or large size, do not range north of New Guinea.

Even though Indonesia is inhabited by many species of venomous snakes, it has no great number of snake bites or of fatalities therefrom. The Pasteur Institute at Bandung, Java, produces a polyvalent antiserum against the venoms of the moccasin, banded krait, and hooded cobra, the principal offenders in western Indonesia. The Queen Saovabha Memorial Institute at Bangkok, Thailand, produces specific antisera against the respective venoms of the moccasin, banded krait, hooded cobra, king cobra, and Russell's viper. The Commonwealth Serum Laboratories at Parkville, Victoria, Australia, turn out specific antisera against the respective venoms of the death adder, taipan, hooded cobra, moccasin, Malayan sea-snake, and the tiger snake (which last does not reach Indonesia). Also from Parkville comes a polyvalent antiserum against the venoms of elapid black snakes and brown snakes.

Unlike most other groups of living things, the lizards and snakes have often profited from man's activities in Indonesia. Except for nocturnal geckos, crepuscular flapfooted lizards, some burrowing skinks, and one or two other species, the Indonesian lizards forage by day and need a good bit of sunlight; and although the snakes are less strongly diurnal, their two most successful families in the islands, the Colubridae and Elapidae, both include a high percentage of day-prowling species. Thus, in the undisturbed rainforest, lizards and snakes are likely to be restricted for the most part to sunnier places, such as river banks, hillsides, and natural openings. Many of these reptiles can thrive where rainforest has been opened up by man, or replaced by *ladang* and *belukar*. As various nocturnal snakes are marsh-dwelling or semiaquatic, they can live about flooded *sawah*. Furthermore, the carnivorous birds and mammals, which often prey on or compete with reptiles, are thinned out around villages and towns. Thus, many reptiles can maintain themselves in parts of the country that have been greatly altered by timbering, agriculture, and settlement. So much cannot be said for the native mammals and birds, most of which take no profit from man's impact upon the environment. Already nearing extinction are the "black ape," a Sumatran leaf monkey called the pig-tailed langur, the dwarf gibbon of Sumatra, the four-striped ground squirrel of Borneo, the Javan and Sumatran rhinos, the babirusa, the anoa, the Bawean deer, the banteng, and the Sumatran serow. Similarly imperiled are three members of the civet family: Hose's palm civet of Borneo, the otter civet of western Indonesia and the Malay Peninsula, and the banded linsang of western Indonesia and the Asian mainland. The cat family, like that of the civets, has fared poorly; the marbled cat, flatheaded cat, and clouded leopard have declined almost into extinction, along with the Sumatran, Javan, and Balinese races of the tiger. Indonesia's only native member of the rabbit family, a pretty little striped animal called the Sumatran hare, is also on the list of rare and vanishing mammals. The orangutan has little chance for survival, and the elephant has been preserved as a wild animal only because it rarely breeds in captivity, the work herds of necessity being replenished from wild stock. Among birds, the maleo of Sulawesi has almost disappeared.

The foregoing list of immediately imperiled mammals and birds includes none from New Guinea, but only because the interior of that great island was but recently opened to outside exploitation. The environmental ravages of such exploitation have been felt most strongly in the Territory of Papua and North-East New Guinea; and if the island's ancient fauna and ecosystems are saved for their esthetic and scientific value, it will be only because Indonesia provides a refuge for them in Irian Barat.

The major problem confronting modern Indonesia is that of bolstering the economy, and this is being done in the usual fashion, through the exploitation of natural resources; but even so, the country might do a better job than, say, the United States in setting aside truly inviolable wildlife sanctuaries where plant and animal populations are preserved for esthetic and scientific reasons, and from which commercial activities of every kind are rigorously excluded. Such a statement will sound unbelievable to the average American, who is probably heir to the old European merchant tradition, and who in any event has seen the modern American bearers of that tradition unceasingly attack and despoil even the lands that are theoretically aside for the preservation of a natural heritage. But a majority of Indonesians, in spite of long exposure to the Arab and then the European merchant tradition (if the two are distinguishable), still respect the soil and the productions thereof, and are not inclined to gut Mother Earth heedlessly. Like the American Indians of old, many Indonesians feel that man is a part of, not an ordained exploiter of, an ecosystem in which all living things are involved; and that a cosmic balance is jeopardized by taking without giving. The Dutch made an effort to conserve the spectacular, vulnerable elements of the islands' flora and fauna, and the Republic of Indonesia was one of the few countries that did not regard emergence from colonial status as an excuse for slaughtering the remaining wildlife. The more isolated ethnic groups of Indonesia often have sacred groves from which surrounding areas are constantly restocked with plants and animals. Of course, such groves rarely escape the eye of a Christian missionary, who insists that they be burned along with all the villagers' artistic productions. Nevertheless, Indonesia is a country where there would be much popular support for a system of real (as opposed to nominal) wildlife sanctuaries, if the desirability of such were made widely known.

This account has so far been concerned with the land vertebrates. But in Indonesia as elsewhere, the backboned animals are far outnumbered in both kinds and individuals by the lower animals. However, only a few invertebrates may be singled out here as being of exceptional interest to local people, visitors, or scientists.

Spiders, called *labah-labah* (Malayan) or *lawa-lawa* (Javanese), are numerous, but only one species is known to deliver a highly venomous bite: the redback spider, a close relative of the American black widow, and similarly a species of the genus Latrodectes. The redback has not been found on Java or Sumatra, but is known from Borneo, Morotai, Timor, Biak, and New Guinea. It can live about rock piles, clearings, and the debris of human occupation; and its wide but spotty range, from New Zealand to the Ryukus, probably reflects frequent introduction in cargo. More characteristic of undisturbed situations are certain big, hairy spiders, given to hunting on the rainforest floor. Although frightening of aspect, they are not inclined to bite man, and are not highly venomous. Sometimes they hide in banana clusters and are inadvertently shipped to Europe, where they are called "banana spiders." Long-legged house spiders, commonly seen on floors and walls in Indonesia and elsewhere, are harmless and may perform a valuable service in devouring small insects. Cobwebs, called *sarang labah-labah* ("spider's nest"), are sometimes thought to stanch bleeding when applied to a wound; the belief is not peculiar to Indonesia but is also met with in India, as well as among some American Indian tribes. In the Indonesian rainforest, the Western visitor will encounter webs of great size and complexity, spun across a trail during the night. The gold-glinting strands have a tensile strength that is astonishing, adequate to hold even a sunbird or a honey-eater. At the edge of the web the spinner hangs, her smooth, elongate body the size of a man's thumb and her legs spanning a good eight inches. It is hard to believe that this giant orb-weaver, a species of Nephila, is inoffensive, and is eaten as a delicacy in many scattered areas from New Guinea to Thailand.

Indonesian scorpions, *kala,* are also less dangerous than one might guess from their sinister appearance. The house scorpion, a small species that finds a home in thatching, is called *kala djinking.* The phrase means "scorpion with upraised posterior," in reference to the menacing, sting-tipped tail whose effect is painful although not dangerous. In the forest is found a gigantic scorpion whose claws suggest those of a crab or lobster, and accordingly it is called *kala bangkang,* "crustacean-like scorpion." (In Javanese, *bangkang* also means stubborn, obstinate, crusty.) For all its size, *kala bangkang* is not dangerous. Indonesia has no scorpion as venomous as those of Arizona or North Africa.

Near Tretes, Java, dancers posture in sight of an active volcano.

*Below:* Coconut and betel-nut palms are scattered through a village of palm-thatched huts in upland New Guinea.

Passing a temple gate on the way from market, a Balinese woman balances
bamboo containers full of grain.

Many interior valleys of New Guinea are treeless and covered with coarse grasses.

The bottle-gourd that was used by ancient man on both sides of the tropical Pacific.

Cattle-drawn cart, of a style commonly used around Djokjakarta, Java.

*Below:* The taipan, world's most dangerous snake, ranges into the south-eastern part of Indonesian New Guinea.

The "horse dance." The Javanese dancer is in a trance, during which he mimics the actions of a horse and rider.

Wilfred T. Neill

Indonesian Tourist Bureau

Elaborate "headdresses" of Balinese women are being taken to the beach as offerings to sea-gods.

A Melanesian village in New Guinea. In many parts of Indonesia, small villages are similarly oriented toward the sea. *Below, left:* Huts of Papuans on the beach near Merauke, Irian Barat. *Below:* Araucaria Creek, an upland stream near Djajapura, Irian Barat. Streams of the rainforest often are clear, cold, and rocky.

Negrito children and their grandfather in a village of upland New Guinea. The bamboo tube is a tobacco pipe, the magazine a gift from the author.

*Below:* Bahau Dyak man of Kalimantan and Karo Batak woman of Sumatra.

*Above, left:* Men of Papuan physical type, near Merauke, Irian Barat.
*Above, right:* The Malay physical type, predominant in central and western Indonesia, is typified by the Javanese dancer.
*Below and left:* Classic photographs from the Archbold Expedition of 1938-1939: first views of "Shangri-La," valley of the Balim River, Irian Barat.

From R. Archbold, A. Rand, and L. Brass, *Bull. Amer. Mus. Nat. Hist.,* Vol. 79 (1942), Art. 3

*Below:* Djokjakarta and Surakarta are centers for the manufacture of hand-painted *batik* fabric. The designs often show Indian influence.

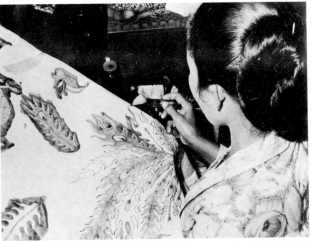

*Far left:* Rising terrace upon terrace, with hundreds of statues and about 3 miles of sculptured reliefs, Java's temple of Borobudur is the world's greatest monument to Buddhism. *Right:* Statue of Buddha in the temple of Mendut near Borobudur.

*Below:* The *Ketjak,* a famous Balinese dance based on an episode from the *Ramayana,* a Hindu epic.

Indonesian Tourist Board

Trans-World Airlines

*Upper:* The war in Irian Barat. Allied raid on Japanese airbase at Galela, Halmahera. *Lower:* Incendiary bombs fall on Japanese airbase at what was then Hollandia, Dutch New Guinea.

★ *Soekakah anak pembatja mendjadi begini?* ★

Tiga boelan sesoedahnja si Djepang membawa 1600 "hei ho" dan "romusha" kepoelau Noemfoor (Pápoea) hanja tinggal hidoep 251.

Jang lainnja mati karena KELAPARAN atau DIPOTONG KEPALANJA, atau mati karena DIPOEKOEL atau DIKOEBOER MASIH HIDOEP atau DIPAKOE KETANAH DAN DITINGGALKAN SAMPAI MATI.

Si Djepang sendiri disitoe gemoek dan segar !

INSJINJOER SOEKARNO ! BAGAIMANA RASA DIHATI TOEAN MELIHAT BOEAH PEKERDJAAN TOEAN INI ??

★

*Upper:* The war with words. A package of Allied leaflets opens in midair, to drift down upon a village. *Lower:* Striking at Sukarno where he was most vulnerable, an Allied leaflet deplores the effect of Japanese conscription on Indonesian youths.

Wilfred T. Neill

*Left:* In Djakarta, the *betjak* or three-wheeled pedicab has long been a popular form of transportation.

Indonesian Tourist Bureau

*Above and opposite page:* Netherlands Indies Civil Administration village set up on Morotai while adjoining Halmahera was still in Japanese hands.

*Below:* Observatory and amphitheatre entrance of the new cultural center in Djakarta.

A Javanese puppeteer holds flat leather puppets used in shadow-plays.

Of Indonesian centipedes, *lipan*, some can inflict a severe bite, others not. A harmless little house centipede, about two or three inches long, is noted for an ability to give off a fluid that glows brightly in the dark. Related to centipedes, but incapable of biting, are the millipedes, *tenggulung*. Some of them can squirt a blistering fluid when disturbed, and so are let alone.

Insects, like flowering plants, reach maximum diversity in the wet tropics, and so abound in Indonesia. In many areas, dragonflies are eaten. Collecting them is often the pastime of a child, who secures the insects by means of a twig that has been gummed with spider webs. The dragonflies are fried in oil, and the child can take pride in having provided the hors d'oeuvre. Certain locusts, *belalang*, are also eaten. Fried and served unshelled, they are somewhat reminiscent of shrimp. The migratory locust, distributed from Europe to the Philippines, occasionally appears in droves, the Indonesian flights reputedly originating in Borneo. Crickets, *djangkrik*, are sometimes penned and encouraged to fight, with much betting on the outcome of the battle. Stick insects and leaf insects, both of which resemble plant parts, are abundant in this land of leafy vegetation. New Guinea, especially, is noted for stick insects and leaf insects of exceptional size and with an uncanny resemblance to twigs or leaves. Praying mantises, too, profit from a camouflaging resemblance to vegetation, often mimicking twigs, leaves, bark, or flowers. Needing no camouflage, protected by secretive ways, are the termites. Called *anai-anai* or *rajap*, they devour rotting wood and house timbers, or even attack living trees. Some termites build a nest above ground on a stump or a tree branch. Such a nest is a huge thing, perhaps a yard across, somewhat earthen in texture, and riddled with the insects' network of tunnels and galleries. Little blind-snakes enter the galleries, presumably to eat the occupants, and the termitaria are dug into by nesting birds of several kinds.

There are in the forest not only wood-eating insects in great variety but also many leaf-eating ones. In the latter category are butterflies and moths, *kupu-kupu*, whose caterpillars usually feed upon leaves. Caterpillars are called *bulu* if hairy, *ulat* if not; and *kepompong* is the chrysalis, the pupa from which the winged adult emerges. In some moths, the pupa is covered with a cocoon whose silk can be unwound, spun into thread, and then woven into cloth. Bombyx, a moth whose caterpillar produces the finest silk, was first domesticated in India or China, but the caterpillar of some other moths, including several of Indonesia, turn out a usable product. The secret of silk manufacture, long withheld from the West, reached Indonesia from India, and the Indonesian name for silk, *sutera,* is from the Sanskrit. ("Suture" is a cognate word in English.) Silken cloth, prized in the islands, was probably more often imported than locally made. Still, one can be sure that in many cases, no more than the raw silken thread was imported; for many old museum specimens and family heirlooms, along with more recent costumes of silk, are woven and decorated in characteristically Indonesian styles. But perhaps in the long run, the silk traffic was most important in establishing routes along which ideas could move. The Silk Road was opened in 122 B.C. to carry Chinese silk westward across Asia to the shores of the Mediterranean, but along it flowed philosophical, religious, astronomical, mathematical, dialectical, and therapeutical concepts—concepts that would in many cases reach tropical southeastern Asia, including Indonesia, by way of the Burma Road and a variety of maritime routes.

Although the adult butterflies and moths of Indonesia may sip nectar, they are not always such dainty feeders; many are attracted to rotting fruit, dog and cattle droppings, or damp ashes. On patches of wet sand, small butterflies with wings of orange, yellow, or white may be accompanied by gaudier swallowtails in sipping moisture from among the sand grains, and even the gigantic birdwing butterflies may join the aggregation. Swallowtails and birdwings are prized by collectors for their size, but even larger are some night-flying moths of the rainforest. Certain long-winged moths are called *gegat* or *ngengat,* a name alluding to their humming flight.

When Alfred Russel Wallace explored Indonesia, he was impressed by the beauty and variety not only of the butterflies and moths but also of the beetles; of the latter he collected more than 83,000 specimens, including representatives of at least 2,000 species that had never before been seen in Europe. Conspicuous in this lot were the metallic wood-borers and the longhorn beetles, whose larvae live under bark or tunnel into wood; for both families abound in a forested land. In one of the wood-borers, the wing covers are so strong and so beautifully iridescent that they are used as jewelry settings. In New Guinea, larvae of the longhorn beetles are gathered and eaten. The tribesmen of that island also use the wing covers of a bright green scarab beetle as headband decoration. But many of the Indonesian beetles are more grotesque than beautiful, provided with horns, exaggerated antennae, or fierce mandibles. One very large beetle is rarely seen except around the containers in which palm sap is being collected; it pulls itself along laboriously with its enormously lengthened front limbs. Even stranger are the fiddle beetles, flattened to hide beneath bark, and nearly transparent. Their grubs live in and eat toadstools. Some nocturnal beetles can give off a flash of light, and their Indonesian name of *kelip-kelip*, "twinkling," is more appropriate than the English name of "firefly." Usually these beetles flash now and then while flying through the dusk, but on Biak a certain kind will gather by the hundreds on a limestone boulder to flash rapidly in unison, and from a distance the insects' communal glow, alternately fading and brightening, suggests a lantern signal.

In the West, the common insects of the darkness are fireflies and a few other beetles, along with moths and mosquitos; and so it is surprising to find that in Indonesia some bees and wasps are also nocturnal. *Penjengat malam*, "night stinger," is the name given to one hornet-like species that will enter houses at night, attracted by the lights therein. The giant honeybee, which builds a dripping comb on a tree branch or the side of a building, will similarly fly after dark. There are also Indonesian bees and wasps of more ordinary habits, among them the common honeybee, called *lebah*. Its honey, *air madu*, is a delicacy, and for that matter so are the bee grubs. Accordingly, *kandang lebah* ("bee stables") are erected so that swarming bees may take up residence in them. Although worldwide today, the honeybee may have come originally from southeastern Asia, and has several close relatives in Indonesia. Some of its more distant relatives in that country produce a honey that is poisonous, but no one is likely to be poisoned, for these species and their nests are easily identifiable. A bigger problem is that of bee-sting. *Induk madu,* a tempting, honey-dripping comb, may be let strictly alone if it is guarded by giant honeybees; and a forest trail may detour widely around a low-hanging hornet nest.

The insect order Hymenoptera, to which the bees and wasps belong, also includes the ants. The latter insects are called *semut;* but if this word is supplied with a prefix denoting action, the resultant expression, *menjemut,* means to swarm, to teem. It is appropriate to focus attention on the ants' teeming societies, for social organization has enabled these insects to assume a major ecological role in the tropics, where they might be thought of as an environmental factor with which other organisms must cope. In temperate lands, where ant species are not very numerous, the biological collector often finds it profitable to turn over logs and rocks, thereby disclosing many secretive little vertebrates and invertebrates; but in Indonesia there are likely to be colonies of stinging ants—and nothing else—beneath every log and rock, in hollow reeds and bamboos, under loosened bark, in tree holes, beneath clustered orchids, and among the fronds of epiphytic ferns. While a few organisms have evolved ways of living with ants, most are excluded from snug hideaways by these swarming, stinging insects. Nesting in termitaria rather than in tree holes, various Indonesian birds secure protection from ants, which do not invade the termites' domain. A few animals, such as the spiny anteaters of New Guinea, the pangolin of western Indonesia, and some narrowmouth frogs of wide distribution, are specialized to prey upon ants. Even among the plants there are adaptations that function to discourage vegetarian or leaf-cutting ants, or to use the carnivorous ones as protectors. In the ant-plants, which abound in Indonesia, the cavities of the plant's bulbous body are of two kinds, one being used by ants as a nursery, the other as a toilet. Some botanists have asserted that the plant takes no profit from the insects' presence, but the biological collector with Indonesian experience could inform them otherwise; for at the slightest disturbance, hordes of ants rush from the plant to attack the disturber, and there is little likelihood that any animal will feed upon the leaves or will tear open the bulbous body for the water that is stored in some of the cavities. In Malayan-speaking areas, one kind of ant is so conspicuous that it has earned a special name, *kerengga*. A large, red species, it builds a nest by gluing leaves together, using its own larvae—which can spin silk —as living glue-tubes. The nest, large as a man's head, hangs conspicuously from a tree branch, and the ants rush out at any disturbance. The Chinese spread the custom of slipping a bag over the nest, breaking off the branch, and rehanging the ant colony on a citrus tree, which the transplanted insects would soon rid of swallowtail caterpillars and other pests. So-called driver or army ants, notorious for migrating periodically over the forest floor, do not live in Indonesia.

The country has many other insect groups, but most of them need not be discussed here. The mosquitos certainly warrant attention, but they have a water-dwelling larval stage, and are better reviewed in connection with aquatic life, the subject of the next chapter.

# CHAPTER IV

# THE WATERS, FRESH AND SALT

A GLANCE at a map of Indonesia will reveal frequent use of the words *danau* and *sungai*. The first of these means a body of standing water, the second of flowing water. But ecological subdivision of the aquatic situations may be carried far beyond this basic one. Thus, *paja* is a heavily forested swamp, *rawang* a thinly forested one, *rawa* a marsh with herbaceous vegetation, *lanau* a mire, *aliran* a brook. *Tasik* is a large lake, *benu* a smaller one, *kolam* a pond, *lungkang* a puddle, *kubang* a mudhole. These and many other words attest to the Indonesian variety of freshwater environments, each with its own fauna; and to the naturally occurring wetlands man adds several kinds of impoundments given over to the raising of crops or edible fishes but often invaded by other organisms. All these teeming bodies of fresh water rest on the land, whose extent, however, does not rival that of the Indonesian salt water. Thus, the aquatic life of the country merits special consideration.

The life of the fresh waters may be taken up first. Some mammals inhabit rivers and lakes; but since they are offshoots of essentially terrestrial groups, they were dealt with in the preceding chapter. One bird family, that of the ducks, geese, and swans, is largely associated with the water. Indonesia has a considerable variety of waterfowl, among them the gray teal, Garganey teal, white-quilled pygmy goose, green pygmy goose, whistling tree-duck, white-headed shelduck, and a black duck resembling the American one. Small wild ducks are called *belibis,* domestic ones *itik* (Malayan) or *bebek* (Javanese). The domestic goose is known as *angsa*—an interesting name, for it is cognate with Anser, the ancient Latin and modern scientific designation of a goose. The word *angsa* was borrowed into Malayan from Sanskrit, and it may be supposed that the domestic goose, like its name, was taken to Indonesia from India. Indonesia has no native swans. However, in the late seventeenth century the Dutch, who knew only the white swans of north temperate lands, were astonished to find a black swan in western Australia. They took the bird to their colonial capital of Batavia on Java, and later to Europe. Domestic swans are called *burung undan,* but the name is also applied to pelicans; it means a bird that bobs about in the water.

Among reptiles, the turtles include a few species of the land and a few of the sea, but the majority live in fresh water. The common turtles (Emydidae), land tortoises, and softshells are families that entered Indonesia from the Asian mainland, while the side-necked turtles entered from Australia. The pit-shell turtle, in a family of its own, is confined to New Guinea. Of the common turtles, about nine species inhabit western Indonesia, only one of them ranging east of Wallace's line. This one, known scientifically as Cuora, is distributed from Sumatra, Java, and Borneo eastward to Ceram. It resembles the American box turtles in being able to withdraw the head, limbs, and tail, and then close the shell completely. Not much of a swimmer but frequenting boggy places, it is familiar to ricefield workers, who call it *penju bulus,* "turtle without appendages." Regarded by Indonesians as an amusing pet, it was probably carried by man to islands east of its original range. Sometimes it is called *baning,* although this name is also used for land tortoises inhabiting Sumatra, Borneo, Sulawesi, and Halmahera. Of Indonesian softshells, two are restricted to the westerly islands, but a third, Pelochelys, has extended its range from the Asian mainland to New Guinea. A powerful swimmer, Pelochelys will enter salt water, where it is sometimes taken by hook and line or in weirs. Common turtles are good food but softshells, *labi-labi,* are superlative, yielding much firm, white meat. In New Guinea the lakes and rivers are inhabited by about nine species of side-necked turtles, members of the primitive family Chelidae. Some of the species are also found in Australia, but none ranges west of the islands that lie on the Sahul Shelf. The hard shell of a side-necked turtle conceals a fair amount of meat, and New Guinea tribesmen, having much interest in small game, gather these reptiles whenever possible. The unique pit-shell turtle, Carettochelys, resembles a large softshell but has more paddle-like forelimbs. It is known only from the Fly River and islands in the Fly delta, but probably reaches Irian Barat.

The crocodilians are another reptile group essentially of the fresh water. *Buaja* is the general name for a crocodilian, not only in Malayan but in many languages from the northern Philippines to Irian Barat. Four species inhabit Indonesia. The Tomistoma or "false gavial" is a remarkable crocodilian confined to Borneo, Sumatra, and the Malay Peninsula. Reaching a length of 15 feet, it is a shy, harmless fish-eater of the rivers. It is called *buaja sepit,* the latter word meaning "narrowed" or "pinched," in allusion to the very narrow snout. Another name, *buaja sendjolong,* compares the reptile to a long-snouted marine fish, a halfbeak known as *sendjolong.* Today very rare, the Tomistoma has been slaughtered for its hide. The other Indonesian crocodilians are true crocodiles, members of the genus Crocodylus. The Siamese crocodile, reaching a length of about 11 feet, is a harmless, freshwater reptile ranging from the Asian mainland to Java and Borneo. It too is imperiled by hide-hunters. The smallest Crocodylus is the New Guinea crocodile, confined to the island for which it is named. About six feet long, it is a timid inhabitant of fresh water, and so inoffensive that tribesmen of the interior will wade and grub about in the mud for it. The existence of this species was not made known to science until 1928, and then only on the basis of two skulls that had been collected 20 years before by an anthropologist investigating the Sepik

135

River tribes. Although most published records for the New Guinea crocodile are confined to the Territory of Papua and North-East New Guinea, the species has been reported once from Irian Barat. It was formerly common in the Lake Murray vicinity near the eastern boundary of Irian Barat, and should range well into the Indonesian part of the island. One hopes so. Australian policy has permitted hide-hunters to extirpate this reptile from the Territories, and it, like most other components of the New Guinea fauna, will survive only if Indonesia protects it. The fourth species of Indonesian crocodilian is the estuarine crocodile, a gigantic reptile distributed from the Asian mainland to northern Australia. The maximum length is about 20 feet. As suggested by its common name, the estuarine crocodile inhabits coastal situations; but it will follow the rivers far inland, a habit first remarked on by Eugène Dubois. In areas where it has been extensively hunted, it is shy; but where local people do not use firearms, it will prey upon man just as it will upon any large animal that ventures into the water. In the New Guinea lowlands, especially, many a person has lost a hand or foot, if not a life, to an estuarine crocodile. In recent years, this species has been greatly reduced in numbers, not because it occasionally attacks man but because it also yields a salable hide. Various crocodile organs figure in the Chinese pharmacopeia, a further inducement for hunters. At night the crocodile's eyes shine with a reddish, ember-like glow in the rays of a flashlight, and so after dark the reptile is easily killed by hunters operating from a powerboat. During the 1950s and 1960s, with the price of crocodile leather climbing, parties of hunters turned from the no longer productive coastal waters to push far up the New Guinea rivers, supplying the tribesmen with flashlights and other gear useful in taking crocodiles, and with salt to preserve the hides. Today, the estuarine crocodile is virtually extinct in the Territories, and uncommon in many parts of Indonesia. It is often referred to by an honorific meaning "scholar."

Among Indonesian lizards and snakes, there are scattered genera and species that live in lakes, swamps, or rivers, but no family that is primarily freshwater; and so the reptiles may be left temporarily in order to consider the amphibians, which usually lay eggs in water and have an aquatic larval stage even if the adult can live on land. Of the amphibians, one major group, the salamanders, does not reach the Asian tropics. A second major group, the caecilians, is made up of limbless burrowers, two species of which range from the Asian mainland to Sumatra, Nias, the Mentawais, Java, and Borneo. Best known is the slimy caecilian, Ichthyophis. Black above with a yellow lateral stripe, and reaching a length of about 15 inches, it superficially resembles an overgrown earthworm. Like a worm it is a burrower in damp places; yet its life history is typically amphibian in that the gelatinous eggs hatch into aquatic larvae, which later metamorphose into the adult form. In parts of Indonesia, as in some other lands, caecilians are thought to crawl up the rectum of a person who sleeps on the ground. The mistaken notion may stem from the confusion of caecilians with large, parasitic worms which pass in the opposite direction.

The really successful group of Indonesian amphibians is that of the frogs, with seven families represented in the country. Of these, the toads, spadefoot toads, and rhacophorid treefrogs are concentrated west of Wallace's line, although a few toads and rhacophorids range east into the Celebesian Transition. The hylid treefrogs and the southern-frogs (Leptodactylidae) are concentrated in Australia and New Guinea, with a few hylids ranging west into the transition. Finally, the narrowmouths (Microhylidae) and common frogs (Ranidae) are present in both western and eastern Indonesia. *Katak* (Malayan) or *kadok* (Javanese) is the name for frogs and toads generally. *Kangkung* or *ketak puru* are toads (Bufo) resembling the familiar American and European species and similarly given to hopping about in yards and gardens; but some Indonesian members of the toad family are web-footed swimmers, while others climb bushes. The skins of certain large toads were imported into Indonesia by the Chinese for use as medicine, and since the skins contain digitalis-like chemicals, epinephrine, and indole bases, no doubt they have some physiological effect when taken internally. Spadefoot toads, family Pelobatidae, live on Sumatra, Java, Borneo, Bali, and the Natunas. Some of them, colored like a dead leaf, are provided with grotesque horns, and so do not resemble the North American members of the family; nor would Indonesian pelobatid tadpoles look familiar, for they are provided with an umbrella-shaped mouth that opens upward, permitting the aquatic larva to feed from the surface film of the water.

The two Indonesian treefrog families, the Rhacophoridae and Hylidae, are not closely related to each other but instead represent separate invasions of the arboreal habitat. Rhacophorids are distributed from the Asian mainland to Sumatra, Java, and Borneo, with a few of the species ranging eastward as far as Sulawesi and Timor. The most famous rhacophorid is the flying frog, a green, yellow, and black species found on the Asian mainland, Sumatra, and Borneo. During Alfred Russel Wallace's stay on Borneo, a Chinese workman presented him with a frog previously unknown to science. When this amphibian's very long toes were extended, the webbing formed a surface apparently broad enough to support gliding flight, and the workman assured Wallace that the frog had "come down, in a slanting direction, from a high tree." Wallace's published report of the episode was received with skepticism, but in recent years it has been found that the frog does indeed glide downward in a slanting direction, buoyed by the extended webbing. Other rhacophorids are not so specialized for arboreal existence. One species, which superficially resembles the hylid "tree toad" of North America, is very common from the mainland of southern Asia east to Sulawesi and Timor. On rainy nights its croaking is heard from bushes and vines around the sawah, or from garden shrubbery and fences. In the water, the female of this species deposits not only her eggs but also a substance that she beats into foam, using her hind limbs for this purpose. In the morning the frogs have vanished, but many foam nests around the sawah margin attest to the nocturnal activity. The hylid treefrogs, so abundant in the New World, are lacking from the Asiatic tropics but reappear in great diversity in the Australian Realm, whence a few species range about as far west as Timor, Ceram, and the Moluccas. In New Guinea the common frogs are largely restricted to upland streams, the narrowmouths are burrowers, the southern frogs are secretive—but hylid treefrogs of the genus Hyla are everywhere. A tiny green one with orange thighs sits all day atop an Alocasia leaf; a small, buffy one, given to frequent color change,

lives in ant plants or else hides beneath the ragged bark of a Mela-
leuca tree; a gigantic green one, almost as big as a bullfrog, croaks
from the branches far overhead; a slender green and brown one
avoids the trees to hop through wet grass. The vagabond treefrog,
black-masked like a highwayman, descends to its breeding ponds
only on one or two nights of the year, when rain fills the holes left
by wind-thrown palms. Cat-eyed treefrogs, members of the hylid
genus Nyctimystes, huddle on boulders and mossy tree trunks near
upland streams. In some of the species the transparent lower eye-
lids are pigmented with black; they are pulled over the eyes when
the frog rests, thus functioning as sunglasses.

From a distributional center in Australia, the leptodactylids or
southern-frogs range westward through New Guinea to a few
smaller islands on the Sahul Shelf. One species, a Lechriodus, is
very common beneath fallen logs near rivers in Irian Barat. It is
remarkably variable in color, being whitish, cream, buff, pink,
green, or dark red, with or without a dorsal stripe of some contrasting hue. Yet, no color phase is conspicuous among the debris
and vegetation of the forest floor, and the frog usually lies motionless when disturbed, relying on camouflage for protection. On New
Guinea, southern-frogs are considerably outnumbered by narrowmouths, members of the frog family Microhylidae. Although concentrated on New Guinea and Borneo, narrowmouths are
represented by at least one or two species in almost any part of Indonesia, their ability to subsist on ants perhaps accounting for
their success. In this country of spectacular animal life, one would
not expect the drab, secretive little narrowmouths to command attention, but a Western visitor may find them doing so, especially in
the *sawah* regions. Imagine a typical small village on, say, the
western end of Bali. Storm clouds, gathering all afternoon, have
broken soon after dark. Rain rattles on the thatched roofs, pours off
the eaves, forms pools in the black and empty streets. From a
street puddle comes a mournful bleat, immediately answered from
the edge of a nearby ricefield. From a garden rises a croaking and
a sharp trilling, from the deepest part of the flooded field a cluck-
ing, from the farther shore an inhumanly hollow laugh. But all
these calls are soon drowned out by hammering notes which multi-

139

ply until the whole *sawah* is aclatter. As the night wears on, the voices from the blackness take on a subtle rhythm, and the listener is lulled to sleep. This is the nocturnal chorus of the frogs, opened by the bleat of one narrowmouth and dominated by the clatter of another, with counterpoint provided by frogs of other families. On Bali a popular orchestral selection is the "Frog Song" in which a Jew's-harp, flute, drum, cymbals, and slit drum combine to imitate the complex rhythm of the frogs' breeding chorus. In western Indonesia, everyone knows *katuk-katuk*, the noisy frogs whose name signifies a variety of hammering sounds. In many settled areas, the wells are provided with a wooden rim only an inch or two high, and during a rainy night the narrowmouths may tumble in. Poor at climbing, they can only float about, to be discovered in the morning.

Narrowmouths provide musical inspiration; the common frogs, family Ranidae, provide meat. In Indonesia as in Europe and the United States, the ranids are the largest frogs that are gathered for the table. For obscure reasons, Westerners throw away half the meat, that of the forelimbs and body, saving only the hind limbs; but butchered more sensibly, a large ranid yields a fair quantity of flesh. In New Guinea, ranids are most abundant in the uplands. Here they are a staple food of the tribesmen, who collect both the tadpoles and the adult frogs. A few Indonesian ranids have extraordinary habits. One such is the crab-eating frog, a Rana distributed from China through Indonesia as far east as Flores. It is unusual among amphibians in that its eggs and larvae can survive a little salinity, and the adults can live in brackish mangrove or nipa swamps, where their nocturnal grunting is often mistaken for that of crocodiles. *Katuk pisang* is a brightly patterned, green and reddish Rana found from the Asian mainland east to Sulawesi. It eludes enemies by bouncing across the surface of the water in the fashion of a skipped stone. Several Indonesian frogs and lizards have the ability to skitter across the surface of the water, traveling 10 or 15 feet before submerging. In some ranids of western Indonesia, those of the genus Staurois, the tadpole clings to a rock in a swift brook of the uplands, held in place by a ventral suction disk.

Now for the fishes of the fresh waters. When the Sunda Shelf was exposed in the Pleistocene, the present rivers of eastern Sumatra and western Borneo were the headwaters of one large river which flowed northward, while the present rivers of northern Java and southern Borneo were the headwaters of another large stream which flowed southward. Soundings have traced the former courses of the two vanished master streams on the ocean floor. Two drainages, interdigitating in their headwaters, can make contact through geological processes that need not be reviewed, and in effect there was in past times a continuity of fresh water from the present Asian mainland to the edge of the Sunda Shelf, with ramifications into Sumatra, Java, and Borneo. Accordingly, many of the mainland freshwater families could range to one or more (usually more) of these three islands, but not beyond. In this category are the minnows, loaches, mountain loaches, half a dozen families of catfishes, nandids, pristolepids, the climbing-perch and its relatives, snakeheads, the single luciocephalid, and the spiny eels. There were, however, two other ways in which Indonesian islands acquired freshwater fishes. First, a good many fish genera or families, although regarded as characteristic of the fresh water, have at least a few members that can tolerate a bit of salinity and that can cross a narrow sea barrier between islands. Thus, a freshwater fish on an oceanic island may have been derived from a salt-tolerant ancestor. Second, if mainland or salt-tolerant freshwater fishes do not reach an island in any variety, the aquatic niches there may be taken over by some offshoot of an essentially marine family. Ignoring a few species transported by man, the freshwater fishes of the Celebesian Transition are descendants of salt-tolerant or marine stocks. For example, topminnows reach fresh waters of Sulawesi and Timor, but their family, the Cyprinodontidae, is noteworthy for ability to withstand salinity and often inhabits coastal waters. One fish family, the Adrianichthyidae, is confined to Lindu and Poso, lakes of Sulawesi, but had topminnow-like ancestry. Sulawesi harbors distinctive freshwater halfbeaks and silversides, but both families also have marine members. Melanotaeniids, from fresh waters of Australia and southern New Guinea, are derived from sil-

141

versides. A peculiar little goby is known from the fresh waters of such scattered islands as Java, Sulawesi, the Philippines, and the Solomons; but gobies are often coastal in habitat.

When the Sahul Shelf was exposed in the Pleistocene, there was a continuity of fresh water from Australia to New Guinea, but this situation may not have greatly altered fish distribution in the Australian Realm, where only two genera of freshwater fishes have no close relatives in the sea. The freshwater fishes of this realm belong mostly to families with marine members, for example, the lampreys, galaxiids, plotosid catfishes, sea-basses, anguillid eels, gobies, and silversides. Doriichthys, a catfish of southern New Guinea, is placed in a family of its own, but it is probably an offshoot of the ariid catfishes which abound in the sea. Just as the forests of New Guinea seem strangely empty of life, so do the fresh waters seem lacking in fishes. Of Australia's two strictly freshwater types of fishes, only one reaches New Guinea, and the offshoots of marine stocks have not been able to exploit the fresh waters of that island very well. High in the mountains of Irian Barat, little gobies dash about in the rocky brooks, but there is nothing comparable to, say, the assemblage of dace, chubs, shiners, suckers, sculpin, madtoms, and darters that might occupy a similar brook in the uplands of eastern North America. Some of the New Guinea mountain tribes have never seen any fish except eels. A backwater in the Irian Barat lowlands might yield a few large catfishes and bony-tongues, along with an eel or two, but nothing comparable to the assemblage of sunfishes, bass, pickerel, bowfin, eel, channel catfish, and bullheads that would take a fisherman's lure in a river backwater of the southeastern United States. Sharks, sawfishes, anchovies, and needlefishes invade the lower courses of large rivers. The Neolithic-level peoples of Irian Barat occupy a land where the freshwater vertebrate fauna, like the terrestrial, is impoverished.

Indonesian freshwater fishes are not well known outside the country, and only a few of them need be singled out. Scleropages, a genus of the bony-tongued fishes (Osteoglossidae), has no relatives in the sea. The genus is distributed from the Asian mainland to Sumatra and Borneo, and from Australia to New Guinea. The bony-tongues are large fishes, some of them up to a yard long and quite stout. Called *kelesa,* they are taken less often with hook and line than with *tempuling,* a steel-tipped spear, or with *seruit,* a harpoon whose barbs are of wood. Freshwater eels, closely related to those of the United States and Europe, are widespread in Indonesia, and like their relatives go down to the sea to breed. *Ikan* is the general name for fishes, while *ikan belut* are eels. Remarkable eels are the synbranchs, genus Synbranchus. They lack pectoral and pelvic fins, their eyes are reduced to pinpoints, their mouth is small and weak, and a single perforation on the ventral midline is their only external sign of gills; yet they thrive in the tropics of four continents, seeming to be equally at home in a muddy rice-field, a clear stream, a coastal swamp, or even cavern waters. One species, ranging from India through Indonesia to Australia, can be found in mangrove and nipa swamps but is more common in *sawah.* Local residents often make small, bottle-shaped eel-traps out of split bamboo, baiting them with minced worms, leaving them overnight in the *sawah,* and the next morning collecting from them a number of small, edible synbranchs. When *sawah* is plowed during a dry spell, these eels are often turned up in numbers. Apparently they can live for long periods in damp soil.

The most widely known of Indonesian freshwater fishes are certain little ones that have reached the aquarium trade. Most of them are collected on Borneo or Sumatra, or less frequently on Java. A majority also range to the Malay Peninsula or beyond, and enter the world market through several large cities of the Orient. Many Indonesian members of the minnow family, Cyprinidae, are seen in European and American aquaria. Among them are the damsel, checkerboard, striped, six-banded, and clown barbs, and one or two other species of Barbus, stout little fishes whose colorful scales flash like mirrors. Slimmer and speedier than the barbs are the Rasboras, at least eight popular species of which come from streams of Sumatra and Borneo. The so-called "black shark," actually a velvety black cyprinid of the genus Labeo, aroused much enthusiasm when it was first imported from Sumatra, Java, and Borneo; and lately another Indonesian cyprinid, the "flying-fox," has interested aquarists. Indonesian loaches include the striped Botia, the clown loach, and several eel-like species such as the coolie loach. A silurid, the glass catfish of Sumatra, Java, Borneo, and the Asian mainland, is the most nearly transparent of fishes; its skeleton is plainly visible, as is a sac in which the internal organs repose. The Indonesian topminnows, Cyprinodontidae, are mostly too drab or otherwise unsuitable for captivity, but an exception is the genus Oryzias, whose members, such as the paddy-fish, medaka, and Java killy, often inhabit ricefields. The live-bearing killifishes, Poeciliidae, are native only to the New World, but one of them, a Gambusia, has proven of great worth in the control of mosquitos, upon whose larvae it feeds. Gambusias have accordingly been introduced into many parts of the Old World, including Indonesia. The country also has some native fishes that are live-bearers, among them the common halfbeak and the slim halfbeak, both inhabiting fresh water but having congeners in the sea. The English name of "halfbeak," like the familial name of Hemirhamphidae, alludes to the prolongation of the lower jaw far beyond the upper. Like halfbeaks, the gobies are principally saltwater, but include two attractive species, called bumblebee gobies, that can live in fresh.

In a review of aquarium fishes, the family Anabantidae warrants separate mention. Its strangest Indonesian member is the climbing perch, *puju-puju*, a small fish which can travel overland and even climb with the aid of spiny gill covers. A much larger anabantid is one known in Java as *gurami*. Reaching a length of two feet, it is often raised in ponds as a food fish. The local name in its English version, "gourami," has been applied or rather misapplied to many small members of the family. Among them are the chocolate, lace, snakeskin, blue, spear-tailed, sparkling, and croaking gouramis, all known from Indonesia. Also inhabiting that country are the kissing gourami and the green kissing gourami. Their turned-out lips are used to eat algae off stones, and their osculation, although inspiring anthropomorphism, is a mutual cleaning. The best-known anabantid is the Siamese fighting fish. Its presence as a wild species in Indonesia may reflect frequent introduction by man, but its generic name, Betta, is from Malayan *ikan betah*, "enduring fish." The males are belligerent toward each other, and if two are placed in the same jar, they fight. The Siamese people may have been the first to have staged these battles and bet upon the outcome, but the custom spread to other oriental regions, including Indonesia. The little battlers are rarely taken from the wild but are of domestic strains recognizably different from their wild ancestor. Some additional strains have been originated by aquarists, selected for color rather than pugnacity. (Indeed, aquarium fishes of many families have been bred for form or color not seen in the wild.) The anabantids, the single luciocephalid, and the snakeheads (Channidae) have a supplementary breathing organ which retains pockets of air in the vicinity of the gills. This is why some of these fishes can move overland, survive transportation from pond to pond, remain active for a time in a small jar, or live all day on display in a fishmarket. Chinese fishmongers, supplying customers' demand for truly fresh fish, will casually slice a living snakehead at intervals during the day, the unfortunate victim continuing to wriggle until most of its elongate body has been sliced away.

Fishes that live in brackish water often can tolerate considerable variation in salinity, for at times their habitat is freshened by rainwater runoff. A good many brackish-water species of Indonesia are kept by aquarists in fresh or lightly salted water. Among them are the archerfishes, Toxotes, whose species are distributed from mainland Asia through Indonesia to Australia, and eastward to many Pacific isles. An archerfish is remarkable for knocking down flies by squirting water droplets at them. Performing readily in an aquarium, a captive archerfish has even been "trained" to extinguish a glowing cigarette in the dark. Less widespread than the toxotids, but present throughout much of Indonesia, are the fishes called scats, or less euphemistically scatophagids. *Kitang* is one Malayan name for them. They are often seen around docks and tidewater villages, where they fatten themselves on the refuse that falls into the water; yet they are dainty in appearance, resembling the marine butterfly fishes to which they are related. The moon scat is a well-known species from New Guinea, the spotted scat from many of the Indonesian islands. But in this land of unusual fishes, none is more remarkable than the members of the family Periophthalmidae. They are to be seen around most of the islands—on land, for these are the famous mudskippers, with frog-like faces and an

145

uncanny ability to hop about over muddy beaches. A mudskipper will moisten its eyes by wiping its fins over them, wet its body by rolling in a shallow puddle, chase an insect across the ground, and even climb into the mangrove roots. *Ikan tembakul* is the commonest name for these odd little fishes, which have evolved in a direction paralleling the Amphibia.

The foregoing list is but a sampling of Indonesian aquarium fishes. The growth of the aquarium trade brings more and more species to the attention of fish fanciers, and occasionally brings to light species that were previously unknown to science. Tropical fishes of most kinds are kept in sparkling, tastefully decorated tanks, and it is amusing to note the circumstances under which the same kinds exist in nature. Often, a wide assortment of jewel-bright fishes may be obtained by one pull of a seine through *sawah* where the water is turbid with mud and *kerbau* droppings.

Flooded fields of Indonesia are often expected to yield not only one or more plant crops but also some kind of edible fish, and if fishes are not naturally present in the *sawah*, they may be deliberately introduced there. The walking catfish, Clarias, is a freshwater species that ranges from the Asian mainland into Sumatra, Java, and Borneo, but that has been carried by man to *sawah* areas farther east. The discovery of a few specimens in Florida, escaped aquarium stock, led to a good bit of sensational journalism in 1969 and 1970, readers being left with the impression that hordes of ravenous creatures were marching across the state, gobbling up dogs in passing. Actually, this is a small and comparatively slender fish, the adults about a pound in weight. Like other catfishes, it will defend itself with its fin-spines when molested. Indonesian children enjoy watching it lurch awkwardly across the ground, but their parents prize it for another reason. Most fishes die soon after being removed from the water, and in this warm, humid land must be eaten quickly before they spoil. In many of the scombroid fishes—tuna, bonito, mackerel, and related species of the sea—the histidine of the tissues may be bacterially converted in just a few hours to saurine, which produces allergy-like reactions in man. But a catch of walking catfishes, sandwiched between wet banana leaves, can be taken in a basket to the market, where after a day on display the fishes are still alive. Recent photographs of the walking catfish have portrayed pinkish individuals, but they are of an albinistic strain favored by aquarists; wild specimens are dark. *Keli* is the Malayan name.

Not only are fishes introduced into *sawah;* special ponds are built in which edible species can be reared. Such ponds are most often seen on Java. In general, fishponds of brackish or salt water are called *tambak*, a word literally meaning a dam or dyke; and *siwakan* are freshwater ponds. It is not unusual to see two or three men walking in the shallows beside a beach, carrying a fine-mesh seine and peering closely at the schools of tiny, darting fishes. The biologist will understand why artificial ponds must be periodically restocked with fry seined from the wild, for some fishes will not breed in confinement; but he will wonder how the seiners·can pick out the kind of fry they want, and how supposedly delicate little fishes can withstand the extreme changes of temperature and salinity to which they probably will be exposed in their transfer from sea to pond. *Belanak*, the gray mullet, is a species often cultivated in impoundments. In some areas, the buttery flesh of a pond-reared *belanak*, carefully freed of bones, is mixed with spices and coconut milk, the mixture then sewn into a *belanak* skin and baked. The result is unsurpassable.

Before turning to the marine fauna, mention should be made of a few invertebrates associated with the fresh water. Leeches, blood-sucking relatives of the earthworm, are common in many bodies of water. In the *sawah*, the buffalo leech fastens itself to the leg of *kerbau* or man. *Lintah* is the name for an aquatic leech, but *lintah darat*, "land leech," is a usurer. There actually is a terrestrial leech, but it is called *patjat*. Especially common in the swamp peat forest, it may crawl over damp ground toward a prospective victim, but more often it clings to trailside vegetation, ready to drop upon a passing animal. Although the *sawah* has leeches, it has no crayfishes, and this is all to the good, for in other lands these crustaceans have proven damaging to rice seedlings. Irian Barat is the only part of Indonesia in which crayfishes live, and there they are confined to the southerly drainage. They are collected and eaten by tribesmen. But in many parts of Indonesia there are small crabs that live in fresh water, and others that scuttle about on the ground or even climb trees to hide in epiphytic vegetation.

Common in flooded *sawah* and other ponds is a giant waterbug about four inches long. Highly predaceous, equipped with hooked forelegs and a sharp beak, it kills small fishes and frogs. For all that it is a swimmer and a flattened bottom-dweller, the giant waterbug can fly, and is sometimes attracted in swarms to city lights. The Chinese brought to Indonesia the custom of gathering these swarming insects and frying them in oil as a delicacy. But of Indonesian insects associated with water, most important are the mosquitos. The adults, called *njamuk,* will fly about, but the larvae, *djentik-djentik,* are water dwellers; and each species of mosquito must locate the proper kind of aquatic situation in which to breed. *Njamuk* are most troublesome in the lowlands, and are likely to be more common around human settlements than in the wilds. One of the best known Malayan words is *kelambu,* a mosquito net. In the form *kolambun* the word exists in Melanesian pidgin, which has a second name for a mosquito net, *taunem.* When the *kelambu* is draped over a bed, its fine mesh prevents entry by mosquitos, although tiny, stinging flies, *rengit,* can pass through it. Rarely are uncivilized peoples seriously discommoded by mosquito bites, to which they become inured; but in some New Guinea lowlands, the tribespeople sleep under dome-shaped piles of matting, preferring the heat and the closeness to the torment of biting mosquitos which swarm after dark. Of mosquito-borne diseases, yellow fever is lacking from Indonesia, dengue present at many scattered localities, yaws transmitted infrequently by insect bite. Malaria, however, has been a public health problem of considerable magnitude. It is transmitted only by the bite of female mosquitos that belong to certain species of the genus Anopheles and that have previously bitten a malaria sufferer. Four species of microorganisms, members of the protozoan genus Plasmodium, actually produce the disease in man. Of these four, one is lacking from most parts of Indonesia except Irian Barat; and a second, the causative agent of quartan malaria, is completely lacking. A third, the agent of benign tertian malaria, is widespread in the lowlands, and so is the fourth, which produces the malignant tertian. A principal Indonesian vector is an

Anopheles that breeds in brackish water, and so some coastal settlements have been notably malarious. In the early days of Batavia, the resident Dutch suffered from what Malayan-speakers appropriately called *demam kura*, "spleen-fever," and would have
suffered more had not most female Anopheles, hatching from
brackish ponds, been sated by the blood of Javanese and immigrant Chinese who lived directly on the coast. Cinchona, with its
antimalarial bark, was introduced into Indonesia long before it
was realized that mosquitos carried *demam kura*, malaria.

Although some insects breed in brackish water, only a few can
live in the sea. The marine world is remarkable for a scarcity of
both insects and flowering plants, two groups that abound on land;
and of the vertebrates, only the fishes are highly diverse in the sea.
But many groups of lower organisms—the brown algae, red algae,
sponges, jellyfishes and their kin, comb jellies, ribbon worms, ar-
rowworms, lampshells, acorn worms and their kin, deep-sea pogon-
ophores, echinoderms, and several others—are largely or in some
cases exclusively marine. Other groups of lower organisms—for example, the blue-green algae, mollusks, jointed worms, and
crustaceans—are common in the sea as well as on land, or in the
fresh water. A great many marine organisms are sedentary, attaching themselves to a reef or other substratum; but they usually have
a larval stage that swims or drifts. Thus, an expanse of deep water
may be no barrier even to a species that is sedentary in the shallows. The South Equatorial Current passes in a westwardly direction through the waters of southern Indonesia and the Indian
Ocean, while farther north the Indian Countercurrent and the
Equatorial Countercurrent move eastward. These great, warm currents must have been important in distributing many species
widely, from the Indian Ocean through Indonesia into Polynesia.
At any rate, the distribution of marine life in Indonesia is less a
matter of geographic regions than of distinctive environmental
zones.

The supratidal zone lies above high tide mark, but within reach
of salt spray, at least during storms. It is invaded by some land organisms, but these need not concern us here. Many crabs, although
bound to the sea by a need for salt water in which to breed, forage

into the supratidal zone or beyond. Most famous of these wanderers is the coconut crab, Birgus, a husky night prowler with powerful claws. According to many books, it will climb a palm to cut off the coconuts, and the local residents construct devices that encourage the crab to tumble out of the tree. But this is another myth. The crab climbs into the Pandanus trees, the nipa palms, and the Indian-mulberries to get at the fruit, and when fully grown has the strength and dexterity to open a fallen coconut. Orthodox Muslims may not eat the coconut crab, but there are other people who do so. The Chinese in Indonesia will tether one of these crustaceans and fatten it on coconut meat. But the species is not wholly vegetarian; it has been known to break off and eat the claw of a land crab, Cardiosoma, another inhabitant of the supratidal zone. Also rambling into and beyond this zone are hermit crabs. Unlike most other crustaceans, the hermit crab has a soft, vulnerable body which it usually hides in a discarded mollusk shell. However, one large, common species of Indonesia, known scientifically as Coenobita, will insert its body into a tin can, a length of bamboo, an old lamp chimney, or any other receptacle that can be entered and dragged about. On Biak, small hermit crabs are abundant in the caves, where they break the silence with the eerie scraping of their limbs and the rattling of their shell-homes against the rock. A real pest in some parts of Indonesia is a crustacean known to local residents as *udang ketak*, "rapping shrimp," and to scientists as Thalassina. When *sawah* agriculture is carried on in low, flat country not far from the sea, these shrimp may bore great holes in the dykes, weakening the earthen structures and sometimes permitting saltwater encroachment.

The intertidal zone, between the high tide mark and the low, is the home of many crabs: the colorful fiddlers with their waving claws, the sand-colored ghost crabs who are less conspicuous than their own shadows, the military crabs who parade in groups along a mudflat, and others. More aquatic species, such as Scylla, often resembling the American blue crab in size, habits, and edibility, enter the intertidal zone when the tide is high. *Akrab* is one name for an aquatic, edible crab, *kepiting* a more widespread name. G. E. Rumpf, a pioneer biologist who spent most of his life on Ambon in the Moluccas, reported that a certain local crab (now called Eriphias) was poisonous to eat. If so, it is about the only crab that cannot be prepared for the table. It is an exciting experience to accompany a Moluccan crabber on his rounds. His success depends on the selection of the proper habitat, time, and tide. Shortly after dark, with the tide just coming in, he goes down to a mudflat, preferably near a river mouth. In one hand he carries a torch, in the other a large cylinder of split bamboo which is open at both ends, wider at the bottom than at the top. As he wades barefoot in the shallow water over the mudflat, his torch reveals many crabs resting or crawling on the bottom. Also resting on the bottom are snakes in unbelievable numbers, often a dozen or more in sight within the narrow circle of dim yellow torchlight. Although rear-fanged, they will not bite, not even if touched; and the crabber ignores them. Time and again he slaps his container down over a crab before it can scuttle away. Then, reaching into the container, he seizes the crab by the back of the shell, brings it out, and jams it into a sack slung from his shoulder. As the tide rises higher on his legs, and on the trunks of the nipa palms that dot the mudflat, one or two larger snakes appear, not sluggish bottom-dwellers but active swimmers, looking black in the torchlight. The man glances at them keenly, identifies them, dismisses them, and goes about his crabbing. By the time the water has risen to his knees, he has filled the sack with *kepiting*.

The small snakes, incidentally, are known scientifically as Cerberus. They belong to a distinctive subfamily of rear-fanged colubrids, the Homalopsinae, with about a dozen species restricted to coastal waters of Indonesia and nearby lands. The larger, blackish snakes belong to a different family, the Acrochordidae, confined to salt waters of Indonesia and adjoining regions. The acrochordid of the mudflats is known scientifically as Acrochordus, and locally as *ular belalai gadjah*, "elephant's-trunk snake." But because it has a loose skin, it is also called *ular karung*, "baggy snake," and under the name of karung it provides a commercial leather. Acrochordids are completely harmless. Indonesia has highly venomous marine snakes, about 30 species making up the family Hydrophidae, but seldom do they swim into the intertidal zone. Their venom functions primarily to overcome finny prey. Most of them are disinclined to bite man, and are handled casually by Chinese, Japanese, and Malay fishermen, who gather them for food and nostrums. But a few of the hydrophid sea-snakes are reputed to be touchy, and accidents have happened when fishermen were hauling in their nets. The commonest Indonesian sea-snake, Enhydrina, has one of the most potent venoms, drop for drop, of any serpent; the substance is used in the manufacture of an antiserum against hydrophid bites generally. Enhydrina follows the Digul River of Irian Barat as far upstream as Tanah Merah. Indonesia is the center of hydrophid distribution, whence at least two common species have reached the Pacific coast of the New World tropics.

From the edge of the land, the sea bottom slopes gradually downward to a depth of about 600 feet, at which point a more abrupt drop begins. The gradually sloping expanse, known as the continental shelf, has much to offer man; for the shelf and the waters over it constitute a zone in which saltwater organisms are strongly concentrated. Throughout the world, the shelf zone is the principal source of seafood and other marine products. Indonesia has no highly organized fisheries, but people who live near the sea usually derive a large part of their sustenance from it, and a coastal community of any size is likely to have a *pasar ikan*, a fish market where a part of each day's catch may be displayed and sold. In some places the shelf is smoothly floored with sediments derived from the land, and huge nets may be used to drag a rich haul of seafood onto the beach. The netting procedure is a fascinating one. During the night, a fleet of vessels takes the net far out, leaving the two ends on the beach at points perhaps a third of a mile apart. In the morning, the villagers split into two groups who begin pulling on the two net lines, while the vessels cruise behind the net to frighten the more active fishes, which might otherwise jump the float-line. As the hours go by, the two groups of pullers approach each other. By afternoon they are close together, the vessels can come in no closer, and the rest of the net is dragged into the shallows with an enormous load of swimming, leaping, thrashing, wriggling sea life. There may be a five-foot shark, *ikan ju*, lunging dangerously until some man grabs it by the tail and whirls it back into the sea. A smaller shark, *tjutjut matjan*, cross-banded with brown and yellow, is thrown away with a grimace of disgust, along with a few fishes of more ordinary appearance. Once the unwanted fishes have been discarded, the women move in to fill their pans and baskets, while a dignified old gentleman, a respected elder, strolls about, assuring by his very presence that everyone takes only a fair share of the catch. Especially prized are hundred of little fishes, for they can be eaten entire before or after drying.

The visitor will be surprised at the considerable number of fishes that are discarded, but the fishermen know that certain species are inedible. The black-tipped sand shark, the white shark, and the hammerhead shark may have poisonous flesh; certainly their liver is highly toxic. Some of the morays are unfit to eat. The black, the white-spotted, and the death puffer have poisonous liver, gonads, intestines, and skin, as is also true of the porcupine fish. A great variety of fishes—surgeonfish, ladyfish, surmullet, sea bass, filefish, triggerfish, squirrelfish, oceanic bonito, wrasse, various snappers, a barracuda, and dozens more—at certain times and places may have poisonous flesh, the eating of which produces a complex of symptoms called ciguatera. The malady has a mortality rate of 70 percent. The ciguatera-producing fishes are characteristic of the coral reefs, but the nature of the connection between reef existence and poisonous flesh is not clear. One might suspect that toxins are accumulated in the flesh through the food chain, for many small reef organisms are poisonous. Just occasionally, the flesh of octopus and squid can also produce ciguatera. But in any event, the islanders know which local organisms are to be kept and which discarded.

The coral reef is a distinctive environment of the shelf zone, just as tropical rainforest is a distinctive environment of the land. Reef life includes red algae, sponges, sea anemones, a variety of corals, mollusks, crustaceans, starfishes, sea urchins, brittle-stars, fishes, and others. Some of the species are not wholly committed to reef life but may occur in other shelf situations or even in other zones. Yet, many species can live nowhere but on a reef, and are limited to areas where the water's depth, temperature, salinity, and clarity meet the rigid requirements of the reef-building corals. Often, more than half the mass of a reef is made up of organisms other than the reef-building corals. A reef may parallel the coastline at a considerable distance offshore, in which case it is called a barrier reef. Of earthly structures produced by living things, by far the largest is the Great Barrier Reef, which begins about 150 miles east of Irian Barat's southeastern tip, and extends southward for more than 1,-000 miles off the Australian coast. A fringing reef is one that more closely borders the land, while an atoll is a ring-like reef enclosing a lagoon.

A linguistic digression: *karang* is the Indonesian name for coral or a coral reef. Whether seen in longitudinal or cross section, a chunk of coral shows an elaborate structure, an impressively neat arrangement of calcareous material. When the word *karang* is supplied with a prefix denoting agency, the resultant expression, *pengarang*, means an author or a composer of music, someone who carefully arranges words or musical notes with the beauty and perfection that marks the work of the coral polyp. Bahasa Indonesia, a language noted for complimentary phraseology, here outdoes itself.

Nets cannot be dragged over a reef, which is usually covered with branching or boulder-like corals and other stony growths; but since the reef's upper surface often lies close to the mean low tide mark, many living things may be left in tidepools when the tide goes out. Various plant juices, mentioned in a previous chapter, can be used in the tidepools, or even in coves and lagoons, to stun fishes. More effective is *dinamit*, dynamite. Sticks of explosive have a way of vanishing from construction sites, and when they do, one can expect a distant thunderous booming, soon followed by unusual activity at the *pasar ikan*.

The edible or otherwise useful organisms of the reef are not limited to the fishes. *Udang karang*, literally "shrimp of the coral," is a spiny lobster without claws but with an abundance of firm, white meat in the tail. It is closely related to the crustacean that is served under the name of lobster in Florida restaurants. *Udang karang* is an important item of diet for coastal people. True shrimp, *udang*, are netted, although not especially from coral areas. The octopus, an inoffensive mollusk for all the sensational yarns about it, sometimes moves by night into shallow water at high tide, and in the deeper water it can be trapped. Its tentacles yield a meat reminiscent of scallops. Other edible mollusks, including conchs, clams, abalones, and scallops, are gathered whenever available. Near the cities, seafood finds its way to the restaurants, there to be prepared in a variety of styles. But in Indonesia. as in other parts of the Orient, the list of locally popular seafoods extends to some that are rarely eaten in the West; sea urchins, for example, and the caviar-like eggs of the horseshoe crab, *belangkas* or *mimi*. Books often mention a marine delicacy known as trepang or bêche-de-mer, but seldom tell its full story. Bêche-de-mer, meaning "sea-worm," is a French version of the Portuguese name for a large sea cucumber, a fleshy mollusk that creeps slug-like along the bottom. Called *teripang* in Malayan, this invertebrate has a poisonous skin, which, however, does not discourage all predators from attack. If any enemy persists in attacking, the sea cucumber will extrude its respiratory and reproductive organs, sometimes its intestines also. The predator bites off these organs and departs satisfied, leaving the eviscerated animal to grow a new set. In Indonesia and other parts of the Southwest Pacific, man is often the predator, pinching off the animal's extruded viscera, eating the morsels raw or saving them for soup. The skin of the sea cucumber may be allowed to crawl away, or it may be squeezed and pounded into a tidepool, thereby stunning a number of fishes. But often the skin is dried or smoked, a procedure that detoxifies it; and so treated, it is the trepang of commerce, a proteinous food used in soups or eaten as tidbits. Although China is the principal market for trepang, the search for edible sea cucumbers extends widely across the Pacific.

The collecting of food about the reefs and flats is not without its perils. While aggressive reef organisms are few, many respond painfully when accidentally touched or stepped on. Fire corals, capable of stinging severely, grow on the reef; and the touch of the "blue-bottle," a gelatinous drifter, can be fatal in just a few minutes. Some of the bristle-worms, common under submerged rocks and coral clumps, can deliver a mildly venomous bite. The pin-

155

cushion sea urchin is covered with long spines which slip needle-like into one's flesh and then break up into fragments, while several other sea urchins have stinging organs rather than penetrating spines. Six Indonesian species of cone shells—the court, tulip, geographic, striated, textile, and marbled cones—can inject a dangerous amount of venom when picked up, and a little blue-striped octopus secretes a neurotoxin rivaling that of a sea-snake. Especially near river mouths, stingrays lie buried in the sand and may strike out with envenomed tail-spines when trod upon. Far worse than these is the stonefish, which in coloration and lumpy texture is indistinguishable from the coral or limestone on which it rests; a jab of its spines may prove fatal.

Here and there, marine organisms are gathered for something other than food. Among many uncivilized tribes of the Irian Barat lowlands, the one indispensable item of a man's costume is a penis sheath made from a conch, a cowrie, or a bailer shell. It is worn partly out of culturally conditioned modesty, but also because a seashell is thought to have supernatural ability to deflect evil influences. Upland tribes, receiving shells over long trade routes, are more likely to use them as ornaments or as evidence of wealth. When the Europeans first began to explore New Guinea, they found the mountain peoples already in possession of at least seven kinds of marine shells. Pinctada, the mother-of-pearl oyster, is made into a crescent-shaped ornament or into a strip that can be inserted through the nasal septum. Melo, the bailer shell, is worn entire, cut into pendants, or kept as a status symbol; a New Guinea uplander may measure his wealth in terms of pigs, sweet potatos, and these huge shells. Nassa, a rock shell, is sewn onto headbands of bark cloth, as is Nassarius, a dog whelk, and a Turbo, the green turban. Cone shells, Conus, are used to make nose discs and rings. Most interestingly, the money cowrie, Cypraea, is sewn in long rows onto strips of bark cloth. The strips, each about six feet long, can be worn for adornment, but they can also be exchanged for goods or services. At one time this cowrie was used as a medium of exchange over a wide expanse of the Southwest Pacific, although gradually it was replaced by coinage, except in remote New Guinea. In Irian Barat, the introduction of many new cowries by

156

expeditions, missionaries, and government officials led not only to a devaluation of the local shells but even to social disintegration of the tribes; for the older shells had been controlled mostly by the tribal leaders and mentors. The decline of the cowrie was further hastened by the arrival of New Guinea guilders, which were regarded as the key to the modern world and its material culture. Also, around the mission stations the young tribesmen learned to "counterfeit" by soaking new cowries in battery acid, giving them a patina that greatly enhanced their value and rendered them indistinguishable from the highly prized old shells. The Obano uprising of 1956, although directed against white influence generally, came about because the people of the Wissel Lakes country, the Enaratoli region of Irian Barat, found their social organization being eroded intolerably by the continued arrival of new shells. But the money cowrie will probably be replaced eventually by the Irian Barat rupiah or some other modern currency, and the old ways will vanish.

The mollusks of the genus Pinctada have been of wide interest around the Indo-Pacific, for they produce pearls of gem grade. Their Indonesian name, *induk mutiara*, means "pearls' mother." The more important Indo-Pacific pearl fisheries have been peripheral to Indonesia—for example, in the waters of Queensland, the Malay Peninsula, and Ceylon. However, the Arafura Sea has been one Indonesian source of pearls, and many other sources probably existed but were over-fished; on the average it is necessary to open about 12,000 Pinctadas to find one gem-grade pearl. Although Pinctada yields the finest saltwater pearls, these gems are produced by several other mollusks, some of them marine but a few freshwater. It is interesting to note that Tridacna, a giant clam of the coral reefs in Indonesia and adjoining regions, reaches a weight of 600 pounds and can secrete a pearl as big as a golfball. However, the Tridacna's pearl is only a curio, not a jewel. Incidentally, the giant clam is another Indonesian organism around which Western writers have woven a myth; it does not menace divers. Various mollusks yield the nacreous substance known as mother-of-pearl, which has been used in the manufacture of buttons, knife handles, and ornaments. The principal Indonesian source of

157

commercial mother-of-pearl has been the Pinctada shell, whose lining is called *kulit mutiara,* "pearly skin." The so-called cat's - eye, used as jewelry, is the blue-green, button-like operculum of the tapestry turban, a common shell of the Indonesian reefs.

Most Indonesian mollusks are distributed widely over the Indo-Pacific region. Many of the species reach the collections of shell enthusiasts the world over. Shells found in Indonesia include abalone, top shells, turbans, nerites, periwinkles, sundials, ceriths, a variety of conchs, spider and scorpion conchs, Tibia shells, moon snails, cowries, helmet shells, and bonnets. Then there are frog shells, Triton's trumpets, hairy Tritons, Murex shells, rock shells, drupe snails, Rapa coral-snails, whelks, spindle shells, olives, vases, miter shells, volutes, cones, nutmegs, augers, turrids, and bubble shells. All of these are gastropods, relatives of the familiar garden snails. Among the bivalve mollusks of Indonesia are wing oysters, hammer oysters, mussels, scallops, giant clams, jewel boxes, lucines, cockles, Venus clams, tellins, and others. The world's most costly shell, a cone called glory-of-the-seas, is known only from a few localities in Indonesia and some nearby island groups. In 1964, the dealers' suggested price for an extremely large glory-of-the-seas cone was $2,000, although today a collector might get a fine specimen for about $750, and a small one for perhaps $400. The enthusiast who buys his shells would be hard put to recognize some of his favorite species if he saw them in life on an Indonesian reef, for the colors have a different appearance when viewed through seawater. An excellent example is the Episcopal miter shell, a common species marked with orange blotches. Under the greenish-blue water, the markings become a neutral drab, resembling shadows on the bottom. Also, shells of all kinds are cleaned before they are marketed, but in life they may be blotched with algae or other growths. Furthermore, in many mollusks the fleshy mantle is colored differently from the shell it conceals. Thus, a cowrie with a pure white, glossy shell may be covered in life with a mantle of inky black or orange-red; and the lips of the giant clam are decorated in life with a mantle strip of brightest green or blue. A bailer shell is so called because it is large enough to be used as a boat-bailer, and its generic name, Melo, likens it to a melon; but the pale shell seems a mere excrescence atop the mollusk's huge, fleshy, dark-hued foot. A file clam, Lima, has a drab, unimpressive shell, yet Indonesians often fear this mollusk, which in life has a menacing appearance. The valves are edged with scarlet tentacles that wave about as the animal flaps its way through a tidepool, and a touch of the tentacles produces an indescribable sticky-tingling sensation.

Beyond the shelf, the sea floor drops off more abruptly to form the continental slope, and this in turn drops off into the ocean's basin. The waters beyond the shelf form a series of vertically aligned zones. The sunlit upper waters constitute a planktonic zone, characterized by drifting organisms of many groups. Least often mentioned, yet in the long run the most important component of the planktonic assemblage, are tiny green drifters which, being provided with chlorophyll, can synthesize carbohydrates and liberate oxygen. They form the basis of the food chain in the planktonic and other zones, and are far more important than land plants in keeping our air oxygenated. Because sunlight is necessary to the photosynthetic process, the needs of the green drifters limit the planktonic zone to the upper waters. Indonesians, so often fishermen or sailors, know this zone well, and have names for most of its animal life. *Pendar laut* is the name given to a phosphoresence of the sea, evident especially on certain dark nights and produced by a planktonic protozoan called Noctiluca. Seen under the microscope, Noctiluca resembles a pearl with a pigtail. For all its small size, it can give off a bright flash of light when disturbed by the waves or by the touch of some larger organism. It is an extraordinary experience to swim by night through *pendar laut,* for the swimmer can see his own arms outlined in greenish light, and his passage leaves a glowing trail through the water. Of course, Noctiluca and other plankton may drift into shallow water over the continental shelf, but when they do, they are soon killed by the different temperature, salinity, or turbidity of the nearshore waters. Some minute planktonic protozoans secrete a calcareous or siliceous shell, and over the ages the slow rain of dead shells builds thick deposits on the bottom, deposits which in geological time may solidify into rock. On the floor of the Bay of Bengal, the

Timor Sea, the northwestern part of the Banda Sea, the South China Sea, and the Bismarck Sea there are expanses of deep ooze composed of Globigerina shells; and on the Indian Ocean bottom southwest of Sumatra there is an expanse of radiolarian ooze. The shells of such planktonic organisms would carpet far more of the ocean if there were not an even heavier deposition of sediments washed down from the land. Fairly coarse sand, gravel, and gritty silt are deposited over much of the Indonesian sea bottom, while the lighter particles of red clay are carried farther from land, accumulating in the Indian Ocean and in parts of the Banda and Celebes Seas.

What they lack in size, the planktonic microorganisms make up in numbers, their total mass being sufficient not only to form thick deposits after they die, but before death to support many other living things, some of gigantic size. The whale shark, largest of fishes, floats at the surface and gorges itself on plankton. Its maximum weight has been estimated at 75 tons. The great manta ray is another harmless plankton-eater of Indonesian waters. The headfish, Mola, a globular species weighing about two tons, supports its bulk on jellyfishes which are a part of the planktonic assemblage. One supposes that an enormous number of jellies must be eaten to provide much nourishment, but then some of these watery invertebrates are themselves of large size, and very abundant. At night when the sea is phosphorescent with Noctiluca, pulsating discs of green light mark the presence of innumerable sun jellies, often a yard or more across. The leatherback sea-turtle, Dermochelys, also feeds wholly upon jellyfishes, apparently unaffected by their stinging tentacles. Perhaps this diet explains why the leatherback's flesh is often poisonous. At times this turtle must leave the deep water to nest on the beach; but Indonesians have frequently spotted it at sea, and call it *katung*, a word that also means "floating about."

The mid-depths, the dark waters just below the planktonic zone, are the home of many fast, streamlined, predaceous fishes that cruise endlessly in search of prey. In this category are various large sharks, mackerels, oceanic bonito, albacore, tuna, marlin, swordfish, and others. Some of these will also move into shallow water—unfortunately so in the case of sharks, certain of which have been known to attack swimmers. The white, Pacific mako, tiger, and Pacific sand sharks are the most dangerous species of Indonesian waters. Also dangerous, but restricted to New Guinean and Australian waters, is the gray nurse shark; and occasional attacks are attributed to the more widespread hammerhead. Although the large fishes of the mid-depths inhabit many seas, it was their occurrence in and near Indonesia that focused Western attention on them; for the early Dutch explorers were among the first to write at any length about sharks, swordfishes, sawfishes, and other monsters of the deep. In some cases, very little more is known today about the habits of these fishes than can be gleaned from the old narratives, although Indonesian sailors and fishermen could no doubt add to the meager store of knowledge. For example, ichthyologists puzzled over the function of the sawfish's rostral appendage, concluding that it must be used to rake through mud in search of mollusks. Yet, in *ikan gergadji*, the common Indonesian sawfish, the flattened appendage does not particularly suggest a rake, for it is provided with heavy, widely spaced teeth along both edges; and the sawfish does not inhabit shallow water with the frequency one expects of a mollusk-eater. Indonesian fishermen often take *ikan gergadji*, encouraged to do so by the Chinese, who value its fins above those of sharks as a soup ingredient; and the great beaks go on sale as curios. Commonly, the beak-teeth are found to be packed with scales and other fish remains; obviously the rostral appendage is used to slash at large fishes.

It was once thought that the biotic resources of the sea were inexhaustible, that marine organisms were not harmed by man's disturbance of the environment, and that more extensive "farming" of the sea would someday be carried on to help feed man's burgeoning population. These suppositions were in error, and it is now apparent that the marine ecosystems will not persist much longer than the terrestrial and freshwater ones. By best estimates the sea has already lost 40 percent of its life as the result of pollution, over-harvesting, and the destruction of natural shorelines. Even in the Southwest Pacific, many groups of marine organisms are declining. This is true, for example, of the whales. In Indonesia these animals are called by the remarkable name of *ikan paus*, the

Pope's fish. Long ago, the beef-like meat of porpoises and other small whales was often sold in the markets in Catholic countries, for it was classified as "fish" and eaten on Friday, even though whales are mammals as much as any cow or pig. The Portuguese led the Indonesians (who, whether Muslim, Hindu, or primitive animist, were interested in and subscribed to food taboos) to see a connection between whales and popery. Three of the Indonesian cetaceans—the sei whale, blue whale, and pygmy blue whale—are on the list of mammals in imminent danger of extinction. Also imperiled is the dugong, not a whale but a relative of the New World sea-cows. The English name is from the Malayan *dujun*. The Malayan-speaking seafarers must have known how herds of ponderous dugong would shoulder each other about when grazing on submerged flats, for this animal's name, duplicated and appropriately prefixed (*berdujun-dujun*), means "pushing forward rudely." Today, no one is likely to see a herd of dugong, for these gentle, unwary beasts have been harpooned and netted relentlessly for their oil and flesh.

The sea-turtles of the family Cheloniidae are also declining. (They are not closely related to the leatherback mentioned previously.) Commonest and largest of the Indonesian cheloniids is the Pacific loggerhead, Caretta. It reputedly attains a weight of about 1,000 pounds, although specimens half that size are rare today. The loggerhead's flesh is eaten, but its eggs are prized even more. On Indonesian beaches, the nests are dug into by man, monitor lizards, and wild pigs. A nest may contain 100 or more eggs, which are edible raw or cooked. Whereas the loggerhead ranges from the shallow water to the open sea, its much smaller relative, the Pacific ridley, Lepidochelys, is seldom found far offshore. The curious name of "ridley" is English and not Asian in origin. Most of the cheloniids are widespread in tropical and warm temperate seas, occasionally straggling northward into colder waters; and because they would live on shipboard, they often reached European markets. One of them, the green turtle, Chelonia, was valued far above the others for the savor of its flesh. The green turtle was named not for external coloration but for its vaguely greenish meat and distinctly greenish fat. In contrast, the other sea-turtles have a reddish, somewhat mammal-like flesh, and so they were called "ruddley" or "reddley" or "ridley," an old English name applied to any animal that stood out by virture of a reddish coloration. The distinction was important because the "reddley" meat was inferior and commanded a much lower price. One supposes that most "reddleys" reaching the markets were loggerheads, but with time the name became applied to the smaller species. The Pacific ridley is eaten in Indonesia, its eggs are collected, and its carapace yields an inferior grade of tortoiseshell. The finest tortoiseshell comes not from a tortoise but from a cheloniid, the Pacific hawksbill, Eretmochelys. Indonesians call this reptile *penju sisik* or *penju kembang*. The first of these names means "scaled sea-turtle" in allusion to the thin, overlapping plates of the shell; the second means "flying sea-turtle," with reference to the flapping stroke whereby the hawksbill makes its rapid way through the water. Once in a while the hawksbill develops poisonous flesh, and this may be why it is locally valued more as a source of eggs and tortoiseshell than of meat. The Pacific green turtle, Chelonia, similarly becomes poisonous at times, but throughout much of tropical Asia its eggs are an important source of proteinous food for man. In 1880 a herpetologist announced the discovery of an Indonesian and Australian sea-turtle congeneric with but specifically distinct from the Pacific green turtle. Not until the 1960s was the distinctiveness of the species granted; but in the meanwhile, Australian travel articles and tourist guides provided many fine illustrations of it, and of its nesting grounds, eggs, and hatchlings. This large, flattened reptile, which might be called the reef sea-turtle, has been found nesting on the Great Barrier Reef and the islands of the Torres Straits. Out of the breeding season it may turn up in Indonesian waters, hundreds of miles from the breeding grounds.

Several countries have lately made efforts to protect sea-turtles, but their survival is improbable. Known Indonesian nesting grounds for sea-turtles, of one species or another, include the Penju Islands of the Banda Sea, and the Togians in Sulawesi's Teluk Tomini. Nesting grounds in Malaysian waters, such as those off the Sabah coast, are probably visited by turtles coming from Indonesia.

163

Man's alteration of the environment not only extirpates many organisms but sometimes permits a more hardy species to become a pest. During 1969 and 1970, much was written about the crown-of-thorns starfish, which suddenly began to endanger coral reefs at localities scattered over the Southwest Pacific. Its population explosion was evident where man had killed some coral by blasting, dredging, and pollution; and where Triton shells (predators on this starfish) had been collected by the thousands for the commercial trade. A reef would erode away if the coral organisms did not continually add to it. The increment is slow, and in a night, one of these starfishes can kill a coral head that took 50 years to grow. Crown-of-thorns outbreaks have been reported for the waters of Borneo and New Guinea, as well as of the Malay Peninsula, Australia, and many archipelagos east of New Guinea.

The foregoing review of Indonesian marine life has been cursory, and a local fisherman could easily expand it. Perhaps he would add the killer whale, the snake-eels which are banded like sea-snakes, the venomous scorpionfish and lionfish, the rabbitfish, which is edible although venomous, the sea-bream, which is netted in greater numbers than any other reef fish. Again, he might add *sotong*, an edible squid; *kurau*, the big threadfin that always finds a buyer in the market; *selimpat*, the sea-snake that coils on the surface of the water like a bit of floating wickerwork; *lidah*, a sole whose name likens it to a tongue; *tudak*, which has green bones and will spear a man with its sharp snout. He would warn of the gigantic rock-grouper, *kerapu*, which can swallow a man; and he might call it *kertang*, dung-splattered, in allusion to its mottled pattern. Or perhaps he would tell of *ikan merah*, a red snapper; of *ikan terbang*, a rose-pink fish that flies through the air; of *terubok*, a shad that is edible only when it goes up the rivers; of *tongkal*, the tuna; of *ikan lajar* whose name appropriately means sailfish. If he is from the shores of the Banda Sea, he will tell of fishes called *ikan lawari batu* and *ikan lawari air*, one more of a bottom-dweller and the other more of a swimmer, both making the finest cut-bait —and each giving off from its head twin beams of light like those of an automobile. His story may sound incredible, but the fishes exist. Called Photoblepharon and Anomalops, they harbor luminous bacteria in a glandular structure beneath each eye, the bacterial glow lighting the fishes' way through the black depths. Scarcely less remarkable than these fishes is the discovery of them long ago by Indonesian fishermen, who cast their nets even down into the deep-sea zone of eternal night.

So much, then, for Indonesia's land and waters, its mineral productions, its climate and vegetation, flora and fauna—these the stage and the setting for man.

# CHAPTER V

# THE PEOPLING OF
# INDONESIA

THE PRESENT physical, cultural, and linguistic diversity of the Indonesian people reflects their country's past history and prehistory. Over the millennia, groups of people would move southeastward into the islands from the Asian mainland. Later groups, culturally more advanced than their predecessors, would arrive to absorb the earlier immigrants or displace them, push them into the remoter islands or the less favorable habitats. Thus, the physical type, folkways, and languages of the earlier immigrants would persist—if at all—only in the mountains, in the deepest forest, on comparatively barren or otherwise unattractive islands, and in lands farthest from the Asian mainland. But as a rule the newcomers themselves would be altered, at least to some degree, by the groups they superseded. With time, complex civilizations developed in several parts of mainland Eurasia, and then small numbers of mainlanders, arriving as merchants, missionaries, scholars, artisans, soldiers, and administrators, were in a position to influence the Indonesian cultures profoundly, the languages moderately, the physical types minimally. Only the populations of the mountains, the deep forests, and the less accessible islands were not quickly affected by the advanced ideas that spread out of India, Arabia, and then western Europe. This view of Indonesian history is exceedingly simplified, and some of the fascinating details will be filled in later. Suffice it now to say that Indonesian ethnic diversity, so great as to be highlighted by the Republic's official motto, must be viewed in historical perspective if it is not to appear chaotic.

The Indonesian story might begin with some comment on the "Java ape-man" whose fossil remains first came to light near Trinil, Java. The circumstances of the find involved Indonesia in several ways. In the 1850s the English naturalist Alfred Russel Wallace cruised among the islands, studying the faunal differences from place to place. After about four years of exploration he arrived in the Arus, where he spent a month and a half recovering from insect bites that had inflamed and infected his legs. During this period of enforced rest he put down on paper some conclusions toward which his Indonesian experiences had led him: that living things are innately variable; that some variations improve but others lessen the individual's chances of surviving the hazards of existence; that since the better-adapted variants are the ones that most often survive and reproduce, a species slowly but constantly changes in the direction of greater fitness for existence within its environment. And since a species may be exposed to different environments in different parts of its geographic range (as is often the case in the far-flung islands of Indonesia), it may develop in divergent ways from place to place. Thus, several species may eventually arise from one. Wallace's proposition appears clear enough today but was daring for its time, when man's intellectual progress was still hobbled by ancient religious dogma.

Much the same line of reasoning was being followed by another English naturalist-explorer, Charles Darwin, who had traveled in South America, the Galapagos, Tahiti, Australia, and New Zealand. In 1858 Wallace and Darwin made a joint announcement of their theory of organic evolution by natural selection. But since the latter scientist wrote at greater length, and subsequently emphasized that the species called man was also the result of adaptive change, the concept came to be associated mostly with Darwin in the public mind. In 1867 the German scientist Ernst Haeckel published a chart portraying the development of animal life from a protoplasmic blob to man. In those days the world had been inadequately explored for animals, the fossil record barely revealed, and so a few gaps in Haeckel's sequence had to be filled by theoretical types. One such type—Haeckel dubbed it Pithecanthropus, from Greek root-words meaning "ape-man"—was a being less human than any living man, more human than any living ape. In the Netherlands, a youth named Marie Eugène François Thomas Dubois was fired with the idea of discovering the fossilized bones of the Pithecanthropus. Such a species must surely have existed, but where? In the Netherlands East Indies, Dubois guessed, or hoped.

Having studied medicine and natural history at Amsterdam, in 1887 Dubois went to the East Indies as a military surgeon, spending his off-duty hours in the quest for prehuman remains. On Sumatra he found fossil beds but they did not yield the Pithecanthropus. Then, turning his attention to Java, in 1891 he visited the island's largest river, the Solo, at a locality near the village of Trinil. The river at this spot was perhaps 50 or 60 feet across, with steep banks from which the trees had long since been cleared and in whose strata fossil bones could be seen. Searching here, by 1892 he had found some near-human teeth, a brain-case with low forehead and apelike brow ridges, and a femur whose straightness and articular surfaces revealed that its owner had walked erect. In a published monograph Dubois named his fossil species *Pithecanthropus erectus*. Explaining why he had expected the ape-man to be found in the East Indies, Dubois said only that apes were all tropical, and that hairlessness would have encouraged a prehuman type to stay in the tropics. But Haeckel had portrayed a Papuan as the next step above the Pithecanthropus, and one might suspect that this choice led the young Hollander to look toward the Southwest Pacific for remains of subhuman primates. Today, Dubois' species is known as *Homo erectus,* and is regarded as a near-man, the immediate precursor of modern man, *Homo sapiens.* About 500,000 years ago, the near-man ranged from southern Africa northward practically to the glacial border in Europe, and eastward across Asia into China and Java. In places, the debris of his camp sites includes not only his own remains but also those of large and small beasts upon which he preyed. Charcoal and burned bone imply that he used fire, and he turned out rude flint-work in patterns that remained unchanged for millennia. He reached Java over land at a time when the Sunda Shelf was above water.

Dubois' work led to extensive paleontological investigation of Java, and from the island have since come numerous exciting finds. Excavation at Sangiran produced the fragmentary remains of an advanced ape, at first called Meganthropus. It now appears to have been an australopithecine, Paranthropus, one of the man-apes better known from Africa. Modjokerto yielded the bones of a near-man, *Homo erectus,* but of an earlier and more primitive variety than Dubois' Trinil type. Additional remains of the latter were found at Sangiran. At Ngandong, not far from Trinil, excavators discovered eleven skulls which, being low-vaulted and heavy-browed, suggested *Homo erectus,* but which were sufficiently advanced to be classified as *Homo sapiens* of an early variety. A bit more advanced, perhaps leading toward the modern Australoid type, were two human skulls from Wadjak. At Tjabengke on Sulawesi, a Pleistocene fossil bed produced the remains of a pygmy elephant, for all its small size an offshoot of the mammoths; and among the bones were rude scrapers and blades of flint.

Not surprisingly, stone artifacts have been encountered far more frequently than the remains of their makers. Deliberately fabricated stone tools antedate both man and near-man, their origin being traceable back some 1,900,000 years to the australopithecine man-apes of Africa. The earliest known flint industry of Indonesia included two tools. One of these is a large pebble from which a series of coarse flakes has been struck, thus producing a sharp edge along a part of the pebble's circumference. The flakes were struck from only one face of the pebble, leaving the other unmodified. Such an implement is called a chopper, but the name is one of convenience; probably the tool was used principally in butchering game. Accompanying the chopper is a smaller implement edged by the removal of flakes from both faces. This simple tool kit is widespread in eastern Asia, but in general it is replaced from India westward by a different kit: the hand-axe and Levallois flake. The chopper tradition eventually spread into Europe, although not by way of southern Asia; while the Patjitan flint industry of Java is a remarkably isolated, eastern outpost of the hand-axe tradition. In other words, the earliest artifacts of Eurasia reveal that continent already to be separated into eastern and western culture areas, although with some overlap of culture traits. No doubt the regional differences in flint tools were paralleled by differences in other productions of which little trace remains in the archeological record.

If we were vouchsafed a firsthand look at the mainland of southern Asia in that remote time when early man was but a roving hunter and gatherer of wild foods, we should find him existing in a variety of physical types; and we should see these types spreading, clashing, mixing, occasionally leaving the mainland to push into the Indonesian islands. The first known human immigrants into Indonesia were the Negritos, a pygmy people resembling the African Negroids in facial features and woolly hair, but rounder of head, more hirsute, and of course much smaller, the men now averaging about 4 feet 8 or 9 inches in stature, the women a few inches shorter than this. Where the Negritos came from, no one knows. When they began their radiation some 30,000 years ago, they had only the limited cultural equipment of the Paleolithic, the Old Stone Age. They were nomads who lived by hunting and gathering, but they established man's hegemony over a major segment of the habitable world, pushing eastward into the Philippines and Japan, as well as southeastward through Indonesia to Australia. Across lands still overrun by the nightmare animals of the Pleistocene, the pygmy people moved, their "little camp-fires, ever brightly, bravely gleaming / In the womb of desolation, where was never man before." The Negritos moved southeastward at a time when both the Sunda and Sahul shelves were above water, and the straits of central Indonesia reduced in width. Often, from one island they could see the next, but surely they crossed water gaps at least 30 miles wide. By 26,000 years ago they had reached Australia. Here they were eventually replaced by Australoids, except for one relict population that survived to the present in the deep forest and around the mission stations of northern Queensland. Negritos with some Australoid admixture also survived into modern times on Tasmania, but they were exterminated by the white settlers, except for a few part-white individuals. On New Guinea the Negritos were eventually pushed into the central highlands by the Papuans, of whom more will be said later; but the genetic influence of the pygmy stock is detectable in many parts of New Guinea and nearby islands.

Farther west, toward central and western Indonesia, traces of Negrito occupation were nearly eradicated by wave after wave of later comers. Cave burials, recently discovered on Borneo, reveal that island to have been inhabited at one time by the pygmy people, as well as by the Malays who still live there. Negrito characteristics are noticeable in tribes of the deep swamps in eastern Sumatra, and of some rugged uplands in the Lesser Sundas. Negrito groups still live in the Andamans, the Malay Peninsula, the Philippines, southern India, and the Assam-Burma forests. The African pygmies, pushed into the Upper Congo rainforest by the expansion of the Negroids, are probably another remnant of early Negrito radiation. In general, relict Negrito groups have abandoned their own languages in favor of those spoken by larger neighbors.

In their movement through Indonesia, the Negritos were followed by Australoids. As shown by fossilized skulls and radiocarbon dates, the Australoids had spread widely over Australia by 12,000 years ago, and they may have first arrived there several millennia before that date. A fossil skull from Aitape, about 95 miles east of Irian Barat, suggests their presence on New Guinea well before the end of the Pleistocene. Sea level was still low and the Sunda and Sahul shelves above water when the Australoids passed through the islands. In Australia, where they displaced the Negritos, they were not themselves overtaken by later peoples until the arrival of white settlers in historic times. But outside Australia, traces of Australoid occupation are scanty. In New Guinea, an occasional Negrito or Papuan has an Australoid cast of features. As such individuals are more numerous in the mountains, the common refuge of vanishing types, it is reasonable to suppose that New

Guinea once had a sizable Australoid population of which little evidence remains. Detailed archeological investigation of New Guinea has begun only recently; and further studies, paralleling those already well under way in Australia, should make it possible to associate certain artifact complexes with one or another group that pushed southeastward through Indonesia at an early date. In the swamps and forests of southern Sumatra, the interior of Borneo and Sulawesi, and scattered uplands of the Moluccas and Lesser Sundas, there exists a physical type that has been called Veddalike, the reference being to the Ceylonese Vedda, a relict group that may have had Australoid and Negrito ancestry. The Wadjak skulls, of Late Pleistocene age, may represent Australoid occupation of Java. On the Asian mainland, Australoid and Veddoid traces are seen in groups of people scattered over India, concentrated toward the southern part of that country and (before the attempted abolition of the caste system) in the lowest castes.

Having moved far out into the islands, the Australoids were isolated from the Asian mainstream of technological progress. They arrived in Australia with a Paleolithic-level culture and retained it until white settlers brought civilization. Probably the Australoids were of two subtypes, one moving ahead of the other. The earlier subtype was comparatively thickset, hirsute, with light brown skin and brown, curly hair. Such people may have resembled the Ainu, the brunet, hairy tribes who were formerly widespread in the Japanese islands (although today the Ainu are considerably mixed with other stocks). The earlier Australoids spread through the Murray Basin and along the eastern, western, and southern coasts of Australia. Being on the best land, they were quickly decimated and dispossessed by the white settlers of historic times. The later Australoid subtype resembled the earlier in having a low vault, heavy browridge, and depressed nasal root, but differed (probably as a result of slight admixture with non-Australoids on the Asian mainland, in Indonesia, or across the Torres Strait) in being taller, darker, and more smooth-skinned. This later group, settling around the Gulf of Carpentaria and along the northern coast of Australia, also pushed southward into the deserts. Their culture, while still Paleolithic, included a larger and more complex artifact inventory

173

than that of their predecessors. Probably they brought the dingo, a dog with wolf-like relatives in India. Since the later Australoids occupied inhospitable tropics and deserts, their lands were not often coveted by white settlers, and they have survived to the present in fair numbers. The language of some north-coastal aborigines is said to have a slight similarity to Papuan speech, as though a few Papuans had reached the southern continent and mingled there with the Australoids; but otherwise, the many tongues of the Australian aborigines form several language families without relatives in other parts of the world.

Negritos and Australoids had moved southward at a time when great glaciers, three or four miles thick, covered much of northern Eurasia and northern North America. But about 10,000 years ago the ice sheets began melting back, returning their water to the sea. Many great beasts of the Pleistocene began to vanish, for reasons having more to do with the rise and spread of man than with climatic change. Eurasian man was faced with a new ecology: a shift toward a warmer and drier climate, a rising sea level, differently distributed vegetation zones, and a fauna that had lost many of its meatiest animals. In response to the changed environment, he worked out a new way of life called the Mesolithic, the Middle Stone Age. He was still a hunter, but of smaller game; and more than ever a gatherer of plant foods, mollusks, and other edible life. Large, permanent settlements were still out of the question for him, since even a small group of people, subsisting entirely by hunting and gathering, can quickly use up the local supply of edible plants and animals. But coastal waters and larger rivers, and to a lesser extent the supratidal and riparian swamps or forests, are highways along which edible organisms constantly move; and so beside the mainland waterways Mesolithic man was able to tarry for quite a while, elaborating his productions in stone, bone, wood, and shell, and perhaps directing a disproportionate amount of attention toward some local plant that yielded abundant starch. The effect of climatic change was felt even in near-equatorial New Guinea, the present ice caps of the Irian Barat peaks being but the remnants of much larger ones that stretched along the highlands in Pleistocene times; and the Australian Realm had some giant marsupials that died out just as so many giant placentals did in Eurasia. Mesolithic culture influences spread from mainland Asia into Indonesia. Some Mesolithic-level culture traits probably were borne by, or reached, the Papuans, who followed the Australoids out into the islands; but the topic need not be reviewed here, for the original Papuan culture, whatever it may have been, was destined for thorough-going revision by a later people, the Melanesians. Yet, the postglacial rise of sea level certainly had one direct effect on the distribution of people and customs in the Southwest Pacific. The Bass Strait formed, separating Tasmania from the Australian mainland, and permitting a basically Negrito group to survive on that island without being wholly replaced by Australoids. More significantly in the present connection, the Torres Strait also formed, separating New Guinea from Australia. Probably a few Papuans reached northern Australia by canoe, but the strait sufficed to keep these people from replacing the Australoids on the Southern continent.

The Papuans today resemble many African Negroids in having woolly hair, a long head, and a dark skin. However, they are smaller, more hirsute, high-nosed, the men inclining toward baldness; and the skin is sometimes more reddish-brown than black. A reddish-brown skin, regarded by many Papuans as desirable, may have been their norm before admixture with darker people. A receding hair line, luxuriant beard, and figure-6 nasal profile often give a Papuan man a strikingly "Semitic" look; and many a young girl, her finely chiseled features dominated by dark and widely spaced eyes beneath heavy eyebrows, would not appear out of place in lands just south of the Mediterranean. The origin of the Papuan physical type has been a puzzle, especially since its former presence in western Indonesia and mainland Asia has not been demonstrated. It is barely possible that the type evolved locally from mixed Negrito and Australoid antecedents, with a later overlay of Melanesian characteristics. Another possibility, perhaps a better one, is that the original Papuans were a distinctive group who bypassed a good bit of their predecessors' route toward New Guinea. It is not necessary to accept the view, so often advanced in the nonscientific literature, that the Papuans are descended from the mythical "lost tribes of Israel" or from some band of far-wandering Arab traders. It is possible that thousands of years ago, the ancestral Papuans moved out of northeastern Africa, following the Monsoon Drift or the Indian Countercurrent—but such speculation may be deferred until archeological studies are much further along. Today, the Papuan physical type predominates on New Guinea and nearby islands, although it is modified here and there, to a greater or less degree, by that of the earlier Negrito or later Melanesian. On archipelagos east and west of New Guinea there is a mixture of physical types, but enclaves of Papuan speech, existing as far west as Alor and as far east as the Solomons, indicate that Papuans have contributed to the mélange. Except for these enclaves, Papuan speech is restricted to mainland New Guinea.

The early Papuans may have lived mostly beside the rivers and coasts of New Guinea, hunting small game, gathering plant foods, and relying heavily on the sago palm for starch. But on the Asian mainland a new way of life was in the making, initiated by the discovery of agriculture. No longer having to spend so much time in a food quest, agricultural man advanced rapidly in his technology and social organization. The Neolithic, the New Stone Age, arose at a number of centers from the eastern Mediterranean to China. And so when the next group of Asian people, the Melanesians, moved into Indonesia, they took with them a Neolithic-level culture far more elaborate than anything their predecessors had known.

Today, typical Melanesians are of medium stature, on the average a little taller than the Papuans, a bit slimmer of build, rounder of head. The Melanesian features stand more or less intermediate between the Malay and Negroid norms. The skin color is occasionally reddish-brown, but more often dark brown to black. Body hair is scanty. The hair of the head, while frizzy, grows quite long, forming a huge ball sometimes five feet in circumference. Often, however, the Melanesian physical type grades into the Papuan, there having been much admixture of the two in New Guinea and elsewhere. It is at first surprising that the Melanesian languages belong to the Malayo-Polynesian Family, for the numerous other languages of this family were carried by people who, like the present-day Malays, Polynesians, and Micronesians, show minimal

Negroid characteristics. The Malayo-Polynesian homeland was Cambodia and Viet Nam. In early historic times, along the Mekong Delta of South Viet Nam, there were some villages occupied by ancestral Malays, but others occupied by a dark-skinned, frizzy-haired people who could have been stay-at-home Melanesians. The Melanesian physical type probably was first approximated in Indochina by a combination of the Malay with the Negrito; for the Malay type once predominated in Indochina, and the Negrito has persisted in the Cardamom Mountains of Cambodia. The present-day Melanesians, restricted to the Southwest Pacific, are more Negroid in appearance than their ancestors, having mixed with earlier peoples in New Guinea and some archipelagoes farther east.

But the appearance of the early Melanesians is less important than their actions. They were not mere island-hoppers but true seamen, taking their sailing vessels to the Bismarcks, the Solomons, the New Hebrides, and New Caledonia, and reaching New Zealand long before the Maori. Landing on the eastern coasts of New Guinea, the Melanesians brought Neolithic wonders: pottery, the bow and arrow, axe blades and other implements of polished stone, the domestic pig, several crop plants, agricultural techniques, betel-chewing, elaborate wood-carving, sea-going outrigger and composite canoes, ceremonial cannibalism and "head-hunting," human sacrifice in connection with major ventures, highly ritualized warfare, secret societies with graded membership, men's club-houses, and a more complex social organization. Tattooing, calendrical observances, cowrie money, and the use of sails—these, too, may first have reached New Guinea with the Melanesians. From points of introduction in eastern New Guinea, Melanesian ideas spread westward through the island, some with more vigor than others. Crop plants and the pig reached almost everyone, and betel-chewing was received nearly as enthusiastically as agriculture and husbandry. On the other hand, pottery-making proved of much more limited appeal. Some of the Papuan tribes remained indifferent to earthenware pots; others preferred to trade for rather than make them; a few learned the ceramic art and became proficient at it. The bow and arrow spread widely but not to everyone, perhaps because New Guinea has no really first-rate bow wood.

Without tracing the spread of other ideas, it may be said, in summary, that the barbaric splendor of New Guinea cultures has resulted from Melanesian influences. The people of Irian Barat, being farthest from the cultural wellspring, received these influences in a somewhat attenuated form.

From the Asian mainland, where technological and societal advances were multiplying, the Malays would follow the Melanesians southeastward into the islands, but they would impress their physical, linguistic, and cultural stamp mostly on western and central Indonesia. New Guinea would not be completely isolated from the mainstream of Eurasian progress, but after the arrival of the Melanesians it would receive scattered visitors rather than groups of settlers. The western half of the island, in particular, would retain its own Neolithic configurations of culture even through the period of European colonial expansion and World War II. It is therefore not amiss to interrupt the historical narrative for a closer look at present-day Irian Barat, where the Neolithic life-ways even now are being confronted with those of civilization.

The physical types have continued to mix. In western New Guinea, Negritos of purest stock are concentrated in the Pegunungan Sudirman. A belt of rough, uninhabited mountains isolates them on the north from the Papuans of the Tariku-Taritatu lake plains, while the snow ridges and the precipitous southern flanks of the Pegunungan Sudirman isolate them from the Papuans of the southern coastal plain. To the west, in the Pegunungan Arfak, the Negrito stock is mixed with Papuan and Melanesian. To the east it is mixed with the Papuan, although populations of scarcely mixed Negritos are scattered almost the full length of New Guinea's central highlands. Whereas the Negrito stock is confined to the mountains, the Melanesian is found near the sea. From their original landing-places in eastern New Guinea, the Melanesians spread westward, keeping mostly to the coasts, where they could better indulge their fondness for trading and fishing. Their westernmost villages on the northern coast are strung out around Teluk Sarera (the former Geelvink Bay). On the southern coast their westernmost villages border the Papuan Gulf, not Indonesian territory. In extreme western Irian Barat, and in fact on Misoöl and Ceram, the

Melanesian physical type is detectable here and there although variously mixed. Except for pygmy Negritos in the remote interior, Melanesians on or very near parts of the north coast, and intermediate groups near Negrito or Melanesian territory, the indigenous population of Irian Barat may be regarded as Papuan. The Papuans, thus defined, occupy the seacoasts and lowlands of northern Irian Barat west of Teluk Sarera; the Vogelkop; all southern Irian Barat; and scattered north-coastal areas east of Teluk Sarera, including the lowlands south of Teluk Jos Sudarso (the former Humboldt Bay). They also occupy the Mamberamo River country, including the vast lake plains of the Tariku and the Taritatu. Finally, Papuans live in parts of the central highlands and piedmont, having followed some of the rivers far upstream to reach habitable valleys.

The distribution of languages in Irian Barat does not exactly parallel that of physical types. As far as is known, even in the remote Pegunungan Sudirman the Negrito groups have abandoned their own original languages, whatever these may have been, in favor of Papuan speech. This is not to say that any one of these groups will speak precisely like nearby Papuans; rather, the numerous Papuan languages are now distributed over people who are physically Negrito, Papuan, and mixed. Or to phrase the matter in another way, over the millennia the New Guinea Negritos have developed versions of Papuan speech, just as the Papuans themselves have done. Linguists have hoped that some trace of the original Negrito languages might be discovered among the little-known pygmy tribes of the Pegunungan Sudirman. In these mountains, the Negritos have developed, or have retained from a very ancient time, a sign language that overcomes the local linguistic diversity, permitting lengthy conversations in complete silence. Just as the original Negrito languages gave way to the Papuan, so have the latter lost a bit of ground to the Malayo-Polynesian. That is to say, the Malayo-Polynesian Family of languages includes Melanesian speech but is distributed to some parts of coastal and lowland Irian Barat where the villagers are of Papuan physical type with only minor evidence of Melanesian admixture. Malayo-Polynesian languages have approached Irian Barat from the Lesser Sundas and

179

the Moluccas as well as from eastern New Guinea. The Malayo-Polynesian Family has 16 groups in Indonesia. One of these, the
South Halmahera–West New Guinea Group, blankets Waigeo, Ba-
tanta, Salawati, and Misoöl, as well as the northern coast of Irian
Barat from about Sansapor eastward to Wonti. There is one en-
clave of this group around Djajapura (the former Sukarnapura or
Hollandia) and Teluk Jos Sudarso, another around Teluk Lakahia
on the south coast. The languages of this group also cross Irian
Barat at its narrowest, extending from the western shores of Teluk
Sarera to the upper part of Teluk Berau (the former McCluer
Gulf) and the upper part of Teluk Arguni (the former Argoeni
Bay). The Ambon-Timor Group of Malayo-Polynesian languages
extends from eastern Sumbawa eastward through the Arus, the
Kais, the Watubelas, and Ceram.

Two trade languages have also approached Irian Barat from opposite directions. One of these, Melaju Pasar or Bazaar Malayan, is
for the most part a simplified Malayan that uses root-words without affixes. Like any lingua franca, Melaju Pasar is no one's native
tongue but is learned as a second language by individuals who
have wide dealings in a polyglot region. The second trade language of New Guinea is Melanesian Pidgin, which is neither a simplified English nor an outgrowth of Chinese Pidgin, but which in
many ways is a reflection of Melanesian thinking; its grammar and
syntax are typically Melanesian. *Pren, man bolong Rom, wantok,
harim nau. Mi kam tasol long plantim Kaesar, mi noken beten
longen*—even Antony's oration at the death of Caesar can be delivered in this remarkable tongue. Melaju Pasar, a familiar trade
language in the Indonesian islands west of New Guinea, is occasionally heard on the north coast of Irian Barat and in nearby islands such as Biak; while the pidgin, created to permit Melanesian
communication with English-speakers, is widely heard on the
north coast of the Territory of North-East New Guinea and in the
Melanesian archipelagos east of New Guinea. Both of these lingua
francas are known around Djajapura and Teluk Jos Sudarso.

The passing of western New Guinea into Indonesian hands presumably will encourage the use there of Bahasa Indonesia, Melaju
Pasar, and possibly English. In eastern New Guinea, the pidgin

and a Melanesian language called Motu have been used to inform the tribesmen of laws made or urged by English-speakers; and English-speaking missionaries, if unappreciative of the pidgin, have usually proselytized in Melanesian tongues such as Yabim (although Kate, a Papuan language, has also served.) A large majority of the New Guineans are Papuan-speakers, yet the commercial and administrative affairs of their island are carried on in Malayo-Polynesian languages, English, and the Pidgin hybrid. This situation does not reflect any inherent inferiority of Papuan speech, but only its subdivision into a great number of mutually unintelligible tongues. In the uplands of eastern New Guinea there are some Papuan languages with as many as 10,000 speakers, but this situation is unusual; for in other parts of the island, each Papuan language is likely to be spoken by no more than a few hundred people. New Guinea has over 500 languages, most of them Papuan. Some of these numerous languages have nothing in common with others of them, beyond being non-Melanesian.

In New Guinea, the boundaries between the physical types have become blurred, and have been crossed by the languages, while culture traits and complexes have diffused widely through the island. However, there is still some correlation between physical type and culture. Thus, the Negritos, where they are most effectively isolated from outside genetic influence, have also been to some degree cut off from the flow of ideas; the Papuans, with their tight interlocking of economy, social organization, and religion, and with their culturally prescribed hostility toward outsiders, suffer exceptionally when confronted by civilization; and the Melanesians, in spite of a comparable interlocking, are more receptive to new ideas, more inclined to look beyond the immediate village confines, and inordinately proud of their language and its wide usefulness. But even so, in any broad summary, the culture traits and complexes of Irian Barat are better discussed individually or on an areal basis, with only minor reference to the physical type or language of the culture-bearers.

Strictly speaking, language is a part of culture, for the latter is taken by anthropologists to include all activities of man that are transmitted socially, not biologically. However, there is ample precedent for setting linguistics apart from the rest of cultural anthropology, which deals especially with family life, community organization, government and law, the arts, religion and magic, technology or material culture, economic life, and ideologies, as well as with methods of utilizing and coping with the environment.

It should be noted at the outset that Irian Barat does not constitute a sharply bounded culture area. By treaties of 1885 and 1895, New Guinea was arbitrarily divided among the colonial powers of Germany, Britain, and the Netherlands. The Netherlands portion eventually passed to Indonesia, the remainder to Britain and then Australia. The boundary between Indonesian and Australian New Guinea is overlapped by physical types, languages, and culture, and even by some tribes. It should also be noted that tribal customs, even though described below in the present tense, are rapidly being modified; some of them are disappearing even while the comments on them are being written or read. Modern culture is diffusing piecemeal to Irian Barat, supplanting some of the old ways; but the diffusion of modern culture proceeds ubiquitously, and so warrants discussion in a broader frame of reference than the regional. Such diffusion will not be considered at this point, where the intention is to give an idea of what is entailed by Neolithic-level life in extreme eastern Indonesia.

Irian Barat covers 162,873 square miles. Anthropologists have not been much interested in dividing this vast region into culture areas, but several such can be recognized on the basis of available data. Their distinctiveness results in part from local adaptation to environment, and in part from the differential spread of culture traits or complexes thereof. Direct settlement by Melanesians often implies the local introduction of many such complexes. The Northwest Coast Area includes the coasts and nearby lowlands of Teluk Sarera, and extends thence westward over the entire Vogelkop (the "bird-head" that forms the western end of New Guinea). The islands of the Biak-Numfoor-Japen group also fall in this division, the cultural peculiarities of which reflect both Melanesian settlement and the eastward diffusion of ideas from the Moluccas. The Northeast Coast Area includes all the north coast and adjoining lowlands from the Mamberamo River eastward across the international boundary to the vicinity of Vanimo. Within this area, the Djajapura vicinity is culturally atypical, having been first a Dutch and then an Indonesian administrative center. There has been Melanesian settlement around Teluk Jos Sudarso; and to further complicate the picture, there once was a settlement of Bronze Age Indonesians, probably Malays, around Lake Sentani, where many bronze implements have been discovered. The Southwest Coast Area is a wide band of country, most of it low and swampy, stretching from about Mimika eastward to Sungai Muli. In this area lies the Casuarina Coast, which received considerable magazine attention in the early 1960s following the disappearance there of Michael Rockefeller. The Mimika and the Asmat, both Papuan, are the best known tribes. The Southeast Coast Area, similarly low and flat, reaches from Dolak (the former Frederik Hendrik Island) eastward across the international boundary about to the Morehead River. The eastern terminus of this area marks a change of environment; farther east, the great swamps give way to higher ground with much *kunai* grassland and a different vertebrate fauna. The Central Highlands Area corresponds to the island's mountainous backbone, extending in an east-west direction for about 400 miles through Irian Barat, and for about an equal distance through Australian New Guinea. In large part, this area's unity reflects adjustment to a montane environment. Between the eastern end of this area and the western, there are a good many cultural differences. Perhaps the area is subdivided by the Strickland River, whose enormous gorges, lying about 75 miles east of Irian Barat, may have been a barrier to the spread of people and ideas in the mountains. The above five areas are distinctive foci of culture traits and complexes; while in the rest of Irian Barat there is probably a mixture of traits from nearby foci. However, it may prove desirable to recognize an Interior Lake Plains Area corresponding to the valleys of the Tariku and the Taritatu; also a Peninsula Area bounded on the north by Teluk Berau, on the east by Teluk Kamrau and Teluk Arguni. A few more culture areas, although centered in Australian New Guinea, cut or lie close to the Irian Barat border, and are worth mentioning here. To the north, the Sepik-Ramu Area covers the drainage basin of the two streams for which it is named, as well as some adjoining lands. Most people of this area are Papuans, but the Melanesians have built villages along the lower course of the Sepik, and a few immigrants from farther west have settled at localities along the coast. As a result of ideas introduced by Melanesians, localities on the Sepik became pottery-making centers, and the Keram River, a tributary, was named for the ceramic work turned out along it by tribespeople. To the south, the Gulf Area stretches from the lower Fly River eastward through the coasts and lowlands of the Gulf of Papua to about the vicinity of Port Moresby. This area includes both Papuan and Melanesian settlements, the latter predominating toward the east. A Middle Fly Area should probably be recognized, centering around Lake Murray, extending a short distance into Irian Barat, and inhabited by Papuans. A Torres Strait Area, made up of such islands as Mulgrave, Banks, Thursday, and Prince of Wales, links New Guinea cultures with those of Australia. New Guinea culture areas lying well east of Irian Barat need not be reviewed.

The indigenous population of Irian Barat is estimated at 800,000, and it is customary to say that this population is divided into hundreds of tribes. It is certainly useful to recognize a tribal level of social organization, more complex than that of nomadic bands of hunters and gatherers but less complex than that of a developing civilization. Still, a trenchant definition of "tribe" is not readily formulated. In general, and with some exceptions, a tribe is a comparatively small group of people who share the same culture, speak the same language and dialect thereof, inhabit or lay claim to a continuous territory, are more or less self-sufficient economically (although frequently trading for some goods), and are politically autonomous. In the last analysis, however, the outer limits of any one tribe are determined by the consensus of its members. These limits may fluctuate from time to time, and may embrace one village or dozens. While members of a tribe speak the same language, it does not follow that a single language is spoken by only one tribe, for the reverse is often the case in Irian Barat, where two adjoining tribes, perhaps hostile to each other, may speak the same language. Political autonomy does not mean that a tribe is a group of people following a single "chief," for the popular Western con-

184

cept of a tribal autocrat has little connection with reality, especially in Irian Barat, where responsibilities, although traditionally falling to certain lineages and clans, are usually borne by several outstanding men within each tribe. These men handle economic, political, and religious affairs, which at the tribal level are not conducted through separate institutions. In Irian Barat and elsewhere, occasionally there emerges a charismatic man who, quite apart from official position or ascribed power, acquires many followers among his own tribe, and perhaps admirers among nearby tribes. Anthropologists, translating from Melanesian, refer to such a person as a "big-man." More power accrues to a big-man than to any tribal functionary, but he must provide for his followers or be deposed. An underlying principle of New Guinea tribal life is reciprocity, which involves not only the exchange of gifts but also the *lex talionis* in case of offense; and the big-man is not exempt.

Almost by definition, a tribe is supported primarily by the domestication of plants, animals, or both; for a local supply of wild foods is easily exhausted, and with rare exceptions, subsistence by hunting and gathering is possible only to nomadic bands who do not reach the tribal level of organization. Exceptions exist where some wild food is surpassingly abundant and continuously available, permitting semisettled village life without agriculture or husbandry. Irian Barat provides such an exception. Among some tribes of the southeastern lowland, agriculture is a minor concern, secondary to the gathering of sago; for a day's work suffices to fell a large sago, split it, and separate perhaps 200 or even 300 pounds of pinkish, edible starch from the inedible fibers. The gathering of sago is an important occupation in the Tariku-Taritatu lake plain, also. But most Irian Barat tribes are settled agriculturists, and pig-farmers as well. Even the most isolated Negritos of the Pegunungan Sudirman raise crops and pigs.

Agriculture took a distinctive course in southeastern Asia, the Indonesian islands, and New Guinea. Elsewhere it usually involved the planting of seeds and the storage of seeds for the next planting season; but in the area of especial concern here, it involved the planting of vegetative parts such as tubers, slips, sprouts, and rootstocks. The dichotomy was ecologically induced.

In a constantly warm, humid climate, many plants normally reproduce by vegetative means, and numerous others can be made to do so even though they usually spread by seeds. Unlike seeds, vegetative propagules must breed true, and so they permit rapid spread of desirable variations. Taro, bananas, sugarcane, and sweet potato, the principal crops of Irian Barat, are propagated vegetatively when under cultivation.

Taro is the primary crop for some tribes, particularly in the lowlands, around the periphery of the central highlands, and on the Vogelkop. Taro needs a good bit of water and is usually grown in ditches or at the edge of swamps. It is sometimes irrigated, the water brought to it in bamboo pipelines. Bananas are raised in most parts of the country, but especially at low and medium elevations. Plantains or cooking bananas are seen more frequently than the sweeter varieties, although one upland banana is so sweet and tender that it can be eaten skin and all. In many areas, banana groves are within the village confines where the fruiting stalks can be protected from possums, rodents, and fruit bats. The sugarcane of Irian Barat, possibly an indigenous species, forms dense stands in damp places, and is widely planted. Not only does the stem yield a sugary juice; the flower tassels are edible when cooked. Breadfruit, papaya, upland rice, cassava, peanuts, lemons, and yams are among the secondary crops, some of them introductions of the historic period. Coconuts are usually gathered from natural stands back of the beach, but along some stretches the palms are lacking, and the coastal tribespeople will plant them around their villages. In the uplands, several kinds of nut-Pandanus may be transplanted from the wilds to the gardens.

The sweet potato warrants separate mention. Although grown in most parts of New Guinea, it becomes the primary crop in the central highlands; and to the mountaineers, the idea of taking a meal may be expressed by the phrase, "eating sweet potato." It is astonishing to see how excellent an economic foundation can be provided by intensive cultivation of this plant. During World War II, airmen of the Fifth Air Force, operating out of Port Moresby, Papua, spotted what they took to be a "lost civilization" hidden away in a mile-high valley of the Oranje Gebergte. The valley, 10

186

miles wide and 40 miles long, was heavily settled, its floor drained by a maze of artificial canals, its cultivated fields divided by neat fences of stone and wood. Low dams of earth permitted the growing of crops even on steep slopes; terraced gardens climbed the mountainsides to vanish in the clouds; walled villages were concentrated beside a river that meandered down the valley. Houses were reported to be of stone, some dome-shaped but others rectangular, roofed with thatch. The fields were dotted with watchtowers made of poles, and a suspension bridge 150 feet long crossed the river rapids. When plans were laid to build an airstrip somewhere in the highlands on the route from Merauke to Hollandia, many aerial photographs were taken of this extraordinary region, which journalists dubbed "Shangri-La." A natural rock formation of the valley was soon dubbed a "Pyramid."

Actually, the locality had been discovered by the Archbold Expedition in 1938, and is now called the Grand Valley of the Balim River. The numerous canals drain the alluvial soil of the valley floor, rendering it dry enough for sweet potatos, which are grown in many varieties. Taro, bananas, cucumbers, beans, spinach, and tobacco are also cultivated, but the sweet potato is the basis of the economy. The inhabitants of the valley, about 70,000 in number and divided into many tribes, are Papuans of ordinary appearance, and their speech belongs to a Papuan language family, Ndani. While intensive cultivation of the sweet potato is usual in the central highlands of both Indonesian and Australian New Guinea, Grand Valley agriculture is advanced beyond anything reported in other parts of the island. When first visited by outsiders, the Grand Valley people had cleared the forests away, removed the stumps and rocks, drained the lowlands by clean-cut canals, built up low areas with dirt from the canals, and terraced the precipitous mountain slopes. They had laid out the fields in checkerboard squares, considered land contours when planting crops, crisscrossed the fields with neat stone fences, and set out rows of Cordyline bushes to control erosion. They were using leaf mulch to warm the soil of the chill uplands. Casuarina trees, noted for an ability to dry the soil by taking up moisture and evaporating it, had been allowed to grow in many low places. Techniques of advanced agriculture diffuse from major centers to outlying regions, and their concentration in Grand Valley is more likely to reflect outside influence than independent invention. The nature of this influence is not apparent, but probably it arrived from the north coast where there are several unexplained cultural manifestations; and significantly, aerial survey indicates the valley to be more readily accessible from the north than from any other direction. Although comparatively advanced, the agriculture of the Grand Valley people has a Melanesian aspect, perhaps with modification by Malays who knew something of mainland Asian techniques.

The problem of New Guinea upland agriculture has been complicated by the supposed New World origin of the sweet potato. Anthropologists have had to assume that this plant spread through an area from western Irian Barat to Hawaii, developed dozens of varieties in the South Pacific, and became the basis of economic life throughout the central highlands of New Guinea, all in the comparatively short time that has elapsed since Europeans began crossing the Pacific. The sweet potato is a morning glory, a member of the genus Ipomoea which, although best represented in the New World, has wild members elsewhere, including Indonesia. There is no botanical reason why the sweet potato could not have been a native Old World plant, especially since it was of very restricted distribution in the New World. It is now known that Neolithic-level culture was first brought to the New World about 5,000 years ago by Japanese who crossed the Pacific from Kyushu to the coast of Ecuador, and the demonstration of this has led archeologists to look more favorably on the artifactual and botanical evidence that several Asiatic peoples made transoceanic voyages centuries before America was discovered by the Norsemen. The common Polynesian name for the sweet potato occurred also in a limited area of the New World, a circumstance suggesting aboriginal contact across the Pacific; but the situation is complicated, for this name, *kumar-*, could be derived from *kumad*, a Sanskrit word for the edible lotus whose thickened rootstock was dug for food in India. The transfer of a name from one root crop to another is a process familiar to students of ethnobotany, and it is not out of the question that unrecorded voyages from India were responsible for spreading both the sweet potato and a name for it. This view may find support not only from the widespread evidence of Hindu-Buddhist influence in the Southwest Pacific, but also from the numerous hints of such influence in the iconography, art, and architecture of the Late Classic cultures of Middle America.

In the uplands of Irian Barat, the alteration of the environment by agricultural man suggests a long history there for the sweet potato, the only New Guinea crop that will support close settlement at high elevations. Vast stretches of the highlands have been deforested, taken over by grasses tall or short. Even in the remote Pegunungan Sudirman, the landscape is frequently reminiscent of shortgrass prairie, miles of open country terminated by precipitous mountain slopes. Stands of evergreen oaks have grown up on numerous abandoned village sites where the soil was altered by long occupation. In scattered areas of heavy settlement, a fine-grained, whitish spear wood may no longer be available except through trade, and a reddish wood of inferior quality may be scarce. Decorative plumes and furs often must be traded for, the small game having been killed out. In places, the local supply of firewood may have been exhausted, the mountaineers now having to bring it down from the cold, dank moss forest. In Grand Valley, the Balim is yellow with silt, and no fish lives in it.

A few highland tribes will laboriously dig up, mulch, and plant the grassland, but most agriculture in Irian Barat is of the typical *ladang* variety, a forest patch being burned and then planted. In this part of the country, one hectare (a little less than two and a half acres) of *ladang* will support 5 to 8 people, but after a few years' use the patch may have to lie fallow for 20 or 30 years before it is productive again. The upper altitudinal limit of cultivation is determined less by the frost line than by the elevation at which the clouds hang over the mountains. The lower montane forest can be cultivated, but not so the moss forest, kept dripping by clouds. In the Pegunungan Sudirman, some of the Negritos are said to live as high as 10,000 feet, but settlement even as high as 9,000 feet is rare, for on most mountains the clouds hang lower than this. A *ladang* is not fertilized except by ash, nor is it plowed. Only human labor is used in farming, and digging sticks are the only tools. A man's digging stick is large, resembling a pointed boat paddle; a woman's is shorter and spear-like. A woman is expected to use her digging stick in self-defense if she is surprised by an enemy warrior while she is working in the fields. Although the fields are generally cleared by men, the crops are tended and gathered by women, since fertility is a female concern. An exception is tobacco; it is usually tended by men, for it is smoked ritually, and ritual is principally a male concern. The tobacco patch is likely to be planted in the center of the village, in an enclosure that only the privileged may enter. Tobacco is of New World origin, and is supposed to have been brought to New Guinea by the Portuguese. Yet, it has reached even the most isolated Negritos of the Pegunungan Sudirman, and more remarkably, it is integrated into ceremonial life. Probably, smoking rituals predated the arrival of tobacco, and were originally based upon other plants.

Some of the tribes build shelters to store taro, sweet potatos, or yams, but storage is risky in a warm, humid land.

The domestic animals of New Guinea are the pig, the dog, and the chicken, the first of these being by far the most important. Although there are areas where wild pigs are hunted, most of these animals live about the villages, and in all parts of Irian Barat are valued highly. When necessary, lactating women may suckle piglets as well as babies. The mountaineers practice selective pig-breeding, conveying the sows to some particularly illustrious boar; and as a result, upland pigs often are of enormous size. In a boar, an upper tusk meets a lower, the two sharpening each other; but the tribesmen may knock out both upper tusks, permitting the lower to grow into semicircles. After the pig's death, the enlarged tusks are made into ornaments. When a pig is to be killed, two men lift it, one by the hind legs and the other by the snout. A third man then kills the animal with an arrow through the lungs. The Negritos and some other small people are not strong enough to hold a large pig in this fashion, and so the animal is trussed and slung from a pole, two men lifting the pole so the archer can perform his task. Various rituals, such as sprinkling of the pig's blood, are performed in order to placate the spirit of the departed animal.

Debts can be settled, and some offenses atoned for, by payment in pigs.

The dog is a domestic breed, medium-sized, yellowish in color. It cannot bark but indulges in a mournful singing, something between a whine and a howl. A village scavenger and a pet of no great worth, the dog is sometimes used for hunting and sometimes for food. The chicken is uncommon, seen mostly in coastal villages. Probably it is a fairly recent introduction.

Wild game is hunted, gathered, and trapped. The most valuable game is the cassowary, which supplies meat, feathers for bonnets, quills for nose ornaments, and bones that can be worked into daggers and tools. The deer is of limited distribution, and may be another fairly recent introduction; few Irian Barat tribes know much about it. As is usual among uncivilized people and occasional among civilized, irrational food taboos are observed. For example, many tribesmen belong to a clan that recognizes a kangaroo or wallaby as its totem, and the totem animal is not hunted. Lizards and snakes are rarely eaten, not even the tasty monitors and pythons, but they are collected for their hides, which are used especially as drumheads. The surprisingly narrow diameter of a New Guinea drum reflects the necessity of stringing it with a reptile skin not more than a foot wide. The commonest trap is a twitch-up snare of ingenious construction. Made simply of branches and vines, it will take a monitor, a wallaby, or a wild pig with equal facility, and can even be built arboreally to take a tree monitor or a possum. It is not baited but is set on a well-worn animal trail, sometimes with drift fences, lines of cut brush that lead an animal into the trap. Along the coast, seafood is gathered by hand from the reefs and shallows, and Derris is used as a fish poison. Angling and netting are activities carried on in the coastal waters, and in those larger rivers which are invaded by some marine fishes. The shores of Lake Sentani are inhabited by about 7,000 people, who often set large, cylindrical, submerged traps for the marine fishes that enter the lake. Women dive into the water to investigate the traps.

Many of the tribespeople do not receive enough dietary salt

from the plant foods on which they rely so heavily, and therefore must trade for this mineral. It is probably not coincidental that heavily settled parts of the uplands have salt springs nearby. In such places, salt production is left to the women. First they beat lengths of banana stem to expel the juices. The interior structure of the stem is sponge-like, and will soak up brine when dropped into a salt spring. So treated, a length of stem is then dried and burned, the salty ash being used as a condiment or traded away in small containers of bamboo. In the uplands, knowledgeable explorers have sometimes paid for local labor with salt, which is received gladly and which does not upset the tribal economy. At the end of the day, the laborers' wives will file by, each with a square of banana leaf on which to receive a lump of salt. Often, the tribespeople seem to feel a craving for the mineral, which they will eat avidly when it is provided. In the mountains, iodides have usually been leached away, and the uplanders occasionally suffer from goiter, a thyroid malfunction resulting from iodine shortage.

Even where settlement is comparatively heavy, communities are small. The people of one tribe may erect several collections of huts, scattered over a few square miles. For example, pigs are kept away from the crops, and the pig-herders might occupy huts a mile or two away from the cultivated fields. Coastal villages, especially of the Melanesians, may be built out in the water, where the huts stand on poles; or sometimes they line the shore. In either case they are situated where there is protection from storm winds and tides. Some villages of the interior are built along the larger rivers, but others are not riparian, although of necessity a village site must be near a source of drinking water. Most huts are of pole-and-thatch construction. A circular floor plan seems to be an ancient one in New Guinea, but the custom of building rectangular huts has invaded the island from both ends. The Negritos of the Pegunungan Sudirman, and many other tribes of the highlands, still build circular huts, while rectangular dwellings are the rule in the lowlands. Some of the upland people use circular huts as family dwellings, rectangular ones as bachelors' quarters. The largest buildings are bachelors' quarters and ceremonial houses, the latter with a high gable at each end. The snuggest dwellings are those of the mountains; they are domed and low, windowless, with a false wall behind the door to keep out drafts. In the Pegunungan Arfak and elsewhere, there are rectangular "skyscraper" huts supported on posts 40 or 50 feet high, and entered by long ladders which may be drawn up after entry. Supplied with food and missiles, such aerial abodes offer protection from enemy raiders.

Of implements made locally, the most important is the stone-bladed axe, for it is used especially to clear *ladang* and to cut house-poles. The Negritos of the Pegunungan Sudirman, and some other mountain peoples farther east, use a simple kind of axe, its wooden handle club-like and provided with a hollow into which the stone blade fits. The blade, of polished greenstone, greywacke, or amphibolite, is oval or lens-shaped in cross section. This type of blade, often called a celt, is found as an archeological specimen at many localities from the mainland of southern Asia through New Guinea. Usually it is accompanied by potsherds, and this is not surprising, for pottery and polished stone implements characterize the Neolithic. Interestingly, the lenticular celt has also been found archeologically on the Cape York Peninsula of Australia, an area that received quite a few Melanesian culture traits. Probably, the simple axe was brought to New Guinea by early Melanesians. If so, it went out of fashion everywhere except in isolated pockets of the mountains, replaced by a composite axe whose polished stone blade is quadrangular or planilateral in cross section. In the more elaborate implements, the quadrangular blade is fitted into a socket which is in turn fastened to a handle, the composite tool being strengthened by wrappings of fiber. This kind of blade can be mounted transversely as an adze or vertically as an axe. Sometimes it is mounted at an angle, or in a swivel socket whose angle can be changed. The composite axe-adze is widespread among Melanesians and Papuans. Less important than this implement is a crescent-shaped knife of polished slate, employed especially in the manufacture of bows and arrows but also used by a man to pull out unwanted whiskers. Either slate or greenstone may be worked into a chisel, which serves particularly when cutting out sockets for axe blades. A specialized implement is the sago-pick, used to separate the sago fibers from the starch. The pick-head, of polished stone, is hafted like an adze blade but is much duller, for a sharp edge would break the fibers into small pieces that would be tedious to remove. Unmounted, the pick-head serves as a pestle. Small pestles of polished stone, ornamented with human or bird figures, have gone out of fashion, and so have small stone mortars, although tribal oldsters recall that they were used in the preparation of arrow poisons. Still fashionable, especially in southeastern Irian Barat, is a mace with a head of polished stone. The head, perforated to accomodate a handle, is usually disc-like but may be star- or flower-shaped. The mace is principally a weapon for striking, but occasionally it is thrown or used to parry a missile.

The art of chipping flint, or some other silicate rock, is much older than that of grinding and polishing stone. Flint-chipping is known widely in New Guinea but apparently was never important there. Flakes may be employed as scraping, cutting, drilling, and tattooing implements. A special kind of axe blade, used in chopping wild sugar cane, is the most elaborate widespread production in chipped stone. One sago pick-head of obsidian has been seen, and there is a report of a flint-tipped arrow that was used as a knife at a boys' circumcision ceremony. Near the Irian Barat–Papua border, hunting arrows may be tipped with neatly made, leaf-shaped points chipped from obsidian.

Arrows are occasionally tipped with slices of human limb bone or with bamboo. However, most New Guinea arrows have a head and foreshaft carved in one piece from a hard wood, myrtle in the uplands but elsewhere black palm. The head-foreshaft of a game arrow is smooth, that of a war arrow carved into rows of small barbs. A barbed arrow is difficult to remove from a wound, although special wooden tweezers are made to facilitate such removal. In some war arrows, the more proximal barbs are reversed in direction so that the missile, once imbedded in flesh, can neither be pulled out nor pushed through without considerable tissue destruction. The tribes of the Tariku-Taritatu lake plain use a latex to attach numerous bone barbs to the head and foreshaft. The bone slivers remain in the wound even if the arrow is removed, and they set up an infection. In Grand Valley, the head of a war arrow is wrapped loosely with orchid fibers which remain in the wound

194

when the shaft is withdrawn. Interesting museum specimens from near Merauke are war arrows whose sharp points were ground down from metal crosses distributed by a missionary. All New Guinea arrows have a very long shaft of light cane. Length is necessary because fletching is not used, and a short, unfletched arrow would wobble in flight. The arrow has no nock, for it must fit against a flat bowstring made from a rattan strip. The bow may be of laurel or Rhododendron in the uplands, but elsewhere it is usually of black palm. This brownish wood has numerous black rods running through it, and these, of extraordinary hardness, impart the desired springiness. The smallest bows, those of the Negritos, are about 5 feet long, while those of the Papuans and Melanesians are about 6 feet. In southeastern Irian Barat, bows are of giant bamboo. Armguards of woven rattan are widely used and much needed, since a bowstring will begin to flay the forearm after a few shots. To protect themselves from arrows, the Negritos and some other mountaineers make a cuirass, a body armor of woven rattan.

The spear-thrower, a device used to hurl a lance with great force, is more ancient than the bow and arrow. Two types of spear-thrower are known from New Guinea, one made of thongs and the other carved from wood or bamboo; but in general, the spear-thrower has been replaced by the bow. A large spear, cast by hand, is still widely used. About 16 to 18 feet long and almost as thick as the thrower's wrist, the spear is usually of black palm, although trees of the myrtle family provide spear wood for some uplanders. The point of the spear usually bears several long series of barbs. A spearman will hold the implement at arm's length, snapping it up and down a few times to test its weight, balance, and spine. To throw it, he runs forward in the fashion of a javelin-thrower, sometimes actually hurling himself to the ground with the effort of the cast. The spear is used in both warfare and hunting. During a fire-drive, a row of spearmen stand in advance of the flames, ready to bag a wild pig, wallaby, or deer; and a thrown spear will transfix even a large boar.

Arrow foreshafts and spears usually are decorated by engraving, often with red or white pigment rubbed into the incisions. Some of the Negritos are reported to limit their artistic efforts to such decoration; but most of the tribes turn out wood carvings such as benches and stools, drums, masks, spirit images, hardwood panels whose intricate designs memorialize deceased individuals, human or animal figures to crown the ridgepole of a ceremonial house, and figurines upon which drums and other paraphernalia are hung. Art is frequently representational, especially of human figures and skulls, animals, and mythological beings; but abstract or symbolic designs are also known. In the uplands there are paintings on the walls of some caves. Cloth is not woven, but tapa cloth is made from bark. Naturally colored or artificially dyed fibers are closely woven into armlets and other ornaments, as well as into wrappings for ceremonial drums and axes. A netted fabric serves for the making of caps and carrying bags. Strips of animal fur, especially from cuscus and flying-fox, are used on headdresses, but animal hides are not tanned or turned into parchment. While a few decorative objects, such as hairpins, pendants, and nose ornaments, are occasionally made from bone, this material is generally reserved for utilitarian items.

Of special interest are carved wooden figures, or other portrayals, of a man-like being with a grotesquely elongated nose. The motif of the long-nosed god appeared in many parts of New Guinea, where it had much significance for the tribesmen; yet, ethnologists were long unable to discover its rationale. But when the motif was traced into the islands west of New Guinea, it gradually changed, became more detailed; and by the time Bali was reached it had become recognizable as Ganesa, the elephant-headed god of the Hindu pantheon. Similarly, the New Guinea *korwar* (described below) was derived from a kind of Buddha statue characteristic of Indochina. It is not known whether Hindus and Buddhists actually reached New Guinea in the great days of Indian colonization, or whether their ideas were taken to the island by Indianized Malays. The latter is more likely.

As might be expected from the recognition of culture areas, certain productions, techniques, and art styles are concentrated in or limited to one or another part of Irian Barat. The region around Teluk Berau is noted for petroglyphs, abstract and realistic designs cut into the rocks. Their age is unknown. Also in this region are rock paintings, some of them with revealing detail. One of them portrays a ship with a high prow, probably a Melanesian vessel. The Vogelkop is noteworthy for tapa cloth with geometric designs that show influence from west of New Guinea. Such designs also appear on bamboo combs and containers, plaitwork, and dance belts of bark. Designs from west of New Guinea likewise are used around Teluk Sarera on boat prows, head rests, bamboo combs and containers, arrows, and *korwar*. Strictly speaking, a *korwar* is an ornamented box in which a human skull is kept; but the box usually forms the head of a carved wooden figure, and so the name has been extended to a variety of figures and figurines turned out locally. In one type of *korwar*, a skull is placed upon the peg-like neck of a figure. In the Sentani vicinity are numerous survivals of the Dong-son art style, which originated in Indochina during the Bronze Age, and which spread over most of Indonesia, brought by Malays. Around Teluk Jos Sudarso, comparable designs are woven into basketry, or carved on bone daggers, tobacco and betel-nut containers, drums, wooden bowls, suspension hooks, paddles, and the gables of sacred houses. This region is also known for bark paintings, in which fishes and monitor lizards are usually portrayed. These attractive paintings are unique in the South Pacific. Wood carving in the round is particularly well developed near Teluk Jos Sudarso, where kneeling figures are carved in addition to standing ones, even a mother-and-child group being attempted by the local wood-carvers. South of this bay, large canoes are made in the Melanesian style, with high, decorated prows, some S-shaped and others vertical. The Sepik-Ramu Area is the principal source of human skulls whose features have been restored with clay or fiber and then painted. These skulls are not head-hunting trophies but mementos of departed relatives.

In the Southwest Coast Area, the land of the Mimika and the Asmat, the most notable production is a large, heavy pole, up to 37 feet high, set in the ground and carved into a veritable arabesque of designs and grotesque human figures. This is called a *bitoro* (Mimika) or *bisj* (Asmat). Also from this region comes a bamboo trumpet used to announce the success of a head-hunting foray. In the Southeast Coast Area, the Marind-Anim are noted for a cult emblem, the *gari*, fan-shaped and up to 9 feet wide, made from the carved stems of sago palm fronds or else from some light wood.

Aboriginal metal-working is now unknown in New Guinea, although there once was a Dong-son center of bronze-working around Lake Sentani in northeastern Irian Barat; and the island has yielded a few perforated stone blades that seem to be copies of the bronze axe-heads that were formerly made at Sentani and on many islands farther west in Indonesia.

Pottery-making, familiar to most Melanesians, was taken up by only a few Papuan tribes. This is unfortunate because in the absence of ceramic vessels, the tribespeople never took much interest in boiling as a method of food preparation; and a great many leaves, sprouts, and berries are edible after boiling but not before. Also, pottery-making is usually left to the women and affords them a creative outlet, the finished vessels being both utilitarian and artistic. Some tribes do not turn out pottery but will trade for it. A pottery-making center grew up on the middle Sepik, at Aibom on Lake Chambri. Here, a local clay is tempered with sand to make the finished vessels harder and more resistant to breaking. No potter's wheel is used, the vessels being built up in coils by hand. Large, round-bottomed or bell-shaped jars and pots are most popular, although other kinds of containers are also made. Many are decorated with incisions, trailed lines, punctations, or appliqué fillets, and perhaps with grotesque faces. Deep incisions may be filled with red, yellow, purple, and white pigments. Aibom pottery is traded far and wide. It may seem strange that uncivilized people would carry the heavy, moderately fragile vessels any great distance through wild country. However, transport is frequently by dugout canoe along the rivers; and furthermore, vessels are not always traded empty but may be offered along with contents such as sago flour. The acme of New Guinea ceramic work is a fire-basket, a huge container with scalloped edges, resembling a gigantic tulip. It is usually decorated below the rim with trailed lines and appliqué work, and may have a gargoyle head modeled on the inside of the rim as though gazing into the flames. A fire-basket is a portable hearth that can be placed where it is needed. Of course it can be used for cooking; but at night when mosquitos rise in clouds from the river swamps, it also creates a welcome indoor smudge.

The fire-making kit is a thong, a stick, and a pinch of tinder. If the thong is sawed against the stick, sufficient heat is generated to ignite the tinder. When not in use, the fire-thong may be worn as a bracelet. A blaze is started to burn off a *ladang*, flush wild game, or rout enemy warriors from cover, as well as to light a cook-fire. The cooking technique is remarkably effective even in the absence of fireproof vessels. A pit, dug into the ground, is lined with palm or treefern fronds; and then fire-heated rocks, handled with wooden tongs, are placed in the pit along with the food that is to be baked. The ends of the fronds are bent over the food and held down with more rocks. Meat is usually cooked along with sago or plantain, and choice tidbits may be wrapped in sections of banana leaf before being placed in the pit. Meat, sweet potatos, and yams emerge perfectly done. Even the coastal Melanesians, well provided with cooking vessels of several kinds, have not abandoned the ancient, admirable technique of pit-baking.

Travel is on foot or by dugout canoe. Long, narrow canoes are widely used on the rivers and swamps, the paddlers standing upright even though the vessels are unstable. On quiet coastal waters of Irian Barat, a lone man will paddle a small outrigger canoe around the reefs in search of seafood. Larger coastal vessels are equipped with outrigger and sail. A famous craft of the Southwest Pacific is the Melanesian *lakatoi*, a sail-mounted raft supported by canoes. In the old days, the Melanesians would make an annual *lakatoi* trading voyage, carrying earthenware pots to the Papuans, who offered sago, plumes, and seashells in return. Maces, bows, arrows, drums, canoes, and tobacco were also carried by Melanesian traders within fairly recent times.

Costume is scanty, even in the cool mountains. In most upland tribes the man wears a penis sheath made from a long, horn-shaped gourd, held in place by a loop of sennit and by a cord that fastens around the waist or chest. Often it is decorated at the tip with a tassel of fur or with a spiny cocoon. In some mountain tribes the upper end of the gourd is used as a betel-nut container. A shorter, less ornamental gourd is worn when the man goes into battle. Among lowland Papuans, the penis sheath is often made from a seashell. Among some Papuans of southeastern Irian Barat, the man does not use a penis sheath but tucks the organ beneath a belt of woven fiber. In a minority of the tribes, a man's brief costume may be of leaves or fiber strips. The Melanesian man wears a sarong-like skirt, originally of tapa cloth. Among Negritos and most Papuans, the woman's costume is a narrow strip of Pandanus or some other fiber, worn very low fore and aft; or two bundles of Cordyline leaves may be hung from a waistcord. In the mountains, a skirt is often made of dangling fiber coils. (Needless to say, native costume is the first aspect of material culture to disappear after the tribes make contact with the modern world; for Christian missionaries are in the vanguard of Western cultural expansion, and today just as in past centuries they are grimly determined to make innocently nude tribespeople feel ashamed of their own bodies. But of the impact of missionaries, more in a later chapter.)

In the mountains, a man confines his hair in a netted cap, perhaps decorated with cowries; while the headgear of the upland woman is a "net-back," a sort of cap prolonged behind into a huge bag of netting. In the net-back she will carry garden produce, a baby, or a piglet, the front border of the garment serving as a tumpline when a load is borne. For all that it is a container, the net-back can properly be termed a garment, for when empty it is worn over the shoulders and back, its warmth much appreciated when a cold mist hangs over the mountains and valleys. Often it is dyed in patterns of red and purple.

The man's ceremonial costume is most elaborate among the Melanesians, least among isolated Negritos. Nowhere in the world is there a headdress to rival the Melanesian *kangal,* a great sunburst of plumes on a framework perhaps 6 feet high. Papuan headdresses, although a bit smaller, are gaudy with feathers, furs, shells, beetle wings, and sometimes ferns. Birds-of-paradise, including plume-bearers and other species, supply the greater part of the feathers that are worked into Melanesian and Papuan headgear; and some of the ceremonial dances appear to mimic the courtship display of these gaudy birds. The simplest headdress, the only one known to some Negritos and upland Papuans, is a bonnet of cassowary feathers. In various Melanesian and Papuan tribes, the woman's finery includes feathered or otherwise ornamented caps, along with a variety of beads and bangles. Among Negritos of the Pegunungan Sudirman, the woman may have no ceremonial wear; she is a little brown hen watching her man strut rooster-like in paint and feathers.

Man, woman, and child may paint the face on ceremonial occasions. Originally, the pigments were yellow clay, red ochre, charcoal, and a white made either from earths or from a kind of seed pod. Among tribes with much Negrito ancestry, the hair may be short-growing in both sexes and not amenable to any particular treatment. The Papuan man often uses latex to convert his medium-length hair into ropy strands. In southeastern Irian Barat and some other areas, woven fibers are braided into a man's hair and allowed to hang down his back, shielding his neck from the blow of a mace. In some Melanesians the hair, although of woolly texture, grows quite long, and is teased out into an enormous ball like an exaggerated "Afro." Although tattooing is known in the interior of the country, it is best developed among the coastal Melanesians, whose women may be tattooed from head to foot with angular patterns. Such tattooing, which is painful, is done at intervals, the pattern taking years to complete. Cicatrization, the deliberate scarring of the skin to produce ornamental welts, is known among the Papuans but is not commonly practiced. In general, it is favored by people whose skin is too dark to show a tattoo.

From what has been said, it is evident that tribal existence is not haphazard or disorganized. On the contrary, it is closely regulated and given coherence by a series of interlocking precepts, and by a social organization which, although varying from one part of Irian Barat to another, always seems complex for so small a group of people. The parent-child relationship is regarded as very important by the tribesmen, of course; but so is the sibling relationship. Much attention is given to lineage, that is to biological kinship, as well as to in-law relationships that link two lineages. Organization of this kind has a counterpart in the civilized world, but is taken more seriously by the tribespeople. A tribal language includes a bewildering complexity of kinship terms; each kind or degree of kinship carries with it certain prescribed responsibilities toward relatives, even remote ones; each marriage sets up a variety of pre-scribed relationships between the groom's relatives and the bride's. A Papuan man does not need to be told, "When you marry the girl, you marry her family too." The bride's parents not only "gain a son" but also acquire a long list of in-laws. Tribal organization likewise includes clans, groups of people who regard themselves as being of common descent. In a lineage, biological relationship is demonstrable; but not so in a clan, whose members are putatively descended from a remote couple, mythological figure, or beast. Some clans, claiming descent from a certain kind of animal, recog-nize that animal as a totem and never molest it. A clan division, the subclan, is likely to be regionally concentrated and therefore more important than the clan proper. The highlanders generally reckon clan descent on the male side, but many lowlanders reckon it on the female. Patrilineal systems are probably ancient in New Guinea, and still predominate in the mountains; matrilineal ones were probably introduced by the Melanesians. Westerners, accus-tomed to emphasizing patrilinearity, are often surprised to learn that in many Neolithic-level tribes, descent may be reckoned on the female side; clan and other affiliations, as well as property, may be passed down from a mother to her children. In some cases, a newly married man leaves his home to move into his bride's hut. In the eastern part of the Vogelkop, systems of reckoning descent have become mixed, some being patrilineal, others matrilineal, still others ambilineal.

Many tribal activities, from major ceremonies to everyday chores, are the prescribed responsibility of some particular seg-ment of the population. This situation becomes clearer when atten-tion is focused on one particular locality. A likely choice is the Star Mountains of eastern Irian Barat, for the region was not reached by explorers until 1959, and a Dutch anthropologist had chance to study the tribal ways before these were at all modified by civiliza-tion. Here, a nuclear family occupies a hut, a collection of which make up a so-called hamlet. Several of these hamlets, each perhaps an hour's walk from another, in turn make up a parish, the largest territorial unit with corporate functions. One hamlet is traditionally if not in actuality the original one, and in it is found the only ceremonial enclosure and the only sacred house, or *iwol*, in the parish. The enclosure is taboo to women except on ceremonial occasions. The *iwol* is entered only by initiated men of some years and standing. In it they carry on a ritual regarded as necessary if taro is to be cultivated successfully. Pork fat, taboo to the uninitiated, is stored in the *iwol*, which must be maintained in perfect order, and which is guarded at night by certain men or their deputies. Occasionally, several parishes gather at one sacred house for a major ceremony at which many pigs are slaughtered and cooked. Each hamlet has its men's clubhouse, the *bokam*, which serves as a gathering place for initiated males and as a dormitory for unmarried or visiting men, widowers, and husbands who have been quarreling with their wives. Each hamlet also has an isolated hut, the *sukam*, where women go to menstruate and have babies. The men's clubhouse is taboo to women, the women's hut to men.

Land is regarded as owned by the parish, but each hamlet occupies the garden land in its vicinity. Several parishes may cooperate in the cultivation of a tract, yet a parish can function as a political unit in warfare against another parish. Deaths, except those of young children and old people, are thought to result from sorcery carried on by someone in another parish. In this region, the clan is little more than a name group, the name passing from father to son. A subclan usually extends through all the parishes that might gather at one sacred house, a lineage through all the hamlets of a parish. Members of a small lineage marry into other lineages, but the local clans are not exclusively out-marrying. A vanishing lineage may merge with a lineage of another clan in the same parish, but not with a lineage of its own clan in another parish; and any such merging requires several generations to complete. When a woman is secluded in the *sukam*, the members of her lineage and the residents of her hamlet must stay away from new gardens to avoid crop failure. When a woman marries, her relatives suffer a loss, and so her father or brother must be reimbursed with pigs, netted carrying bags, shells, and axes. When a man marries, his mother and sisters make the carrying bags that he must offer; and indirectly they supply all the other needed items, for they have raised the pigs, some of which he can exchange for shells and axes. And so tribal life goes, through a series of carefully defined responsibilities and interdictions.

Furthermore, Irian Barat tribespeople usually believe their territory to be inhabited by spirits who must also be dealt with in prescribed ways. Omnipresent are the ghosts of the recent dead, not necessarily malign, perhaps even protective if duly acknowledged, but rather inclined to punish infractions of custom. When someone dies, a relative will chop off a finger joint to placate the spirit of the departed. While any close relative may supply the needed joint, the usual donor is a small girl or a woman, for a man should save a few fingers to handle the bow and arrow. An old grandmother, one who has known many bereavements, may have only a few finger-stumps left. The sacrifice of a finger joint is a very ancient and widespread practice whose arrival in New Guinea probably far antedated the coming of the Melanesians. Paleolithic Europeans decorated cave walls with pictures of mutilated hands; and in the United States, the Crow Indians were lopping off finger joints as late as the nineteenth century. In Irian Barat, cremation may be the oldest method whereby a body is disposed of. The Negritos of the Pegunungan Sudirman still practice cremation, but among most other people, the body is either interred or exposed. Often it is returned to after the flesh has decayed, and the skull salvaged to be kept in the village. A man may wear around his neck the skull of his mother, who protects him after her death just as she did in life. Numerous skulls in a village, polished by much handling to the sheen of ivory, are not head-hunting trophies but the melancholy relics of departed kin who, in a sense, still participate in tribal affairs. Even the ghosts of dead pigs receive some attention, and symbolic shields may be fashioned to ward them off.

In addition to the shades of pigs and ancestors, the world of the Irian Barat tribespeople is inhabited by less readily identifiable spirits who take up residence in unpredictable places, and who may behave capriciously. Or perhaps this is phrasing the situation wrongly. Perhaps it would be better to say that almost any natural or man-made object—a boulder, a cave, a tree, a shrub, a stretch of forest or riverbank, a certain spot in the trail, a seashell, a weapon, a headdress—may harbor a spirit who can influence human affairs. Oddly, in Irian Barat such animistic beliefs are less important than ancestor-worship, while the reverse is true in western Indonesia. Ancestral or other spirits are to some extent manipulable through offerings or rituals, but someone in another village will manipulate the supernatural improperly or vindictively, to bring on mishaps and catastrophes of nature. Animism, ancestor-worship, sorcery—these are the tribal tenets. A fourth widespread theme is that of duality, occasionally of a logical sort but usually not. That is to say, on the one hand there may be such things as superiority, the big-man, the father, maleness, the spirit, semen, chastity, purity, bachelorhood, ritual seclusion, "male" crops, wild game, the sacred house, the right side of the thorax and the right hand, the sun, the sky-dwellers, a reddish skin, immortality, and a ✸ settlement with kin. Respectively opposed to these are inferiority, the rubbish-man (another term borrowed from Melanesian), the mother, femaleness, flesh and blood, milk, sexuality, pollution, husbandhood, domestic life, "female" crops, the pig, the secular dwelling house, the left side of the thorax and the left hand, the moon, the earth-dwellers, a dark skin, mortality, and the deep forest with demons.

Watched over by ancestral spirits, bound by regulations, and anticipating catastrophe if custom is violated, the tribespeople of Irian Barat are thoughtful and law-abiding within their own frame of reference. An antisocial act is rarely committed within the tribe, and if it is, retribution is exacted—perhaps exacted not just from the offender but also in some fashion from other people who are linked with him by lineage, clan, or other segment of society. It is erroneous to call such people lawless or savage, even though their culture permits or even calls for hostility toward strangers and nearby tribes. Westerners often have failed to understand intertribal hostilities and related practices such as cannibalism and headhunting. An American anthropologist, who in 1926 followed the Mamberamo River and the Tariku to reach the Pegunungan Sudirman, wrote, "The natives do not fight in an organized manner, nor even intelligently. Although small parties of our expedition were frequently attacked, and we had 16 men killed, the excitable natives usually betrayed their ambushes by shouting and by firing their arrows too soon." To the average Westerner of the twentieth century, almost any stratagem of warfare would seem acceptable if it took a toll of the enemy; but not to the Irian Barat tribesmen, whose armed clashes are carried on with great formality. The opposing parties agree beforehand on the time and place of battle; hostilities follow a prescribed pattern, the warriors religiously obeying an etiquette of war; and the battle can be terminated by mutual consent, to be followed by elaborate peace-making ceremonies. Intertribal warfare has been appropriately likened to Western sports. However, sports are a mere catering to the aggressive impulses of participants and spectators; the ritualized combats of the tribesmen are a social obligation, a defense of tribal territory, an exacting of retribution for some encroachment or offense.

Cannibalism is an adjunct to warfare. While it was known to Paleolithic peoples, it was chiefly a Neolithic development, concerned primarily with magic, with an effort to demean an enemy by taking his strength and *elán vitál*. The practice was introduced into New Guinea by the Melanesians, and, like so many other customs of similar origin, is more characteristic of the eastern part of the island. Some Papuans of Australian New Guinea, perhaps encouraged by a chronic dietary lack of animal protein, carried cannibalism into the realm of gastronomy, relying heavily on enemy tribes as a source of meat, and becoming connoisseurs of the cuts and tidbits that can be taken from a human carcass roasted with sago. The Fly River country has been especially notorious for gastronomic cannibalism. But for most New Guinea tribes, the eating of human flesh is a rite surrounded by taboos. Thus, a warrior may be prohibited from eating the flesh of an enemy he himself has killed; or women might be totally excluded from cannibalistic feasts. From points of introduction on the eastern coasts of New Guinea, the practice of cannibalism spread westward more readily in the lowlands than in the mountains. It never reached the Negritos of the Pegunungan Sudirman, and is of no more than sporadic occurrence among the Papuans who occupy the eastern end of Irian Barat's central highlands.

Head-hunting is more than a manifestation of intertribal hostility. Severed heads are ceremonially treated, and are displayed in the hope that they will divert malign influences from the neighborhood. Heads are occasionally those of strangers, more often those of people from enemy villages. Contrary to widespread supposition, Old World headhunters do not shrink the trophies they bring in, this being a practice only of certain American Indians in Ecuador and nearby parts of Peru. In New Guinea, the skin of a human head is occasionally mounted over one end of a war drum, but usually only the skull is kept, to be decorated with paint, shells, or tassels. Large sticks, encrusted with cowries, may be set into the eye sockets. As a head is not quickly severed with primitive implements, a warrior in the heat of battle may remove only a token bit of scalp from a fallen enemy; and on ceremonial occasions a headhunter may wear or carry something to symbolize each head he has taken. Thus, a hornbill's beak may be fastened into a bonnet, or a tassel of parrot feathers hung to the spatula that is used for dipping betel-nut. Like cannibalism, head-hunting was introduced into New Guinea by the Melanesians, and spread westward more readily in the lowlands than in the mountains. Until recent times, the practice was also known in remoter parts of central and western Indonesia, so may have diffused to Irian Barat from two directions. According to original Melanesian belief, a freshly taken human head was necessary to consecrate the building of a new sacred house, the launching of a war canoe, or some other important undertaking; and if necessary, the Melanesians would sacrifice one of their own people to obtain the head. Few Papuan tribes, if any, adopted this custom of sacrifice, but many of them took to collecting the heads of enemies and strangers. In the eastern half of the island, head-hunting became widespread. In the western half, it never reached the Negritos of the Pegunungan Sudirman nor some upland Papuans, but diffused widely in the low country both north and south of the mountains. Head-hunting is not yet a thing of the past in Irian Barat but will probably continue for some time to come, especially in the swamps of the southeast and the lowlands around Teluk Sarera and Teluk Berau. Modern uprisings, directed against the colonial powers and their successors in New Guinea, will not be considered at this point, for they involve something more than tribal ways.

The New Guinea tribespeople have been hostile toward outsiders; the Dutch were preoccupied with economically more rewarding islands farther west; the Indonesians proper are confronted with problems of their own. Thus, Irian Barat is just now undergoing the traumatic passage from the New Stone Age directly to modernity. Not so central and western Indonesia, which remained in the mainstream of Eurasian cultural advance, and which has changed progressively. Now to consider the events that have moulded the Greater Sundas, the Lesser Sundas, and the Moluccas, islands where the texture of history is exceedingly deep.

The first great migration into Indonesia, that of the Negritos, took place because the islands were there, to be won by the venturesome. The last such movement, that of the Malays, took place out of necessity. For as the Neolithic spread in Eurasia, many peoples were pushed aside by stronger or more aggressive neighbors; and among the groups so displaced were the ancestral Malays and their kin. They had been living in what are now Cambodia and Viet Nam, but found themselves under increasing pressure from the north. Their exodus must have begun not long after that of the Melanesians, for many groups of them bore a Neolithic-level culture much like that of their immediate predecessors. In some part the exodus of the Malays took place overland and coastally down the great peninsula that would eventually bear their name, but in another part it involved a crossing of the South China Sea and various straits of Indonesia. To Borneo and Sumatra the Malays spread, then to Java and Sulawesi, dispossessing earlier immigrants, absorbing them or forcing them into marginal habitats. Farther to the southeast, the Malays impressed their physical, linguistic, and cultural stamp upon the Moluccas and the Lesser Sundas, but were themselves modified by Papuans and Melanesians already entrenched there. A few Malays settled upon Wuvulu, Arua, Ningo, the Luf Islands, and the Kamiets, specks of land west of the Admiralties, administered now by Australia. New Guinea, bristling with the spears and arrows of tribal warriors, brought the southward movement of the early Malays to a halt, although they carried a good many culture traits to the north coast of the great island.

Some of the migrants from Indochina bypassed New Guinea to spread into the archipelagos farther east, passing through the Melanesian isles, swapping a few genes and culture traits with the Melanesians, and arriving at New Zealand to become the Maori. On New Zealand they met, dispossessed, and finally absorbed the Maoriori, their Melanesian predecessors. Still other migrants from Indochina pointed their vessels toward the sunrise, pushing beyond Melanesia to more distant islands on which they became the Polynesians. From the Tuamotus they sailed yet farther east to reach Easter Island, at which point they were about three-quarters of the way across the Pacific. Perhaps a few boatloads of them completed the transoceanic crossing to arrive on the Pacific coast of the New World, but this is not a part of the present story. From Polynesia the emigrants also reached a chain of volcanic islands in mid-Pacific, to become the first Hawaiians.

Nor was this all of the Malayo-Polynesian radiation from Indochina, not by any means. Some of these people arrived at archipelagos far northeast of New Guinea, there to settle as Micronesians. Closer to the Asian mainland, the Malay wave swept over the Philippines, which had a large population of Negritos to be absorbed except at scattered localities. Still farther north, the Malays probably reached Japan, but peripheral traces of their presence have been obscured by later developments, and Taiwan (Formosa) is the northernmost island they assuredly settled upon. The Malays also sailed westward from Indonesia, crossing the Indian Ocean to Madagascar (now the Malagasy Republic) which they occupied entirely, and where they later became somewhat mixed with Negroids and Arabs.

Some of the ancestral Malays and their kin did not leave their Asian mainland home but stayed in Cambodia and Viet Nam. Here they received many advanced ideas, and soon passed from the Neolithic level to that of an early, bronze-using civilization. But people continued to push southward into the Indochina Peninsula, following several routes. The ancestral Malays of the Mekong and the Tonle Sap, harried on the north by the Khmer, began another exodus. These civilized Malays, having been exposed to more genetic influence from the rapidly expanding Mongoloid physical type, differed from the earlier ones in being broader of face, rounder of head. And to judge from their descendants, the later Malays were also straighter of hair, and occasionally provided with the epicanthic skin-fold which imparts a characteristic appearance to the Mongoloid eye. Unlike the Neolithic-level Malays, the civilized ones in most cases did not disperse far and wide across the seas. Probably they did not need to do so, for their advanced culture permitted them to usurp coastal areas of the Greater Sundas. And usurp they did, pushing aside the early Malays who had displaced still earlier peoples. Small groups of the civilized Malays sailed eastward into the Lesser Sundas and the Moluccas, to trade and explore if not to settle; and they introduced many culture traits which spread from island to island, a few even to New Guinea.

Anthropologists have used the term "proto-Malay" to designate basically Caucasoid Malays who went to Indonesia with a Neolithic-level culture and whose stock is best represented today in the interior of Sumatra and Borneo (for example, by the Batak and Dyak). The contrasting term, "deutero-Malay," accordingly designates the more Mongoloid Malays who took Bronze Age civilization into Indonesia from Indochina, and whose stock is best represented today around the coastal trading centers of the Greater Sundas. This arrangement begs the question of origins outside Indonesia, and it is probably well to do so here. No doubt, late prehistoric and protohistoric Indochina resembled historic Indonesia in that some peoples did not participate fully in cultural advances. In the days when some Malays were exporting civilization to the Greater Sundas, there were Indochinese tribes who had not advanced beyond the Neolithic level. Pressure on Indochina from the north, in the form of border aggressions and a southward flow of immigrants, did not cease; and even after the exodus of the civilized Malays, groups left Indochina bearing Malayo-Polynesian languages but still a Neolithic-level culture. Some parts of the Malayo-Polynesian world could have been populated by cultural laggards who left late.

But in any event, the last great migrations into Indonesia were those of the Malays, Neolithic-level and newly civilized. The culture would continue to change in the western and central islands, but the physical types and the languages there were largely determined by these migrations, and so might be summarized as they exist today. The physical types have continued to mix, and no sizable percentage of the Indonesian population could be sorted convincingly into proto- and deutero-Malay types. The most one can say is that the physical type of the later Malays is concentrated in the coastal districts of the large, western islands, while that of the early Malays is concentrated in the interior of these islands. Although culture is not under discussion at this point, it is worth noting that on the larger islands, the coastal settlements of the later Malays eventually became the nuclei of trading kingdoms, while the interior settlements of the early Malays became centers of agriculture; thus, cultural differences have helped to prevent a complete merging of the two physical types which were not trenchantly different to begin with. On the smaller islands east of the Greater Sundas, the Malays became numerically, linguistically, and culturally dominant, but received much genetic influence from Papuan or Melanesian predecessors. In the Moluccas, as well as in the Lesser Sundas east of central Flores, there have remained some groups of people in whom an old, non-Malay strain runs strongly. The Dutch called such people the Alfoer. This name, also rendered Alfur, Alfuro, or Arafura, was adopted by the Dutch from the Portuguese fora, "outsider," with the Arabic article al-. Much earlier, the Chinese had designated such non-Malays the K'un-lun, and supplied some interesting remarks on them. The K'un-lun, who were dark skinned and woolly haired, thrived in the mountains and on the sea but not on the intervening lowlands. The maritime K'un-lun, great traders and seamen, were always ready to supply boats and crews, and their language had become a lingua franca among the polyglot islands of the eastern seas. The Chinese suspected that the dark peoples had discovered a mystic connection between mountain and ocean; but today it seems possible that the K'un-lun of the mountains were Papuans who had been pushed back into the interior of some islands, while the K'un-lun of the sea

were surely the Melanesians. The distinction between the two
would become obscure as their islands were taken over by Malays.

Outside Indonesia, the Malay physical type is detectable, of
course, as far away as Madagascar, New Zealand, and Easter Island. Depending on locality, it is slightly or greatly modified by
absorption of other peoples. On the Asian mainland, from the
Malay Peninsula and the Indochina Peninsula northward into
southern China, the population (except for relict groups such as
Negritos) is physically quite similar to Indonesian Malays, although diverse languages and cultures are now found in this region.

In the lands of the South Pacific and the Indian Ocean, many
ways of life have developed, and today the term Malay would seldom be extended to the modern Madagascans, Polynesians, Micronesians, or Maoris. Yet, the common descent of these peoples,
and others, is revealed by linguistic similarities. As the late Sukarno phased it, "The Ma- of Malaya, the Ma- of Madagascar, the
Ma- of Madura and Manila, the Ma- of Maori—all are the same."
Eastern Taiwan, Hawaii, Easter Island, New Zealand, the Melanesian south coast of Papua, and Madagascar are on the periphery of
the Malayo-Polynesian speech area, at whose heart lie Indonesia,
Malaysia, and the Philippines along with the Micronesian, Melanesian, and Polynesian archipelagos. West of Irian Barat, the Malayo-
Polynesian Family of languages blankets Indonesia except for
two areas: Alor in the Lesser Sundas, and the general vicinity of
northern Halmahera in the Moluccas. Several Papuan tongues persist on Alor, while languages of the distinctive North Halmaheran
Family cover the two large northern peninsulas of Halmahera and
the nearby islands of Morotai, Ternate, and Tidore. The speakers
of North Halmaheran are the people who were first and most frequently called Alfoers, and their speech was probably derived in
considerable part from that of very early Papuans. On the Indochina Peninsula, the Cham tongue retains a Malayo-Polynesian
base, although modified by Khmer, which belongs to a different
family. Some "Montagnards" of Viet Nam speak Cham. The distribution of Malayo-Polynesian speech in Irian Barat has already
been outlined.

In Indonesia alone, the Malayo-Polynesian Family includes more than 250 languages, these falling into about 16 groups. An important group is the Sumatran, whose 15 languages cover the Mentawais, Sumatra, the Riaus and Linggas, Bangka, Belitung, and the lowlands of Kalimantan, with a few enclaves elsewhere. Included in the Sumatran Group are the Atjehnese of northern Sumatra, the Batak centered around Sumatra's Lake Toba, the Minangkabau of central Sumatra, and the Malayan. The last exists in four dialects: Riau Malayan, which extends from the lowlands of eastern Sumatra to those of Kalimantan; Djakarta Malayan, which has developed in and around the capital city; Kubu, with scattered enclaves in southeastern Sumatra; and Moluccan Malayan, which is heard on a few small islands such as the Bandas and the Watubelas. Of these four dialects, Riau is regarded as the purest, the classical Malayan tongue. From Sumatra it crosses Selat Melaka (the Strait of Malacca) to the southern part of the Malay Peninsula. Riau Malayan is the principal literary language of Indonesia, and as such is understood by educated Indonesians generally. Modernized, it is Bahasa Indonesia, the official tongue, while greatly simplified it is Melaju Pasar, a trade language widely known in Indonesia and heard at seaports from China to New Guinea. Still other dialects of Malayan exist in the Malay Peninsula but need not be reviewed. So-called Baba Malayan was developed in Singapore and the Malay Peninsula by Chinese entrepreneurs and businessmen, most of whom also spoke English.

A second important language group of Indonesia is the Javanese. It includes the Sundanese speech of southwestern Java, the Madurese of Madura and extreme eastern Java, and the Javanese, which covers the central section of Java. Javanese also extends westward along the northern coast of Java, but is split by the large enclave of Djakarta Malayan, which has borrowed many Javanese and Sundanese usages. A third group, the Bornean, occupies the interior of Kalimantan and non-Indonesian Borneo. Some of its many languages are spoken by the people generally called Dyaks. Within the territory of the Bornean Group there are scattered enclaves of Malayan. Also belonging to the Bornean Group is the language of the Badjau, sea nomads with no home on land. The Balinese Group includes the Balinese of Bali and Penida, the Sasak of Lombok, and the Sumbawan of Mojo and the large western peninsula of Sumbawa. The Philippines Group links the southern Philippines with the Talauds, the Sangihes, and northern Sulawesi. (The Philippines are blanketed by Malayo-Polynesian groups and languages in exceptional diversity.) Farther west on the northern peninsula of Sulawesi, the Philippines Group gives way to the Gorontalo Group, and the latter in turn to the Tomini Group. In central Sulawesi is the Toradja Group, with the Loinang Group at the end of the island's east-central peninsula. Banggai, spoken in the Banggai Archipelago, is placed in the Loinang Group, but is very distinctive. The southeastern peninsula of Sulawesi is the homeland of the Bungku-Laki Group, and the southwestern of the South Celebes Group, while the Muna-Butung Group covers the smaller islands from Muna and the Tukangbesis southward to Kalao and neighboring islets. In the lesser Sundas, the Bima-Sumba Group extends from eastern Sumbawa eastward through most of Flores and all of Sumba. A very large group, the Ambon-Timor, with 22 languages, stretches from eastern Flores eastward through the Tanimbars, the Kais, the Arus, Ceram, Ambon, and Buru; as noted, it is interrupted by a Papuan enclave on Alor. The Sula-Batjan Group is confined to the Sulas, the Obis, and Batjan, with a Malayan enclave on Obi. Finally, the South Halmahera Group carries the Malayo-Polynesian Family from southern Halmahera eastward to Waigeo, Salawati, Misoöl, and Irian Barat, as described in connection with the Melanesians.

Recalling that each of the foregoing groups includes several to many mutually unintelligible languages, the linguistic complexity of Indonesia becomes evident. Yet, such complexity is not excessive in proportion to the country's vast extent, and is roughly comparable to that of Europe, which has a long list of Indo-European and other languages. In Indonesia, the distribution of the Malayo-Polynesian languages is not strongly correlated with physical geography. The water gaps of the country have been highways rather than barriers; a single Malayo-Polynesian language may reach several islands, and a majority of the groups do so. Nor is the distribution of Indonesian tongues strongly correlated with political geography, for the country's boundaries are crossed by groups and even by some individual languages. But often a single language is restricted to and helps define a single ethnic group, the name of a language sometimes being that of a distinctive people also. Well-known examples are the Atjehnese, Batak, Minangkabau, Badjau, Balinese, Makasarese, and Buginese.

The spread of the Malays was not completed in a few years or even a few decades. About the time some Malays were bringing Bronze Age civilization to western Indonesia, others were just bringing the Neolithic to Madagascar and had not yet reached New Zealand, Hawaii, or Easter Island. Hence, the spread of the Malayo-Polynesian languages was not accomplished rapidly, and the present distribution pattern of these languages in Indonesia had to emerge gradually as dominant peoples extirpated or absorbed subordinate ones. Even the dominant peoples would eventually enlarge their vocabularies with words borrowed from several Asian and European tongues. In the meanwhile, many cultural changes would come about.

Descendants of the early Malays maintained a Neolithic culture until modern times in scattered parts of Indonesia. Such people reveal the life of the early Malays to have been much like that of the Melanesians. There was a similar reliance on the cultivation of tropical crops in *ladang*, and on the raising of pigs. There was a similar division of the people into tribes, with emphasis on clan and kinship; there was intertribal warfare and head-hunting; there was ancestor worship, animism, sorcery, and a belief in mystic duality. Weapons, tools, household utensils, and ornaments of the early Malays were not substantially different from the ones that were taken to New Guinea by the Melanesians. To the early Malays' economic, societal, ideological, and technological base were added advanced culture traits leading toward civilization. The sequence in which they were added is easier to determine on the Indochina Peninsula than on the islands of Indonesia, where many customs survived long after passing out of fashion elsewhere.

Consider, for example, the problem offered by megaliths, enormous stone columns that were laboriously moved and placed upright. The practice of erecting these columns reached Indochina in late Neolithic times, perhaps around 2500 B.C. At first, two kinds of megaliths were in favor: the dolmen, which was supported by a lintel, and the menhir, which stood without support. The columns were often arranged in circles or lines, with seats, walks, and dwellings nearby. At a later date, a stone sarcophagus might be built in connection with a megalith. The custom of erecting megaliths could have first diffused into Indonesia before the Neolithic was over in any part of Indochina; but it was carried mostly by the later Malays with a Bronze Age civilization. Eventually, stone columns were being erected not only on many islands of western and central Indonesia, but a few even in Melanesian New Guinea and the archipelagos farther east. Once built, a megalith might function as a permanent setting for changing beliefs. At Pakauman in eastern Java, a megalithic grave was still in use as late as the ninth century A.D., for it contained Chinese pottery of that period, along with glass beads and tools of bronze and iron. At several localities in Java, megaliths were carved to represent figures from the Hindu pantheon; and on Sulawesi, Nias, Flores, and Sumba, megaliths have been erected in modern times.

At any rate, one of the earliest civilizations of tropical southeastern Asia was developed by the ancestral Malays in Indochina. The Mekong Delta of South Viet Nam, the Tonle Sap region of Cambodia, and the east coast of both South and North Viet Nam— these were Malayo-Polynesian areas at one time, occupied by the people who would later dominate western and central Indonesia. Such areas were not simply abandoned by wholesale emigration to the islands. Continually absorbing Khmer immigrants from the north, and adopting Hindu-Buddhist culture, they were probably still ruled by ancestral Malays and their kin when the Chinese first began to keep written records of conditions in southeastern Asia. But the early Chinese accounts of Indochina, dating from the first few centuries A.D., are too late to provide the desired insight into a way of life that was carried to Indonesia by the deutero-Malays; for such an insight one must turn to archeological studies in Indochina and the Greater Sundas.

Of exceptional consequence was excavation at Dông-so'n, a village now in North Viet Nam just south of the old Tonkin border.

216

(Thanh Hoa is the nearest large, well-known community of modern times.) Uncovered here were a great variety of artifacts, the relics of an early civilization; and archeologists came to write of the Dong-son culture (omitting diacritical marks). The designation is one of convenience; it does not imply that the culture necessarily originated in the exact area where it was first discovered, or that the modern village was occupied by lineal descendants of the people whose ancient settlement was investigated. The Dong-son culture was adumbrated in the eighth century B.C., crystallized in the seventh century B.C., and around 500 B.C. carried by deutero-Malays to the Greater Sundas and the western part of the Lesser Sundas. Dong-son traits eventually spread selectively to islands still farther east, a few even to the north coast of New Guinea. A significant feature of the Dong-son culture was the use of bronze. The casting of this metal, a hard alloy of copper and tin, permitted the manufacture of fine new weapons, tools, utensils, and ornaments. (Dong-son bronze also included a high percentage of lead, up to 25 percent.)

Dong-son bronze work included drums, bells, buckles, daggers, axes, spearheads, figurines, and imitations of woven panniers and fish baskets. One type of axe blade, asymmetrical in cross section, was probably made expressly for cutting bamboo. This kind of blade, which was also turned out in polished stone, probably originated in China, where it had a prototype; but a second variety of bronze axe blade, pediform and with decorated side-panels, seems to have been peculiar to the Dong-son culture. Most of the Dong-son implements went out of style at the end of the Bronze Age, but the drums continued to be made for many centuries thereafter. The original Dong-son drums, fortunately distinguishable from later copies, are remarkable instruments. They might well be called drum-shaped gongs, for they are entirely of metal. Some are of great size and probably were suspended from a bamboo or wooden framework. The larger ones, at least, were mould-made, cast in the usual metallurgical fashion; but smaller ones may have been turned out by the *ciré-perdue* or "lost wax" method. The Dong-son bronze drums had somewhat of an hourglass shape, with a tympanum on one end only; and New Guinea drums, even though more elongate, wooden, and strung at one end with reptile skin, show a generic similarity to the Dong-son. The New Guinea instruments, of Melanesian origin, provide a clue to the shape of a prototypic wooden drum that was eventually duplicated and improved upon in bronze. Dong-son drums were usually decorated over the ends and sides with delicately executed reliefs: abstract or stylized designs, along with portrayals of flora, fauna, mythological beings, and people. The more realistic portrayals reveal significant details of early costume, tools, agriculture, household equipment, weapons, and musical instruments. One frequent theme of the reliefs is a spirit ship, carrying the souls of the dead to some hereafter-land. This theme is identifiable because it lingered into modern times in southeastern Asia, both on the mainland and in the islands. The Toradja of Sulawesi preserved it in incantatory rites, Borneans in wood carvings, Sumatrans in textiles. Some Borneans (and American Indians) came to leave a dead body in a spirit canoe elevated on posts.

People in Java and Sumatra acquired a few bronze drums that were made in Indochina, but cast many others for themselves and for export to the Lesser Sundas and the Moluccas. There were stylistic changes in the drums as time went by. These instruments were treasured at remoter localities long after they had been forgotten elsewhere. In later times they were assigned new uses: some were buried in the ground to insure crop fertility, or banged on to bring rain, or stood on end to serve as altars. An extraordinary number of bronze drums have turned up on Alor, where they are called *mokko* and have been used as currency in modern times.

Of course the Dong-son culture involved more than bronze work. Gold work, *ikat* or tie-dyeing of textile fibers, terracing of mountain slopes, new styles of dwellings, stone statues, female figures in low relief on stone graves, new varieties of handmade pottery, the potter's wheel and wheel-turned wares, plank-built boats, urn burials—these too probably were first introduced into Indonesia as components of the Dong-son culture. But a definite statement is hard to make, for several reasons. Much of southeastern Asia is poorly known archeologically, and recent excavations have focused attention on Thailand as a possible center from which

Neolithic and then Bronze Age culture began to spread at an early date. Perhaps more importantly in the present connection, Indian and Chinese influences reached Indonesia around Dong-son times, thus complicating the problem of Bronze Age beginnings in the islands. Urn burial, originating in China, diffused to Indochina and then Indonesia, but could also have been taken directly to some of the islands by Chinese adventurers. The important technique of *sawah* agriculture was probably known to the Bronze Age people at the Dong-son type-site, but its spread in Indonesia can be credited mostly to Indians at a somewhat later date. Excavation at the mainland type-site yielded one plowshare, but the widespread use of draft animals in Indonesia postdated the Dong-son period. A few iron tools characterize the end of this period, but local life was not much altered by the use of iron, for bronze was satisfactory for most purposes, and it also had beauty. Many Dong-son objects were carefully fashioned in attractive bronze for ceremonial use, with utilitarian counterparts in wood, stone, or other ordinary material. With the Dong-son traits of material culture went a comparably advanced social organization, but its details cannot be determined from the archeological record.

The Dong-son period came to an end in the first century A.D., but the Dong-son left its stamp on later cultures of Viet Nam, Laos, Cambodia, Thailand, Burma, Malaysia, and Indonesia. The statuary and architecture of Indonesia's Buddhist and Hindu period would not be an exact copy of the Indian, but would at first be superimposed upon the Dong-son megalithic tradition. Bronze Age designs and grotesque figures would persist to the present in Indonesian art, and some figures of the *wajang kulit*, the puppet shadow-play, would stem not from Indian but from Dong-son legends. Modern ceremonial weapons would show derivation from Bronze Age prototypes, and Indonesians would retain the Dong-son emphasis on fine craftsmanship with simple tools.

There are, however, some Indonesian themes that clearly derive from China. An archeological problem, still unsolved, is the extent to which the Dong-son culture had Chinese antecedents. Dong-son shows many similarities to the Hallstatt culture of the Danube region, the Thracian and Cimmerian cultures of Hungary, the Bal-

219

kans, and southern Russia, the late Bronze Age of northern Europe, and the early Iron Age of the Caucasus. These similarities, and Chinese history, suggest that there was an actual movement of peoples eastward from Europe and the Caucasus, introducing the Bronze Age into southeastern Asia, and modifying.an older, preexisting Bronze Age farther north in China. The Shang Dynasty, roughly 1700-1100 B.C., was an agricultural society that flourished in the valley of China's Yellow River, where its people cast exceptionally fine bronze implements, worshipped their ancestors, raised crops and livestock, produced silk, glazed their pottery, gathered cowries for trade money, and had a highly developed system of writing. The succeeding dynasty, the Chou, about 1100 to 256 B.C., brought the Yangtze valley under its domination, and sent trading expeditions to Indochina. The Bronze Age levels of the Dong-son type-site yielded a few trade items from Chou China: a sword, mirrors, jade objects. Chou influences reached Indonesia almost simultaneously with Dong-son, and persisted for centuries on some of the islands. In the art styles and handicrafts of Borneo and Flores, especially, Chou influence would remain detectable into modern times. In China the Chou Dynasty was succeeded by the brief (221–206 B.C.) but notably expansionist Ch'in. Annals of the Ch'in Dynasty mention cloves, which courtiers had to chew before approaching the emperor. Since cloves at that time grew only in the Moluccas, Chinese trade with Indonesia may be assumed. The Han Dynasty, 202 B.C. to 220 A.D., greatly expanded China's boundaries and demanded tribute from distant kingdoms, a Han emperor even sending to Sumatra for a living rhinoceros. At Pasemah, an archeological site of eastern Sumatra, megaliths and stone graves are accompanied by statuary and reliefs deriving from the early Han Dynasty.

Chinese written records, coupled with archeological excavations, throw some light on developments immediately following the Dong-son period. The continued growth of China forced more and more people southward into Indochina, but during the first few centuries A.D. Malayo-Polynesian influence remained strong there. According to Chinese accounts, a thriving state grew up in the Mekong Delta. The indigenous name of this state is not known, but the Chinese dubbed it Fu-nan, "Lord of the Mountain," in a belief that its people worshipped volcanos. Fu-nan had been Indianized, and had absorbed an ever-increasing number of Khmers, but Malayo-Polynesians formed a part of its ruling class and a large part of its population. According to Chinese sources, Fu-nan exercised naval control over shipping in the Greater Sundas, especially in Sumatran waters. Evidently, then, the Indonesians were still in contact with their Indochina kin. On the northeast coast of the Indochina Peninsula, centered in the vicinity of present Hue, was another state, which the Chinese dubbed Lini-i. Around the end of the second century A.D., India established a merchant colony here, and its influences resulted in the growth of a thoroughly Indianized state called Champa. Champa's first capital, Indrapura, was near present Da Nang. The Champans became a trading and seafaring people who did not draw a very sharp line between commerce and piracy. Malayo-Polynesians probably formed at least a part of the Champan ruling class and a majority of the population. Fu-nan lasted for only a few centuries before succumbing to the Khmers, but Champa survived for a thousand years before falling to Viets from Annam. The Cham, modern descendants of the Champans, are now clustered, unassimilated, around Phan Rang in South Viet Nam; as noted, their language retains a Malayo-Polynesian base.

It may be surprising that in the latter part of the Dong-son period or soon after, Rome made contact with Indonesia. Sea and caravan routes linked Rome with the East. The Romans knew of a distant land which they called Chryse, and beyond it was Seres where silk was produced. Near the end of the first century A.D. a shipping manual was written, probably by a Roman sea captain who had retired to Alexandria. Sail east (he wrote), keeping the land always to the port side and the sea to starboard. "The very last land as one travels eastward" is Chryse, noted for tortoiseshell; while to the north of Chryse is a land that sends raw silk, silk thread, and silken goods by caravan to Bactria and thence to the Coromandel coast of India. In the second century A.D. the Roman emperor Marcus Aurelius sent a mission to China by way of Viet Nam. Roman coins, lamps, tin discs, and engraved stones, dating from this century, have come to light at scattered localities in the Indochina Peninsula. At Go Oc-Eo in the Mekong Delta of South Viet Nam, a trading center of old Fu-nan has been excavated, yielding objects from the Mediterranean, the Near East, and India, along with others of local manufacture.

Indonesia was involved, albeit somewhat peripherally, in a trade that linked several early Eurasian centers; for the island Malays could offer a variety of luxury goods. Spices, gems, perfumes, fine timbers, tortoiseshell, gold, silver, ivory, rhino horn, and various nostrums were carried from Indonesia to both Rome and China, flourishing civilizations that could afford such products. Also, shipping had advanced to a point where profit could be made from such activities as the warehousing of goods, as well as the provisioning, outfitting, and repairing of ships. Selat Melaka was the gateway from the Pacific to the Indian Ocean, and the ports of Sumatra and Java must have been important way stations in an East-West maritime traffic whose magnitude is just becoming evident.

It can be seen that many characteristics of modern Indonesia were established or foreshadowed by the third or fourth century A.D. The distribution of the physical types was determined: mostly the Papuan in Irian Barat, mostly the Malay elsewhere in the country, the deutero-Malay concentrated coastally and the proto-Malay interiorly, the Melanesian on the Irian Barat north coast, the Australoid virtually obliterated, the Negrito pushed back into the mountains, a mixed type here and there in the Moluccas and the eastern part of the Lesser Sundas. A persistent linguistic dichotomy was established along geographic lines, with Papuan languages predominating in Irian Barat but Malayo-Polynesian ones elsewhere. Yet, the two speech areas were linked, in that there were Papuan and North Halmaheran enclaves in the Malayo-Polynesian area, and Malayo-Polynesian enclaves (Melanesian tongues) in the Papuan. A persistent cultural dichotomy was also brought about along geographic lines, in that Irian Barat remained at a Neolithic level until modern times, while central and especially western Indonesia continued to participate in Eurasian advances. Yet, the country was sufficiently large, and the ecology sufficiently diverse, to permit the survival of many life-ways. Thus, a few tribes retained or reverted to Paleolithic-level hunting and gathering; others continued to live by the waterways in Mesolithic fashion, relying more on sago and other gathered foods than on cultivated crops; still others found Neolithic-level agriculture and husbandry adequate for their needs; and some, although perhaps working more in iron than in bronze, did not pass very far beyond the Dong-son level. The distinction between a coastal trading center and an agricultural area was established in Dong-son times and proved lasting, although it was later refined. Champa if not Fu-nan was a forerunner of the Indianized states that would develop in Indonesia, and the Champan brand of piracy would reappear on the Indonesian seas every time the coasts were not strongly governed. Sumatra, even though a comparatively undeveloped island, began to attain importance soon after the Dong-son period because its east coast and northern tip guarded the Selat Melaka, the safest and best outlet to the Indian Ocean. Shipment of cloves and peppers, from Indonesia to various early kingdoms, would grow into a spice trade over which Western nations would quarrel. And a Western concept of Indonesia, as a land to be despoiled of its riches, can be traced back to the days of the Roman Empire; for Chryse, like El Dorado, is a name meaning "the Golden," and conjuring up a vision of wealth for the taking.

During the first few centuries A.D., parts of Eurasia became so linked that events in one area might soon have repercussions 6,000 miles away. The destiny of Indonesia was to be affected by happenings in distant China and Rome. In its territorial extent, population, and cultural level, the Han Dynasty of China was the equal of its Western contemporary, the Roman Empire. Han China and imperial Rome both came under attack by northern barbarians, struggled to preserve frontiers, and depleted the treasury by militaristic ventures. In both Han China and Rome, generals acquired great power, and the civil administration came to be dominated by the military. In both countries, the civilians' scanty resources were taxed, the coinage was depreciated, and protest groups multiplied. Intellectual life ceased, and there was a rapid decline in skill and taste. In the third century A.D. the Han Dynasty collapsed, to be followed by nearly four centuries of impotent struggle and social unrest. Also in this century, the Roman governmental and economic systems collapsed, although the Empire of the West struggled on for another century or so. With China and Rome in decline, the way was open for some other power to dominate the East-West traffic. Strategically placed and long civilized, India would do so, and would expand its influence in lands along the trade routes. With this emergence of India, Indonesian life would enter a new phase.

CHAPTER VI

# THE INDIAN, ISLAMIC, AND PORTUGUESE PERIODS

MODERN Indonesians often look back on the Indian period of their country's history as a sort of Golden Age. Having won its freedom from the Dutch, Indonesia probably would have called itself by some old Indian or Hindu-Javanese name such as Dvipantara or Nusantara, if these designations had originally been of sufficient geographic scope. Place-names of Indian derivation are still scattered over western Indonesia, and borrowed Sanskrit words abound, especially in the Malayan, Sundanese, Javanese, Madurese, and Balinese languages. The Greater Sundas are dotted with ruins and restorations dating from Buddhist and Hindu times: temples, monuments, statues, tombs. Archeologists studying these constructions often are aided by written records in both Indonesian and Indian languages. Nevertheless, some aspects of the period need further investigation, especially since Indonesian contact was not with a static but with an ever-changing India.

The earliest known inhabitants of India were Negritos who had a Paleolithic culture and who were displaced from many parts of the country by Australoids. Later, several groups of people arrived to further dispossess the Negritos along with the Australoids and Veddoid mixtures. The usurpers were of two or three physical types, of which the best known is the Dravidian. The early Dravidians, basically similar to the Mediterranean peoples of southern Europe, probably were brunet Caucasoids with a high nose and straight to wavy hair; but as time went by, they became considerably mixed with earlier stocks. Many unsolved problems relate to the development of the Neolithic, and then of an early civilization, in India. One widely accepted view of the situation is about as follows: The Dravidians entered India from the west, and so passed through lands where the Neolithic way of life supposedly was first developed. These lands were, of course, the so-called Fertile Crescent, which stretched from the eastern Mediterranean northward and then eastward through Turkey, and thence southeastward through parts of Iraq and Iran. Neolithic culture traits were rapidly introduced into India, by the Dravidians or along the route they had followed. As the Fertile Crescent was the first area to reach the Neolithic level, so was it the first to develop a civilization; and influences from it led some Dravidians, and contemporaries with whom they had mixed, to develop their own version of civilization in the valley of the Indus River. (The valley is now within Pakistan; but for present purposes, Pakistan and Bangladesh may be treated with India as parts of the Indian subcontinent.)

However, the foregoing interpretation of Indian prehistory, although widely accepted, may turn out to require considerable modification. Vast expanses of Asia have not been explored archeologically, and it could not be asserted flatly that the Fertile Crescent led all the rest of the world in cultural advances. Recent archeological work suggests the possibility that both the Neolithic and the Bronze Age are at least as old in Thailand as in the Fertile Crescent, and it is possible that India received many cultural stimuli from lands farther east. Indeed, as far as present knowledge goes, India could have been the hearth, not merely the recipient, of advanced traits in much variety. The most that one can say with assurance is that the Neolithic, and then civilization, spread rapidly in an area extending from the Mediterranean to China; and the scattered Eurasian regions that partook of these advances may also have contributed to them.

As for problems within India, that country's remarkably early civilization seems to have developed in large part out of local antecedents; and while this civilization, the Harappan, received cultural stimuli from other regions, it was not simply imported into the country by foreign invaders from the Fertile Crescent or anywhere else. Harappan cities have yielded human skeletal remains assignable to several physical types, but it is hard to say which of these remains, if any, are those of the city-builders. It is not out of the question that the Harappans were of some ancient Indian stock, perhaps predominantly Australoid.

At any rate, the principal sites of this Indian civilization were at Mohenjo-Daro in Sind, and at Harappa 400 miles north in the Punjab. Many other sites of the Indus Valley civilization have been discovered, revealing an urban culture on a scale vaster than that of Mesopotamia or Egypt. There were walled citadels, ceremonial terraces and monumental gateways, broad streets laid out at right angles, bath-houses, shops, granaries, flour mills, wells, one- and two-story houses. Construction was with well-fired bricks made to a standard size. The city builders were good sanitary engineers, providing bathrooms, sewers, covered drainage canals, cesspools, even rubbish chutes leading from houses to outside bins. The economic foundation included wheat, barley, sesame, dates, peas, and melons. Cotton was raised, spun, and woven. Domestic animals were numerous, including the zebu or humped bull, a short-horned bull, the water buffalo, goat, sheep, pig, dog, cat, camel, horse, ass, elephant, and fowl. Transport was by wheeled vehicle and by boat. There was trade with Sumer, central Asia, southern India, and the western shores of the Bay of Bengal. Copper and bronze were used for weapons and tools, gold and silver for jewelry. Weapons were few, however, suggesting that the people were not warlike. Pottery was wheel-turned, well made although mostly utilitarian and unimaginative. A pictographic writing was in use. The religious system, as disclosed by statuary, engraved seals, and clay figurines, foreshadowed that of later India, for a Mother Goddess was worshipped, the bull was sacred, and one local god was a prototype of

Shiva. Only a strong, centralized government could have built this complex urban civilization. The rulers, probably priest-kings, were autocratic and conservative, for all the Indus Valley cities were remarkably alike, and they changed very little with time.

This early civilization flourished from about 2300 B.C. to 1600 B.C. Its decline may have in part reflected its rigidity and placidity, but its downfall was at the hands of the Aryans. These people were tall Caucasoids, light-skinned, some probably with blue-gray eyes and chestnut or brown hair. They came from the steppes of southern Russia, moving east of the Caspian into Iran, and thence eastward through the mountain passes into northwestern India. Agricultural and pastoral, the Aryans were in search of a new home. They arrived in India as a series of waves over a period of several hundred years, conquering the lands of the Indus, then the Jumna, next the Ganges. They fought in the Homeric fashion, the commoners on foot, the aristocrats from chariots, using bow and arrow, sword, and axe. Glorying in warfare, they would even fight each other, and in times of peace the warriors kept fit by hunting such dangerous game as lion and wild boar. Strongly racist in their views, the Aryans were contemptuous of any darker peoples, whose cities were looked upon as treasure troves to be looted. In their early writings, the Aryans usually refer to their Indian predecessors as "black-skins" or "flat-noses."

The Middle East and India together were the homeland of several so-called "revealed" faiths, religious creeds and sects alleged to have had divine inspiration. Beginning perhaps around 1500 B.C. or not long thereafter, the Aryans in northern India began to compose the *Rigveda*, a collection of hymns and magic spells attributed to such inspiration. At first these were handed down orally, but eventually they were written in the Aryans' language, Sanskrit. For several centuries, down to about 1000 B.C., the Aryans continued to enlarge the *Rigveda*. In time, to it were added the *Samaveda*, a hymn-book; the *Yajurveda*, with prose prayers and spells; and finally the *Atharvaveda*, with incantations reflecting Dravidian influence. This body of literature is called the Vedas. (The word Veda simply means "knowledge"; its Sanskrit root-word, *vid*, is cognate with English "wit," "wise," and "vision.") The Brahmanas, theologi-

228

cal treatises and rituals, appeared from the eighth century B.C. on; and around the sixth century B.C. the Upanishads were composed as divinely inspired philosophical and metaphysical tracts. Finally, the Sutras embodied much law, ceremonial, and ritual.

From the various Sanskrit writings one can get some idea of Aryan thought and its gradual modification through contact with Dravidians and other peoples. The early Aryan attitude toward life, as shown by the religion, was vigorous, optimistic, and objective. The gods were nature gods, benevolent enough if approached with the proper rituals. Indra was the most human of the Aryan deities: pot-bellied and strong-armed, a great eater and drinker, a hero-warrior who rode in a golden chariot and was armed with a thunderbolt. Varuna (possibly identical with Uranus) was an exalted sky deity who ruled the universe and saw into the hearts of men, while Rudra dispensed rain and controlled the whirlwind. Agni was a personification of fire, and the hearth of each house was his altar. And there were other gods. But Aryan thought was altered by that of the Dravidians and of the mixed peoples who had built the Indus Valley civilization. It is customary to say that from a combination of Aryan, Dravidian, and Harappan beliefs, Hinduism was born, although there may also have been continuing influence from the Middle East.

One concept of the early Aryans was that of a holy trinity, the first triad being Varuna, Mitra, and Aryaman, all probably of Iranian origin. More characteristically Aryan was the triad composed of Vayu, Agni, and Surya; or of Indra, Agni, and Surya. (Modern Indonesian personal names sometimes hearken back to these Vedic deities.) It is likely that a single, ancient body of metaphysical speculation gave rise to both the Christian and the early Aryan notions of three gods in one, but parallels between the Christian Trinity and the Aryan Trimurti ("trinity" in Sanskrit) have been overdrawn in Western literature; for trinitarianism in the Western sense was at best a minor development within the complex Hindu polytheism.

The history of Indian theology need not be detailed here. Suffice it to say that the Aryans eventually focused their speculations upon three gods: Brahma, Vishnu, and Shiva. Brahma was the supreme god and creator, somewhat remote although every man's soul was a part of him. Vishnu was the preserver of the world and had many incarnations, one of them being Krishna, who was dark in color and probably of Dravidian origin. Devotion to Krishna led to personal salvation. Shiva, third member of the triad, personified death and destruction, and was to be feared rather than adored. Shiva had begun as a diety of the Indus Valley civilization, but was identified with the Aryan Rudra. At the base of Hindu metaphysics was the concept of a world soul, Brahman or *atman*. (The latter Sanskrit word is cognate with English "animate.") Man's spirit was taken to be a part of something immortal and universal, a notion appearing about a century later in Greek writings also. *Samsara* was metempsychosis, repeated rebirth of the soul. Nothing was permanent, for even the gods must die; but even death was not permanent, for the soul was continuously reborn into one body after another. The sum of past actions, *karma*, determined the present abode of the soul. *Moksha*, a cessation of rebirth and a union with Brahman, was the ultimate aim, but could be attained only through the realization that the world was illusion. Matter must be disavowed and life regarded as a burden to be escaped. Early, orthodox Hinduism was thus a religion of pessimism, quite unlike the buoyant views held by the Aryans when they first came to India, and written down by them in the *Rigveda*.

The doctrine of *karma*, whereby a man's condition was predestined as a result of behavior in previous incarnations, had great possibilities for control of the masses by an elite, since protest of the status quo could be considered sacrilege. Other Aryan concepts contributed even more to social stability. At first the Aryans merely drew a color line, *varna*. They themselves were on one side of the line, while on the other side were all the darker peoples. The Indus Valley civilization had made considerable use of slaves who were obtained principally from early stocks, and so the slave peoples were automatically placed on the dark side of the color line. Today, the term *varna* is sometimes used to designate a class group, four of which were erected by the Aryans. Highest of these groups was the Brahman, its members forming a priestly and scholarly elite whose esoteric knowledge was thought capable of influencing and even coercing the gods. Below the Brahmans were the Kshatriyas, made up of secular and military commanders. (To modern Indonesians, whose heritage includes Hindu thought, *ksatria* is a nobleman or knight, and *ksatriaan* could be translated as chivalry.) Next came the Vaishyas, the commoners such as farmers, traders, and artisans; and still farther down the scale were the Shudras, who were slaves, serfs, servants, menials generally. The first three classes were made up of Aryans, the fourth of non-Aryans. Finally, some people were outside the class system, and their very touch might be defiling.

In India, as in Indonesia, some ethnic groups had been pushed back into unfavorable habitats or out-of-the-way places, and many others had taken up a specialized way of life in adjustment to the immediate environment. In other words, the Hindus found a ready-made basis upon which the defined class groups might be subdivided, in time, into a graded series of castes. Subcastes and mixed castes were eventually recognized, while positions were made for new immigrants into the country. Some castes were based on occupation, such as barber, washerman, or bard; others followed tribal lines and included descendants of early stocks; still others were sectarian, or otherwise produced by fission from an already existing caste. "Untouchability" was a convenient limbo for the offspring of unions that were not approved by society, and for people expelled from their caste for offenses. Each class had its own *dharma*, a set of rules governing marriage, diet, other customs, sometimes occupation. *Dharma* was supposed to have divine approval; and caste membership, determined by birth, was inalterable except through expulsion into untouchable status. Although ramifying in complex ways, the caste system retained strong racist overtones, at least in that the fair-skinned Aryans were at the top while the dark aborigines were at the bottom. It is interesting to note that many centuries after the Aryans had devised this social system, the early Portuguese explorers gave it a name that had much the same connotation as the Sanskrit *varna*. The Portuguese word was *casta*, meaning "race" or "color," and it was as a result of Portuguese insight that Westerners came to speak of a "caste" system in India.

The early, orthodox Hinduism, or Brahmanism as it is sometimes called, imposed a social system that was not received everywhere with the same enthusiasm, although opposition to it came from directions that might not have been anticipated. To the south, where the aboriginal stocks and lower castes were concentrated, the system generally held firm. It was to the north that unrest developed, partly because new peoples continued to arrive through the mountain passes but also because the secular rulers were perturbed by the growing strength of the Brahmans. In the Ganges Basin, especially, there arose many schools of more or less anti-Brahmanistic thought, claiming divine inspiration and assuredly having princely blessing. Schism began as early as the sixth century B.C. The Upanishads, later called Vedanta, "Vedas' end," were more of Kshatriya than Brahman origin, and from them grew an ideology that opposed polytheism, rejected ritual, lauded inquiry over dogma, and concerned itself especially with man's spirit as a part of the universal soul. Turning from good works and priestly mediation, Upanishadic Brahmanism advocated a personal, mystic approach to Brahman, who might be reached through moral behavior, devotion to one god, meditation, and asceticism. But the Upanishadic variety of Brahmanism reflected the non-Aryan pessimism and world-weariness, proclaiming that the world was illusion, *maya;* escape from life was desirable but was obtainable only by the few. Another school of thought was founded by Vardhamana, a princely Kshatriya born in the sixth century B.C., perhaps as early as 540 B.C. In middle age he abandoned worldy life, took to meditation and asceticism, and received enlightenment. Thereafter he was called Mahavira, "Great Hero," and his doctrine came to be known as Jainism. Mahavira preached not in courtly Sanskrit but in a commoners' dialect, condemning Brahman tyranny, ignoring the Vedas, and disavowing the caste system. Recognizing no deities, he believed that a supernatural force resided in men, beasts, plants, minerals, the earth, fire, and various manifestations of nature. Souls of men, beasts, etc. were all reincarnated, and all looked forward to breaking the material bonds. *Ahimsa,* nonviolence, was therefore imperative: harm neither a person nor any other living thing. Poverty, chastity, honesty, truth, and respect for all living things—these led a man into right thinking, which, with contemplation and the suppression of earthly passions, might break the cycle of rebirth. Like orthodox and Upanishadic Brahmanism, Jainism was pessimistic, regarding life as a burden to be escaped.

The Indian period of Indonesia is often referred to as a Hindu or Hinduist period. To the average Westerner such reference would suggest Brahmanism with a rigid caste structure and three gods, but it will be seen that Hinduism became a faith of surpassing flexibility. Jainism, taken to be reformed Hinduism, and some other sects dispensed with deities entirely; while on the other hand, the three principal Hindu gods could encompass a wide pantheon, since many other gods could be designated as reincarnations of Hindu ones. Furthermore, the deities were sometimes imagined as having a personal life, with retainers, consorts, and progeny; thus, the old cult of the Mother Goddess could be retained by regarding her as a god's consort or mother; and some tribal god, if not qualifying as an incarnation of a Hindu deity, could be identified as the offspring of a divine union. Animism could be subsumed under Hinduism, for example through the Jainist view that a soul resided in rocks, trees, etc. Animistic worship of the bull, which began with the Neolithic predecessors of the Harappans, did not conflict with Hinduism, for the animal could be thought of as symbolizing or as having been ridden by a god. Phallic worship was easily linked with the bull and a powerful male deity, Shiva. On a more secular level, it was possible to question Brahman authority and ritual, to modify the caste system or disavow it; and dissenters were not silenced. In Indonesia, the deutero-Malay bearers of the Dong-son culture were ready to advance beyond the Bronze Age, and the direction of their advance was determined by contact with India. Aryan-Harappan-Dravidian thought had progressed beyond the Indonesian, but not so far beyond that contact with it would be traumatic; and the flexibility of Indian metaphysics was such that Dong-son Indonesians could incorporate their beliefs in it without being made to feel embarrassingly backward. Thus, the spread of Indian culture was generally welcomed in southeastern Asia, and there is reason to think that deutero-Malay principalities of Indonesia invited Indian participation in their development.

One further theological development in India must be recounted. A major creed was founded by Siddhartha, of the family Gautama. A princely Kshatriya, he was born in 563 B.C. in the Himalayan foothills near the Nepal border. Even before middle age he became depressed with widespread human misery, and so abandoned earthly ways to embark upon a life of asceticism and meditation. Failing to receive the desired enlightenment, he gave up the regimen. According to tradition, he was sitting under a pipul-tree (a Ficus that had been sacred to animistic Harappans) when he was assailed by Mara, the prince of darkness, who tried to frighten and tempt him away from his urge to save suffering humanity. Withstanding the assault, Siddhartha received the desired revelation and thereafter was the Buddha, the "enlightened one." The Buddha taught the Middle Way, an avoidance of extreme self-indulgence but also of self-torturing asceticism. He taught the Eightfold Path: kindness to all living things, purity of heart, truthfulness, and charity, as well as abstention from fault-finding, covetousness, hatred, and violence. He taught certain commandments: do not kill, steal, commit adultery, lie, speak evil, stir up trouble, become angry, or embrace heresy. Later, the Buddha stated the Four Noble Truths: that existence is sorrow, sorrow stems from desire and the thirst for continued existence, the sorrow and thirst that lead to rebirth must be removed, and they can be removed by following the Eightfold Path. Thus, Buddhism is pessimistic, declaring all existence to be sorrow, human existence pain. Yet, deliverance is possible, and not just to a few but to all. The Buddha never tried to be an overt social reformer. He did not preach against the caste system but simply ignored it; nor did he specifically reject the Hindu gods. He had little to say about *atman* or about a supreme deity. But he spread the idea that man is not a helpless slave of the supernatural; he can achieve his own salvation through a combination of works and knowledge. The Buddha's teachings were written down first in Pali (a language related to Sanskrit) as the *Tripitaka*, "three baskets." Around the *Tripitaka* were collected the *Jatakas*, tales about the life and times of the Buddha. Centuries later, many of these tales—the marriage feast, the prodigal son, the temptation by the devil, the dining with sinners, the rich young man seeking deliverance, the woman at the well, and others—would be worked into the Christian mythology.

The *Tripitaka* and the *Jatakas* form the basis of Theravada Buddhism. Even in the most advanced modern countries, an intellectual religion is beyond many people, who must have mystical, magical mumbo-jumbo instead; and it is not surprising that the Buddha's lofty approach was debased after his death. Dubbed the Hinayana, "lesser vehicle," the original message was replaced by the Mahayana, "greater vehicle," in which the Buddha, who never taught a Deity, was himself converted into one. With this step Buddhism was turned back toward Hinduism, for the Buddha could be regarded as an incarnation of a Hindu deity, and a tribal god could be retained as a reincarnation of the Buddha. In time, Buddhism practically vanished from its homeland, but not before it was exported to many lands, including Indonesia. Indian missionaries took Buddhism to the east, while the Persians, whose temporary conquest of India was beginning in the Buddha's day, carried Hindu-Buddhist thought to the west where it later reappeared in several guises.

Then came the Buddha's antithesis, the young Alexander of Macedon, bitter and uncertain of his paternity, but certain that he would use his inherited power, the strength that his elders had built, to conquer the world and establish himself as its deity. Entering India from the west, he did indeed oust the Persians and establish a Greek rule, albeit a brief one. This curious interlude in Indian history had two effects in Indonesia. One was minor: many centuries thereafter, Sumatran and Malaccan rulers would claim descent from Iskander, that is from al-Iskander, Alexander. The other effect was more important. Indian religious art and sculpture had indicated the Buddha's presence only by an empty throne or by footprints, but the Greeks introduced the idea that deities could be portrayed as people. And so the Buddha was portrayed in India —sometimes as a sleek Apollo, other times as a Greek philosopher complete with a robe in classical folds. Graeco-Buddhist art reached Indonesia. There could be no better example of cultural synthesis than an Indonesian sculpture clearly deriving from the megalithic tradition, but showing the deified Indian sage with the pose and features of an Olympian. And under Greek influence the stupa, originally a mound covering a pinch of the Buddha's ashes or some other holy relic, was elaborated into an architectural work of which a stone hemisphere was the most important feature.

It is customary to say that by the first century A.D., Indonesia had become known to India, Rome, and China; but this date is a conservative one. The *Rigveda* mentions voyages eastward around the shores of the Bay of Bengal, and it is likely that the Greater Sundas were known to the early Aryans. The *Jatakas* mention trading voyages eastward around the bay shores to the Malay Peninsula and Sumatra. The Indians were in search of luxury goods for their western trade, and offered cotton cloth which was in much demand in southeastern Asia. An eastward movement of Indians began around the fourth century B.C., points of departure first being from Kalinga (later called Orissa) on the northern shores of the Bay of Bengal. Points of departure for later movements were progressively farther south along the bay's west shore. Even today in Indonesia, Indians are called *Kalinga,* a circumstance suggesting early contact with the state of that name (although other interpretations are possible). Migrants from India were not numerous in Indonesia, but they took important positions there, led the process of Indianization, and facilitated trade. Late in the fourth century B.C., India was strongly united under Chandragupta Maurya. Early in the third century B.C., Chandragupta's grandson, Ashoka, wiped out 100,000 unruly Dravidians in Orissa, became remorseful, and adopted Buddhism which he put into practice and exported to many lands through missionaries. Although Buddhism would decline in India, it would take root in Indonesia and elsewhere. Beginning in the second century B.C., the Scythians moved into the southern Punjab and began to conquer India. The Scythians were allied with the Parthians who had enemies farther west, and the Scythian takeover severed Indian trade connections to the west; so connections to the east therefore became more important. In the first century A.D., the Dong-son period came to an end in Indonesia through the accumulation of ideas from India; and by the opening of the second century A.D., with Indianization spreading from Sumatra to Java, Borneo, and southern Sulawesi, the Greater Sundas were metamorphosing into Dvipantara, the "island empire." Political subdivisions within Dvipantara were emerging, with Java and southern Sumatra set apart as Yavadvipa. There is mention of a Sumatran state called Srivijaya (Sriwidjaja in Indonesian spelling), destined to rise.

Around this time, southern India became important as a way-station in the east-west maritime traffic, because the Arabs and Greeks had discovered the reliability of the southwest monsoonal winds. Previously, western ships had reached India by a long voyage around the coasts of the Arabian Sea, but it became evident that in the proper season, a large ship could sail directly from Arabia to India in less than three weeks. Goods reached India from the west in Arab, Egyptian, and Greek vessels, but were transshipped to the lands farther east in Indian vessels with Indian crew and passengers. Thus, Indonesian trade relationships were especially with India. One major sea lane, an easterly continuation of the monsoon route, left Kattiara (near modern Tuticorin), swung southward around Ceylon, crossed the Bay of Bengal to the Nicobars, then passed to the Atjeh coast of northern Sumatra, and so on across the Selat Melaka to the Malay Peninsula. A branch route extended down the coast of the peninsula to the Riaus. By the fourth century A.D., in parts of the Malay Peninsula closely connected with Indonesia, people were using the South Indian Pallava script to carve Mahayana Buddhist inscriptions. By the fifth century A.D., numerous pirate ships were preying on the rich traffic in the Selat Melaka. A Chinese monk, Fa Hsien, noted that there was little Buddhism in Indonesia, but that there were Brahmanist cults on Java and Sumatra, with Shiva-worship predominating. During this century, Dvipantara was becoming divided into several rival states or kingdoms. (Modern political terminology cannot be applied accurately to early Asian territorial subdivisions, which were spheres of influence rather than sharply bounded areas.) Southeastern Sumatra was called Jaya, and north of it was Malayu, or Melaju in modern Indonesian spelling. At the western end of Java was the state of Taruma; could it have been named for *tarum*, the indigoplant prized and cultivated by Indians for its rich blue dye? Traditionally, Buddhism reached Sumatra in the year 424 A.D., and the island has yielded Buddhist inscriptions dating from approximately this time. Other inscriptions reveal Brahmanist and Hindu beliefs in western and central Java during the fifth century A.D., and the development of a Hindu state in eastern Borneo. Buddhist inscriptions, as well as Hindu and Buddhist images in the Gupta style, are also known from eastern Borneo at this time.

By the sixth century A.D., Dvipantara was a complex of Indianized kingdoms. The west coast of Sumatra was Jambudvipa, inland and north of which was Menangkabu, in other words the country of the Minangkabau, who resisted many aspects of Indianization but who were too numerous to be ignored. Yavadvipa was now called Java, with Taruma at its western end and a state called Kalinga at its center. Bali became known and Indianized, while Borneo and Sulawesi continued to form Dvipantara's eastern periphery. But the most important developments were in southeastern Sumatra, part of which was occupied by a kingdom called Malayur or Malayu, with a focus near present Djambi. South of Malayu was Sriwidjaja, with its focus near present Palembang. Strategically located to guard the Selat Melaka, Sriwidjaja was a crucial link in trade all the way from Arabia to China, and it flourished accordingly. Its rulers were Mahayana Buddhists, and the Buddhist faith was nourished in Indonesia even while declining in India. By the seventh century A.D., Sriwidjaja had surpassed Fu-nan as the dominant political and commercial power in tropical southeastern Asia. The boundaries of Sriwidjaja were extended to encompass Bangka and western Java, but the kingdom's influence was felt more widely. With the rise of Sriwidjaja, Indonesia was no longer the mere recipient of peoples and ideas from mainland Asia, but was a cultural center to which other lands could look for enlightenment. In the meanwhile, Buddhism had spread to China; and Palembang, a Buddhist center in Sriwidjajan times, became an important stopping-place for Chinese Buddhists en route to the holy lands of India.

The Dong-son and earlier periods of Indonesia are known principally from tangible relics, and so it is gratifying to be able to discuss the Indian period in terms of metaphysical and philosophical concepts, especially since these were, in a manner of speaking, among India's most significant exports to the Far East. But advanced ideas flourish best in an appropriate economic and social setting, and India's material contributions to Indonesia must not be overlooked. From the beginning of the Indian period if not sooner, Indonesia was involved with some complex cultural diffusions. As mentioned previously, the generally accepted view is that the Middle East reached the Neolithic level, and then the level of civilization, a bit ahead of any other area. From a Middle East center, the Neolithic and then early civilization spread west around the Mediterranean and east to the Yellow River of China, leaving tropical southeastern Asia as a sort of backwater into which ideas drifted slowly. But agriculture, pottery, and polished stone tools—hallmarks of the Neolithic—were known in Thailand at an extremely early date, and bronze implements appeared there about as soon as they did in Mesopotamia. Thus, the deutero-Malay bearers of the Dong-son culture may have taken to the islands some advanced ideas which, in the present state of knowledge, are credited to the Indian period but which might have arrived earlier, from Thailand. The situation is further complicated by the Indianization of Indochina, and the likelihood that many Indian ideas reached Indonesia not directly but by way of Indochina.

At any rate, it is possible to cite cultural changes that were wrought in Indonesia by the Indians, whether through the introduction of new practices or through emphasis on preexisting ones. While rice may have first been domesticated in Thailand, wet-rice cultivation in *sawah* is associated with India. The Harappans and early Aryans had cultivated such grains as wheat and barley, but by 450 B.C. the Tamils of India's southwestern tropics were producing a surplus of rice for export to Greece. A century or so later, Chandragupta's empire was relying heavily on rice, two crops of which could be harvested annually. While the technique of wet-rice cultivation perhaps reached Indonesia in Dong-son times, it spread during the Indian period, and the *sawah* areas of the country are practically coextensive with those of Indian influence. As already noted, the arrival of the deutero-Malays established a cultural dichotomy in Indonesia, in that their settlements became the nuclei of trading kingdoms while the rest of the country remained agricultural. This scheme was further refined during the Indian period, in that some areas were given over to wet-rice in *sawah* while others remained centers of *ladang* agriculture. The trichotomy has persisted to the present, and works on modern Indonesia usually recognize three broad categories into which most of the population can be subdivided: (1) The wet-rice growers, who are by far the most numerous, and whose way of life has been minimally altered by the tides of history; (2) the coastal peoples, originally traders, still inclined toward pursuits that can be carried on near the sea, and the principal Indonesian heirs to Muslim religion and merchant tradition; and (3) the interior or otherwise isolated tribespeople, gatherers of sago or else *ladang* cultivators of dry-rice, maize, or root crops, sometimes Westernized by Christian missionaries, to whose proselytization they were exceptionally vulnerable.

To the Indians must also go the credit for popularizing wheeled vehicles and draft animals in Indonesia. The wheel is often cited as one of man's most significant discoveries, but it did not particularly interest peoples who had no domestic hoofed beasts. Bullocks and *kerbau* were useful not only in drawing carts but also in plowing, a valuable agricultural practice but one that is impractical with human labor only. The horse, also introduced in Indian times, probably was more showy than useful. Wheel-turning of pottery, while perhaps dating back to Dong-son times, was encouraged during the Indian period. It is a superior technique to hand-modeling in that it is comparatively rapid, one potter readily supplying the needs of an entire village, and developing the ceramic art as a specialty. Although the Dong-son smiths worked magnificently in bronze, they had much to learn from the Indians, whose castings in iron could not be excelled. During the Indian period, tapa cloth was replaced in parts of Dvipantara by woven goods, mostly cottons but also silks for the elite; and the art of weaving was given local impetus.

Materials, objects, and techniques, first introduced into Indonesia by the Indians, often were called by their Sanskrit name. Accordingly, it is revealing to look at a few Sanskrit-derived words in Malayan. *Angsa* is a domestic goose, *dadih* is curds or curdled milk, *gembala* a shepherd—words indicative of animal husbandry.

Although indigenous names for the elephant exist in Indonesia, its commonest name, *gadjah*, is from the Sanskrit; and so is the word *kusa*, an elephant-goad. Troops of war elephants made a great impression on the Indonesians, and were regarded as irresistible. *Nila* is the indigo plant's bluish dye; and *tjuka* is vinegar from wine. The word *badja* originally meant something added for its strength-giving quality, especially manure added to the soil, or some chemical added to iron to harden it. Today, *badja* means manure, or steel, or a dentifrice made from coconut milk and iron rust, used for blackening and supposedly strengthening the teeth. In Malayan, glass is called by a Sanskrit-derived name, *katja*, the glazier's art having introduced by the Indians. *Rata* is a chariot, *gergadji* a saw, *ketjapi* a harp or lyre, *djentera* a wheel, *suasa* a gold-copper alloy, *sutera* silk; Sanskrit loan-words all.

As a matter of fact, Sanskrit loan-words reveal much more about the Indian period than details of material culture. Strictly speaking, the speech of the early Aryans might be called Vedic, for the term Sanskrit, "perfected," was not coined until the fourth century B.C. when the language had become the property of the Brahman priests and scholars. In the meanwhile, popular dialects called the Prakrits had emerged, and from them grew important modern Indian languages such as Hindi, Bengali, Marathi, Punjabi, Kashmiri, and others. There is a close parallel with the way in which classical Latin persisted as a priestly tongue in Europe, while Latin vulgate was transformed into various Romance languages such as French, Spanish, Italian, Portuguese, and Rumanian. Borrowings into Malayan seem mostly to be from the actual Sanskrit, not a Prakrit; and it is clear that the Indianization of Indonesia was being directed by Brahman priests and scholars, not by merchants or military men. A great many of these borrowings obviously are from the priestly jargon: words meaning religion, negligence, perverse, withstand, almsgiving, evil, sin, sorrow, incense, incarnation, falsehood, covetousness, hell, fasting, ritual, suffering, fidelity, heaven, penance, asceticism, tribulation, adversary, assimilated, tranquility, the heavens, evil spirit, magic spell, supernatural power, book of spells, god, goddess, nymph, goblin. The list could be added to, but even without addition one can easily imagine the nature of a Brahmanic sermon in the days of Dvipantara. Further Malayan borrowings from Sanskrit today appear scholarly, although Brahman scholarship was not readily separable from religion. In this category are words meaning wisdom, the earth, the Milky Way, a cubit, a letter of the alphabet, a teacher (*guru*), a scholar, an astrologer, an eclipse, the game of chess. Still other borrowings from Sanskrit have a legal air: words meaning witness or evidence, injury, judicial discussion, stratagem, a fine, jail, property or wealth, investigate or inquire, guesswork, instance or precedent, a stake for impalement of criminals.

As might be expected from the Aryan outlook, Malayan abounds with Sanskrit-derived terms relating to position, rank, social standing, and regal pomp. Thus, *abentara* is a court herald, *anugerah* is a gift to an inferior, *bahtera* is a state barge, *makota* a crown, *karunja* a gift from a god or a king (but now any favor), *menteri* a minister, *penggawa* a court official, *permaisuri* (literally "appearing beautiful") a queen, *perwira* a hero or warrior (but today simply meaning gallant). *Bangsawan* means of noble birth, *hina* is common or low, *dina* is mean or unfortunate, *mulia* is illustrious. While Malayan had words meaning husband and wife, the corresponding Sanskrit terms, respectively *suami* and *isteri*, were borrowed as being especially polite designations.

The Sanskrit loan-words now have a distinctive Bahasa Indonesia spelling, and some of them no longer have quite their original meanings. *Bahasa* is now the generally used word for "language," but a clue to its earlier connotation is provided by the phrase *kurang bahasa*, actually "rudeness" but literally an "insufficiency of speech." When the word *bahasa* was borrowed into Malayan, it had the meaning of courtly speech which was inseparable from courtly manners. *Sahaja*, or *saja* in Bahasa Indonesia, is now translated as "I" and generally used as the polite first-person singular; but it once had the meaning of "servant," and was used when speaking of one's self to a ruler. Several Malayan words, borrowed from Sanskrit, were intended for use in describing the activities of royalty, leaving the Malayo-Polynesian equivalents to describe the behavior of the masses. There is a parallel to the way Latinities acquired prestige at the expense of Anglo-Saxonisms after the Norman conquest of England.

The cultural heart of Dvipantara was southern Sumatra east of the Pegunungan Barisan, along with western and central Java. There were also close ties with Suvarnadvipa, the southwestern part of the Malay Peninsula. The principal languages of this general area—Malayan, Sundanese, and Javanese—were the ones most noticeably affected by Indian thought, although Madurese, Balinese, Makasarese, and Buginese also came to know Sanskrit influence. Most strongly affected by Indian concepts was Javanese, which developed different vocabularies to express the same idea, a choice among them depending on the age, official position, and social status of the person addressed. (Sukarno once stated that he could recognize 13 Javanese "speech levels.") It had far more speakers than any other Indonesian language, but this complexity and extreme emphasis on class distinction led to its rejection as the official language of modern Indonesia.

In the days of Dvipantara, a lingua franca was needed in the islands. Sanskrit would not serve, for it was the special property of the elite; and so the use of Malayan was encouraged. Sriwidjajan inscriptions from Sumatra are in this tongue. Of special interest are the Gandasuli inscriptions of central Java, dating from 827 and 832 A.D., for even though they are in the heart of the Javanese speech area, they are in Malayan. A literature began to grow as several Indonesian languages made use of scripts from India.

The Indian period saw considerable change within Indonesia. Theravada Buddhism reached the islands, but was replaced on Sumatra and Java by Mahayana Buddhism. Sumatra remained primarily Buddhist, but Hinduism eventually prevailed on Java. Traffic with India varied, sometimes being largely with Gujarat, at other times with Orissa or Bengal. The balance of power fluctuated in the islands, and the eighth century was marked by the appearance of new kingdoms. Mataram arose in central Java to vie with Sriwidjaja. Under a ruler named Sandjaja (reigned 732–760), Mataram extended its authority into western Java, parts of Sumatra, and Bali. On the Dieng Plateau of Java, temples were built to Shiva, favorite deity of Mataram which was Brahmanist in religion and culture. Toward the latter part of the eighth century, the Sailendra Dynasty (reigned 760–860 in Java) unified the Sumatran and Javan kingdoms, and around 772 A.D., in Java near the present

Djokjakarta, the second Sailendra began constructing Borobudur, the greatest monument to Mahayana Buddhism. No western cathedral rivals it in magnitude. A vast and elaborated stupa built around a hilltop, Borobudur includes 2,000,000 cubic feet of dressed stone, 20,000 square feet of low reliefs illustrating Buddhist texts, more than 500 images of the Buddha, galleries, and terraces with stairs. Although Persian, Babylonian, and Greek influences can be seen in Borobudur's art and architecture, the monument has many peculiarly Indonesian characteristics; for example, the reliefs depict Javanese people in a Javan setting. Borobudur may have been erected to encourage Buddhism, the Sailendras' faith, in a land where Shiva-worship was spreading. During the Sailendras' reign, much Sanskrit literature was translated into Javanese. By the ninth century there was syncretism in Java, the people regarding Shiva and the Buddha as incarnations of the same being. Late in the ninth century, the Sailendra empire split into Javan and Sumatran components, so that for a time one branch of the Sailendra family ruled Sriwidjaja, and another central Java. The fortunes of the Javanese Sailendras declined, but the kingdom of Mataram thrived under new rulers who returned to Brahmanistic Shiva worship and who built some appropriate monuments, those of Prambanan near Djokjakarta. The largest of these monuments is to Shiva but others are to Vishnu and Brahma. The Mataram capital was moved to East Java, where the kingdom grew politically and culturally, and where a Hindu-Javanese literature was composed. The daughter of a Mataram prince married a Balinese prince, and took with her to Bali the beliefs of her people.

Meanwhile, on Sumatra the Sailendras carried Sriwidjaja to new heights, especially through monopoly of the spice trade, which was becoming internationally important. Sailendra authority spread to Malayu on Sumatra, Johore on the Malay Peninsula, ports on the Selat Sunda, and some parts of Java. A Sriwidjajan prince even became ruler of Cambodia, extending Indonesian influence in Indochina. The Khmer empire, with a capital at Angkor, was begun by a Sailendra, Jayavarman II. Sriwidjajan colonies were established in the Moluccas and the southern Philippines, while commercial settlements were founded on Borneo and the Sulus to handle trade with China's T'ang and Sung dynasties. Eventually, Sriwidjajan commercial settlements were established as far away as Formosa and Hainan.

The acme of Sriwidjajan political and commercial importance was attained by the early eleventh century. Around that time, Sriwidjaja temporarily conquered Mataram and destroyed its capital; but then Sriwidjaja was itself attacked from India, by Tamils from the Indian state of Chola. Much had changed in India, where the Dravidians of the Deccan and the Tamil Plateau, late to receive Aryan influence, had come into their own. Three Tamil states arose, each trying to conquer the other two. One of them, Chola, attacked Ceylon, and received tribute from Malacca and Java. In the year 1025 under Rajendra Choladeva I, Chola launched a great fleet against Sriwidjaja, the Malay Peninsula, northern Sumatra, and the Nicobars, lands from which pressure could be brought to bear on the Selat Melaka and the traffic that had to pass through it. The Cholans smashed through to Palembang at the heart of Sriwidjaja, but the kingdom recovered from the blow, and was able to withstand succeeding Cholan raids over a period of 35 years. Yet, during this time, Sriwidjaja lost its hold on Mataram, and thereafter declined slowly. Malayu, centered around Djambi but a near-vassal to Java, rose as Sriwidjajan power waned. East Java also grew stronger, especially under the king Airlangga (ruled 1019–1049) whose capital was at Kediri. East Java controlled the Moluccas, traded with Borneo and Sumatra, and reduced Bali and Ternate to vassalage. At that time, the religion of East Java was Hinduism, with emphasis on Vishnu worship; but the priests grew too strong for the liking of the rulers, and from the resulting power struggle a new dynasty emerged. In 1222 A.D. the East Java capital was transferred to Singhasari (Singosari) near present Malang. Its official faith was the Buddha-Shiva syncretism. Dvipantara came to be known as Singhasari, East Javanese influence extending as far as parts of Sumatra, the Malay Peninsula, eastern Borneo, and the Moluccas.

The last ruler of Singhasari, the warrior-king Kertanegara, strengthened his kingdom, and fortunate it was that he could do so, for a new and dangerous force was abroad in Asia: the Mongols of Kublai Khan. The ships of the great Khan reached Java, bringing an envoy who demanded submission, and Kertanegara sent him back with a negative reply tattooed across his face. The insult would be avenged by Kublai Khan. But while the Khan was gathering a punitive fleet at Canton, Kertanegara was slain by palace rivals, and his son-in-law, Widjaja, founded a new dynasty with a capital at what was then a minor town, Madjapahit. When a thousand troop-ships of the Khan reached Java in 1293, Widjaja welcomed the Mongols and guided them to Kediri, convincing them that the Kediri ruler had been responsible for mistreating their envoy. The Khan's troops took Kediri, but their ranks were thinned and dispersed in the process. Then Widjaja threw his fresh Madjapahit soldiery against the tired Mongols, who suffered heavy losses and who evacuated the island as rapidly as possible. The Mongol hordes had been able to plant their sun-and-moon standard far and wide across Eurasia, under the broad blue sky which they worshipped animistically; but they went down to bitter defeat when confronted with the guile and the military strength of Widjaja. And for generations thereafter, Indonesian boys might be given a name meaning "Widjaja the Victorious."

The new Javan state, called Madjapahit after its first capital, soon forged ahead of all others, especially in the days of Hajam Wuruk (ruled 1350–1389). Under the guidance of Gadjah Mada, chief minister from 1331 to 1364, Madjapahit extended its sphere of influence widely, eventually encompassing southeastern Sumatra, Bangka and Belitung, the Anambas and the Natunas, all of Java but the western end, Madura, Bali, eastern Timor, western Ceram, Buru, the Sulas and Banggais, Obi, Batjan, western Halmahera, extreme northern and extreme southern Sulawesi, the Tukangbesis, southwestern Kalimantan, and perhaps a few localities in western Irian Barat. Outside the present limits of Indonesia, the influence of the Java-based kingdom extended to the southeastern part of the Malay Peninsula, and to an island just off the peninsula's tip. On this island was a small but quite old settlement which Sumatrans had founded around the year 1200 and had called Tumasik. Some day the island would become famous as Singapore, but that day was far in the future. Madjapahit claimed hegemony over much of

the Malay Peninsula and the Philippines, and established a protec-
torate over Siam, Cambodia, Champa, and Viet Nam. Naturally,
the original community named Madjapahit expanded as the capital
of a growing empire, and so did Madjapahit's north-coastal outlet,
Surabaja. In 1377 the forces of Madjapahit took the old Sriwidjajan
capital of Palembang, and there was no power in tropical southeastern Asia to contest that of Madjapahit. Outside Java this empire was mainly a coastal one, entrenched in the trading provinces
and having only minor effect on the lives of interior tribespeople.
Governors and troops were stationed in the trading centers, which
were forced to pay heavy tribute.

Hinduism, with emphasis on Shiva-worship, coexisted with Buddhism in Madjapahit, but these were religions chiefly of the secular
and priestly elite, the masses retaining animism or whatever beliefs
they chose. In Madjapahit there was some division of church and
state, the priesthood being subordinate to the worldly rulers. Several cultural trends of the Indian period reached a culmination in
Madjapahit times, one of them being deification of the kings. In
statuary these men were portrayed in godly guise as though they
might be incarnations of deities; and when a *radja* died, his ashes
were apportioned out to various mausoleums as holy relics. It was
in the days of Madjapahit that Indonesian sculpture, architecture,
religion, and philosophy departed most obviously from Indian prototypes, assuming distinctive characteristics of their own. No wonder, then, that modern Indonesians regard Madjapahit as a national and historical symbol, especially since it was heading
toward Indonesian unification.

Yet, for all its promise, Madjapahit flourished scarcely more than
a century, and its really great period was much shorter, roughly
1335–1380. Looking back on Asian events, it is easy to accept the
Chinese view of history, whereby a dynasty would rise, extend its
dominion, thrive for a time, succumb to venality, and then fall—an
inevitable cycle. In 1389 there were rival claimants for the throne
of Madjapahit, which was soon ripped apart by strife and civil
war; and by 1410 the once-great empire had withdrawn to parts of
Java and one or two nearby islands. By 1428 it was no more than a
minor principality with foci at Djokjakarta and Surakarta (Solo).

Thus reduced, Madjapahit remained an enclave of Hindu-Javanese culture until the early part of the Islamic period. During the years 1513–1528, it was attacked by a coalition of Javan states that had newly turned Muslim, and its rulers fled to Bali.

Seldom does one historical or cultural period pass quickly into the next. While one period seems to be continuing unabated, certain forces may be gathering that will terminate it. While Madjapahit was still thriving, there appeared on the scene two outside forces that would some day dominate Indonesia. One of these was the West, in the person of Marco Polo, who visited Sumatra in 1292. Polo's book of travel would stimulate Western interest in the possibilities of the Indies. The other exogenous force, of more immediate consequence, was the arrival from Gujarat of many Arabs bearing a religion previously little known in the islands—Islam.

Islam was an old faith and a mighty cultural force long before Madjapahit times. At least as far back as the sixth century A.D., Mecca had been the principal city of Arabia, its trade connections reaching by land and sea to India, Europe, and eastern Africa. In those days most of the Arabs worshipped tribal gods. A cubical building of Mecca, the Ka'aba, was a pagan shrine containing the holiest of relics, among them a block of meteoritic iron. In the Ka'aba were statues of 300 tribal deities, including an exceptionally important one called Allah. Thus, Mecca was already an Arab commercial and religious center at the birth of Muhammad, about 569 A.D. Muhammad was of the Quraish, the aristocracy who controlled Meccan finance and religion, and who governed the town through a council made up of influential families. While still very young, Muhammad was successively bereft of his father, his mother, and a grandfather, ending in the care of a paternal uncle. With no fortune of his own, the young Muhammad tended sheep, bought and sold in Mecca, and eventually became a caravaneer for a wealthy widow, Khadijah, whom he subsequently married and by whom he had six children. On trips to Syria he came in contact with many Christians, and noted the strength of the Christian Byzantine empire. Closer to home he met some Christian Arabs and a few Jewish Arabs—strange-sounding designations today—as well as various Christian and Jewish traders visiting Mecca; and in the desert were *hanif*, Arab ascetics who had developed some personal brand of monotheism. Relieved by marriage of financial worries, Muhammad took to meditating in a cave on Mount Hira, sometimes alone and sometimes with his family. There, according to tradition, in the year 610 he was visited by the angel Gabriel; and a *hanif*, consulted by and related to Muhammad's wife, announced that the visitation was similar to the one that had been accorded to Moses. By 613 Muhammad had been vouchsafed a second revelation and was preaching in Mecca.

Muhammad did not reject in toto the earlier "revealed" writings of the Middle East, but regarded them as striving toward a full enlightenment which only he could supply. Accordingly, the Koran, his collected sermons, includes familiar characters from the Judaeo-Christian mythology—Adam, Noah, the Pharaoh, Mary, Jesus, Solomon, Abraham, Ishmael, Jacob, David, and others— although in different roles. But the Koran also contains noble truths. Muhammad taught that there was but one God, Allah, solitary and sovereign, to be thanked and worshipped by man. Before Allah all men were equal. And death was not the end; for a day of judgment would come when every man must account for his earthly deeds. Allah was merciful and patient, but personal salvation depended upon acceptance of him as the one God, and of Muhammad as his prophet; the alternative was damnation and hellfire. Charity was the will of Allah, and alms should be given to the needy; the rich should share with the poor. Frequent and humble prayers were necessary, and certain fasts were to be observed. Pilgrimage to Mecca, and specifically to the Ka'aba, should be made at least once in a lifetime.

In 22 years of preaching, with many tribulations and setbacks, Muhammad fused a Hebraic kind of monotheism with a latent Arabian sense of national identity. It was a synthesis behind which the Arabs could unite and expand. Less than ten years after Muhammad's death, Islam—"submission" to Allah—was shaking the foundations of Byzantium and Persia. Over the centuries, Islam spread west to Spain and east to the Indus, a culture and a way of life as well as a faith. During this time, India was invaded by many peoples. Persians, Greeks, Scythians, Kushans, White Huns

—all poured in, each establishing a greater or lesser degree of governmental control. Indian states, forever trying to conquer one another, flourished and declined. In the tenth century A.D. the Muslims arrived, and India's disunited north fell to them. ("Muslim" is derived from the same Arabic word as Islam, and means "one who submits.") From bases in the north, the Muslims launched their power against the western Deccan, where they met greater resistance. Many would-be conquerors of India were eventually absorbed into the teeming population, but not so the Muslims, who were held apart by their uncompromising monotheism, hatred of idolatry, and doctrine of social equality. Newly Islamized Turks, pushing into northern India, were exceptionally fanatical as new converts often are, and plundered the country mercilessly. During the early thirteenth century, Bengal was captured by the Muslims. But around that time, in lands west of India, Islam was having trouble with infidels. Sultan Saladin had been able to defeat the Christian crusaders and to take Jerusalem in 1187, but the onslaught of Genghis Khan, beginning in 1221, was irresistible. Persia was ravaged by the Mongols, and in 1258 Bagdad fell to the hordes of Hulagu Khan, grandson of Genghis. A great Islamic center was thus in pagan hands, but Muhammad himself had known setbacks, and losses in the Middle East could be offset by gains in India and the Far East. Accordingly, the Arabs strengthened their positions in India, where they were able not only to hold the Mongols at bay but also to take Gujarat before the thirteenth century was out.

How was Indonesia affected by these events of the Arabic world? As far back as the fourth century A.D., long before the birth of Muhammad, there had been at least a few Arabs in Indonesia, for Arabia was a major link in an east-west trade that also involved the islands. Muslim Arabs from India and the Abbasid caliphate were in Indonesia by the eighth century, supervising their portion of this trade; and by the middle of the tenth century there was a small Muslim state in northern Sumatra. It should be noted that the development of a Muslim state in Indonesia, whether a tiny principality or a large kingdom, required no massive influx of Arabs but only the conversion of the state's *radja* to Islam; for the ruler's faith, whether Buddhism, Hinduism, or Islam, became the official creed and usually determined the religious orientation of the people. When Marco Polo visited Sumatra (which he called "Lesser Java") in 1292, he noted one small kingdom whose inhabitants "are for the most part idolaters, but many of those who dwell in the seaport towns have been converted to the religion of Mahomet, by the Saracen merchants who constantly frequent them." This was probably Pasai, where the Muslim traveler Ibn Battuta spent two weeks in 1345. Battuta reported the ruler to be a convert with much interest in Islamic learning, and also noted that Arabs were handling a specialized trade across the Selat Melaka: the exchange of Sumatran cloth for the fragrant, resinous, and reputedly panacean aloes wood (Aquilaria) of Malacca.

In the fourteenth century, far more Arabs entered Indonesia than ever before; for the Muslims in India, blocked to the west by the Mongols, turned their energies more toward eastern trade, especially after taking Gujarat and its great port of Cambay. The coming of Arabs in fair numbers from Gujarat, and in lesser numbers from Bengal and the Persian Gulf ports, heralded the end of Indonesia's Indian period; for even though these Arabs were mostly from India, their thinking was Arabic, and it ushered in what may be called the Islamic period.

But there were indigenous as well as exogenous factors involved with the easterly spread of Islam. After Sriwidjaja declined, Java became the dominant island of Indonesia, and held this position thereafter. Its chief rival was Malacca, or Melaka as the Indonesians now spell it, on the southwestern coast of the Malay Peninsula. Malacca's history had been much like that of parts of the Greater Sundas: settlement by Malays from the Indochina homeland, then Indianization, and finally development into a kingdom with a commercially competitive and territorially aggressive outlook. Malacca was threatened from the north by a militaristic Siam to which it had to pay tribute, and was menaced in another fashion from the south by the commercial strength of Java and Sumatra. Just as modern Asian kingdoms call upon one or another great power for support against a neighbor, so did Malacca call upon the Arabs for commercial and the Chinese for military assistance. The Chinese sent naval vessels to protect Malaccan shipping, and the Arabs sent *shahbandar*, harbor masters, who were very successful in expediting Malaccan trade. On more than one occasion, a Sumatran aristocrat, favorable to if not converted to Islam, migrated to Malacca; and a Pasai princess married the Malaccan ruler and raised their children as Muslims. With Islamic rulers, Malacca soon became a Muslim state, and a center from which Islam could be exported to Indonesia when called for.

It was soon called for. The Arabs controlled a large part of the east-west trade, were on excellent terms with the Chinese, and had superior competence in the technical aspects of warehousing, shipping, and merchandising; but the Indonesian rulers, of course, had to open their principalities to Islam if they were to have the Arabs' cooperation. In 1413 the Chinese envoy Cheng Ho visited Sumatra and noted the progress of Islam there, although the old Sriwidjajan capital of Palembang was still Buddhist. On Java, Madjapahit called for *shahbandar* to supervise mercantile affairs. With the *shahbandar* came their families and staff, followed by *wali*, who were religious teachers, by *kidjai*, who were more secular teachers, and by *ulama*, who were scholars and jurists. Along the north coast of Java a number of independent kingdoms had developed as a result of participation in the spice trade, and their rulers were appalled by the way in which Islam infused new life into Sumatra, Malacca, and Madjapahit. The princelings of North Java called for Muslim support, and in order to receive it they accepted Islam. The first major North Java city to turn Muslim was Demak, in 1477; and in 1480 Tjirebon was founded specifically as a Muslim settlement. By 1487, Demak and Tjirebon, joined by other Muslim states of North Java and Madura, attacked what was left of Madjapahit. The states of North Java and Madura, bordering the route to the Moluccan spice islands, became centers from which Islam could spread farther east. By the end of the fifteenth century, there were 20 Muslim kingdoms scattered over Java, Sumatra, Madura, Borneo, Sulawesi, the Moluccas, the Philippines, and the Malay Peninsula. Soon thereafter, Tjirebon conquered and forcibly converted the principalities of West Java. The common people were not consulted about a state's official religion, but they profited

when a Hindu kingdom turned Muslim, for the government became a bit more democratic.

In some ways the Islamic period of Indonesia paralleled the Indian. Its dominant characteristics were similarly introduced from
without, by people who were interested both in profit and prosely-
tism, and its impact was first felt in the coastal trading centers. A
phase of warring kingdoms, beginning as soon as Indianized states
were strong enough to make war, continued through the Islamic
period, and trends toward unification were only temporary. Just as
Hinduism had its Brahmans, so did Islam have its Sayyids (*said* in
Indonesian spelling) who, as descendants of Muhammad, made up
a class of leaders.

In its early centuries, the Muslim creed was profoundly different
from Hinduism, not only being unequivocally monotheistic but
also surpassing even the Judaeo-Christian dogmas in dispensing
with tales of mystical creations, births, resurrections, transforma-
tions, cures, serpents, apparitions, numbers, and symbols. Although
the Koran includes a few Judaeo-Christian myths, such as Noah's
ark and Aaron's rod, the work is mostly preceptual, outlining codes
of behavior. It is astonishing that as far back as the early seventh
century, there existed a people who could rally behind a religious
system that did not blur its ethical and moralistic precepts with innumerable tales of magical episodes. But of course the Arabs were
a remarkably sagacious people who contributed greatly to the
early development of mathematics, astronomy, geography, medicine, music, ethics, law, government, and philosophy. They saved
the best of early Greek thought when Europeans allowed it to die
out or even suppressed it; and the European Renaissance owes far
more to Muslim contact than is generally realized in the West. Yet
in Indonesia Muhammad's rational religion did not clash with
Hindu mysticism as fiercely or as frequently as might be surmised.
Needless to say, Islam developed schisms as it spread geographically. At quite an early date it diverged into *sunni* (orthodox) and
*shia* branches. More significantly in the present connection, there
also arose the *sufi* Muslim philosophy which, although regarded as
orthodox, emphasized individual contemplation and personal devotion leading toward what might loosely be called sainthood. Simi-

lar philosophies existed in both Christianity and Hinduism. In India, the *sufi* Muslims and *bhakti* Hindus used this more personalized approach to build an ideological bridge between seemingly incompatible religious systems. From the thirteenth to the eighteenth century, the *sufi* were the principal Islamic missionaries, and are thought to have played a dominant role in the conversion of Indonesia.

In short, although Islam was a dramatically uncompromising faith at the start, it became more permissive in India as time went by. Then, taken to Indonesia, it was further modified on some islands. Such modification was possible partly because repetition of the *shahada* was the only ineluctable requirement of Islam. This credo, called *kalimat sjahadat* in Malayan, was the statement, "I testify that there is no God but Allah, and Muhammad is His prophet." Today, 90 percent of the Indonesians are classified as Muslims, but among them are many levels of belief. Take, for example, the situation on Java, where about half the Indonesians are concentrated. Roughly a third of the Javanese are *santri*, orthodox Muslims who pray five times daily, attend services at the mosque on Friday, fast through the daylight hours of the fasting month called Ramadan, observe the prescribed food taboos, memorize verses from the Koran, and visit Mecca if circumstances permit. The Javanese *santri* carry on the traditions of the North Java trading kingdoms. On the other hand, the Javanese *prijaji*, although considered Muslim, are interested in metaphysical philosophy, social graces, artistic proficiency, and verbal skills—a Hindu heritage. The *prijaji* carry on the traditions of the old Javanese aristocracy, although today they might be white-collar workers rather than gentry. The Javanese *abangan*, while nominally Muslim, are basically animistic, believing spirits to reside in a variety of living things and inanimate objects, and staving off the evil influence of such spirits through a combination of offerings, consultation with a *dukun* (medicine man), and right thinking. The *abangan* are mostly peasant cultivators. Outside of Java, other variants of Islamic faith exist. In general, the *santri* level is approximated wherever the communities became strongly involved with the coastal trade of the Islamic period: eastern Sumatra and parts of the

Malay Peninsula, the Atjeh country of northern Sumatra, Bangka and Belitung, the Riaus and Linggas, the lowlands and river valleys of Borneo, southern Sulawesi and the Gorontalo country of northern Sulawesi, Ternate, Tidore, the Batjans, the Gorams, Madura, and Sumbawa, with scattered enclaves elsewhere. But differences are detectable from place to place within this group of islands. For example, the Atjehnese have been more fiercely Muslim than some other peoples, while the nominally Muslim Minangkabau are noted for their emphasis on *adat*, the customary law of the village, a law older than the Islamic and sometimes in conflict with it.

Indonesian languages were first written in scripts derived from India. During the Islamic period, Arabic scripts replaced the Indian ones, and Arabic literary styles provided models upon which a local literature was based. About 650 Arabic words were borrowed into Malayan, and it is remarkable how often they parallel the earlier borrowings from Sanskrit. Many of the Arabic loanwords reflect the priestly jargon: words meaning trinity, miracle, fidelity, amen (*amin*), transitory or worldly, immoral, psalm, lust, holy, ablutions, throne (of God), sacrifice, Islamic tradition, created beings, act of charity, temptation, essence, religious fervor, martyr, destiny, sect, parable, and prophet. Legalistic loan-words from the Arabic include those meaning lawsuit, circumstance, adult (in the legal sense), truth, claim, null and void, partnership, deputy or agent, legal guardian, living expenses, and alimony. Like the Sanskrit-speakers before them, the Arabs did not find Malayan words adequate to express concepts of time or duration, and so supplied their own. Sanskrit had already provided words meaning eventide, always, at the time when, anciently, beginning, continually, immemorial, once upon a time, first of all, and epoch. Perhaps these expressions were not widely used by the masses, for the Arabs added their own words meaning endless, end of time, eternal, beginning, forenoon, early part of the evening, time, period of time, epoch, and day (24-hour period). The Arab calendar prevailed in Indonesia for a while. The Muslim Era, *tarikh hidjrat*, was considered to date from the Hegira, the departure of Muhammad from Mecca to Medina, an event that took place in the year

622 A.D. by Christian reckoning. Twelve lunar months were recognized by the Arabs, their Arabic names being adopted into Malayan and other languages of Indonesia. These names are still remembered, especially in the Malay Peninsula; but in Indonesia the Dutch promulgated the Western calendar, and there the ninth lunar month is the only one that is now generally called by its Arabic designation, Ramadan.

The days of the week are still known in Indonesia by their Arabic names. Beginning with Sunday, these are *Ahad*, "first"; *Senin*, "second"; *Selasa*, "third"; *Rebo* or *Arba*, "fourth"; *Kamis*, "fifth"; *Djumaat*, "assembly"; and *Sabtu*, "Sabbath." The name of a weekday is usually preceded by the word *hari*, the Arabic for "day" in the sense of a 24-hour period. (Another method of naming the weekdays, one devised by Chinese businessmen in large cities of Indonesia and the Malay Peninsula, is also in use.) *Subuh, lohor, asar, magrib,* and *isja* were the Arabic loan-words for the five prayer-periods of the day: dawn to sun-up, midday, afternoon, sunset, and dusk to dawn. *Asar* has come to mean the noon services, and *magrib* the westerly direction, toward the setting sun. The Arabic language included a number of sounds not present in Malayan, and the pronunciation of Arabic loan-words was usually altered to fit Malayan speech patterns. In Bahasa Indonesia, Malayanized pronunciations and spellings are approved, and diacritical marks are omitted. Thus, the names of the weekdays, and many other Arabic loan-words in Malayan, may differ a bit from their original Arabic form.

Arabic borrowings into Malayan include only a few words from the scholarly jargon, and not many that have to do with rank or position, except for a few relating to official posts. Some material things were first made known or popularized in Indonesia during the Islamic period, and are still called by Arabic names. Thus, *sjaer* is a type of barley, *zufa* is the hyssop used by Hebrews and Arabs in purification rites, *ambar* is amber, *zait* or *zaitun* the olive, *antelas* satin, *afiun* opium, *kirbat* (sometimes corrupted to *gereba*) a waterskin, *zamrud* or *djamrud* an emerald, *zirafah* or *zarafat* a giraffe. The Arabs expanded the Indonesians' geographic horizons, and several countries are still called by their Arabic designations,

256

among them Abyssinia, Saudi Arabia, Egypt, and Iran. One Malayan name for Greece, Junan, is cognate with "Ionia."

The Arabic loan-words, like the Sanskrit, seldom relate to the arts, but this means only that the indigenous Malayan vocabulary was adequate for expressing most of the concepts involved. It is generally held that the emphasis was on the performing arts during the Indian period and on the written arts during the Islamic period; but the dichotomy is not as sharp as might at first appear. It is true that the modern Javanese *santri* are interested in poems, family or dynastic histories, and morality tales in the Arabic tradition, while being content to leave the dance, drama, and music to the *prijaji*. However, much literature of the Indian period failed to survive, and recent studies suggest Arab modification if not origin of at least a few traditional dances. While the average Westerner, not musically trained, perhaps would not detect regional variations in the traditional orchestral music of the Greater Sundas, in some areas and selections an Arab influence is recognizable. This is not to question the largely pre-Arabic origin of Javanese and Balinese drama, puppet plays, dances, musical instruments, and orchestral tuning systems. It is certain that sculpture, painting, and allied representational arts were not given such impetus by the arrival of the Arabs as they had been by the earlier arrival of the Indians. It was not the Koran but Arab tradition that frowned on the portrayal of living things. In the early decades of Islam, the Arabs felt that the concept of a Supreme Being would be debased if He were depicted as a human being; and their concern with historical accuracy led them to oppose the depicting of Muhammad, since his exact appearance was not known. Probably an abhorrence of animistic idols and totems led to an even broader rejection of realistic portrayals. While at certain times and places the Muslims did not mind semiabstract floral patterns, or even paintings of men and beasts, it was generally held that artists should confine themselves to flat ornamentation in more or less geometric style, in other words pure arabesque. A brief passage or expression from the Koran, done in the graceful Arabic script, could also be presented artistically. Thus, the Arabs' religious and secular writings did not provide the Indonesians with the aesthetic inspiration they had gotten from Buddhist and Hindu texts or from Indian epics such as the *Mahabharata* and the *Ramayana*.

Although the Indian period was much longer than the Islamic, each developed gradually, and each took almost a century to get fully under way in Indonesia. Obviously, then, one must be arbitrary in assigning calendar dates to these periods, for actually they are culture phases with some temporal overlap, and certain practices of one phase continued into the next. In East Java, a small Hindu kingdom survived to the beginning of the Portuguese period, and Bali has remained Hindu-animist to the present. Hindu thinking modifies the activities of nominal Muslims in Java and other islands, while animistic beliefs everywhere lend color and zest to what might otherwise be workaday existence. And as mentioned previously, various ethnic groups did not share in many advances of the Indian or Islamic period, but remained essentially at some earlier level. Nor should it be forgotten, in this effort to define periods, that the Indonesians themselves provided the ideological, technical, and economic foundation to which Indian and Arab ideas could be added. Even in the areas where exogenous influences were most frequently and strongly felt, many cultural themes run strongly and continously from the early Indian period well into Dutch colonial times. Buddhist-Hindu and Islamic culture were all given a characteristically Indonesian aspect in the islands, the Indonesians impressing their own stamp upon Indian and Arabic art, sculpture, architecture, literature, philosophy, and religion. Even borrowed Sanskrit and Arab words were changed in pronunciation and in shades of meaning. For a thousand years, say 700 to 1700 A.D., Indonesia had a smoother continuity of culture than might be deduced from the recognition of periods. The foregoing provisos are implicit in the statement that the Islamic period began in the fourteenth century with the arrival of many Arabs from Gujarat.

Islamic culture gathered momentum in Indonesia throughout the fifteenth century, and for about a dozen years thereafter. Then came the Portuguese.

What a saga remains to be told: the voyaging of the Portuguese southward around Africa, eastward across the Indian Ocean, and so to the Indies. Today we would give much to know just what ideas, manufactures, crop plants, domestic animals, parasitic organisms, and other cargo were spread by these adventurers in the closing years of the fifteenth century and in the first decade or two thereafter. But probably we shall never know, for the details of the voyages were kept secret as a result of Spanish-Portuguese rivalry. Tangible traces of early Portuguese expansion are not conspicuous in the Orient. Of Portugal's Asian empire there remain only Macao on the South China coast, and Portuguese Timor with a few nearby enclaves. Yet, Western views of the East, and of the African lands along the route thereto, were profoundly influenced by the early Portuguese explorers and traders. Histories, dealing mostly with war and commerce, do not make this clear; but a look at languages, including English, is revealing. A tribesman of southern Africa is said to live in a "kraal" and to brandish an "assegai"; but the first of these words is Portuguese *curral*, a sheep pen. The second is Portuguese *azagaia*, a lance; the Portuguese borrowed the word from the Berbers long before pushing into the Orient. South African tribesmen are called "Kaffirs" because the Portuguese spread an Arabic word, *kafir*, that meant "unbeliever." "Sjambok," a whip, is a word the Portuguese got probably from the Malays (Malayan *tjambuk*), who in turn had gotten it from the Persians. *Feitiço*, artificial, is the term the Portuguese applied to the idols of the heathen; in English it became "fetish." Portuguese *palavra*, speech, became "palaver" on the African coast of the Indian Ocean. It was the Portuguese who named the tip of Africa *Cabo de Boa Esperança*, Cape of Good Hope; for once the cape had been rounded, there was good hope of reaching the Indies. An Indian nurse is an "ayah," yet from the start the word was Portuguese, not Indian. As already noted, the cobra and the betel-nut bear Portuguese names, and the Indian "caste" system was so characterized by the Portuguese. A Chinese official is called a "mandarin," but the word is Portuguese *mandarim;* the Portuguese got it from the Malays (Malayan *menteri,* a Sanskrit loan-word). The most widely spoken Chinese language, the courtly Mandarin, accordingly bears an Indo-European name that was passed from Sanskrit into Malayan, then into Portuguese and so back into many Indo-European tongues. "Joss" is merely the Portuguese *Deus,* God. "Tempura" is a Japanese specialty, but the name is from Portuguese *tempora;* the *Quattuor Tempora,* four occasions, were the Ember-days when the Portuguese would eat no meat but would accept bits of shrimp and other seafoods in batter. "Bonze" is an English designation for a priest, especially a Buddhist priest, of China, Japan, or Korea; the word was originally Chinese (*fan seng,* a monk), but the Portuguese version, *bonzo,* is responsible for the English usage.

Other pseudo-Asiatic words could be cited, further revealing the extent to which we still see the Orient through Portuguese eyes. Portuguese place-names also turn up widely in the East. The name of Ceylon's capital was altered by the Portuguese to Colombo, thus honoring Columbus. Flores ("flowers"), an island in the Lesser Sundas, bears a name the Portuguese applied to a number of places. Selat Patinti, the tortuous and tiresome passage between Halmahera and Batjan, was once the Paçiençia Strait. Far up the Asian coast, Formosa (Ilha Formosa, "beautiful island") and the Pescadores ("fishermen") likewise have Portuguese names; and China would probably still be called Cathay had not the Portuguese popularized an alternative designation. In the first four chapters of this book, the Portuguese were mentioned in a dozen specifically Indonesian connections. This being the case, it is surprising to encounter, mostly in older works, the assertion that the Portuguese sailed Indonesian waters chiefly as pirates, having little effect on trade and less on culture. The assertion exists because the Portuguese were not often writers, and their period of dominance in Indonesia is known largely from the writings of their enemies, the Dutch.

It was the spice trade that lured the Portuguese to the Orient. As mentioned in Chapter II, the spices of the East Indies were known in Europe long before the Portuguese found the sea route to the Indies. They were regarded as medicines, aphrodisiacs, and status symbols; and they were necessary to preserve and flavor the stinking meat of the European markets. Nutmeg and cloves, especially effective in preserving and flavoring, in those days came only from the Moluccas; and mace was produced along with nutmeg. The Portuguese became determined to follow the spice trade back to its source, and to wrest it away from the Muslims. In addition, they hoped to discover and establish friendly relationships with a mythical Christian kingdom, that of "Prester John," from whom they expected help in confronting Islam. During the period 1416–1460, Portugal's Prince Henry, nicknamed the Navigator although he stayed at home, encouraged mathematics, astronomy, and navigational science, as well as exploration of the Atlantic Ocean and the African west coast. Madeira, the Azores, and the Cape Verdes were discovered, and the mainland coast was explored southward for nearly 2,000 miles. Constructing bases along their route, the Portuguese began to exploit whatever commodities they could find: slaves, peppers, ivory, gold. By 1483, Diogo Cão had found the mouth of the Congo; and by 1488, Bartholomeu Diaz had reached what he called the Cape of Storms, a landmark his more optimistic followers dubbed the Cape of Good Hope.

When the Portuguese rounded this, the *Cabo de Boa Esperança*, there was indeed good hope of reaching the Indies; for the seas that lay before them had been criss-crossed and the islands charted by Malays, Javanese, Arabs, and Chinese. Pushing their way into the Indian Ocean and then the Southwest Pacific, the Portuguese were not slowed by a need for constant soundings or the laborious mapping of currents and coastlines; they had only to obtain maps and to recruit navigators from the local people. A decade after Diaz, Vasco da Gama had taken a Portuguese fleet around the cape, up the African east coast, and across the Indian Ocean to India, piloted on the last leg of his journey by an Arab from Gujarat. By 1500 the Portuguese were clashing with the Moplah, the Muslim traders, along the coast of India. By 1502 the Portuguese had established themselves at Cochin on the Madras coast, and just seven years later they appointed Affonso d'Albuquerque as their Viceroy of India.

Albuquerque's bitter hatred of Islam is easier to understand when one recalls that Portugal had fought for centuries against Muslim domination. The Viceroy dreamed of diverting the Nile at its headwaters, bringing drought and famine to Egypt, and opening the way to an attack on Mecca itself. More practically, he decided to occupy several strong positions, bulwarks for an empire to be. In 1510 the Portuguese were at Goa, in 1511 at Macao; and now Albuquerque was ready to move against Malacca, which guarded one of the great "bottlenecks" of world shipping. By 1512 Malacca had fallen to the Portuguese, and the islands of Indonesia lay before them. Shortly before the fall of Malacca, Albuquerque had captured a Javanese pilot who owned a splendid chart of Indonesia, showing the position of the smaller islands that lay south and east of the Greater Sundas; and so before 1512 was out, the Portuguese were in the Moluccas.

In time, these Europeans entrenched themselves not only in many parts of the Orient but also on both coasts of Africa, as well as on several islands of the eastern Atlantic. Among other functions, the African and Atlantic settlements provided stepping-stones between Portugal and the Far East, and bases from which naval units could be launched to protect Portuguese shipping. Large stretches of the African east coast were ruled not by tribal chieftains but by Muslim sultans whose trade connections stretched to Indonesia or beyond, and the history of Indonesia was therefore affected to some degree by events all along the Portuguese trade route. However, subsequent discussion will, for the most part, be restricted to happenings in the Orient.

And there was no lack of happenings, large or small but always colorful, in the tropical lands where the Christian-Muslim conflict, already centuries old, was opening a new and more easterly battleground. A curious story, but one in keeping with the spirit of the times, is of an Indonesian known only as "Malacca Henry." A seafarer, he was most likely nicknamed after the Navigator. Not much was recorded about him. He came from the Moluccas, and probably was a dark Alfur, for he was captured and sold into slavery. In southeastern Asia, both the mainland and the islands, Negrito and other dark aboriginal groups were often called by a name meaning "slaves," and slavery was an ancient practice in this part of the world. Even well into Dutch colonial times, the Balinese and other people of western Indonesia were raiding into the more easterly islands, bringing back coffles of Alfurs and Papuans. The Islamic doctrine of social equality was not regarded as applicable to pagans, and when the Portuguese took Malacca, they fell heir to an

Arab slave market. They could use it, especially at this time when the spice trade was not yet theirs in its entirety. As the Spanish sardonically commented, *"Esclavos, no clavos";* slaves, not cloves. Henry was among the slaves who had been brought to Malacca for sale, and he was eventually purchased by a Portuguese nobleman, Fernão de Magalhães, who had taken part in the capture of the town. This nobleman dreamed of sailing west from Europe to reach the Moluccas, rounding South America, which had to terminate somewhere. Finding no support from his own sovereign, he turned to the Spanish emperor, Charles V of Austria, who provided five ships for the venture. In those days, even the longest voyages were not costly except in terms of men, and Magalhães—Magellan, as he is now called—assembled a tatterdemalion crew, among them the slave Henry.

In 1519 Magellan set sail from Sanlúcar de Barrameda, crossing the Atlantic and reaching the southern tip of South America, where he lost one ship by desertion and another by wreck. At last finding the strait that now bears his name, he crossed the Pacific, reaching Guam and then the Philippines in 1521. While Magellan was on his way, the Portuguese had received trading privileges at Martaban, Burma, and had made their first landing on Timor in the Lesser Sundas. Magellan stopped at Cebu in the Philippines, and Henry's ability to understand some part of the local speech was the first proof that the expedition had indeed reached the East by sailing west. Allying himself with the Cebuans, Magellan joined them in a war against the nearby Mactan islanders, and was killed along with a number of his men. The survivors, Henry among them, loaded the contents of the three battered ships into two, then burned the stripped one. Of the two remaining ships, one, the *Trinidad,* tried to make Panama but was beaten back to the Moluccas by unfavorable winds. There the crewmen were imprisoned by the Portuguese, who by now were already well entrenched in those islands. The other ship, the *Victoria,* loaded a cargo of cloves and nutmeg in the Moluccas, hoping then to round Africa and return to Spain. But note that in making it back home to Moluccan waters, Henry became an unsung hero, the first man ever to sail completely around the world. Not until about a year later did the

*Victoria* finally reach Spain. There, its cargo of spices sold for about six cents a pound, more than repaying the expenses of the voyage, discounting the loss of 245 men out of the original 280. What finally became of Henry the Circumnavigator, no one troubled to record.

Of two follow-up voyages from Spain, one barely reached the Moluccas, the other never rounded South America. Yet, Spain decided not to follow the Portuguese around Africa but to cross the Pacific from Mexico. This decision finally led the Spanish to take over the Philippines, and to establish trade relations with China, while leaving Indonesia to the Portuguese. The relationship between Spain and Portugal was anomalous in that they were competitors in practice, but non-competitive allies in theory. Both had accepted the authority of a series of papal bulls, and the Treaty of Tordesillas, whereby they could divide the New World between them along the meridian of 46° 37' west longitude. But however it was numbered, this meridian extended around the globe, and the rivals thought they had also better use it to divide the Orient between them. By such reasoning, the Moluccas were Portuguese territory, but in those days no one could reckon longitude accurately. In 1530 the Portuguese acquired the Indian island of Salsette and founded Bombay on the nearby mainland. Before the end of the 1540s they were in Japan, and casting covetous glances at the Philippines, which were in a convenient place to receive both Chinese silk and Moluccan spices. However, wishing primarily to control the spice trade at its Moluccan source, the Portuguese decided to concentrate their efforts in Indonesia, thus presenting the world with a fait accompli if the elusive meridian turned out to be unfavorably located.

Portuguese expansion into Indonesia was bitterly contested by local rulers. The sultans of Ternate and Tidore, both of them Islamic merchant-princes, struggled with the Europeans for monopoly of the spice traffic. The sultan of Malacca, ousted from his domain by the Portuguese, fell back to Bintan in the Riaus, and from this base set about building a new kingdom at Johore; but much of his former commercial strength and political influence passed to the sultan of Atjeh, in northern Sumatra. The Atjehnese leader vied with the Portuguese for control of the sea lanes through the Selat Melaka, and succeeded in monopolizing the Sumatran pepper trade. As the years went by, both Atjeh and Johore launched attacks against Malacca; but the Portuguese grip could not be broken, and the peninsular stronghold continued to guard the Portuguese shipments of cloves, nutmeg, mace, and lesser products of the land. However resentful the sultans were at being thrust aside, their subjects in the Moluccas were better off after the Portuguese take-over. That is to say, the common people of these islands had not profited from the sale of spices. Rather, they had been forced to plant, tend, and harvest these commercial crops, regularly delivering stated and usually exorbitant quantities to the sultans, who reaped the profits. In contrast, the Portuguese did not force the villagers to produce anything, but simply bought whatever was available. During the Portuguese period, the Moluccan peasants had their first opportunity in generations to clear more *ladang* for their own foodstuffs, and to put in a reasonable amount of time on their own welfare and concerns. During this period, spice production declined but Moluccan islanders enjoyed a somewhat higher standard of living; and the Portuguese were satisfied.

Madjapahit had begun to collapse long before the arrival of the Portuguese, and by 1525 its last remnants were being shared by various Javanese Muslim states. One of these, Demak, had built up a Moluccan trade in earlier times under the patronage of Malacca. Now, with Malacca in Portuguese hands, Demak expanded independently. With the Portuguese guarding the Selat Melaka, the Selat Sunda or Sunda Strait became important as an alternative gateway for Muslim traffic between the islands and the lands farther west. It may be asked why one or two straits should appear so important when many others existed through the archipelago. Indonesia forms a barrier between the Indian Ocean and the Pacific, and the gaps in this barrier, the straits, are passageways through which the tides must sweep with increased speed as they move across the oceans. A very narrow strait, such as the Selat Bali, could become a veritable raceway. Furthermore, in a narrow strait a sailing ship might easily be driven aground by unfavorable winds. The Selat Melaka, very broad and somewhat sheltered by its bordering lands, was the first choice in maritime gateways, the narrower and more exposed Selat Sunda a poor but necessary second. The northwestern tip of Java had been occupied by a comparatively minor state called Banten (Bantam), with a focus at Serang; but when the Selat Sunda began to assume increasing importance, the sultan of Demak built a westerly outpost and commerical establishment in Banten, at the coastal settlement of the same name. Banten and Demak kept the Selat Sunda open for Muslim shipping, and dominated what traffic remained to the Javanese.

In some ways, Demak was a successor to Madjapahit; but whereas the old state had been Hinduized, the new one was Muslim. The creed of Islam was still spreading in Indonesia, following the trade routes to their end in the Arus. And when the Atjehnese rose to power, they virtually forced Islam upon the Minangkabau of western Sumatra.

Although strong in coastal cities, the Muslim faith was slow to move inland. In central Java, somewhat away from direct Islamic or Portuguese influences, a new state arose, calling itself by an old name, Mataram. Like the earlier Mataram, the new one centered near Djokjakarta. It will be recalled that this part of the island, aloof from the spice traffic, had an economy based solidly upon *sawah*-grown rice. As the kingdoms of coastal North Java declined under the Portuguese onslaught, the new Mataram increased in power and influence, finally outstripping Demak.

The Portuguese eventually set up a string of forts and trading centers, from the Moluccas and Timor westward through Sulawesi and Flores to western Java and northern Sumatra. Farther west, scattered bases guarded the route to Indian entrepôts such as Cochin and Calicut on the Malabar coast. There, Indonesian spices could be loaded along with Indian produce for shipment back to Portugal, while Goa served as an administrative center from which Portuguese affairs in the East were handled. These affairs were commercial, and did not involve territorial expansion beyond what was necessary to build trading centers and protect them. Although a small nation, with only about a million inhabitants, Portugal succeeded in monopolizing what was then the world's most lucrative trade. Much of this success was due to Albuquerque's geopolitical

266

abilities at the start of the Portuguese period. Not only did he establish bases at strategic locations, but he also recruited a native soldiery with Portuguese officers, and arranged treaties whereby local sovereigns could ostensibly remain all-powerful while in practice leaving the problems to the Portuguese. Albuquerque's abilities did not characterize his Portuguese successors in office, but in later times his strategy was emulated by the Dutch, British, and French in the Orient.

Among the colorful visitors to Indonesia was Luis Vas de Camões, a Portuguese nobleman and precocious student of the classics at Coimbra. As a poet and gallant he had seen the Portuguese royal court at its most brilliant, for wealth was pouring in from the Indies, and oriental potentates were visiting to pay homage to John III and Catherine. In turn an exile in Santarem, a soldier against the Muslims in North Africa, and a street-brawler in Portugal, Camões was jailed in 1552 for wounding a court official, but pardoned on the condition that he take service in the East. He went to Goa, where he polished his reputation as a poet and soldier, then to Ternate for over a year. Soon afterward, at Macao, he began composing his greatest work, *Os Lusíadas*. Shipwrecked at the mouth of the Mekong, imprisoned off and on for flouting authority, he finished the Lusiads in Mozambique. Returning sick and destitute to Portugal in 1570, the poet-patriot was granted a small pension, and his epic was approved by the censor of the Holy Inquisition. Today, some of Camões' roundels and sonnets are regarded as among the finest in the Portuguese language, while *Os Lusíadas*, telling of Da Gama's voyage and Portugal's glory, is a national epic of the first magnitude.

Other people who were sent to the Indies included Jesuit priests, whose order had lately been founded by Ignatius Loyola. They got nowhere in their efforts to impress Islamic scholars, who were firmly monotheistic. Call it Trinity, Trimurti, or anything else, these Muslims said, the concept of three gods is polytheism, whether or not they are "in one"; and additional supplication of the Virgin Mary is but a return to the ancient cult of the warm Mother Goddess who has wide appeal and who appears under many aliases. And what is the difference, the Muslims asked, between a pantheon of demigods and a calendar of saints? For all are lesser supernaturals who are supplicated and who are supposed to preside over this and that. And prayer before crucifixes, icons, statues, and other portrayals of deities and semi-deities—is this not idolatry? Also, Christianity had already become noted for a discrepancy between high-minded doctrine and bloody practice. Not that other faiths were blameless in this regard, but Portugal at that very time was in the clutch of the Holy Inquisition, a reign of terror directed against Muslims, Jews, Protestants, and intellectuals, with frightful torture and genocide in the name of Jesus. What a contrast with India, peaceful and united under Akbar, greatest of the Mughul emperors, who actually encouraged theological seminars and debates. When the Jesuits failed to convert the Muslims by argument, the Portuguese tried a different approach, that of sinking boatloads of devout pilgrims on their way to Mecca.

To understand the Portuguese period of Indonesia, it is well to remember that excesses in the name of religion were characteristic of Portugal and to a lesser degree of Goa, but not especially of the Portuguese settlements at the Indonesian termini of the trade routes. Away from the administrative centers, at least some of the Portuguese were tolerant, establishing amiable relations with the local populace. In this connection, it is interesting to note the Portuguese loan-words that still exist in Malayan. A flag is *bendera,* a clock or watch *arlodji,* butter *mentega,* a salad *selada,* a saddle *sela,* a bullet *pelor* or *peluru,* a cupboard *almari,* a window *djendela.* A towel is *tuala,* a festival *pesta,* cheese *kedju,* shoes *sepatus,* a soldier *serdadu.* A work-break is *tempo,* a fork *garpu,* a violin *viola* or *biola,* a pump *bomba,* a ball *bola,* a doll *boneka.* A hat is *tjepiau,* dice *dadu,* a crowbar *alabangka,* a bench *bangku.* All of these words were taken from the Portuguese, as were the Malayan words for thimble, velvet, sponge-cake, eggplant, buoy, Police Inspector, foreman, badge, pin, ribbon, hammock litter, awning, shirt, flintlock, ell, auction, flatiron, and iron bucket. Malayan *sinjo* or *sinjur,* meaning a young gentleman, is from the Portuguese *senhor.* When Spanish dollars arrived in Indonesia, they were called by a Portuguese name. Even a few adjectives and abstract nouns were borrowed from the Portuguese; thus, *falsu* is Malayan for spurious or counterfeit, and *antero* means all, whole, or entire. *Paderi*, priest, and *geredja*, church, are among the few Portuguese religious terms adopted into Malayan. In some areas, Sunday is *hari minggu*, from Portuguese *Domingo*, Lord.

Portuguese loan-words in Malayan are down-to-earth, dealing not with rarefied concepts but with everyday life on the common level. The Portuguese and the islanders talked about housing, furniture, children's toys, cooking, and clothing; about public affairs and events; about work and relaxation from it. Furthermore, Malayan is a language focused in western Indonesia and the Malay Peninsula, while the Portuguese held their empire longest in the Moluccas and the Lesser Sundas. In languages of the Moluccas, additional Portuguese loan-words are numerous. Alfred Russel Wallace was the first to note this situation. Of his 1857 visit to the Kais, he wrote, "It is interesting to observe the influence of the early Portuguese trade with these countries in the words of their language . . . *Lenco* for handkerchief, and *faca* for knife, are here used to the exclusion of the proper Malay terms." And the Ambonese, Wallace said, are "a mixture of at least three races: Portuguese, Malay, and Papuan . . . The Portuguese element decidedly predominates . . . as indicated by features, habits, and the retention of many Portuguese words . . . Their language still has much more Portuguese than Dutch in it." Recording some of the Ambonese language, Wallace noted Portuguese loan-words meaning pigeon, forehead, hours, pin, chair, handkerchief, cool, flour, sleep, family, talk, you, even, brother-in-law, sir, and madam. The local people had no idea that these familiar words were exogenous. In the Arus, among people who were predominantly of the Papuan physical type, Wallace also heard a good many Portuguese expressions. He concluded that the Portuguese "had a marvelous power of colonization, and a capacity for impressing their national characteristics on every country they conquered, or in which they effected merely a temporary settlement." It is indeed true that in several of the Spice Islands, for example Ternate, Ambon, and Batjan, there was creolization, the indigenous physical type, language, and culture all being modified by the Portuguese. In Wallace's time, creolized ethnic groups were called *Orang Serani*, from the Arabic loan-word *Nasrani*, Christian.

The tobacco plant, and its common Indonesian name of *tembakau*, were brought by the Portuguese from the New World. As mentioned earlier, one Malayan name for wheat, *terigu*, is from the Portuguese. In eastern Indonesia, maize is often called *milo*, yet another Portuguese loan-word.

Old churches and forts, some still in good condition, also attest to the former presence of the Portuguese in many areas from which they have since withdrawn. In the Moluccas and the Lesser Sundas, Portuguese helmets, swords, and ornaments are treasured as heirlooms by certain Indonesian families who are descended from island sultans. The armor of the Nias islanders, now used only ceremonially, may have had a Portuguese prototype. In the seas around Sulawesi, high-pooped sailing vessels called *palari* are copies of the old Portuguese caravels, and in many parts of the Orient the local boatwrights still employ Portuguese techniques and sometimes vocabulary.

But Portuguese dominion over the Indies was transitory. Portugal itself declined, while throughout the Indies there was administrative laxity, personal speculation in commodities, and undue reliance on non-Portuguese personnel. On Ternate, one of the two main clove-raising islands, the Portuguese had built a permanent, garrisoned base, and had concluded a mutually profitable, seemingly ironclad treaty with the local Muslim sultan. The other main clove-raising island, Tidore, was just southeast of Ternate but was governed by its own sultan; and as might be expected, the two petty rulers were more enemies than allies. The Spanish, by now well entrenched in the Philippines, and still hopeful of some day taking the Moluccas, found it easy to create dissension by supporting Tidore against the Portuguese-Ternatean alliance. In 1570 the Portuguese murdered the sultan of Ternate, with the idea of extracting extra concessions from his successor; but the islanders revolted and by 1574 had expelled the Portuguese. Expulsion from Ternate presaged a more general decline in Portuguese fortunes. Other Europeans were pushing into the Orient. Spanish, Dutch,

French, British, and Danish ships were to be seen in Indonesian waters, along with pirate fleets of both Asian and European origin. The Dutch proved especially aggressive. The Portuguese period, which may be taken to date from 1512, lasted about a century, and was terminated by the arrival of the Dutch in force.

CHAPTER VII

# THE DUTCH PERIOD

THE ENTRY of the Dutch into Indonesia came about as a result of political struggles in Europe, which like Asia was a land of perpetually warring kingdoms. In the latter half of the 1500s, Spain ruled Sicily and a good part of Italy, as well as the Low Countries, which are now divided into the Netherlands, Belgium, and Luxembourg. The people of the Low Countries were much involved with shipping among the ports of Europe, for which activities they were favorably located from a geographic standpoint. As a part of the empire of Charles V—the monarch himself from Ghent in Flanders—the Low Countries practically monopolized the carrying trade of northern Europe. Lisbon and Seville were open to them, and there they could purchase goods for resale and distribution. In addition to produce from the Indies and the New World, the cargo ships of Amsterdam, The Hague, Rotterdam, and Antwerp carried grain from northern Germany and the Eastland, timber from Norway, iron and copper from Sweden, herrings from the great North Seas fisheries, salt from Portugal and the Biscay coast, and wine from the German vineyards, as well as

273

woolen cloth, coal, and malting barley from England. The six-teenth century was that of the European Commercial Revolution, brought about by overseas expansion into the East Indies, Africa, the New World, and other lands; and the Low Countries profited through participation in the volume of trade, profited so greatly as to provide most of the financial support for Charles V and his wars. In Antwerp and Rotterdam, local merchants mingled with those from Portugal, Spain, Italy, Germany, England, and the Hansa. In 1531 the first great European stock exchange, the Bourse, was established at Antwerp. Here the wealthy could rein-vest their capital in whatever commodities appealed to them. Groups of soberly clad businessmen sipped black Java coffee and discussed the newly introduced techniques of double-entry book-keeping, cargo insurance, life insurance, and trading in futures.

Yet, with the arrival of the Protestant Reformation, eight north-erly provinces of the Low Countries united behind Calvinism, took up arms against Charles V, broke free after five years of fighting, and in 1581 organized themselves into the Netherlands. The new country was often called Holland, after its most heavily settled, westernmost province. During those years of fighting, many Neth-erlands ships had been seized in Spain. More importantly, Spain had acquired Portugal (in 1580), and had struck at the unruly Dutch by closing Lisbon to them, so that they could take no fur-ther profit from the East Indian trade. A notably determined peo-ple from earliest historic times, the Dutch decided to move into the Orient and wrest this trade away from the Portuguese. Prospects for the venture were good, for during the Holy Inquisition, Portu-gal had expelled or exterminated virtually all her non-Catholics and intellectuals, and was much weakened thereby. Many Se-phardic Jews fled to the Netherlands, where they were welcomed and where they made significant contributions in several fields, es-pecially the economic. The Inquisition was waging a grim battle to hold man in the Dark Ages, but the Age of Reason was nonetheless under way. "Africa begins at the Pyrenees," northern Europeans exclaimed, and turned to the new brands of science, philosophy, religion, and politics.

In the Netherlands there had been much progress in cartography, navigation, geographical knowledge, and boat-building. Gerhard Kremer, a Fleming who in 1544 had narrowly escaped being burned alive for his liberal views, devised a method of showing the world's curved surface on a piece of flat paper, in such a way that a straight line drawn on the map would correspond to a single compass heading on the earth. Jan Linschoten, formerly a secretary to the archbishop of Goa, wrote the *Itinerario*, an encyclopedia of the East Indies, with a description of the spice trade and of Portuguese strength and weakness. Proud of their role in the defeat of the Spanish Armada (1588), and encouraged by the waning of Spanish and Portuguese sea power, the Dutch were ready to move into the Indies. But from what direction? Looking for a new route, a northeast passage above Eurasia, they found Spitzbergen and impassable ice. Crossing the Atlantic in search of a northwest passage, they found Hudson Bay and more ice. Experimenting with the North Russia route to China, they discovered the climate to be intolerable. To follow Magellan around South America was out of the question at this time, what with the presence of Drake, Frobisher, and other Elizabethan freebooters in the western Atlantic; and so to capture the spice trade, the Dutch would have to sail the Portuguese route southward around Africa. A Dutch squadron had trailed the Portuguese to the Cape Verdes in 1585, but no ship from the Netherlands had ever gone the rest of the way. However, there were Dutch private companies ready to back such a voyage, and a man, Cornelis van Houtman, available to take the first Dutch fleet around the Cape of Good Hope. History portrays van Houtman as ruffianly, but he had served with the Portuguese and knew something of the tropical waters. And whatever the judgment of history, he did what he set out to do. Although losing 145 men out of 250, he brought his four ships around Africa, across the Indian Ocean, and into Banten in 1596.

Banten, on the northwestern tip of Java, was then in its heyday. Having established a relationship of hostile coexistence with the Portuguese, it had become an open market where anyone could trade if he was willing to pay the high prices that prevailed. Here the pepper crop from Atjeh and West Java entered the world market, along with other commodities that had bypassed the declining

Portuguese. On Banten's docks, bearded Arabs from India and the Middle East mingled with pale Chinese who served the Wan-li emperor in the last years of the crumbling Ming Dynasty. And there were bustling Japanese merchants, proud now because their country was in the ascendancy, their ships plying the waters of Indonesia and the African east coast. The Japanese had recently invaded Korea and had been hoping to take all China, not knowing that the Manchus were already gathering to do the same thing. In Banten's markets there were Annamese and Siamese, bolder now that China's grip was weakening. Even the Portuguese could trade here if they cared to pay the prices; and they did. The Portuguese traders at Banten were delighted to see fellow Europeans, van Houtman's men; but while the Dutch crew were celebrating their safe arrival, their captain signed a treaty with the sultan of Banten, pledging Dutch aid against the Portuguese. When news of the Dutch arrival reached Goa, the Portuguese administrators knew exactly what was afoot and sent ships to punish Banten; but Portuguese strength had declined to the point where the sultan was able to beat off the punitive expedition. In 1597 van Houtman returned safely to the Netherlands with a profitable cargo, touching off a boom and feverish speculation.

Between 1598 and 1605, a dozen expeditions, totaling 65 ships, were launched from the Netherlands to the Indies, backed by competing companies. Most of the ships dealt at Banten, but one pushed into the Moluccas, loading cloves, nutmeg, and mace at Ambon and the Bandas in 1599. Still, the situation was not promising if rival Dutch companies had to compete among themselves; and so in 1602 the Dutch Estates General granted a charter to the Vereenigde Oost-Indische Compagnie, the United East-India Company, to trade, make treaties, build forts, maintain troops, and operate courts of law in all the lands from the Cape of Good Hope to the Straits of Magellan. The Compagnie was a joint stock company whose shares found ready sale and rose astronomically in value as the years went by; one of the original stockholders was able to leave his heirs eight tons of gold as profit from his investment. In the year of its founding, the Compagnie opened an office at Johore near the tip of the Malay Peninsula.

Also in 1602, a Dutch fleet defeated a Portuguese squadron off Banten. Once the Compagnie was in action, the Dutch began systematically to attack the Portuguese from Lisbon to the Moluccas. In 1605 the Dutch slipped into Ambon, where by promises and bribes they obtained from the local sultan a small, fortified base. In 1606, while a part of the Dutch fleet blockaded Lisbon, another part launched an attack at Malacca but was beaten off. Now the Dutch were moving rapidly. In 1607 they gained a foothold on Sumatra, in 1608 defeated a Spanish fleet off Gibraltar, and in 1609 sank a Portuguese fleet in the Selat Melaka just off Malacca. The Portuguese might hold their peninsular base a while longer, but with so many ships on the bottom, they could not keep the Dutch out of the Moluccas. Before the year was out, the Dutch had established themselves in the Bandas, from which stronghold they soon drew the sultans of Ternate and Tidore into their orbit. Making clear its intention of monopolizing the spice traffic, the Compagnie attacked all shipping in Indonesian waters, sinking Indian, Malay, Javanese, Portuguese, Japanese, Chinese, Siamese, and Annamese vessels impartially.

Even though the Portuguese still held Malacca and Timor, by 1610 their period of dominance in Indonesia was at an end, and the Dutch period was beginning. The responsibility of the Compagnie was toward its profit-minded stockholders, who were not much interested in settling Indonesia, or in proselytizing, or in ruling the indigenes in matters other than commerce. Nor were they interested in owning any more land than was needed to build and protect their so-called factories, the trading posts. The days of Compagnie dominance are known mostly from the writings of factors and agents, merchants, seamen, soldiers, and business administrators from the Netherlands. Understandably, these people were concerned mostly with the economics and logistics of the East Indian trade, and they leave the impression that the indigenes were doing nothing much beyond responding in one fashion or another to Dutch stimuli. This view is extreme, but certainly the Indonesian kingdoms continued to quarrel with each other and to develop internal rifts. This is why they were such easy prey for any strong external power that chose to control them.

277

The task of building a Dutch commercial empire was assigned to Jan Pieterszon Coen, a strict and saturnine Calvinist with burning ambition. Coen had taken two ships to the Indies and had served as factor at Banten, but in 1618 he was appointed governor-general. The following year, he made a move that would alter Indonesian history. On the northwest coast of Java was a sort of no-man's-land over which Banten and Mataram were squabbling. There was a blunt promontory called Tandjung Periuk—Cooking-Pot Cape—and just west of it a good harbor into which a small stream, the Tjiliwong, emptied. Nearby was a Javanese town which the Dutch understood to be called Djakatra (Djakarta in modern usage). Clearing the town away, the Dutch began their own settlement, resurrecting for it an old Latin name that had once been applied to southwestern Holland and Flanders. And so on the northwest coast of Java, the settlement of Batavia was founded as Compagnie headquarters. A broad canal was dug, crossed by a high-arching bridge and bordered by tall, steep-roofed houses, all in the Amsterdam fashion.

The Dutch had also been active in India, establishing a factory at Pulicat on the east coast in 1609, and at Surat on the west coast in 1615. Surat was not far from the Portuguese base of Damão, but more disturbing to the Dutch was the presence of British agents. For in 1600 the English East-India Company had been founded, and in 1611 had opened a factory at Surat. In theory Britain and the Netherlands were allies against Spain and Portugal: by treaty terms, a combined Anglo-Dutch fleet would cruise Asian waters, and trade would be shared between the two Protestant nations. But in practice the Anglo-Dutch alliance broke down as soon as it became obvious that the Portuguese could be displaced from Indonesia. Coen was hostile to the British, declaring that the only way to stay friends with them was to give them the whole earth. This he had no intention of doing, and in 1619 a Dutch fleet attacked four British ships near Banten, sinking one of them. The British soon retaliated by attacking the new Dutch base of Batavia, but were driven off. Two years later, a joint Anglo-Dutch force, sent against the Spanish in Manila, collapsed as the rival commanders squabbled.

In 1621 Coen ordered an attack on Banda, a part of whose clove crop was still bypassing the Dutch. The governor-general destroyed clove plantations, executed many of the islanders and carried others into slavery, gave their lands to Compagnie employees, and blocked off the rice supply. Every year or so thereafter, the Dutch sent armed raids through the Moluccas to destroy any surplus spices. In 1622 the Compagnie ships attacked Macao but were driven off by combined Portuguese and Chinese forces. Although crippled, the Dutch fleet next turned north to seize the Pescadores. In these islands the Compagnie found itself under constant attack by the Chinese, and so agreed to depart in return for a base on Formosa. Accordingly, on the southwest coast of Formosa the Dutch built Fort Zeelandia, an extraordinary bastion with solid brick walls six to eight feet thick. Coen's purpose in these waters was to obtain Chinese trade, from which he was barred by a Portuguese-Chinese agreement. In 1623 he arrested the entire staff of a British factory on Ambon: one Portuguese, nine Japanese, and ten Englishmen. These men were charged with having tried to take Ambon, and were executed after torture and a perfunctory trial. In 1624, news of the Ambon massacre reached England, where the English East-India Company printed and distributed an account of it, complete with a woodcut of an Englishman being flayed and burned by Dutch soldiers. The resulting public outcry led England to give up its pretence of cooperating with the Netherlands in the exploitation of the Indies.

In 1627 Mataram rallied its forces to strike at Batavia, but the Dutch could not be dislodged. Two years later, Coen died of cholera at Batavia, and several years went by before his successor was chosen. In 1633 the Dutch began making annual forays into the Selat Melaka, and in 1636 when Anthony van Diemen became governor-general, he kept up the practice. By this time there was no Portuguese fleet to speak of in Asian waters, only scattered ships to be picked off. Ordering a blockade of Goa and the Malabar Coast, van Diemen then began to occupy Ceylon. In 1639 the Dutch defeated a joint Spanish-Portuguese fleet in the English Channel. By 1640 the Compagnie was established in Bengal, India; Arakan and Pegu, Lower Burma; and Cho Chu, Tonkin (now North Viet Nam).

279

In that year Portugal broke away from Spain, but the Portuguese in the Orient took little profit from the changed political situation in Europe. Well entrenched at many localities in the East, the Dutch were now ready to strike again at Malacca. For 130 years the Portuguese had held Malacca against the attacks of Johore and Atjeh, but in 1641 it fell to the Dutch. Wishing to develop Batavia as the focus of oriental trade, the Dutch decided to retain Malacca only as a fortress, a base from which the Selat Melaka could be guarded.

Even before the founding of the Vereenigde Oost-Indische Compagnie, Dutch pioneers (the Boers) had been moving into the Cape region of southern Africa. In 1641 the Compagnie built a way-station at the Cape, where ships could be refurbished and sailors refreshed on the immensely long voyage between Batavia and Amsterdam. In 1652 three Dutch ships arrived at the Cape with orders to make it into a permanent settlement, and so the Cape Colony was born. It would be administered from Batavia, where Jan Matsuycker had succeeded van Diemen as governor-general. The Dutch had long wanted faster ways to the Indies. Back in 1616, William Schouten van Hoorn had discovered how to round South America without passing through the treacherous Straits of Magellan; but after the Cape Colony was founded, Compagnie seamen learned that they could follow the westerlies from the Cape to the longitude of Java and then turn north.

Having taken Malacca, the Dutch reduced Atjehnese power in Sumatra, a development gratifying to the Minangkabau who had been restive under Atjeh's domination. Although trading freely at some ports and for some goods, the Compagnie carried out its plan of monopolizing the Moluccan spice trade, and also monopolized the pepper trade of Atjeh and India's Malabar coast. A clandestine traffic, intended to bypass the Dutch, developed at Makasar on Sulawesi; but in 1668 the Dutch captured Makasar, attaining complete control over production and shipping of Moluccan spices. As Compagnie influence spread in Sulawesi, one group of people, the fiercely independent Bugis, sailed away to the Malay Peninsula where some of them founded new settlements, and where others were welcomed into the service of the local sultans. In time, the

Bugis came to dominate several of the sultanates. And in time the Dutch would meet these people again.

The trading empire of the Compagnie eventually extended from the Cape of Good Hope to Ceylon, Indonesia, Samoa, and Japan. The empire's capital, Batavia, became the entrepôt of most inter-Asian maritime trade, the point at which Indonesian, Persian, Indian, Ceylonese, and Japanese products were transshipped. Batavia's walled castle was now garrisoned by 1,200 men; canals had multiplied, and bridges, and houses in Dutch style; a Chinatown was growing up near the harbor. Both Banten and Mataram tried repeatedly to oust the Dutch from the settlement, but the two Javanese states could not drop their own rivalry long enough to operate effectively against the tenacious Europeans. In spite of Dutch presence, Banten did manage to grow and to strengthen its trading contacts with the Arab world; but then it developed internal problems, with rival claimants for the sultanate. The sultan's oldest son, disinherited in favor of a younger brother, called on the Dutch for help, and by taking sides in this power struggle, the Compagnie was able at a single stroke to secure important trading concessions and to split Banten. Thereafter, Banten's former influence passed to the Compagnie.

Mataram, too, had internal problems. Under its greatest sultan, Sunan Agung, this state had attained considerable power, based not on trade but on the control of land and the rice crop. Sunan Agung had tried to drive the Dutch into the sea, but without success. Mataram, viewing itself as a continuation of Madjapahit, retained as much as it could of the old, Hinduized way of life; and dominating several nearby provinces, it became a center of Javanese culture. But Sunan Agung could not ignore Islam which was gaining ground perhaps in reaction to Dutch presence, and so he petitioned Mecca for recognition as sultan. (A *sultan* was a Muslim ruler, just as a *radja* was a Hindu one.) In 1645 Sunan Agung was succeeded by Amangkurat I, who devoted himself to reducing the strength of vassal princes in outlying provinces, and to reducing the influence of Islamic teachers in Mataram. These policies led in 1674 to a revolt in which Amangkurat I was deposed. He sought the protection of the Dutch, who took steps to restore him to the throne, but he died before this objective was obtained. The Compagnie then agreed to support his legitimate successor, Adipati Anom, in return for vast commercial concessions and the ownership of a north-coastal strip that included Semarang. When this arrangement was carried out, Mataram was split into two sultanates, pro- and anti-Adipati factions focused respectively at Djokjakarta and Surakarta—and neither faction able to defy the Dutch. As time went by, both sultanates came to rely more and more on Dutch support.

It will be seen that the Vereenigde Oost-Indische Compagnie, arriving in Indonesia ostensibly to trade, soon established various beach-heads, by force of arms if necessary; and then became involved with the internal affairs of Indonesian states, manipulating these to their own advantage, and making virtual puppets of some native rulers. Soon, *"Jan Compagnie"* would go a step further in its domination of Indonesia. As the seventeenth century drew to a close, European enthusiasm for Moluccan spices was waning. A great variety of produce was reaching Europe from the Orient and the New World, while a traffic in slaves, begun by the Portuguese, was flourishing. In the changing commerical climate, the Compagnie reassessed its position. Coen and his immediate successors had emphasized a carrying trade of the kind that had sustained the Dutch economy in Europe; but within Asia such trade was now comparatively unprofitable, for the real money was in the shipment of produce from the Asian soil directly to European ports. One crop that interested the Dutch was coffee. As mentioned in Chapter II, around this time the Dutch discovered that coffee trees would thrive in the Javan uplands, where plantations of them were set out. Intending to build up a coffee trade, the Dutch asserted a right to collect tribute from all Javanese areas under their control. The idea was not new in Indonesia, or for that matter in any other part of southeastern Asia, for all manner of native rulers had generally done the same. But beginning in 1723, in the Preanger region south of Batavia, the tribute to the Dutch would have to be coffee. This region was dotted with volcanos, including Salak, the twin peaks of Gedeh and Pangrango, and the remarkable Tangkuban Perahu near Bandung (see Chapter I). As a result of much volcanic activity, the soils of the Preanger region were exceptionally rich and would yield a fine harvest of coffee beans; but to make sure the crop was properly raised and delivered, the Compagnie appointed Dutch supervisors. This was the beginning of a Dutch administrative system in Indonesia.

It was also the beginning of an arrangement whereby the islands would be exploited agriculturally, and the islanders forced to turn out produce, to make up for Compagnie losses resulting from a decline in the spice trade. Soon, not only coffee but also sugar, indigo, pepper, tea, and cotton had to be raised under two systems, one of "forced delivery" and the other of "contingents." By the forced delivery system, the native puppet rulers in return for Dutch protection would supply fixed quantities of tropical produce. By the contingents system, the rulers would provide export goods in a quantity that fluctuated according to demand in Europe. If prices were low on the exchange at Amsterdam, the Dutch might raise them by destroying coffee and spices. Both systems put a heavy burden on the peasant cultivators, but the Dutch, working only through the native regents, did not concern themselves with such matters.

Another important episode of the early 1700s was the formal acquisition of New Guinea by the Dutch. The discovery and coastal exploration of that great island had come about as a result of the Moluccan spice trade. A few Portugese and Spanish expeditions had reached New Guinea before the coming of the Dutch. The first Dutch ship, that of Willem Jansz, sailed from Banten in 1605, reaching the Kai and Aru islands, northern Australia, and the New Guinea mainland. Nine of Jansz' crew were killed and eaten by New Guinea tribesmen. In 1616, Jacques LeMaire and William Schouten van Hoorn explored the Bismarck Archipelago, then landed on the north coast of New Guinea, where many of their crewmen were killed by the natives. In 1623, Jan Carstensz cruised the south coast of the island, losing ten men to native attacks. In 1636, Thomas Pool explored the southwestern coast, where he was killed by tribesmen. Operating out of Batavia, Abel Tasman skirted both coasts of New Guinea in 1642, and tried unsuccessfully to find a passage between the island and Australia. (Such a passage had been found long before by Luis Vaz de Torres, but his account of travels was not well known at that time.) In 1714, the sultan of Tidore formally ceded New Guinea to the Compagnie, although of course the sultan had no actual authority over the huge island where a million Papuans, Melanesians, and Negritos held to their ancient ways. In years to come, Britain and Germany would challenge the validity of the cession.

Although the Compagnie became widely entrenched in the lands of the Indian Ocean and the Pacific, its fortunes declined during the 1700s. To some degree this situation reflected changing conditions in countries far from Indonesia. In Europe, new attitudes and techniques were leading rapidly toward the Industrial Revolution. Spain was declining, Prussia rising, France expanding northward to menace the Netherlands. In European waters, Compagnie ships were more than ever liable to be attacked, for the British and the French, especially, were bitterly resentful of Dutch trade monopolies in the East. Closer to Indonesia, the subcontinent of India was again in turmoil. The Mughal empire had withered away; now Hindus and Muslims clashed, while the newly arisen Sikhs questioned both the Vedas and the Koran. The Turkoman ruler of Persia brought his hordes through Khyber Pass to descend upon Delhi, and after him came the Afghans to ravage the countryside. In India's divided land, the British, French, Danish, and Portuguese were all able to hold bases from which to compete among themselves and with the Dutch. Formosa was captured by the piratical Koxinga, and Japan closed herself to outsiders.

The Compagnie also had problems in Indonesia, where its employees took to speculating in hopes of greater personal profit. Native seamen, forced out of business by the Dutch monopoly, turned pirate and hijacked many a valuable cargo. In the Moluccas, where the company's grip had been especially rigid, a part of the populace rebelled as best it could against the Dutch system of forced peonage. Even more troublesome were the Bugis, who had built up a considerable fighting strength in Johore, Kedah, and the Riaus. In 1756 and again in 1784, the Bugis attacked the Dutch fort at Malacca. Both times they were beaten off, but they constantly harried Dutch shipping in the Selat Melaka. The military and naval skills of the Bugis, along with their ability to rouse the sultans against the Dutch, did much to discourage the Compagnie from extending its operations into the Malay Peninsula. Also, the Compagnie found that the big islands of Sumatra and Borneo were ungovernable; only scattered outposts could be maintained there. Batavia turned out to be an unhealthy place in which to live, for as its population grew, so grew the likelihood that diseases would be introduced. Malaria, especially, was the scourge of Batavia, although dysentery was also troublesome. A sociological problem was posed by so-called "barrack-room matings" as many of the Dutch began acquiring wives from the local population.

The contingents and forced delivery systems were not enough to bolster the declining fortunes of the Compagnie. Casting about for some other way to increase profits, the Dutch turned their attention to the Chinese, who had known of and traded in Indonesia for centuries. The constant population pressure in eastern Asia , which had pushed the Malays and other peoples southward, had also affected the South Chinese. Practically unnoticed, there had long been a trickle of Chinese into the Malay Peninsula and Indonesia, where they were not assimilated but maintained many of their original ways. J. P. Coen had been the first Dutchman to urge the importation of Chinese into Indonesia. He felt that the islands should be colonized, preferably by Dutch but alternatively by Chinese and Japanese. His views reflected a chance to observe the industry of the Chinese who had settled at Batavia, and the military prowess of Japanese soldiers in the pay of the Compagnie. Coen even advocated the kidnapping of Chinese if they would not voluntarily settle in the islands. In Coen's day the Compagnie stockholders were not much interested in colonists of any kind, but now, in the 1700s, the Dutch encouraged Chinese immigration. The immigrants were mostly from China's south-coastal provinces of Kwangtung and Fukien. Some were Hakka, an aloof people who farmed the poor soil of mountain valleys west of Canton, and who in a thousand years had not mingled with nearby lowlanders. Others were Hokkien, often refugees from the unsuccessful Fan San Rebellion against the Manchus. Still others were Cantonese. Many of the immigrants were peasants, frugal and adaptable, inured to day-long toil, skillful at extracting a profit from the soil. Some, however, were shopkeepers, traders, bankers, moneylenders, artisans, plantation overseers. Most Indonesians were respectful of the earth and its wildlife, and so preferred to work harmoniously with nature; but the Chinese understood the Dutch urge to exploit natural resources as far as possible, and readily grasped the business practices of the Compagnie. Accordingly, the Compagnie leased whole villages and large tracts of land to the Chinese, turning over to them a variety of entrepreneurial tasks. This was the beginning of Indonesia's "plural society," with the Dutch at the top, the indigenous peoples at the bottom, and the Chinese as a middle class between the two. The history of Indonesia would be profoundly affected by the continued arrival of Chinese; but on that subject, more later. At this point it suffices to note that the industry of the Chinese could not salvage the failing Compagnie.

As company profits declined, the avid stockholders turned to measures that proved penny-wise and pound-foolish. By cutting salaries they attracted less competent personnel, while the established employees were more than ever tempted to indulge in speculation, graft, smuggling, and corruption. Because funds for ship repair were withheld, many repairable vessels were sunk lest they fall into the wrong hands. The Dutch fleet was no longer able to patrol the Indonesian seas, and there were sightings of vessels from England, Denmark, and even the very young United States of America. By 1780 the Vereenigde Oost-Indische Compagnie was virtually bankrupt, but efforts were made in Amsterdam to disguise the situation in the hope that it might improve. In 1795 the French conquered Holland and renamed it the Batavian Republic (with reference, of course, to the Batavia of antiquity, not the Javan city). The next year, the Compagnie admitted its failure and suspended dividends. The new Dutch government was organized along lines suitable to the French. In 1798 it revoked the Compagnie's charter, assumed its debts and assets, and took over Indonesia. Now the islands would be administered by the Dutch government in a fashion that suited Napoleon.

Arabs and Indians, even the Portuguese to a lesser extent, had tried to share their own culture with the Indonesians; but not so the minions of the Compagnie, who were concerned only with making a profit. The Compagnie had a considerable effect on Indonesian culture, but only incidentally so, as a result of economic activities. Some new crop plants were introduced, plantation agriculture was spread, the influence of native rulers was sapped, a Chinese middle class installed, an administrative system roughed out. Dutch concentration on Java, carried over from Compagnie into colonial times, exacerbated the differences between that island and all the others. Dutch words were not borrowed into Indonesian languages in the days of the Compagnie. Disdaining to learn Melaju Pasar or to teach Dutch, the Compagnie employees conversed with the indigenes in a simplified Portuguese, an ironic situation.

Reference is sometimes made to a "Dutch colonial period" in Indonesia, presumably beginning when the islands became a colony administered by the Netherlands rather than by the United East-India Company. However, from the standpoint of this work, in which sequential culture phases have been described, there is no reason to subdivide the Dutch period at a time when the administrative reins were passed to the Dutch government.

The nineteenth century opened auspiciously for Indonesia, at least in that reform was the order of the day. Hermann Daendels, a Dutch lawyer who had served under Napoleon, was sent by that emperor to Java, with instructions to strengthen its defenses against the British but also to institute administrative and legal reforms. To facilitate troop movements in Java, Daendels commenced work on a road from Batavia to Surabaja. He brought the puppet rulers under the direct control of Dutch officials, centralized the colonial government more strongly, took steps against graft and corruption, and established courts of law that recognized *adat*, the customary law of the villages. He abolished forced delivery of spices but not of other products. Daendels' reforms were bitterly opposed by some powerful factions in the Netherlands, and the lawyer was recalled in 1810.

That same year, Napoleon formally annexed the Netherlands to France, and so the Dutch possessions came to be regarded by the British as enemy territory. In 1811 an expedition under Lord

Minto, the British governor-general in India, landed 12,000 men on Java and quickly brought about the surrender of the entire island. Thomas Stamford Raffles, appointed British lieutenant-governor in Indonesia, carried out some of Daendels' reforms and initiated others. Raffles tried to do away with the native regents, substituting a European bureaucracy. In a move the Dutch would not have approved, he abolished the contingents and forced delivery systems in their entirety, instituting in their stead a free market in which peasant cultivators could participate as desired. He was willing to rent out farmlands, from which the farmers could take a profit after having paid the rent. Raffles' policies were successful, not only raising the Javanese standard of living but also increasing revenues eightfold.

Raffles was an extraordinary man, on the one hand an empire-builder, on the other a humanitarian and versatile scientist. Born on a ship in the West Indies, and with but little formal education, at the age of 14 he had become a clerk in the London office of the English East-India Company. Working 13 hours a day with documents from the British possessions in the Orient, the young Raffles somehow found time to learn French and the natural sciences. In 1805 he was sent to Penang to be assistant secretary to a new governor, and prepared himself for the post by learning Malayan. Stationed at several localities in the East, Raffles was given more and more authority. In addition, he studied the local flora and fauna, amassing scientific collections for shipment to England. Insects, scorpions, centipedes, mollusks, fishes, snakes, birds, even tigers and orangutans—all were collected and preserved for study. Near Malacca, the biological activities of Raffles may have puzzled the local sultans, but they appreciated his genuine enthusiasm for the land and its wildlife, and were easily persuaded to favor the British cause over the Dutch. It was Raffles who suggested to Lord Minto that the British occupy Java, which was but thinly garrisoned. This accomplished, it was Lord Minto who appointed Raffles lieutenant-governor of the islands.

The death of Raffles' wife in 1814 left the naturalist-administrator despondent, and he relieved his depression by even more intensive study and exploration of the islands. Although weakened by fever, he crossed Java on foot from the Java Sea to the Indian Ocean. He observed a volcanic eruption at close range, and uncovered Borobudur, the great Buddhist monument which the Muslim Indonesians had allowed to vanish beneath jungle growth. Studying the complex Javanese language, he wrote *History of Java,* and encouraged restoration and study of the ancient temples and ruins that dotted Java.

Like Daendels before him, Raffles was severely criticized for his liberalism, and probably would have been recalled even if Java had remained in British hands. But as it happened, the Napoleonic Wars ended; and at the Congress of Vienna, where various European affairs were settled, the British decided that a strong Netherlands was necessary to restore a balance of power on the continent. Java was returned to the Dutch, and in 1816 Raffles was ordered back to London. Not exactly in disgrace, he was nevertheless called upon to account for some details of his administration, and was demoted to governor of "Bencoolen" (Bengkulu), a Sumatran settlement that the British had decided to keep for a time. Here he abolished slavery and administrative abuses, reorganized the local government, founded schools, and greatly improved the living conditions locally. Although debilitated by fevers, he continued his biological explorations, discovering the pitcher-plant Nepenthes, the giant flower now called *Raffesia arnoldii,* and the Malayan tapir. He boldly visited the Batak, who were notorious cannibals at that time, and scrupulously recorded the recipe for the sauce they used on human flesh. (It was *sambal,* made of ground red hot *tjili* pepper with lemon juice and salt.) Raffles married again, and his children had wondrous playmates: tiger cubs, colorful birds, white gibbons, purring and playful clouded leopards, a sun bear that drank champagne. He claimed that he was through with politics, but in 1819 he recognized the potential importance of an island at the tip of the Malay Peninsula, insisting to his superiors that its acquisition was vital to British interests in the Far East. Once occupied by a village called Tumasik, the island had long been abandoned. Raffles founded a settlement there: Singapore, the Lion City, a name derived from Sanskrit but honoring the British lion. In just two or three years it was thriving, and was destined speedily to become the most important commercial center between Calcutta and Hongkong.

While involved with the Singapore project, Raffles lost three of his six children in six months time, to tropical diseases. Sending his youngest child back to England, he provided the new settlement with governmental organization, schools, and a botanical garden. Then, returning to Bengkulu, he assembled a priceless load of scientific material to take back with him to England: Malayan books and manuscripts, musical instruments, paintings and sculpture, stuffed animals, a tame tapir, thousands of drawings, a detailed map of Sumatra, notes for a projected history of that island and Borneo, human skulls from Batak cannibal feasts. Raffles left Bengkulu in 1824 with this collection, but when he was only 50 miles out of port, a seaman with a torch decided to tap a cask of brandy. In those days, the potency of an alcoholic brew was "proved" by its inflammability. Taking fire from sparks, the cask started a blaze that spread rapidly and sank the ship. The passengers and crew saved themselves in lifeboats, but everything else was lost. Making his way back to Bengkulu, Raffles amassed a second but smaller scientific collection. He got it back to England, where he was congratulated for building Singapore, but was presented by his superiors with a bill for a staggering 22,000 pounds; for his liberalism still had bitter opponents in high places, and his political enemies asserted that this sum of government money had been spent by him without justification. Attempting to reconstruct, mostly from memory, a financial statement of his past twelve years in office, he yet found time to create the Zoological Society of London, still an eminent scientific organization. In 1826, on the morning of his forty-fifth birthday, the empire-builder died at home, of a stroke. Singapore, today an independent nation with a population exceeding 2,000,000, is his greatest monument.

British presence in Java was but a brief interlude within the Dutch period, for with the return of the Dutch to the islands in 1816, the reforms of Daendels and Raffles were quickly abrogated. In 1824 the Netherlands Trading Company was formed at The Hague, devoted to the very opposite of free trade. This company, which is to say the Dutch government, was much in need of cash, for the price of coffee had slumped and a revolt in Belgium had proven costly. The Javanese were intolerably provoked by the company's failure to honor Raffles' commitments, especially in regard to the renting of land; and in 1825 an Indonesian emerged to challenge the right of European nations to manipulate his island as they saw fit. He was Diponegoro, a Javanese prince from Djokjakarta, and in that year he proclaimed war against the Dutch. It was the kind of war the Arabs called *jahad,* and the Malays *perang sabil*—a Muslim holy war against unbelievers, with Paradise assured for every Javanese who fell in battle. Diponegoro waged a guerrilla struggle for over five years before he was captured. This war cost the Netherlands a great deal of money and manpower. In 1830, Johannes Vandenbosch proposed the infamous "culture system," whereby the financial crisis would be eased by more rigorous exploitation of the Indies. The phrase "culture system" is the usual but awkward translation from the Dutch, "cultivation system" being a better term. Indonesia, or as much of it as possible, would be turned into vast, state-owned plantations, operated somewhat like the slave plantations of the southeastern United States. Coffee, sugar, indigo, tea, tobacco, cotton, pepper, cassava, kapok, cinnamon, and quinine would be cultivated by forced labor, and stated quotas of every crop would have to be delivered. Java was the greatest sufferer from this scheme, for the island was entirely in Dutch hands. Between 1840 and 1848, the proceeds of the cultivation system bolstered Holland's sagging economy, reduced her debts, and enabled her to increase her merchant marine; and no one protested when famine swept over the villages of Javanese who were not permitted to raise adequate food for themselves. For with affairs of the Indies left to the Netherlands Trading Company, which reported directly to the king, Hollanders at home knew little of events in the islands.

Encouraged by the success of the cultivation system, during the 1840s the Dutch extended their control in Sumatra, Borneo, and western New Guinea. The year 1848 saw political upheaval and constitutional reforms in the Netherlands, but for a time the only significant change in colonial affairs was the annual presentation of a report to the Dutch parliament. By 1854 the Netherlands had adopted a Colonial Constitution regulating forced labor and slavery, establishing a civil service, discussing the idea of schools in Indonesia, and making it possible for Europeans to lease certain lands in the islands. But it remained for a writer, Edward Douwes Dekker, to focus attention on the abuses of the cultivation system. Returning to the Netherlands after several years in Java, and writing under the pseudonym of Multatuli, in 1860 he published *Max Havelaar*, a work whose impact has been likened to that of *Uncle Tom's Cabin*. Public opinion was aroused, and the Dutch parliament was sensitive to it. In 1864 the colonial budget came under careful parliamentary scrutiny, and steps were taken to abandon the cultivation system—to abandon it very slowly, however. First, tea was taken off the system, then indigo, tobacco, and cinnamon. By 1870 only coffee and sugar, the most valuable commodities, were still under the system.

The Dutch profited greatly by the opening of the Suez Canal in 1869, for shipping expenses were reduced between the Indies and the Netherlands. With the establishment of a new pattern of maritime traffic, connecting Indonesia with the Red Sea lands, many Arabs went to the islands. Some of them were concerned with rejuvenating Islam in Indonesia, and their efforts along these lines were welcomed by certain ethnic groups. The Dutch, operating through the native sultans and punishing village heads if quotas were not met, had somewhat estranged the people from their own rulers, and the Islamic teachers provided a new leadership.

Although the views of Dutch liberals had to some degree improved living conditions for the islanders, political and social affairs remained about the same. Holding that free enterprise and the profit motive would promote the general welfare without formal planning, the liberals urged withdrawal of the Dutch government from certain colonial activities, leaving private enterprise to exploit the overseas holdings of the Netherlands. Under a system of private enterprise, the liberals pointed out, the government would receive money from rents and customs, while the colonies would purchase goods from the mother country. Under an agrarian reform law of 1870, private plantations could be leased to Europeans in Indonesia. As a result, much capital flowed from Europe to the

East Indies, most of it into sugar but some into the tin of Bangka and Belitung. In 1888 petroleum was discovered in Sumatra and Borneo, bringing more capital; and in 1890 the Royal Dutch Oil Company was founded. As the twentieth century approached, the introduced rubber tree and nut palm were bringing capital from the Netherlands, Britain, the United States, France, Belgium, and Germany. As Europe and the United States became highly industrialized, there seemed no limit to the demand for tropical produce, and the Dutch enjoyed unsurpassed prosperity. But if any financial gain accrued to the indigenous peoples of Indonesia, it was soon negated by population growth; for the population of Java had doubled between 1815 and 1860, and had more than doubled again by the beginning of the twentieth century. Also, Chinese continued moving into the Malay Peninsula, Singapore, and Indonesia, generally remaining unassimilated and swelling the middle class.

Around the beginning of the twentieth century, Dutch attention shifted from Java toward the other islands of Indonesia. Borneo had been more troublesome than otherwise. The Dutch had been driven from the island during the Napoleonic Wars, and Raffles had sent Alexander Hare from Java to treat with the sultan of Bandjarmasin. When the Dutch had returned to Borneo in 1816, they had found the way blocked not by indigenes but by Chinese miners who dominated parts of the east coast. In 1853 the Dutch had launched an attack against the Bornean Chinese, who had fought for three years before being defeated. Sumatra had proven even more troublesome. As far back as the 1830s there had been uprisings in that island. The *Paderi,* who in spite of the name were not Catholic priests but zealous Islamic reformers, had tried to displace the *adat* chiefs among the Minangkabau. The Dutch, realizing the danger of a revitalized Islam to their regime, had taken sides with the chiefs, fighting for years before the Minangkabau country was quieted. Next, Islamic reformers had begun working among the Atjehnese, and the Dutch had been powerless to interfere; but in 1824 the British and the Dutch had agreed to maintain an independent Atjeh as a buffer between them. The Atjehnese carried piracy to a fine art in the Selat Melaka, and by 1873, their depredations having become intolerable, they found themselves under attack by the Dutch. The Atjeh War lasted over 30 years, costing a quarter of a million lives. But aside from the discovery of natural resources in Borneo and Sumatra, there was a reason why the colonial government thought it well to strengthen its position in those islands, as well as in lesser, more easterly islands, even though local peoples might prove uncooperative. This reason was the fear of encroachment by other colonial powers; for at the beginning of the twentieth century, Germany was in northeastern New Guinea, Britain in Australia and southeastern New Guinea, Portugal still in and near eastern Timor, Britain in Brunei and North Borneo, the British-affiliated Brooke dynasty of "white *radjas*" in Sarawak, Britain in Singapore, Christmas Island, and the Andamans. The United States had replaced Spain in the Philippines, while Britain had replaced Denmark in the Nicobars and the Clunie-Ross family in the Cocos Islands. Thus, Dutch holdings were ringed about by those of other nations, in a pattern that had little correlation with physiography or the distribution of ethnic groups. By 1907, when the British agreed to withdraw from Sumatra, the Netherlands East Indies had taken on the outlines it would thereafter maintain, and would someday pass on to an Indonesian republic.

The Netherlands East Indies was ruled through a governor-general at Batavia, assisted by a cabinet and an advisory council both composed entirely of Hollanders. There was no popular representation at this time, but some effort was made to save the peasants from the worst effects of a money economy. Non-Indonesians could only rent, not buy, the land. Actual or potential *sawah*, as well as plots suitable for sugar or tobacco, could be leased only on an annual basis, in theory assuring that sufficient land would remain available for the peasants' food crops. Actual or potential *ladang* was leased on a long-term basis to large-scale operators who would develop plantations mostly of tea or rubber. Coffee was still grown under the cultivation system. Land rent was controlled; and to limit the influence of moneylenders, the colonial government set up pawnshops, as well as village banks where loans for agricultural supplies were made at moderate rates. The Village Act of 1906 restored to the villages the responsibility for social welfare, a move theoretically shoring up the damaged social structure, and relieving the Dutch of many problems. *Adat* law was recognized in local affairs.

The Dutch period in Indonesia brought with it the seeds of its own destruction, even though these were slow to take root and grow. For the West had produced not just empire-builders but also liberal philosophers, men of great intellectual stature who concerned themselves with economics, politics, science, human relations, the rights and responsibilities of man; and such brightly shining facets of Western thought could not be concealed by any number of profit-oriented merchants or administrators. A look at Indonesian census figures for the last half of colonial times will reveal an astonishingly large number of people classified as Dutch, and one might suppose that there had been a mass migration from Holland to the islands. This was not the case. Although some Dutch women came out to the Indies, the Dutchmen often took wives from the indigenous population, and raised large families. The offspring of such unions were legally regarded and classified as Dutch citizens, and the "Dutch" of the Indonesian census rolls were in large part island-born and of mixed ancestry. Such people were called Eurasians, Indo-Europeans, or Indos. Understandably, Dutch colonials often wanted their children to receive a Western-style education; and as a result, some island-born, Dutch-descended youths were sent to European schools, or to Dutch schools that were set up in larger colonial settlements of the Indies. About the only thing the colonial government could do with educated, Dutch-descended Indonesians was emphasize their "Dutchness," keep them and their ideas as far away from the general public as possible, and make positions for them in the civil service where they could be watched. Also, a few Indonesian royal families, cooperating closely with the Dutch, had been able to retain some wealth and to educate their own scions. Accordingly, by the opening of the twentieth century, there were some Western-educated Indonesians, at least a few of whom had pondered Adam Smith, Quesnay, Malthus, Ricardo, Owen, Saint-Simon, Mill, Marx, Engels—the controversial, worldly philosophers.

By the sort of coincidence that Indonesians and writers love, it was in the first year of the new century, 1901, that a child was born most auspiciously, at sunrise on the sixth day of the sixth month. The child's mother, Idaju, had been a Balinese temple dancer of Brahman descent, but she had adopted Islam in order to marry Raden Soekemi Sosrodihardjo, a Muslim Javanese who was teaching in a government primary school at Singaradja in northern Bali. Although Sosrodihardjo was notably heterodox, in fact a theosophist in the Hindu tradition, the union was locally opposed; for to the Balinese, marriage into some other ethnic group was well-nigh unthinkable. After paying a substantial fine in Singaradja for their transgression, the young couple removed to Surabaja in Java, where their first child, a girl, was born in 1899. On June 6, 1901, their second child, a boy, was born at sunrise. The boy was given the name of Kusno—just that, for in Indonesia a father's name was not forced upon his child, or a husband's name upon a wife. An Indonesian might have one name or half-a-dozen, but they were bestowed and not inherited, except in the case of Dutch-descended families who followed Western custom, and of some Chinese families.

In the year of Kusno's birth, the Dutch adopted the so-called Ethical Policy toward the Indies, its adoption reflecting an admission that the Netherlands, having profited for 300 years by exploiting Indonesia, should now do something for the islanders in return. The policy was implemented as a sort of welfare program, theoretically aiming at economic, social, and political progress. New bureaus were founded, concerning themselves chiefly with agriculture, irrigation, public works, village sanitation, and personal hygiene. An unsuccessful effort was made to induce emigration from overcrowded Java to the out-islands. Token attention was given to public education, but there were scarcely any jobs for educated Indonesians except in the civil service, and in practice the Dutch tried to make certain that there was no "intellectual proletariat" to agitate for further reforms. Indonesian life in the early years of the Ethical Policy is exemplified by the story of Sosrodihardjo and his family.

Although Idaju was the niece of the last *radja* of Singaradja, and Sosrodihardjo a descendant of the sultan of Kediri (hence the title Raden, applied to someone of direct royal descent), the couple were very poor as were most Indonesians at that time. Sosrodi-hardjo's pay as a teacher was 25 rupiahs a month, of which 10 went for the rent of a room on Djalan Pahlawan in Surabaja. The official rate of the rupiah was 45 to the dollar. In 1907 the family moved to Modjokerto, there to share a leaky shanty with a Javanese woman, Sarinah. For the Indonesians emphasized *gotong rojong*, mutual assistance in meeting life's problems, and many families sheltered one or two extra people. Sarinah helped care for the children, and in later life Kusno remembered her fondly. Deprived and sickly, envious of Chinese boys who could afford to shoot firecrackers on Muslim holidays, Kusno was entertained principally by his mother's stories of Balinese exploits. Idaju told of the battle of Puputan, where the boy's great-grandfather and many other Balinese arrayed themselves in their finest ceremonial costumes and died in a suicidal effort to keep the Dutch from taking their lovely island. She told how the last *radja* of Singaradja was invited onto a Dutch warship for a talk, but was forcibly detained and then banished while the Dutch confiscated his kingdom, home, fortune, and possessions. After school hours, Sosrodihardjo taught Kusno reading and Hindu philosophy, but also told how the boy's paternal great-great-great-grandmother had fought and died alongside Diponegoro in the Java War.

The family's Modjokerto quarters, the most inexpensive to be found, were in a bottomland that was inundated each rainy season by flood waters and sewage. Kusno, already weakened by malaria and dysentery, came down with the typhus. Sosrodihardjo lay on a mat under the boy's bed for ten weeks with the hope of focusing prayer and mystical emanations on the ailing child. Kusno recovered.

Elsewhere in Java, there were vague stirrings of discontent. In 1908 a group of Javanese medical students in Batavia formed a society called Budi Utomo, "High Endeavor." Carefully nonpolitical, it reaffirmed the dignity of the Javanese and the excellence of their culture. A few years later, in 1912, E. F. E. Douwes Dekker, called Setiabudi, formed the Indische Partij, the Indies Party. An Indo-Dutch grandnephew of the famous Multatuli, this Dekker urged Indonesian citizenship for all native-born people, and dared to speak that forbidden word, "independence." The Dutch quickly exiled all the leaders of the Indies Party to the Netherlands. The governor-general in Batavia could exile any person simply by proclaiming him a menace to the colonial regime; no trial was necessary. Also in 1912 a group called Muhammadijah was organized, nonpolitical and urging religious reforms in the direction of orthodox Islam. And in this portentous year, a Javanese man named Oemar Said Tjokroaminoto became first chairman of a group called Sarekat Islam. This society had started out as a merchants' protective association, Sarekat Dagang Islam, intended to help Indonesian batik and textile entrepreneurs meet the growing competition of the Chinese. Composed principally of *santri*, the SDI grew into a religious and political organization with multifarious interests, and in 1912 changed its name to Islamic Union, Sarekat Islam. Tjokroaminoto was charismatic, and of sufficiently high *prijaji* birth to have received a Western education. As a Muslim, he had made the *hadj*, the prescribed pilgrimage to Mecca, and so was always addressed as Hadji; but he was also a mystic in the old Javanese-Hindu tradition.

In 1914, Communism was introduced into Indonesia by a Dutchman, Hendrik Sneevliet, who under the name of Maring also became the first Comintern agent in China. Sneevliet founded the Indies Social Democratic Association, Indonesia's first Communist party. Infiltration of other organizations was a Communist tactic, and Tjokroaminoto found his leadership of Sarekat Islam contested not only by the orthodox Hadji Agus Salim of Sumatra, but also by Alimin, a Communist. But the Javanese masses were firmly behind Tjokroaminoto, who was whispered to be the legendary *ratu adil*, a "righteous prince" who would free the land from its oppressors. Today it is easy to see that the nearly simultaneous emergence of Budi Utomo, the Indies Party, the Muhammadijah, and Sarekat Islam constituted an overt indication of dissatisfaction among all major segments of Javanese society, from the *prijaji* and the Western-educated elite through the *santri* and the *abangan*.

Around this time, Sosrodihardjo became disturbed over Kusno's seemingly hopeless existence, and decided that the boy's lot would be improved by a new and luckier name. The *Mahabharata* provided one. Among the best-loved tales of the *Mahabharata* was that of a man whose name meant "Ear." The story, reminiscent of both the ancient Greek and the Judaeo-Christian mythology, related that a virgin became pregnant from the rays of the sun god who, rather than have the girl be deflowered in reverse by a normal delivery, extracted the baby from her ear. The miraculously conceived and delivered child, a boy, was therefore called Karna, "Ear." In later life he became a hero, in fact the very prototype of heroes. The Javanese version of "Karna" was "Karno"; and a Sanskrit-derived Javanese prefix, "Su-" (or rather "Soe-" in the Dutch-influenced spelling of that day) meant "best." And so the child Kusno was given the new and more promising name of Sukarno, best hero. Sosrodihardjo found it hard to support his children, and the young Sukarno was sent to stay with his grandmother, who made and sold batik at Tulungagung, about 60 miles southwest of Modjokerto. Believing that the boy had supernatural powers of healing, she put him to licking the afflicted parts of ailing villagers, and decided that he would be a clairvoyant. But alas for aval ambitions; Sukarno turned out to be a visionary of quite a different sort.

Sosrodihardjo had always wanted the boy to be educated in a Dutch college, seemingly a hopeless ambition. To attend one of these colleges, a student must have been graduated from a Dutch secondary school; and to enroll in the latter he must have been graduated from a Dutch primary school. However, few Indonesians could send their children to a Dutch primary school, which was open principally to the Dutch or Indo-Dutch offspring of civil servants and to a few scions of cooperative Indonesian royalty. For the masses, the Dutch had built a scattering of so-called Inland Primary Schools, usually running only through the fifth grade. ("Inland" was a euphemism for "native" in the pejorative sense.) Accordingly, this grade was the highest that was likely to be attained by Indonesian children, most of whom in fact did not have even an Inland Primary School in their neighborhood. As a further bar to educational advancement of the masses, the Inland Primary Schools were the only ones at which Indonesians did not have to pay tuition. Sukarno had attended an Inland Primary School of which his father was Headmaster; or rather was *Menteri Guru*, for an Indonesian was not allowed to call himself Headmaster. At Sosrodihardjo's school, the work of the first three grades was done in Javanese and the last two in Malayan, with Dutch lessons twice weekly. Sosrodihardjo prevailed upon the Headmaster of a nearby Dutch primary school to accept Sukarno, who was, however, demoted a grade because he spoke poor Dutch. Scrimping even more, Sosrodihardjo got up a few rupiahs to pay a woman for coaching the boy in the needed language.

Sukarno was finishing the work of the primary school when World War I broke out. The conflict had little direct effect on the Netherlands East Indies. Holland remained neutral, although suffering considerably as a result of her geographic position between Germany and the Allies. In 1914, Australian troops moved into northeastern New Guinea; thereafter, Indonesia would not have German neighbors.

When Sukarno finished the Dutch primary school, his father determined to enter him in what was then the finest secondary school of eastern Java, the Hogere Burger School in Surabaja. The boy was scholastically qualified to enter, but there remained the problem of finances. Sosrodihardjo would continue to scrimp; Idaju would take in boarders, as well as hand-paint and sell batik. Sukarno's older sister, Soekarmini, had married and was living about 30 miles away. Her husband, Poegoeh, was employed in the Irrigation Office of the Department of Public Works, and would be able to send a little money for the boy on whom the family's hopes were pinned. Then there was the matter of housing for Sukarno in Surabaja. Sosrodihardjo had a Surabajan friend with whom the boy could live: Tjokroaminoto. And so at the age of 15, his few possessions in a small bag, Sukarno was sent away to live with the family of Tjokroaminoto. But before the boy left, his mother stretched him out on the ground and stepped over him, back and forth three times, in the belief that a mystic life-giving force would pass into him and keep him well.

By 1916 Surabaja was a bustling port city full of merchants, laborers, and sailors. There were many *kampong*, which might be thought of as country villages transferred to the city and huddled there, slum-like. Tjokroaminoto lived with a wife and four young children in a ramshackle house, half of which was turned over to a number of students including Sukarno. In 1917 Sosrodihardjo was promoted to a better job at Blitar, and was able to send his son the equivalent of $1.50 monthly, for pocket money. Sukarno's only luxury was the cinema, where for three cents he could have one of the poorer seats behind the screen, and where he learned to read the Dutch subtitles backward. It was indeed a luxury, for three cents was more than the average daily wage of a Javanese peasant. But most of Sukarno's time was spent in studying, and in visiting the library of a local theosophical society. More significantly, he was permitted to listen to the political discussions that went on endlessly at Tjokroaminoto's house. And so the youth lived, frequently homesick, studying Western thought in school and theosophical mysticism in the library, daily embittered by Dutch racism—"No Dogs or Inlanders Allowed," proclaimed notices on swimming pools. Of 300 students in the Hogere Burger School, only 20 were "inlanders" like Sukarno, the others being Dutch.

There exist a few high-school photographs of Sukarno. They show him to be a small youth with the delicate features of his Balinese mother, his round face dominated by large, dark eyes. He looks alert, intelligent, sensitive, of course grave for these pictures, a little sad. His Western-style coat, high collar, and bow tie contrast with his Surabaja-style turban. For group photographs the "inlanders" were segregated, and in such pictures Sukarno looks very young and vulnerable among older Javanese with closed faces; but he was active in school affairs, within the limits imposed by the racist attitudes of the times. He joined a study club, a debating club, and a dramatic society, as well as Tri Koro Darmo ("Three Holy Objectives") and Young Java, youth groups devoted to charitable works and the furthering of Javanese culture. The young men who made up Tri Koro Darmo and Young Java were idealistic—the "three holy objectives" were social, political, and economic freedom for Indonesia—but they were in no position to bring about immediate reforms.

Sukarno's studiousness, his enthusiasm for youth groups, his devotion to Tjokroaminoto's family, his brief amours with Dutch girls, his idealism—these may now seem to reflect the predictable attitudes of a pleasantly normal high-school lad; but it must be remembered that Sukarno and his few "inlander" classmates were deadly serious, in some matters wise beyond their years, and conscious of the gravity of their position. For in those days, only a few hundred "inlanders," out of Indonesia's teeming millions, had broken through the barriers that stood in the way of an education beyond the primary level; and in a very real sense these youths were the hope of a brighter future for the multitude. While still in the Hogere Burger School, Sukarno was shouldering responsibility. He became secretary, then chairman of Young Java. He proposed marriage to a willing Dutch girl, with a predictable reaction from her father. Tjokroaminoto's wife died, and the students she had mothered left the house of mourning; but Sukarno entered into a contract of *kawin gantung* with the motherless daughter of the bereaved man. *Kawin gantung* was a marriage which, although legally and religiously binding, was not consummated for some reason, in this case because the girl was too young. Thus, a part of Tjokroaminoto's family burden was passed to Sukarno, who, as Tjokroaminoto's son-in-law, became more closely involved with the affairs of Sarekat Islam. Under the pen-name of Bima (another hero of the *Mahabharata*), Sukarno wrote over 500 inflammatory articles for *Utusan Hindia* ("Messenger of the Indies"), Tjokroaminoto's publication. Sosrodihardjo never learned that his son was Bima who advocated overthrow of the Dutch government; nor did Idaju learn, for she could neither read nor write.

Even before finishing high school, Sukarno had come to understand how the masses love symbols and slogans, which can be responded to emotionally without the necessity of rational analysis. At a meeting of Young Java he proposed the wearing of the *petji* as a symbol of nationalistic aspirations. The name *petji* or *pitji* was a Malayan and Javanese version of a Dutch loan-word meaning "little cap," and the object itself was a cap favored mostly by impoverished city-dwellers. In those days, a majority of Javanese men wore a kind of turban or exaggerated kerchief, its color and style chosen to match the *kain sarung* ("sarong") and to indicate ethnic affiliation; while Javanese intellectuals often went bareheaded, having accepted the Dutch view that traditional headgear was a sign of backwardness. Sukarno had well judged the temperament of the masses; in a very short while, a black velveteen *petji* had been adopted by most Javanese men, and the doffing of it in public was considered rude.

In 1921 Sukarno was graduated from high school and made plans to attend a university in the Netherlands; but his mother would not consent to his leaving the islands, where she felt his destiny lay, and he settled for a technical college at Bandung, where he lived with a married couple, friends of Tjokroaminoto. Around this time Sukarno created a special name to designate the Javanese masses. Although they formed the lowest socioeconomic stratum of the population, they were not exactly proletarians in the usual sense, for they owned means of production such as garden plots, draft animals, agricultural implements, and fishing gear. Sukarno dubbed them "Marhaens" after a very common Javanese personal name, and regarded himself as a Marhaenist.

Soon after enrolling at Bandung, Sukarno was confronted with a difficult choice. Many labor guilds had been organized, and one of them in Garut, West Java, went on strike. It was Indonesia's first strike, and the legal questions surrounding it became known as the Afdeling Case. The Dutch colonial government passed a law that anyone inciting to strike could be imprisoned for six years, and suddenly arrested Tjokroaminoto as having fomented this one. Tjokroaminoto's affairs, children, and new wife were left to languish in Surabaja. To the dismay of his own relatives, Sukarno chose to withdraw from college in order to support Tjokroaminoto's family and carry on some part of his work. Taking a job in a Surabaja railway office, Sukarno missed no opportunity of talking to passengers about nationalism. For Tjokroaminoto's family he supervised a *slametan,* a highly regarded ritual feast in which food is offered to a variety of Islamic, Hindu, and animistic spirits; he also supervised the *sunat,* ritual circumcision, of Tjokroaminoto's young son Anwar. As it happened, the Sarekat Islam leader was released from jail in 1922, and Sukarno returned to college.

He soon divorced Tjokroaminoto's daughter in the Islamic fashion. This required the man to pronounce three *talak,* or repudiations. First was the statement, "I divorce you, one stage." Thereafter, a period of 100 days would pass, during which reconciliation was possible. Then, a like statement as second stage virtually confirmed the separation. The third *talak*, "I divorce you," was final, and the couple could never remarry unless the woman had an interim marriage to another man. The girl was returned to her father's home, where she later married a student. In 1922 Sukarno gave an impassioned speech at a Bandung political rally, and drew police attention to himself. Warned by the dean of the college to stay quiet or suffer expulsion, Sukarno buckled down to his studies in the field of civil engineering. The Bandung couple with whom Sukarno lived went through a divorce, and in 1923 the woman, Inggit Garnasih, married Sukarno. In years to come, she would share many of his triumphs and tribulations.

Of the large student body at Bandung, only eleven were "inlanders," and even their number was reduced with time. In 1926, Sukarno was one of three Indonesians who were graduated. His degree was Master of Engineering, and for many years thereafter he was called *Insjinjoer* (Engineer) Sukarno. While he was in college, other Indonesians had been working in their own way toward independence. The year that he was graduated, the First Congress of Indonesian Youth was held to extoll Indonesian culture; and the Minangkabau poet Muhammad Yamin, principal speaker, found that he had to address the polyglot listeners in Dutch, their only common language. Attention was thus drawn to the need for a national language.

In college, Sukarno had found the emphasis chiefly on skills that benefited the Dutch. Although he studied German and one or two other academic subjects, he had mostly been taught how to design irrigation systems, lay out towns and plantations, and build roads in a way that would mostly effectively bring produce to ports. Mathematics, his poorest subject, had dealt mostly with geodetics and surveying techniques. Wolf Shoemaker, a Dutch engineering professor whom Sukarno admired for his open-mindedness, advised him to accept a position in the Department of Public Works; but Sukarno refused. Artistic and creative, and having done especially well in architecture, he did accept a commission to design and build a house for a District Chief of the Department. Dispensing with traditional Dutch styles, so poorly suited to the tropics, Sukarno built a functional house that was much talked about. Other commissions were proffered but he refused them, for they came either from the Dutch or from Indo-Dutch civil servants. Having been graduated, he received no more financial aid from his relatives; and, declining to work for the Dutch regime, he accepted a position teaching history and mathematics at the Ksatria Institute, run by Douwes Dekker Setiabudi, who had been allowed to return from exile. However, all classes were regularly monitored by the Dutch; and when he refused to modify his lectures on the evils of colonialism, Sukarno was dismissed on orders from above. He opened an engineering office in Bandung with Anwari (not to be confused with Tjokroaminoto's son Anwar), who had graduated with him.

Like the British, the Dutch were fond of social clubs, and in Bandung's comparatively enlightened atmosphere Sukarno was allowed to join one; but as an "inlander" he was barred from holding office. Resigning on this account, and followed in his resignation by other Indonesians, in 1926 he opened a study club run by himself, Anwari, and three young lawyers—Isqaq, Sunaryo, and Sartono—who had just returned from studies in Europe. Sartono was destined soon to become Sukarno's defense attorney as the young engineering graduate continued to inveigh against Dutch rule. The five staged their meetings in a house on what was then Regentsweg, now Djalan Kabupaten. As the club grew, and branches sprang up in other cities, Sukarno issued a club paper, *Suluh Indonesia Muda* ("Torch of Indonesian Youth"). Also in 1926, Sarekat Islam split, one faction remaining under Tjokroaminoto, but the other, larger and Communist-dominated, remodeling itself as Sarekat Rakjat ("People's Union"). The Communists at this time attempted a revolution but the Dutch quickly crushed it and exiled 2,000 revolutionaries. The Indonesian masses became despondent, for Sarekat Islam, which seemed their only hope for independence, had been much weakened by the split. Stepping quickly into the breach, Sukarno and six other study club members organized the Partai Nasionalis Indonesia, the Indonesian National

Party, urging immediate independence. A branch chairman of the PNI was Ali Sastroamidjojo, who years later would become Sukarno's first ambassador to the United States.

Sukarno rapidly emerged as the head of the PNI. Although identifying himself with the masses, he had the interests and verbal skills of the *prijaji*. He was a good artist, a forceful writer, an accomplished linguist who could converse in five languages. In later years, exiled by the Dutch, he proved himself a talented playwright, actor, and producer; even in early Bandung days he developed his speeches in the fashion of a play, each leading to a dramatic and inarguable conclusion. His memory for people, places, events, and facts was unsurpassed. Yet, he could move easily among the masses, his personality inspiring trust and confidence, and his insight into human affairs penetrating. Whole crowds were captivated by him, his colorful metaphors seeming to bring new life and meaning to the most prosaic topics. Soetan Takdir Alisjahbana, who came to be known as the "dean of Indonesian letters," was a student in the Advanced Teachers' Training College at Tegallega, a Bandung suburb, in 1927, and often passed the house on Regentsweg where Sukarno and his four close associates met. Alisjahbana has written that the five young intellectuals were even then the pride, hope, and guide of a new generation of Indonesians, for whom they symbolized an awakening, a new era; and that the superior strength of Sukarno's personality was already evident.

Sukarno traveled around the Bandung area lecturing, trailed everywhere by the police. In a whimsical gesture of which his associates did not approve, he organized the Bandung prostitutes to spy on the police and report what political raids were in planning. Sukarno and Inggit were still very poor, taking in boarders to help meet expenses; for not much business was brought to an engineer who was under surveillance. In 1928 the Second Congress of Indonesian Youth was held in Batavia, pledging devotion to one nation which was to be called Indonesia—a usage that had been forbidden by the Dutch, who accepted only the name Netherlands East Indies. The Congress also pledged devotion to a national language, to be called the Indonesian language, Bahasa Indonesia. Sukarno spread the ideals of the Congress to the many branches of the PNI, where the members sang the newly composed national anthem, *Indonesia Raja* ("Great Indonesia"). In that year, Sukarno was denounced in the Volksraad—the Dutch-dominated Indonesian parliament—and he responded by federating his PNI with all other major nationalistic parties, forming the Permufakatan Partai-partai Politik Indonesia ("Alliance of Indonesian Political Parties"). As chairman of the combined organization he was able to lecture more widely.

Sukarno's approach at this time was something like that of Mohandas Karamchand Gandhi, the Mahatma ("Great Soul") who at that same time was working for Indian independence from Britain. Rallying the masses behind him, Sukarno revealed to the world the piteous conditions under which they lived, cut through the euphemism and hypocrisy of colonial pronouncements, and appealed in the name of humanity for the freedoms the Westerners claimed to value. He did not specifically advocate violence but rather warned that it would come if there were not sweeping reforms. Probably this essentially nonviolent approach explains why Sukarno was left to talk for a while, although more than 2,000 of his activist colleagues were hustled off to die in malarious concentration camps at Tanah Merah, Tanah Tinggi, and elsewhere. Also, the Netherlands were not wholly lacking in liberals and humanitarians, even though their influence was considerably attenuated toward the Indies; and in Indonesia, talk about future independence was tolerable—barely—as long as it did not lead to immediate action. But with the stockmarket crash of October 1929, ushering in the Great Depression, the Netherlands immediately determined to recoup its financial losses by more rigorous exploitation of the Indies; and the possibility of eventual Indonesian independence could no longer be even hinted at. Colonial school curricula were stripped of courses that did not obviously lead to more effective utilization of Indonesian natural resources and labor. The islands were quickly turned into a police state with press and mail censorship, an informer network, tight police control, and mass arrests under cover of darkness. Before 1929 was out, orders were given to suppress Sukarno. In Surakarta he gave a speech. Late that night he was arrested by 50 policemen armed with rifles, and locked in

Margangsan, a prison for the insane. From there he was taken to Bantjeuj jail in Bandung, where he learned that a series of carefully planned, simultaneous raids had imprisoned thousands of his followers, including 40 top men. Although the PPPI had no arms, the trumped-up charge against it was that of planning an armed revolt, to take place in early 1930. In prison, Sukarno wrote *Indonesia Menggugat* ("Indonesia Accuses"), a political history of the islands and a protest against colonialism. After eight months' incarceration, he was brought to trial and sentenced to four years behind the stone walls of Sukamiskin Prison at Bandung. The choice of Sukamiskin, which was primarily for Dutch law-breakers, reflected the colonial government's fear that Sukarno might inflame Indonesian prisoners, most of whom had been convicted only of political offenses against the colonial regime. Sukarno took to studying the Koran, the only literature available to him. In the Netherlands there was much protest against the unfairness of the long sentence, which was then commuted by the governor-general to two years. In late 1931 Sukarno was released from prison. Special police patrols were detailed, to prevent mass demonstrations.

There exist some photographs of Sukarno in the days immediately following his release from Sukamiskin. His clothes hang on him loosely, and his eyes blaze strangely in his emaciated face. Catching the first train to Surabaja, within twenty-four hours of his release he was addressing the Greater Indonesian Congress, assuring the delegates that Bung Karno—"Brother 'Karno"—was with them again. Much had happened in his absence. The PNI had been outlawed, crushed; some of his lieutenants had formed "Partindo," the Partai Indonesia, but it was not thriving. Two Netherlands-educated Indonesians, Soetan Sjahrir and Mohammad Hatta, had tried to win Sukarno's support to themselves, forming the Pendidikan Nasional Indonesia. The name of this new party meant "Indonesian National Education," but its initials, PNI, were intended to recall Sukarno's independence party. Seeing how the original PNI had collapsed with the jailing of Sukarno and a few others, Hatta urged no further reliance on charismatic leaders, but instead on a system of trained cadres who could indoctrinate and educate the masses, slowly leading them to freedom at some indefi-

308

nite time in the future. Hatta would only move cautiously, and Sukarno would not wait. In 1932 Sukarno joined Partindo and was
elected chairman. To support himself financially he established an
architectural bureau with Rooseno who was also a teacher, and the
two designed several small buildings in Bandung. Aided by Mas-
kun, who had been active in the original PNI, Sukarno prepared a
Partindo organ, *Fakiran Rakjat* ("The People's Needs"), and published it from his own house. With Bung Karno free and vocal
again, nationalistic fervor swept across Java stronger than ever before.

The colonial government made it a crime to read *Fakiran Rakjat*
or to wear the *petji*. Sukarno countered by writing *Mentjapai Indonesia Merdeka,* "Toward Indonesian Independence." This pam-
phlet was banned and confiscated, and houses raided to discover
readers. Any group of more than three people might be hauled off
to jail. Eight months after his release from Sukamiskin, Sukarno
was at Md. Husni Thamrin's house in Batavia, when he was again
arrested "in the name of the Queen." He was returned to Sukamiskin where he was kept in a small, solitary cage for eight months;
and this time the verdict was exile, presumably for life, to the remote fishing village of Endeh on Flores. The choice of Endeh reflected the Dutch fear that he might inflame the thousands of exiles
in the more widely used concentration camps. Sukarno was allowed three minutes to say good-bye to his mother and father, who
had sacrificed so much for him. Into exile with him would go
Inggit, her baby niece whom she and Sukarno had adopted, and
her mother whom they had also sheltered.

At first shunned by local people who were under Dutch scrutiny,
and being scarcely able to bear idleness, Sukarno suffered greatly
during his first few years of exile. He took to writing plays, penning twelve of them between 1934 and 1938. His warmly human
personality winning the confidence of the Endehnese and even the
local Dutch, Sukarno managed to organize a dramatic society, the
Kelimutu Show Club, and to convert a barn into a theater. Playing
to large audiences which included both Dutch and Endehnese, the
group actually made money. Sukarno was also allowed to peddle
batik imported from a shop in Bandung—a subtle gesture of the

colonial government, designed to reveal this upstart *prijaji* as a moneygrubber in the Dutch tradition. Inggit, more than a decade older than Sukarno, had borne no children, and so the couple adopted two girls in Flores; and an Endehnese boy also attached himself to the household.

There were occasional letters from home, one of them bringing the depressing information that Tjokroaminoto was dying. Sukarno himself was suffering from chronic malaria, and the day came when he could not rise. When news of this reached Batavia, Thamrin quickly published the information that the colonial government was allowing Bung Karno to die of malaria in exile. In 1938, after nearly five years on Flores, the ailing Sukarno was removed to Bengkulu, Sumatra, and in that healthier town he recovered. At first he had trouble making friends with the highly conservative, orthodox Muslim inhabitants of Bengkulu, who had mostly supported Muhammadijah; but winning them over, he was eventually asked to teach in one of their schools, and he organized a Java-Sumatra interisland seminar on Islamic reform. He wrote more plays, started a debating club, and was able to live a fairly normal life as long as he desisted from revolutionary activities. Under the pennames of Guntur and Abdurrachman he wrote a few articles. When Germany invaded Holland in 1940 at the beginning of World War II, he was allowed to write under his own name, for like many Indonesians he could find little sympathy for the Nazis. Thus, from exile in Bengkulu, he was permitted to send articles to a newspaper published by Tjokroaminoto's son Anwar. In 1941 Sukarno wrote that patriotism must not be based on the narrow brand of nationalism that glorifies a nation above the people who compose it.

Japan had actually been at war longer than Germany. In 1931 the Japanese had attacked Manchuria, in 1937 North China, in early 1939 Hainan and the Spratling Islands. When Germany invaded the Netherlands, Japan laid plans to move south into Indonesia. In January 1942, she landed troops on Borneo and Sulawesi, crossed into Burma from Thailand, set up a base on New Britain, and captured the Malay Peninsula from the British. In February she marched into the great British fortress of Singapore, and took

Sumatra with its rich oilfields. Japanese troops entered Sumatra from the east, arriving at Palembang; and word came that they were moving westward on Bengkulu—were in fact already at Lubuklinggau, a railway junction between Palembang and Bengkulu. The colonial government then ordered that Sukarno be evacuated, lest he fall into the hands of the Japanese and prove an asset to them. For this man, so long hounded by the Dutch, already jailed or exiled by them for a total of almost twelve years, could hardly have been expected to lead his people against the Japanese, who in any event were sweeping as irresistibly as a tidal wave across the Pacific. Sumatra was being evacuated from Padang on the island's west coast. Under armed guard, Sukarno and his family were taken north to Mukomuko, whence they had to walk most of the remaining 130 miles to Padang, prisoners and guards trudging along together through a land of frightened people.

Padang was in chaos, with thousands of civilian and military refugees awaiting transportation to Australia, their time running out as Japanese troops, tanks, and armored cars crossed the island. A plane scheduled to take Sukarno away did not arrive, and his panic-stricken guards abandoned him in the exodus. It was a serious mistake for the Dutch. After locating a former Bengkulu friend, Waworunto, with whom he could live, Sukarno visited a large trading organization, called a meeting of it, turned the meeting into a mass rally, urged the people to remain calm when the Japanese arrived, and said a lengthy Islamic prayer.

A week later the Japanese thundered into Padang. Their coming was viewed with mixed emotions, but the predominant one was relief that the hated Dutch regime was at an end. An Indonesian flag, bicolor, a broad red stripe above a white, had been designed; and soon it was flying from hundreds of staffs in Padang. The Japanese quickly pulled the unauthorized banners down. And, as the Dutch had feared, they sought out Sukarno, proposing that he help administer Indonesian affairs for them.

Before the end of February 1942, Japan had overwhelmed the Allied naval forces in the Battle of the Java Sea. In early March, one Japanese force took Rangoon in Burma, a second landed at Salamaua and Lae in northeastern New Guinea, and a third over-

ran Java. Japanese headquarters were established at Bandung. Sukarno had not reached an agreement with his new captors, but
after they took Java it was obvious that they would control all Indonesia. Although designating the islands as part of a "Southern
Resources Area" to be exploited for the war effort, the Japanese
promised eventual freedom for Indonesia, and spoke much about
Asians united against white imperialists, about a Greater East Asia
Co-Prosperity Sphere. Sukarno was allowed to return to Java,
where he quickly sought out family, friends, and colleagues. He
learned that no strong leader had emerged in his absence; the people would still follow Bung Karno. Like Sukarno, Mohammad
Hatta and Sjahrir had been exiled by the Dutch and freed by the
Japanese. Meeting privately, these three men concurred that the
Japanese would inevitably govern the islands through Indonesian
leaders. Putting aside their differences, they agreed among themselves to accept the burden of leadership, and to work toward Indonesian independence as far as circumstances would permit.
Hatta was qualified to handle affairs on a diplomatic level, Sjahrir
to manipulate the underground organizations, Sukarno to appear
openly and to rally the masses. Obviously the Japanese would not
tolerate overtly infractious Indonesian leaders; and Sukarno, in
particular, would be exposing himself to charges of collaboration.
But no doubt all three of these men felt that they could cope with
the Japanese, who at that time spoke reassuringly of independence,
and who had gratified the islanders by imprisoning a vast number
of Dutch and Indo-Dutch civil servants. Never afraid of challenge,
and accustomed to moving boldly, Sukarno accepted the Japanese
proposal that he become the nominal head of the Indonesian government. Now he would work for independence within Japanese-
imposed rather than Dutch-imposed limits. He could not have fore-
seen that the Asian overlords would prove more heartless than the
Dutch had ever been.

Nationalistic sentiment had persisted while Sukarno was in exile,
but had taken a new course. The Dutch had crushed the more extreme nationalist groups while ignoring the moderate ones, and the
trend had been toward broad-based political parties that hoped to
influence the Volksraad, the Parliament. Parindra, the Greater In-

donesian Party, was a union of conservative groups, while Gerindo, the Indonesian People's Movement, represented the moderate left. The MIAI was a combination of Muhammadijah with the conservative Muslim Nahdatul Ulama; and the PII, Indonesian Islamic Party, was a political arm of the Muslim front. Moderate and radical nationalists had united as Gapi, the Indonesian Political Concentration, to press for a Volksraad composed of Indonesians. The Madjelis Rakjat Indonesia, the Council of the Indonesian People, combined secular and religious groups who wanted an Indonesian parliament, national language, anthem, and flag. All these organizations had emerged between 1935 and 1941. In early 1943 the Japanese sponsored the creation of the Putera, the Center of People's Power, to include all the former nationalist parties; and later in that year they supported the Masjumi (Madjelis Sjuro Muslimin Indonesia), the Council of Indonesian Muslim Associations, which was to include all the Islamic parties. At least superficially, the Japanese were backing the nationalists and the *santri*, the two groups least identified with Dutch rule. But Japan's occupation of Indonesia was a military one, the more easterly islands being administered by the Japanese navy and the more westerly ones by the army, whose methods were notably brutal. Indonesian workers were forced to wear an identification tag and bow to Japanese soldiers. Women were rounded up and sent to Japanese soldiers' brothels. Under the infamous systems of *hei-ho* and *romusha*, Indonesian men were conscripted by the hundreds of thousands, torn from their families, sent to soldier or to work wherever the Japanese saw fit. The men were shipped to Sumatra to work in the oilfields; to Borneo to dig in the mines; to dozens of ports to unload ships; to Irian Barat, Halmahera, and other islands to build airdromes; to Burma where they slaved and died alongside prisoners of war rebuilding the ancient Burma Road. Spies and paid informers were everywhere. Protestors were picked up by the dreaded Kempeitai, the Japanese Secret Police, and tortured as a lesson to those who would not obey. Sukarno himself was bloodied about the head by a Japanese military patrol because a member of his household did not extinguish the lights quickly enough when a blackout was signaled. He was constantly spied upon. Harsh direc-

313

tives were issued in his name, but the majority of Indonesians understood his position and did not lose faith in him.

There was not much that he could do for his people. As the Japanese confiscated food and medical supplies, he promulgated information about the use of wild foods and herbs. Drawing on the lore of his boyhood days, he told how citronella grass could be planted around a house to discourage mosquitos; how the herb called *ketepeng* could be made to yield an anti-malarial; how the mucilaginous sap of a blue-flowered Commelina is soothing to blisters and burns; how the coarse *alang-alang* grass contains a febrifuge. He told how Inggit had planted a dooryard plot of maize, and urged that other families follow her example. Through Sukarno, the Sendenbu (Bureau of Propaganda) spread the news that the rice shortage was to be blamed not on the Japanese but on the Dutch who had converted so much potential *sawah* into fields of export crops; for with Allied ships lurking in the Bay of Bengal, rice shipments from Burma and India were temporarily cut off. Sukarno was allowed to address enormous gatherings, but his speeches were carefully scrutinized in advance. Nevertheless, with his keen knowledge of Indonesian metaphor and traditional literature, he was often able to inject nationalistic sentiments into what the Japanese took for bland pronouncements.

During the terrible years of Japanese occupation, an underground resistance developed in Java. Many of its members were captured and tortured by the Kempeitai, but Sukarno was able to bring about the release of some partizans by having them paroled to him. Among the people so rescued were Anwar, who had been caught listening to a clandestine radio broadcast; Darmasetyawan, who was a nephew of Sukarno's nearest contact with the underground; the lawyer and patriot Sujudi; and Amir Sjarifuddin, who was an underground leader. Subversion of Japanese objectives also came about from an unexpected direction as a group of Indonesian intellectuals began to capitalize on Japanese unfamiliarity with the languages of the island.

The story is a remarkable one. A national language, Bahasa Indonesia, had long been urged by Indonesian youths and intellectuals. While some Dutch colonial officials had favored the idea, many had been cool to it for it had nationalistic implications; and the Dutch language had sufficed for colonial purposes. The Japanese were faced with a dilemma; for on the one hand they had forbidden the Dutch language, arresting anyone heard conversing in it, but on the other hand they wanted to propagandize even the remotest villagers by radio, leaflets, and newspapers. Although intending eventually to make their own language the national one, the Japanese realized that it would take years to accomplish this aim; and in the meanwhile they would have to encourage an indigenous language in order to reach the polyglot population. While adding courses in Japanese to every school curriculum, in latter 1942 the Asian conquerors inaugurated the Komisi Bahasa Indonesia, the Commission for an Indonesian Language. It was obvious that such a language would have to be based on Malayan. This was the native tongue of only about 5,000,000 Indonesians at that time, but it served as a lingua franca, a second language, for uncounted others, and was spoken also in the Malay Penninsula, Singapore, and parts of Borneo lying beyond Indonesian territory.

The history of Malayan was a distinguished one. From its homeland on opposite sides of the Selat Melaka, this language had been spread widely by Sriwidjaja, and had reached the more easterly islands before the coming of the Europeans. Pigafetta, Magellan's Italian navigator, had compiled a glossary of it in Tidore, and van Linschoten had written that Malayan enjoyed the same prestige in the Indies as French in Europe. Furthermore, Malayan had been a vehicle for the spread of Islam in Indonesia, as well as for the islands' first Christian propaganda, that of Francisco Xavier in the Moluccas. The task of the Komisi would be to add to this useful language a large number of terms, mostly Western-derived, relating to modern culture; to set down the grammatic and orthographic norms; and to resolve certain conflicting usages that had developed in different parts of the Malayan-speaking world.

Takdir Alisjahbana, Amir Hamzah, and Armijn Pané were among the scholars appointed to the Komisi. These three pioneers of modern-style literature in Indonesia, all of them Sumatrans, had edited *Pudjangga Baru*, "New Writer," a literary magazine with wide cultural and political support. Alisjahbana, trained as a lawyer but self-educated in many fields, had been associated with the Government Publishing House in Batavia. Hamzah, son of a sultan, had translated much Indian and Persian literature into Malayan; had edited articles in Chinese, Hindi, Japanese, and Turkish; and was considered the finest poet of Dutch colonial times. Pané was the finest prose writer of those times, and his book *Belenggu* ("Bondage") had created a furor for its frankness when published in 1940 in *Pudjangga Baru*. Sukarno and Hatta were added to the Komisi to give it authority, and two Japanese to keep watch; but growing bored, the Japanese attended only a few meetings, then left the Indonesians to develop the project as they saw fit. Without neglecting linguistic aims, the scholars used this organization to further nationalistic ones, subtly undercutting various Japanese directives. Besides facilitating communication, Bahasa Indonesia became a strong nationalistic symbol, unifying the people to a remarkable degree. The Japanese finally realized that they had been deceived, and sent some Komisi scholars to jail, where they remained until the end of World War II.

Other Japanese-supported projects were also turned to nationalistic ends. The army of occupation had encouraged the formation of youth, military, and paramilitary groups, for these are usually easy to indoctrinate. Most important of such groups was the Peta, the Volunteer Army, trained by Japanese but manned and officered by Indonesians. Lacking in overall command, the Peta tended to break up into more or less autonomous fragments, some of which proved unruly.

By 1943 Sukarno was ill again, tormented by recurring malaria and kidney stones, as well as by the conflicting demands of his anomalous position. He was now in his early forties, Inggit in her fifties. The childless couple were divorced, and Sukarno married Fatmawati, the daughter of a former Muhammadijah leader at Bengkulu. She had been one of Sukarno's pupils while he was teaching in Sumatran exile. He was married by proxy, and it was weeks before he could arrange for Fatmawati's transportation to Java. Fatmawati bore Sukarno's first child, a boy who was named Guntur Soekarnoputra (Thunder Sukarno's Princely Son). Sosrodihardjo died soon after his grandson was born, but Idaju continued to live in Blitar.

Late in 1943, Sukarno and Hatta were flown to Japan to be greeted by Japan's Premier Tojo, and were taken on a tour designed to impress them with Japanese military and industrial strength. Sukarno, never before out of Indonesia, was indeed impressed, but not so the widely traveled Hatta. When a Greater East Asia Conference was called in November 1943, political leaders were invited from China, Thailand, Manchukuo, the Philippines, and Burma; but Sukarno was not asked to attend. Kenryo Sato, Tojo's adviser, later reported the Japanese premier to have said that Indonesia was "not quite ready to handle all that treasure."

In 1944 a small part of the Peta staged a revolt in Blitar. The choice of this town probably represented an effort to involve Sukarno, whose mother and relatives lived there; but the Indonesian leader had to remain aloof, and the Japanese quickly put down the uprising.

In latter 1943 and through 1944, Allied forces retook many islands from the Japanese. The Allied strategy involved two interlocked campaigns. One of them, the Central Pacific offensive under Nimitz, was designed partly to tighten an economic blockade around the enemy, but also to establish bases from which air power could strike at Japan proper and from which invasion forces could be launched. The Southwest Pacific offensive under MacArthur was intended to "island-hop," cutting Japan off from her insular conquests and resources, and retaking the Philippines. Fortunately, the large, heavily settled islands of western Indonesia were not in the path of the Allies' two-pronged drive from Australia and Papua northward toward the Japanese homeland. Near the southern end of her wartime empire, Japan had occupied many former British settlements in North-East New Guinea; all the former Dutch settlements of mainland Irian Barat; and several localities in what were then the Schouten Eilanden. Landing strips or airdromes were built at most Japanese bases, and these became targets for Allied bombing attacks. Lae and Salamau were retaken

317

from the Japanese, Allied ground troops moving up from Port Moresby to the Huon Gulf and lower Markham Valley areas. Missions were flown over Sio, Saidor, Rabaul in New Britain, Madang, Alexishafen, the Bogadjim Road, Wewak, Aitape, Vanimo. And over Irian Barat: Manokwari, Babo, Sansapor, Jefman-Sorong, Kokas, Fakfak, Timoeka, and the airdromes of Biak in the Schouten Eilanden. Hollandia, which had been the administrative center of the former Netherlands New Guinea, was bombed with incendiaries whose effect was obscured for a time by the dense pall of smoke that hung over the town. Every Japanese base of the Irian Barat region, with the exception of Seroei (now Serui) on Japen Island, was put out of action. Hollandia was taken over by Allied ground troops, Biak converted into a major American base, Merauke occupied briefly for special missions; but the Allied drive was now toward the Moluccas and the Philippines. Japan's Galela Drome on Halmahera proved no easy target, but American troops soon landed on nearby Morotai, and the war passed northward out of Indonesian territory.

Among little-known aspects of the Pacific war was the occasional bombardment of the enemy and the civilian population with printed leaflets. The procedure may have been started by the Japanese, who showered Australian troops with leaflets portraying American air force officers as rapists menacing Australian women whose men were away in battle. People of several nationalities, mostly with considerable experience in the Pacific islands and with knowledge of Pacific languages, prepared Allied leaflets in Melanesian Pidgin, Malayan, English, and Japanese, to be dropped by Fifth Air Force bombers. Messages in pidgin often were illustrated with portrayals of good luck symbols such as a twist of tobacco leaves or a carved wooden headrest, for it was hoped that illiterate tribesmen would be moved to save these broadsides until they could be read by, say, a "mission boy" or a "police boy" who had been abandoned when New Guinea was evacuated by European civilians. Pidgin leaflets told of Allied military advances, urged aid to forced-down Allied fliers, and warned that the Japanese would confiscate villages, women, pigs, and crops. Messages in Malayan, dropped on Indonesia, were of a very different nature, intended mostly to drive a wedge between Sukarno and his followers. The leaflets were often addressed to *Insjinjoer* Sukarno, thus hinting that his most significant attainment was an engineering degree from a Dutch-operated university. While not attacking him directly, they did so subtly at a point where he was most vulnerable: the Japanese conscription in his name of *hei-ho* soldiers and *romusha* laborers. A typical message was headed, "*Soekakah anak pembatja mendjadi begini?*" This meant, roughly, "Do you want your literate youths becoming (laborers) like this?" Accompanying photographs portrayed starving, diseased conscripts on Numfoor, and the information was supplied that "Three months after the Japanese brought 1600 *hei-ho* and *romusha* to Numfoor, only 251 remained alive." The reverse side of the leaflet showed the surviving conscripts being treated and fed at a NICA camp. NICA, the Nederlandsch-Indische Civiele Administratie, was an organization that followed the Allied troops into eastern Indonesia in anticipation of reestablishing Dutch hegemony.

However, the Indonesians were not affected by the propaganda. By latter 1944 the Japanese realized that they would get only minimal Indonesian cooperation unless they showed more enthusiasm for the islands' independence. The Putera had recently been disbanded for devoting most of its attention to nationalism rather than Japanese victory, and had been replaced by a new structure, Djawa Hohokai. The latter organization, with Sukarno as chairman, was more tightly controlled than the Putera had been, but was readied to take over the governmental reins of an independent Indonesia. Early in 1945, Sukarno and Hatta were flown to Makasar on Sulawesi for secret talks about the actual form that would be taken by a free Indonesia. Sukarno favored a single nation, while Hatta would chop the islands into separate states. On Sulawesi, Sukarno contracted a variety of malaria he had so far escaped.

Flown back to Java, Sukarno and Hatta found heated discussion there over the configuration of a new government. Some Muslims wanted a theocracy, while the Balinese urged a monarchy with Sukarno as king. Nationalists, Federalists, Unitarians, Javanese *aban-*

gan, peasants from the out-islands, santri from Java, traders from Sumatra and Sulawesi, prijaji intellectuals, Western-educated elite, labor unions, a Catholic party, a Protestant party, youth organizations, the Army—these and other groups each had a different idea about the size, shape, partitioning, and administering of the Indonesia-to-be. While the Japanese eyed him grimly, Sukarno cut through the chaos by a speech proposing the *Pantja Sila*, the "five principles" upon which the new state would be founded. In the order he presented them, these were (1) *Kebangsaan*, nationalism; (2) *Kemanusiaan*, internationalism as manifested by humanitarianism or respect for human values; (3) *Kerakjatan*, representative government or democracy; (4) *Keadilan Sosial*, social justice; and (5) *Ketuhanan*, belief in one God within a context of religious freedom. (The apparent alliteration of the five words reflects only the circumstance that an abstract noun is formed in Malayan by prefixing a root-word with *ke-* and suffixing it with *-an*.) Sukarno explained that Indonesia would be a nation but not rabidly nationalistic in the sense of scorning other peoples. Problems would be solved by *musjawarat* and *mufakat*, deliberation and agreement through Islamic-style consultation. The Christian minority would be heeded in proportion to its social importance. Democracy would be not just political but also economic and social. Belief in one God meant that in this predominantly Muslim land, Christianity or any other monotheistic creed would be acceptable, and the followers of one deity should respect the beliefs of those who followed a different one. Sukarno went on to say that the *Pantja Sila*, while amenable to much further division, could also be summarized by the ancient Indonesian precept of *gotong rojong:* rich and poor, Muslim and Christian, Indonesian and non-Indonesian all working together.

The proposal was warmly received, but after the famous *Pantja Sila* speech the Japanese privately and coldly told Sukarno that they themselves would determine the nature of a new Indonesian government, and it would be under the divine emperor of Japan. Yet, on August 14, 1945, Sukarno and Hatta were flown mysteriously to Saigon, there to meet a Japanese official who surprisingly

announced that Sukarno was free to form an Indonesian government as he saw fit. Perplexed by the strange atmosphere of this
meeting, Sukarno learned in Saigon that the Americans had demol-
ished Hiroshima and Nagasaki with atomic bombs, and that Japan
was surrendering.

Flown back to Java, Sukarno was approached on the night of
August 15 by Chairul Saleh, Sukarni, and other youths who, with
the backing of Sjahrir, had been urging revolt against the Japanese. They wanted Sukarno to proclaim independence, rather than
waiting to have it granted by the Japanese. Sukarno replied that
he would make this proclamation at the proper time, specifically
on August 17, two days away. Dissatisfied, the young men returned
in the early morning hours, heavily armed, and kidnapped Sukarno
along with his family. Seizing Hatta also, the *pemuda* ("youths")
took their captives to a hideout at Rengasdenklok, a locality controlled by an unruly segment of the Peta. The quixotic *pemuda*
hoped to touch off a revolt in Djakarta, a revolt they thought
would spread and permit them to say that they had wrested Indonesia from its conquerors. They would say, also, that they had carried Sukarno and Hatta to safety, knowing that Djakarta would go
up in flames; or else would claim to have forced the two men into
declaring independence. Alas for the *"pemuda* insurrection." Japan
had just surrendered unconditionally, and Djakartans would not
riot without Bung Karno. Details of the kidnapping leaked out,
and on the evening of August 16, one of Sukarno's friends, Achmad
Subardjo, drove up to Rengasdenklok in a battered Czech Skoda.
Subardjo carried Sukarno, his family, and Hatta back to Djakarta,
accompanied by two carloads of sheepish *pemuda.*

Very early on August 17, Sukarno and Hatta hastened to the palace where the Japanese authorities were staying, only to be told
that independence was now out of the question; for in surrendering, Japan had agreed that Indonesia would be handed over to the
Allies without change of government. Hastily, Sukarno and Hatta
found a blank sheet of paper and an unoccupied anteroom. Across
the top of the paper Sukarno wrote *Proklamasi,* "Proclamation,"
and underscored it twice. Then he began to write in Bahasa Indo-

nesia the words he had so long dreamed of penning: *Kami bangsa Indonesia dengan ini* . . .

> We the people of Indonesia hereby declare Indonesia's independence. Matters concerning the transfer of power and other matters will be executed in an orderly manner and in the shortest possible time.
>
> Djakarta 17-8-'45
>
> On behalf of the Indonesian people
>
> (Signed)  Soekarno.Hatta

# CHAPTER VIII

# THE FORTUNES OF
# THE REPUBLIC

AUGUST 17, 1945, is the date celebrated by Indonesians, just as July 4, 1776, is celebrated in the United States; but of course Sukarno's proclamation did not automatically bring about independence. The Netherlands had suffered during the war. The polders of the IJssel Meer had been flooded, the Walcheren dykes breached, the harbors blocked with sunken ships and the wreckage of coastal installations. The industries had been bombed; 280,000 civilians had been killed, and many of the survivors were hungry and destitute. As she had done before, the Netherlands determined to recoup great losses by the exploitation of Indonesia; and the islanders, like the American patriots of 1776, would have to take up arms to attain freedom.

Sukarno had dreamed of signing an Indonesian declaration of independence on finest parchment with a consecrated pen in the throne room of Queen Juliana's palace, attended by diplomats in striped trousers and by bejeweled ladies. Haggard from sleepless nights and burning with malaria, he signed it in an anteroom off the foyer of a Japanese admiral's quarters, in his haste and fatigue scratching out two words and rewriting them more accurately; but the document is the more gripping for its stark simplicity. Sukarno later admitted that he penned it not triumphantly but in fear that his hand had been forced too soon; for the Japanese troops were still the strongest power in the land, and potentially dangerous.

Going back to his quarters at Pegangsaan Timur 56, Sukarno wrote dozens of directives to government leaders, alerting them to a public announcement of his proclamation. Then he collapsed; and while he slept, the news of his action spread. Hundreds of people armed themselves with bamboo spears, cleavers, mattocks, whatever they could find, and surrounded his quarters to protect him from Japanese reprisals; the local Peta garrison deployed itself around the neighborhood with antitank weapons. Barisan Pelopor, a youth army of which Sukarno was chairman, was mobilized; and five professional bodyguards, trained in the Indonesian fighting art of *pentjak silat,* were assigned to watch over him. Other youths used Japanese mimeograph machines to run off thousands of copies of the news. After a few hours' rest, Sukarno roused, dressed himself in a simple white tunic and trousers, and donned a black *petji.* Then, flanked but not closely by Hatta, and by the Peta captain Latief in a Japanese-style uniform, Sukarno read the proclamation into a microphone that had been stolen from a Japanese radio station. Fatmawati had sewn a *Merah Putih,* the red-and-white Indonesian flag, and Latief hoisted it to the top of a bamboo pole. There was no music, no band, but everyone sang *Indonesia Raja.* Adam Malik, who was employed by Domei, the Japanese news agency, but who had been working for the underground, used a Japanese shortwave transmitter to send a Morse code announcement of independence. This was picked up by stations elsewhere in Indonesia, and was spread widely.

Sukarno was *presiden,* that is, president of the *Republik Indonesia,* Hatta the vice-president. Within a week they had promulgated a constitution calling for a republican form of government, a cabinet responsible to the president, and a representative council elected popularly. Until elections could be held, the KNIP, the Central Indonesian National Committee representing various social groups, would advise the president. Competing political parties were regarded as undesirable during the emergency, and the nation's political forces were combined into a single front headed by Achmad Subardjo. Flanked by Hatta and Subardjo, Sukarno held a press conference. One Western reporter, probably confusing Sukarno with Subardjo, began to write of "Achmed Soekarno." The readership, believing that everyone followed the Western system of given name and patronym, was interested to learn Sukarno's "first name" at last. The error eventually crept into some encyclopedias, which refer to "Achmed" or "Akmet" Soekarno.

The Dutch had set up NICA centers in parts of Indonesia, for example Morotai, that had been taken by the Allies, but were in no position to accept the official Japanese surrender of the islands. This task fell to the British who, arriving in September, recognized the new Republic, such recognition being necessary to bring about the release of vast numbers of Dutch prisoners of war. Behind the British came Dutch soldiers and administrators, to be joined in some cases by newly released prisoners. The Dutch quickly tried to institute a reign of terror in order to break the spirit of the Indonesians. Dutch patrols marched the streets, shot many civilians, broke into homes and burned them, shanghaied men to work in distant camps, robbed trains. By December, approximately 8,000 Djakartan civilians had been slaughtered. In later years the Dutch attempted to justify the butchery by claiming that they had not realized how Indonesia's people had changed, and supposed Sukarno's government to have been merely a Japanese creation.

Soon after the arrival of the British and the Dutch, the Indonesians organized the People's Army of the Republic. There was fighting in many parts of Java, as well as in Sumatra and Bali. The Republic's first major battle took place in later October 1945. Indonesian troops had occupied Surabaja, but the British demanded that they lay down their arms and surrender unconditionally. *Sekali Merdeka Tetap Merdeka*—"Once Free, Forever Free." This was the war-cry of the Republic; and the Indonesian soldiers, although mostly inexperienced, cut down the British troops. Surabaja's streets were littered with the dead and dying. Sukarno and Hatta flew to Surabaja, where the former instructed the Indonesian soldiers to accept a cease-fire while the matter was being negotiated.

325

But a few days later, the British general commanding the Surabaja forces was assassinated by persons unknown; and while Sukarno was trying to negotiate, the British reopened the battle. Their air force bombed the town, their battleships pounded it from the sea, their troops poured ashore behind the shelter of the residents. This episode, and similar ones during the early days of the Allied occupation, led Sukarno and his people to mistrust and dislike the British. As the days went by, Surabaja was evacuated by civilians, many of whom were bombed and strafed on the highways. On November 10 the Indonesians launched a counterattack, aided by a Chinese Defense Army which the ethnic Chinese of Java had organized at Sukarno's request. About 600 Indian troops defected from the British and joined the Indonesians. Sukarno sent a tape-recorded appeal to London and a protest to the United Nations, as well as a cable to President Truman pointing out that United States trucks and equipment were being used by British troops against Indonesians. He found no help from those Allies who at the beginning of World War II had promulgated the high-sounding Four Freedoms and the Atlantic Charter with its promise of self-determination for all.

The Dutch several times tried to assassinate Sukarno, the British to arrest him. Much Allied propaganda was disseminated to make him out a heartless collaborator with the Japanese, and therefore a war criminal; but the Indonesian people were firmly behind Bung Karno. Indonesian troops fought the Battle of Surabaja until November 30, 1945, by which time their ranks had been decimated.

Also during latter 1945, several Indonesian communities and ethnic groups took it upon themselves to remedy injustices of long standing. Ever since they lost the Atjeh War, the Atjehnese of North Sumatra had been ruled by puppets of the Dutch. Taking advantage of slack governmental controls in the first few weeks after Japanese surrender, radical Muslims overthrew and in fact virtually exterminated this aristocracy; and the success of the revolt led secular rebels of East Sumatra to overthrow the local *adat* chiefs who had been cat's-paws of the Dutch. In Java, which was better controlled by Sukarno's hastily installed governmental network, there were only minor outbreaks, directed against Europeans, Chinese, and unpopular village heads or administrators. Kalimantan, Sulawesi, and eastern Indonesia remained comparatively quiet, for these areas had been spared the full impact of Dutch exploitation, and had been administered during the war years by the Japanese navy, which had discouraged any kind of indigenous political organization. Also, well before the surrender, the easterly islands had been occupied by Allied troops, bringing with them NICA officials who had reestablished a measure of Dutch control.

And of course, even at the heart of the new and embattled Republic there were political opponents, if not of Sukarno and Hatta, at least of Subardjo and his subordinates. Most vocal of these opponents were Sjahrir and the moderately leftist Gerindo leader Amir Sjarifuddin, who capitalized upon their anti-Japanese reputations by demanding a share of power. Other leaders asserted the desire for a multiparty system. Both demands were met; and before 1945 was out, several political parties were organized. Sjahrir and Sjarifuddin combined their supporters into the Partai Socialis, the Socialist Party, not very large but exceedingly well organized; and Sjahrir became the first prime minister of the Republic. A PNI reappeared, not Sukarno's famous old party but a new one that profited by taking the same name, Partai Nasionalis Indonesia. A new Masjumi gathered wider support than any other party, but was loosely organized. The Communist PKI, which had gone underground during the occupation, surfaced very tentatively, most of its members temporarily joining other leftist groups; for the fifth principle of Sukarno's *Pantja Sila,* monotheism, militated against the avowedly atheistic Communists. Armed youth organizations created by the Japanese metamorphosed into the Muslim Hizbullah, the socialist Pesindo, and the radically nationalist Barisan Banteng. These groups defended the Republic but pressed their own interests as well.

In January 1946, menaced by the British and the Dutch, Sukarno moved his capital to Djokjakarta, leaving the Europeans to occupy Djakarta; for the capital was sure to be attacked, and he could not have defended it at that time. Djokjakarta, a center of Javanese culture, was in a major rice-producing region, and its sultan was one of the few Javanese traditional rulers to retain considerable influence. The sultan's *kraton,* royal palace, became the capital building of the new Republic. Thousands of Djakartans left their homes and followed Sukarno to Djokjakarta. Smuggling rice, rubber, gold, and silver through a Dutch blockade of Java and Sumatra, Sukarno gradually built up the economy of Republic with goods from Singapore, Hong Kong, Manila, Bangkok, and Indian ports. The British, anxious to withdraw from their awkward position, bought rice, tin, and rubber for resale to the Dutch, and petitioned The Hague for a resolution of the confrontation. The Republic's forces were joined by soldiers of fortune and young idealists. In the latter category was an American, Bob Freberg, who advised in the purchase of two airplanes, Dakotas, from Hong Kong, and who became Sukarno's personal pilot. (Freberg later crashed while flying money to Palembang for support of Sumatran insurgents.) While the Republic consolidated its position, the Dutch occupied tin-rich Bangka and Belitung, as well as key towns of Java, Sumatra, and Bali.

Stalemated, Sukarno and the Dutch opened a series of negotiations which brought armed clashes to a temporary halt. Prime Minister Sjahrir, strongly anti-Japanese and somewhat pro-Dutch, was an acceptable envoy to conferences in Holland. In April 1946, the Hoge Veluwe conference failed to reach any agreement. Among Indonesians there was widespread objection to making any concessions to the Dutch; and taking advantage of this attitude and the chaotic times, the Communists tried once again to seize the islands. The nationalist-Communist leader Tan Malaka, a European-educated schoolteacher from Sumatra, organized the Persatuan Perdjuangan ("Union for Struggle"), urging abolition of political parties and refusal to negotiate with the Dutch. In this he was backed especially by many youth groups, and by military or political opponents of Sjahrir. Tan Malaka's adherents managed to bring about resignation of the cabinet, but were forced to accept a new cabinet under Sjahrir. Then they attempted a coup, and were arrested in July 1946. However, they had succeeded in promoting divisiveness; for Sukarno's government officers regarded negotiation as vital to survival of the Republic, while their political opponents could flaunt an anti-negotiation stand.

A series of Indonesian-Dutch talks culminated in the Linggadjati Pact of March 1947. The Indonesians wanted full authority in the islands, while the Dutch favored a federal, commonwealth arrangement. The pact recognized a United States of Indonesia, with three member states: (1) The Republic of Indonesia, made up of Java, Sumatra, and Madura; (2) Kalimantan; and (3) the former Netherlands East Indies islands east of Java and Kalimantan. The first of these would be under Indonesian control, the other two Dutch. When the details of the agreement were made known, controversy arose over their interpretation. To Sukarno, "free" and "independent" were synonyms, but the Dutch held that the USI would be free under Queen Juliana of the Netherlands; and the word "cooperation," used so frequently in the 17 articles of the pact, was obviously open to varying interpretations. Opposition to the agreement brought on the resignation of Sjahrir, who was replaced by Amir Sjarifuddin. It was widely felt that the Dutch were merely using the pact to buy time and international goodwill, without actually intending to give up any part of Indonesia. At any rate, while the argument over interpretation was going on, the Dutch began what they euphemistically called "Pacification Exercises" in the more easterly islands, where they were firmly entrenched. In the notorious Westerling Affair, a Dutch captain was accused of "pacifying" 40,000 Sulawesians by butchering, beheading, or shooting them. The captain fled to the Netherlands, where the affair was eventually described as an abortive revolution, by Dutch soldiers with the backing of Muslim dissidents. NICA troops, ostensibly in search of guerrillas, "pacified" a civilian mission hospital by shooting women, children, and patients. After dozens of such atrocities, the Dutch commenced "Mopping-Up Operations," shelling Medan, Palembang, Modjokerto, and other cities. On July 21, 1947, Dutch tanks, troops, ships, and bombers attacked Sumatra, Madura, and Java, closing in on Djokjakarta. Sukarno retreated to the hills near Madiun, taking with him his family, which now included a daughter, Megawati, who had been born the preceding January. From the Madiun base he made frequent appearances in Djokjakarta, and the general populace knew nothing of his absences.

Egypt and Australia boycotted Dutch ships in protest of the ag-

329

gression, and Nehru of India deplored it before the world. The Ukraine had introduced the Indonesian question into the United Nations in 1946, and it was now turned over by the Security Council to a Committee of Good Offices, which brought the combatants together for a conference aboard the U.S.S. *Renville*. The *Renville* Agreement cut further into Indonesian holdings, annexing West Java, East Sumatra, and Madura to the Dutch-held part of the islands. Public opposition to this agreement brought about Sjarifuddin's resignation and a reshuffling of the cabinet. The Benteng Republik ("Republican Fortress"), with strong support from the PNI, the Masjumi, and the Tan Malaka faction of nationalist-Communists, had opposed the *Renville* Agreement when out of power; but PNI and Masjumi members now coming into power, they reversed their position and supported it. To bypass parliamentary opposition, the cabinet was placed under Hatta and made directly responsible to Sukarno without going through the KNIP. The Sajap Kiri ("Left Wing"), with socialist, labor, Communist, and Pesindo support, had favored the agreement, but turned against it when removed from office. A breach widened between Sjahrir and Sjarifuddin. Sjahrir formed the PSI, the Indonesian Socialist Party, which supported Hatta; while Sjarifuddin organized the FDR, the People's Democratic Front, with left-wing, labor, Pesindo, and military backing. The apparently pro-Dutch position of the United States led the FDR to turn more and more toward the Soviets for support. In 1948 the former PKI leader Muso returned from exile in Russia, reorganized the FDR into a larger and more aggressive PKI, and in September of that year tried to spark an uprising by seizing Madiun in east-central Java. Muso, Sjarifuddin, and other leftist leaders were killed in the abortive coup, which was put down by Sukarno's forces. The PKI went underground again, and Sukarno acquired popularity in the United States for his anti-Communist stand.

But taking advantage of the turmoil, the Dutch launched an attack on Djokjakarta in December 1948, bombing and strafing the city, and landing paratroops. Although he had several hours advance warning, Sukarno decided not to flee. Sending his youthful Commander-in-Chief, General Sudirman, to defend the city's perimeter, he stayed to put into effect an emergency plan whereby the Republic's government would be transferred to Sumatra, and to cable the Indonesian embassy in Delhi about the turn of events. When the Dutch troops broke through to the *kraton*, Sukarno had finished burning secret documents and was awaiting them. Head high, lean and trim in his best military tunic and black *petji*, he marched off into another exile, this time to Berastagi in northern Sumatra. And this time he could not take his family. He was kept behind barbed wire and a patrol of armed guards, in what the Dutch called "protective custody." Sjahrir and the aging Hadji Agus Salim were confined with him. Although confronted by heavily armed Dutch forces and divided by political opportunists, with Bung Karno a prisoner the Indonesian people rose up more determinedly than ever before, launching endless guerrilla attacks with which the Dutch could not cope. Sukarno, Sjahrir, and Salim were transferred from the vulnerable Berastagi to a cliff house overlooking Lake Toba at Prapat. Sjahrir reached some kind of agreement with his captors and was released. There were unsuccessful guerrilla efforts to rescue Sukarno, who was transferred with the Hadji to Bangka, where they found Hatta, Ali Sastromidjojo, air marshal Suryadarma, and other former associates who had been imprisoned by the Dutch. In March the guerrillas recaptured Djokjakarta, and the world began to hear more about Indonesia's plight. The Security Council announced that the Dutch had launched a sneak attack while the *Renville* Agreement was still in force; the parallel to Pearl Harbor was obvious. The Council called for the restoration of the Republic's government and full independence for Indonesia. The Committee of Good Offices was reconstituted into the more effective United Nations Committee for Indonesia, and 19 Asian countries banded together to boycott the Dutch, whose activities were also criticized by Britain. It was revealed that the money being spent by the Netherlands, in her effort to crush the Indonesian patriots, roughly equalled the sum she was receiving from the United States under the Marshall Plan—an embarrassing arithmetic. The United States, gratified by the way Sukarno had put down the Communist uprising of Tan Malaka, shut off funds to the Netherlands.

In the meanwhile, the Republic's government continued to operate under wartime conditions. Leaving the cities to the Dutch, Indonesian guerrillas gained control of towns, villages, highways, the hills, the food supply; and what they could not control they sabotaged. There was no way guerrilla activities could be halted except by a word from Bung Karno, and so the Dutch arranged a parley with him at the tin-mining town of Montok on Bangka. This led to the so-called Roem-Royen agreement, reached by van Royen representing Holland and Dr. Muhammad Roem representing Indonesia. Sukarno and Roem agreed to recall the guerrillas, and a Round Table Conference at The Hague was scheduled for August, to discuss transfer of sovereignty to Indonesia. That conference dragged on for months, the Dutch striving for every possible concession. The Republic's government agreed to assume the debts of the former Netherlands East Indies regime—$1,130,000,000, a staggering burden for a nation emerging from colonial status after years of fighting. On December 27, 1948, the transfer of sovereignty was completed. The former Netherlands East Indies would be independent, and the status of Netherlands New Guinea would be reviewed within a year. On December 28, Bung Karno was flown back to Djakarta, to be welcomed by millions as the *Presiden* of a free Indonesia.

However, the Dutch period in Indonesia, already about 350 years old, was not at an end. The Dutch still wielded considerable influence in the more easterly islands, where they had handpicked the leaders, and they intended to exploit Netherlands New Guinea as they had the former Netherlands East Indies.

As a result of the Round Table Conference, the Republic of the United States of Indonesia was created, composed of 16 member states, one of which was the original, revolutionary Republic of Indonesia. The other 15 states were of Dutch origin. Sukarno was president and Hatta the prime minister of the RUSI. Hatta's position was now very strong, for he had played a major role in crushing the Communists at Madiun, and enjoyed the trust of the Indonesian army, the Americans, the Dutch, and the 15 Dutch-created states of the RUSI. One by one these states chose to give up separate identity in order to merge with the RI, the only opposition to unification coming from the southern Moluccas where formerly pagan Alfur tribesmen had been creolized and turned into Christians. There was and would continue to be local agitation for a separate Republic of the South Moluccas. Nevertheless, by August 1950, the RUSI had been converted to a unitary Republic of Indonesia. Hatta's cabinet was then replaced by that of the Masjumi leader Muhammad Natsir, and Hatta was returned to the post of vice-president. Natsir's cabinet was replaced in 1951 by that of Sukiman, also of the Masjumi. In that year, Thomas E. Dewey visited Indonesia and reported that the fledgling republic was poverty-stricken but determined to maintain its independent status; that it wanted to remain friends with its Asian neighbors; that it foresaw and hoped to stay aloof from a massive showdown involving Russia and the United States. In 1952, Sukiman's cabinet was succeeded by that of Wilopo, a PNI leader.

The various cabinets, although toppling rapidly, had been doing a remarkably good job, constitutional democracy operating effectively in the new Republic of Indonesia. The press was free, courts were independent of the government, cabinet critics were not silenced on nationalistic grounds. Nonpolitical administration characterized many parts of the governmental organization. Communications were restored, banditry and rebel activity curtailed, small and medium-scale industry built up along with rice production. Educational facilities were greatly expanded at all levels, and in 1951 the new Gadjah Mada University at Djokjakarta conferred an honorary doctorate upon Sukarno. Bahasa Indonesia was perfected and promulgated. Less successful were efforts to remove squatters from foreign-owned estates, to reduce the civil service, and to pacify the fanatically Muslim Darul Islam guerrillas, who held territory in West Java and South Sulawesi. Export industries, revitalized by the Korean War, slumped at that war's end; and the Indonesian cabinet members' popularity declined as did the exports. But the principal mistake of the members had been their failure to become crowd-pleasing orators whipping up nationalistic fervor; for the country was still full of revolutionaries looking for excitement in politics, and they found the statesmanly cabinet members too drab. Accordingly, the balance of power shifted from Hatta and those of his general orientation to Sukarno and the more radical components of the army and the nationalist groups. In the "October 17 Affair" of 1952, Colonel Abdul Haris Nasution, a pro-Hatta man, surrounded the Istana Merdeka, the Freedom Palace housing Sukarno's headquarters, with troops, tanks, and armored cars, in an effort to force abolition of the parliamentary system. Sukarno told the soldiers to go home, which they did; and then he discharged Nasution. (But not inclined to hold grudges against Indonesian activists, Sukarno later chose Nasution as defense minister, and appointed kidnapper Chairul Saleh a second deputy premier.)

Another newsworthy event of 1952 was the arrival in Indonesia of Eleanor Roosevelt, in connection with the work of the United Nations Economic and Social Council.

The failure of Nasution's coup further strengthened Sukarno, and the pro-Hatta faction suffered a major defeat when the Wilopo cabinet fell in 1953. Bung Karno still could move the masses with a word. Among the interesting events of this year was a march on the Freedom Palace by feminists. The situation was not quite as a Westerner might imagine it, however. The concept of an Asian woman as a downtrodden slave, and as likely to "age" rapidly, is a myth invented long years ago by Christian missionaries who in fact were burning to circumscribe her freedom of choice in a good many matters. From the militaristic Jingo of Japan to Madame Bandaranaike of modern Ceylon, from China's dowager empress Tz'u Hsi to India's Indira Gandhi, Asian women have ruled nations.

Indonesian history and folklore told of many famous women. Between 1641 and 1699, the throne of Atjeh was occupied by queens. Tjut Nja's Dien, a widow who carried on her husband's struggles against the Dutch in the Atjeh War, was killed in action and became a heroine of the nationalist movement. The Minangkabau princess Bundo Kandung was famous for her political wisdom, and her exploits were celebrated in the *Kaba Tjindue Mato;* while another Minangkabau princess, Sabai Nang Halus, was remembered for having headed an army to avenge her father. In South Sulawesi, women chiefs had been numerous, one of them leading a revolt against the Dutch around the beginning of the twentieth century; and Balinese girls had been hailed as *Dewa Agung,* "great god," in major ceremonies at Klungkung. Adji Sitti, divorced wife of the sultan of Kutai, had reigned over the Kotabangun district of Kalimantan; and Dyak women of Kalimantan participated in public affairs to the same degree as the men. The history of Java was full of honored women in such affairs, and the *Mahabharata* hero Srikandi in Java and Bali was turned into a heroine.

*Adat* was usually very favorable to women. This was true even in the patrilineal societies (e.g., those of the Batak, Nias Islanders, South Sumatrans, Lombokese, and some Maluku groups) as well as the ambilineal ones (e.g., the Toradja, Javanese, Minahasans, Dyaks) and the scattering of matrilineal ones. In fact, among the strongly matrilineal Minangkabau, the men had been protesting that they were *"sapati abu diateh tunggua,"* "like ashes on a stump" for all the consideration they got around the villages. Islam had been a notably masculine faith at its inception, Bedouin-like in extolling the patriarch, the warrior, the poet, the orator, the begetter of many sons, while relegating women to inferior status; but even by the opening of the twentieth century, Indonesia was the most advanced of all Muslim nations in relieving women of such restrictions as purdah and the wearing of the veil. (Some Sumatran women in fact later demanded the right to wear a veil.) In the years when Indonesia was struggling toward independence, Sukarno had urged feminist groups to align and move forward with nationalism, and they had done so. Most youth organizations included members of both sexes. There were women in the Sukarno government of 1953, and many outstanding feminists were related by blood or marriage to prominent politicians of the times.

The husky matrons who marched past the Freedom Palace, swinging their clenched fists in military fashion and brandishing signs for the benefit of photographers, were protesting for a variety of reasons. Some disliked the divorce laws, whereby a man could dissolve a union by pronouncing the *talak.* In practice, this pronouncement was not made casually, but only after due consultation with in-laws, and due consideration of child care, dowry and property rights, and related matters; but the *talak* was a male privilege in that a woman could initiate a divorce only by applying to a *wali*, a sort of judge. More widely disturbing to the feminists was the *talik*. Under *adat*, marriage was a moving rite celebrating passage from celibacy to matrimony; but under Islamic law, it was a business-like contract in which the groom received the bride's services, in return for which he would fulfill certain obligations. The word *talik* meant, roughly, the fulfillment of these obligations; and if the man did not live up to his contract, the woman could consider herself divorced. Some of the feminists thought this arrangement gave a man too easy a way out, especially since divorced women were a drug on the market. *Kawin gantung*, betrothal or "hanging marriage" of the kind Sukarno had once entered into, was objected to even though it was usually initiated by a young girl's mother. Another bone of contention was the seclusion of upper-class girls during the usually somewhat irrational period between the onset of puberty and the arrival of a husband. Years before, Raden Adjeng Kartini (1879–1904), daughter of the regent of Djepara, had written a series of letters in Dutch to a Dutch feminist, Stella Zeehandelaar, whom she never met. The missives consisted mostly of self-dramatization, self-pity at the terrible fate of having to be a pampered, waited-upon, and guarded princess—the "poor little rich girl" theme. Long after Kartini's death, her letters were published with some editing, and the princess became a sort of patron saint of the Indonesian feminist movement. Yet another source of dissatisfaction was polygyny, not so much per se as because it multiplied the likelihood of divorce. In general, both *adat* and Islamic law permitted polygyny. Although Muhammad had not personally embraced it until after the death of Khadijah, he had eventually married nine women, and had decreed that any man might have up to four wives if he treated them all equally.

The feminist movement was further complicated by Christian missionaries who were looking for any social injustice that could be ascribed to Islam, and by the Communists who had infiltrated many youth and women's organizations. The nominally nonpolitical "Gerwani" (Gerakan Wanita Indonesia, Indonesian Women's Movement) would some day be revealed under shocking circumstances as a Communist front—but that was a few years in the future. Sukarno, a lusty man in the tradition of Muhammad, said of the 1953 marchers that the good Muslim ladies were trying to rewrite the Prophet's Koran; and soon thereafter he took a second wife, Hartini. She and Fatmawati were given separate homes.

Also in 1953, Wilopo's cabinet was followed by that of Ali Sastroamidjojo, whose political views were close to those of Sukarno. During the few years of the first Sastroamidjojo cabinet (1953–1955), two important steps were taken. Ever since the end of World War II, the United States and the Communist world had grown further apart, many nations siding with one or the other of these two in the "cold war." The United States had been pressuring Indonesia to align militarily against the Communists, offering aid money under conditions the Indonesians found ideologically unpalatable; for the islanders were committed to neutrality, and felt very strongly about choosing their own course in international affairs. Indeed, the Sukiman cabinet had been brought down partly because it had accepted conditions along with aid. Sukarno was taken with the idea of an African, Asian, and Latin American bloc of uncommitted nations, a third force strong enough to resist the pressure of both cold war opponents. Accordingly, he organized the First Afro-Asian Conference, held in Bandung in early 1955. It was a great success as far as attendance went, with such leaders as Nehru and Chou En-lai present; but as it happened, most of the Afro-Asian nations were wrapped up in their own affairs and were not able to unite in any effective action at that time.

In addition to staging this meeting, Sukarno reopened the question of Netherlands New Guinea. By terms of the 1949 Round Table Agreement, the fate of the colony was to have been decided within a year; yet nothing had been done about the situation, and the Dutch were entrenching themselves in the area more firmly than ever before. In 1954 Sukarno petitioned the United Nations for action on the matter. None was taken, but Holland broke what remaining relations she had with Indonesia. In 1955, Sastroamidjojo's cabinet was replaced by that of Burhanuddin Harahap of the Masjumi. Sukarno again petitioned the United Nations for resolution of the Irian Barat question. Other problems confronting Bung

Karno in that year were a Darul Islam rebellion against the Atj-ehnese of North Sumatra, and some political maneuvering that could have lost him a bit of Muslim support. The Muslims had originally hailed Sukarno's *Pantja Sila*, for it was the only states-man-like proposal to be advanced when the Japanese promised In-donesian freedom. But many Muslim groups admired conservatism, a right-wing posture, and government along Islamic lines; and so political dissidents could convincingly portray these groups as coming to reject so liberal a document as the *Pantja Sila*. Once this propaganda had been spread, it was then easy to represent the *Pantja Sila* as anti-Muslim property, and its author as a spokesman for one side of a political struggle rather than a nonpartisan head of state. But Sukarno was not to be maneuvered into any such po-sition. He quickly reassured the Muslims by making the *hadj*, the ceremonial pilgrimage to Mecca. Also in this year it became evi-dent that the Communists had gained great strength by aligning themselves with nationalism and Sukarno. Dipa Nusantara Aidit, a Communist who had fled Indonesia after the abortive coup at Madiun, had returned. Arrested and then released, he had reorga-nized the PKI into a body with perhaps 1,000,000 members. (He claimed 16,000,000.) In latter 1955, elections for parliament and the constitutional assembly revealed the ideological trends. The na-tionalists, PNI, received 22.3 percent of the vote, the Muslim Mas-jumi 20.9, the conservative Muslim Nahdatul Ulama 18.4, the Com-munist PKI 16.4. Of these, the PNI, NU, and PKI received support mostly from Java, with the Masjumi strong in the out-islands. The socialists were also strongest outside Java. Sastroamidjojo returned to head a cabinet coalition of the PNI, the NU, and the Masjumi.

The performance of the newly elected officials was disappoint-ing. Military commanders in North Sulawesi and South Sumatra soon began large-scale smuggling operations to avoid an unfavora-ble exchange rate with Java. These operations were broken up, but the officers involved were not punished. In 1956 Colonel Zulkifli Lubis tried unsuccessfully to stage a military coup in Djakarta, and urged a military dictatorship. For years Sukarno had been the binding force of the pathetically divided new nation. Faced now with a new threat, and seeing the multiparty system hamstrung by factional bickering, he determined to take the reins of government. Returning from a trip to Washington, Moscow, and Peking, he declared that Indonesian political parties were selfish and should be abolished; that his new aim for the country was "Guided Democracy." There were immediate objections to Sukarno's plans. Hatta resigned, while military commanders in North, Central, and South Sumatra staged bloodless coups overthrowing Djakarta-appointed officials. A counterrevolt in North Sumatra returned the Djakarta regime there, but the other two provinces remained in the control of the military, who charged neglect and undue leniency toward Communists. In sympathy with the rebels, the Masjumi withdrew from Sukarno's government, exacerbating the split between Java and the out-islands. In February 1957, Sukarno outlined his *Konsepsi*, "conception" of government. Western-style democracy, he said, was not suitable for Indonesia with its low levels of prosperity and literacy. What was needed was a cabinet in the tradition of *gotong rojong*, and in which all major parties would participate; plus a high advisory body, a Dewan Nasional or National Council, representing functional groups such as labor, the peasants, entrepreneurs, youth, and so on. The council would operate through consensus rather than voting.

The PNI, some minor nationalist groups, and the Communists supported Sukarno's plan, but not so the Muslims and moderates. The army, now under Nasution who had attained the rank of general, became arbiter between the two factions. Aidit deployed his Communist organization with painted slogans and sound trucks, but Nasution ordered an end to the demonstrations. There were military coups in four provinces east of Java, and the second Sastroamidjojo cabinet resigned. Sukarno placed the whole country under martial law, and personally chose a new government. The new cabinet, headed by Djuanda, included two Communist sympathizers but no PKI members. Two ministers were given to a new party that called itself the Generation of '45, headed by Chairul Saleh, Sukarno's onetime kidnapper. The Generation of '45 was a union of youth, labor, and veterans' organizations. In mid-1957, the provincial elections of Java revealed the Communists to be in the lead there, with 27.4 percent of the total vote.

339

Sukarno and 18 nations of the Afro-Asian bloc had repeatedly brought the New Guinea question before the United Nations but to no avail. In November 1957, Sukarno announced that he would resort to other means to resolve the issue. While he laid plans to take Irian Barat, Darul Islam was plotting to assassinate him because his government was based on the *Pantja Sila*, not Islam. Darul Islam was headed at this time by a rebel chieftain named Kartosuwirio. On November 30, Sukarno was present at a fund-raising bazaar for the Tjikini School which was attended by his children Guntur and Megawati. There were 500 guests, uncounted spectators, balloons, confetti, music, games, singing, an auction, a playlet. Into this gathering, Darul Islam assassins threw numerous grenades, killing 9 people and wounding 150. Although his automobile was damaged, Sukarno was unhurt, and the legend of his invincibility grew. (It was widely rumored that he was a reincarnation of Vishnu.) Within twenty-four hours, his intelligence service had rounded up the four assassins, although Kartosuwirio remained at large. In later years, Sukarno passed unscathed through four more assassination attempts.

In December 1957, left-wing employees of an interisland shipping line, owned by the Dutch, hoisted the Communists' red flag over it. The action gave Djuanda a pretext to order expulsion of the Dutch and to seize plantations, banks, and businesses owned by them. Most were seized by SOBSI, the PKI-controlled labor union. At this time there were about 46,000 Dutch citizens still in Indonesia, most of them Indo-Dutch, physically indistinguishable from the general populace. They fled to Holland or to the United States, traveling usually in family groups in the Indonesian fashion, often with wives, relatives, and adopted children some of whom had no Dutch ancestry. When Dutch property was officially nationalized, Sukarno and the army shared the spoils, the PKI choosing to lie low for a while because it had little strength outside Java. Publicly supporting the Djakarta government but undercutting it at the village level, the Communists laid plans for the day when they would have to confront the army. Such confrontation would not be easy; for the armed forces supervised customs, imports and exports, immigration and the movement of aliens, transportation, communications, and the operation of nationalized estates, as well as matters of censorship, the investigation of corruption, and political activities. The army and the civil police were powerful under Sukarno's new regime. The military could requisition anything it needed, giving it great economic influence also.

In early 1958 Sukarno visited Thailand, where he was told that a revolt against him was brewing in the out-islands. Soon after he returned to Djakarta, this revolt began in Sumatra and Sulawesi, led by Sumitro Djojohadikusumo and two former cabinet heads, Natsir and Harahap. These three had Masjumi sponsorship. Claiming to feel endangered by army-backed youth groups in Djakarta, Natsir and others had removed to Padang in Sumatra. Through Colonel Husein, the local commander, they issued Sukarno an ultimatum on February 10, 1958: form a new cabinet within five days, with either Hatta or the Sultan of Djokjakarta as head, or the regionalists would establish a government of their own. The demand was not met, and so the Revolutionary Government of the Republic of Indonesia, the PRRI, was proclaimed in Padang, with the Masjumi leader Sjafruddin Prawiranegara as prime minister. The revolt was directed against the Djakarta government, and reflected a desire for more out-island, socialist, and Muslim power; but by designating it as anti-Communist, its fomenters were able to receive United States arms and planes. The American secretary of state Dulles expressed sympathy for the rebels. In early April, rebel planes bombed a church and other buildings on the Christian island of Ambon. Indonesian anti-aircraft gunners shot down a B-52 piloted by an American, Allen Pope, who, surviving the crash, claimed to be merely an anti-Communist soldier of fortune. Sukarno pardoned him after hearing a plea from his wife, mother, and sister.

The Indonesian Civil War was under way. With the United States arming the rebels, Sukarno had sent Nasution to eastern Europe to buy munitions, and now deployed the navy to isolate the rebellious regions. These regions were principally Central Sumatra and North Sulawesi, a good many other provinces of the out-islands being more or less uninvolved. American enthusiasm for the venture waned as rebel commanders squabbled among themselves, and proved themselves unable to govern any more satisfactorily than Djakarta. The Padang government requested the United States to freeze Djakarta's overseas funds, but this was not done; and the Caltex oil company, with installations in Central Sumatra, continued to make foreign exchange payments to Djakarta. Sukarno negotiated with Hatta, but sent a few bombers against rebel outposts, and began landing troops on Sumatra where they met little resistance. On April 17 the Djakartans took Padang, and on May 5 Bukittinggi. The rebellion was virtually over in Sumatra; and by the end of July it was over in Sulawesi except for guerrilla activity and the continued liberation of overseas propaganda. Although brief, this war had a profound effect on the future course of events. Previously, the regionalists had been a significant force because in some matters they could tip the balance between Sukarno and the army, the two main foci of power. Now, however, the regionalists were culprits; and their main parties, the Masjumi and the socialists, were in disgrace. And with the collapse of the Padang government, the United States began supplying arms to Djakarta, equipping the army for a showdown with the Communists.

With the regionalists overthrown and the army somewhat divided within itself, Sukarno assumed more and more power in late 1958 and through 1959. The PKI aligned itself with him for protection from the army, and could offer in exchange for this protection its unsurpassed organization and communications network ramifying to the village level. However, Sukarno suspended political parties altogether, a move that was a setback both for the PKI and for those who were trying to identify him as a Communist. Some observers of the political scene then tried to identify him as a dictator, but other observers were equally insistent that Indonesia was heading toward a military dictatorship in the fashion of Burma, Pakistan, and the Sudan. Sukarno expelled 40,000 Chinese for violation of an edict prohibiting aliens from carrying on commercial activities in the villages. The edict had been on the books for years, but this sudden enforcement of it disturbed the PKI, since both immigrant and native-born Chinese were for the most part loyal to Communist China rather than Nationalist China. In early 1960, Khrushchev arrived in Indonesia, but his visit was not a success. Sukarno, an enthusiastic patron of the representative and performing arts, took the Russian premier to some lengthy Indonesian ballets where he dozed off now and then. Krushchev said that Communism advances not by broadening its base among the masses, but by militant action. His speech before the parliament was applauded only when he mentioned the Irian Barat issue, and then only by a few Communists in the audience. Disgruntled by the proceedings, Sukarno was somewhat mollified when Khrushchev promised a twelve-year credit of $250,000,000 at 2½ percent interest.

Although temporarily inactivated, the major political parties of Indonesia had retained their organization; and soon after Khrushchev left, the PKI, the PNI, the NU, and the Masjumi combined forces—strange coalition—to oppose a budget submitted by Sukarno. Thereupon, Sukarno abolished parliament and announced a new political creed: *Manipol-Usdek*. The word was a complex acronym. *Manipol* referred to the Political Manifesto of the Republic, to which he had alluded in an Independence Day speech in 1959. *U* was for *Undang-undang Dasar' 45*, a return to the constitution of 1945. *S* was *Socialisme à la Indonesia*, socialism in the Indonesian fashion. *D* was *Demokrasi Terpimpin*, guided democracy; *E* was *Ekonomi Terpimpin*, guided economy; and *K* was *Kepribadian Indonesia*, Indonesian identity. In response to Sukarno's proclamation of Manipol-Usdek, the Darul Islam made another assassination attempt, strafing two of his residences with a MIG-17. Unharmed and undaunted, in June he appointed a *gotong rojong* parliament of 283 members representing 9 political parties and 20 functional groups. In August he added 326 more members, and formed the Madjelis Permusjawaratan Rakjat Sementara, the People's Provisional Consultative Congress. Composed half of parliament members and half of Sukarno appointees, the MPRS was the highest governmental authority in the land. He outlawed the Masjumi and the PSI, squelched all the other parties, placed restrictions on the press, banned "foreign influences," suppressed a few (surprisingly few) Indonesian intellectuals and journalists, jailed a few politicians including Sjahrir.

Army leaders, impressed with Sukarno's concept of representation by functional groups, set up a series of Cooperative Bodies, intended to align labor, youth, and other groups with the army. Having repeatedly but ineffectually petitioned the United Nations for a resolution of the Irian Barat problem, Sukarno announced *Konfrontasi*, direct confrontation of the Dutch over the matter. Quickly following his lead, the army combined all its Cooperative Bodies into the FNPIB, the National Front for the Liberation of Irian Barat. Not to be used in any such way, Sukarno disbanded the FNPIB in 1960, replacing it with his own National Front. The army countered by creating the Badan Pembina Potensi Karja, the "Body to Develop the Potential of Functional Groups," and managed to secure representation in parliament.

Sukarno having emerged as a man of power and determination, he was invited to the United States in 1961 for a day's talk with President Kennedy. Sukarno was as old as the twentieth century. His millions of followers called him Pak now, a friendly abbreviation of *Bapak*, "father." He had added a few pounds, his black *petji* hid a receding hairline, and his optical prescription was ground into his sunglasses. But he was natty in the military-style costume that he favored, ebullient as ever, grinning disarmingly, and flourishing his elaborately carved swagger-stick as he chatted with Kennedy and Johnson. Indonesian newspapers, which often read as though they were describing events in some Tolkienesque Middle-earth, explained that there would be dire results if Sukarno ever lost that swagger-stick, for it concealed a shiny black jewel of great magical potency.

On a previous trip to the United States, Sukarno had been offended to be met at the airport only by minor functionaries, and to be kept waiting at the White House until he threatened to leave; his talk with Eisenhower had been strained. But the Indonesian leader liked Kennedy, and was delighted to be taken for a ride in the presidential helicopter. In later years, one of Sukarno's most prized possessions was a similar helicopter, a gift from Kennedy. As a visitor, Sukarno presented a sharp contrast to the dour, puritanical Khrushchev who had made American headlines in 1959. Bung Karno liked Disneyland, Hollywood, the movie stars, drum-majorettes, the well-stocked shops, journalists with whom he could wisecrack, the people generally. His only unfavorable reaction to Americans—a reaction commonly evoked from foreign visitors and occasionally from a native son—concerned their tendency to reverse the biologically normal role of the sexes, the men so often being subservient to domineering wives. Not that the situation came as a surprise to him; for the comparatively unmasculine nature of the American man was internationally remarked upon, and even in Javan villages the initials U.S.A. were jokingly interpreted as an acronym of a phrase meaning "under the skirts." At the conclusion of Sukarno's American tour, he was immeasurably gratified by Kennedy's expression of willingness to visit Indonesia; for Sukarno had been bitterly humiliated by Eisenhower's refusal to visit Djakarta even though in the neighboring capital of Manila. Sukarno was building a special guest house for Kennedy when the American president was shot down by an assassin.

Sukarno's trips of 1961 included a flight to Vienna, to be operated on for kidney stones. Late that year he ordered mobilization for a showdown in Irian Barat, and early in the next year dropped paratroops who clashed there with Dutch forces. (Indonesia's campaign in Irian Barat was coordinated by an officer of whom the entire world would soon hear. His name was Suharto.) The United Nations was roused to action, and with the United States persuaded the Dutch to withdraw from New Guinea. For a brief while Irian Barat was turned over to the United Nations, but in May 1963, Indonesia was given control of it. With the transfer of sovereignty, Indonesia assumed its present outlines, and Dutch colonialism was at an end in the Southwest Pacific. The transfer included a promise that the inhabitants of Irian Barat would be allowed self-determination by January 1, 1970.

After this victory, Sukarno received vast sums of "aid" from nations, especially Russia and the U.S.A., that were competing for his favor. Completely out of his depth in economics, the "dismal science," he did not use much of this money where it should have been used. Highways and railway lines should have been repaired, mineral resources exploited, housing provided for a burgeoning population, schools strengthened, public health measures intensified. But declaring that Western nations would never respect Indo-

345

nesia as an equal unless they were treated to vast projects and architectural monuments in Western style, he embarked on some grandiose ventures. There would be an obelisk higher than the one in Washington, D.C.; there would be a majestic Hotel Indonesia where diplomats and wealthy tourists would be proud to stay; there would be Istiqlal, one of the greatest and most beautiful mosques in the world. And there would be a stadium in which Asian and African nations could hold their own version of the Olympic games. Indonesia's neglected economy declined, and with it the exchange rate of the rupiah. In 1959 the rupiah had been devalued to the official rate of 45 to the U.S. dollar, but the black market gave a better idea of the value in which it was held. The latter rate declined progressively, reaching 1,200 to the dollar by the end of 1962. (By the end of 1965 it would reach 12,000 to the dollar.) The peasants struggled along as ever, but the bourgeoisie were hard hit, many of them turning to graft and corruption. Nevertheless, there were certain gains by the early 1960s, for peace had been brought to the entire country of Indonesia. Not only had the PRRI and the Permesta surrendered, but the Darul Islam was finally suppressed in West Java, and its leader Kartasuwirio executed in 1963. The rebellion of Daud Beureueh in Atjeh and of Kahar Muzakar in South Sulawesi were also put down. An Indonesian veterans' organization urged that Sukarno be appointed President for Life; and the idea being widely approved, steps were taken to put it into effect.

As the Irian Barat issue was laid to rest, the Malaysian one arose. In 1962, Sukarno surreptitiously supported a nationalist uprising in Brunei, led by Azabari, who had been a captain in the Indonesian army. The Philippines were also involved in a complicated boundary dispute with British North Borneo (Sabah). Both Indonesia and the Philippines therefore protested when the British and the Malayan prime ministers announced their intention to form, by the end of August 1963, a Federation of Malaysia, to include Brunei, Sarawak, Sabah, Singapore, and Malaya. In the summer of 1963, the two protesting nations agreed to accept the concept of Malaysia if a United Nations referendum demonstrated popular support for it in Sabah and Sarawak. Such a referendum was begun by U Thant but was not yet well under way as the August 31 deadline neared. Sukarno protested again but was granted only a brief delay by Britain and Malaya, who announced that Malaysia would be formed on September 16 even though the referendum would not be completed by that time. Faced with what he took to be United Nations ineffectuality, Sukarno proclaimed a new *konfrontasi*, this time against Malaya; and as usual the Indonesian masses supported him enthusiastically, some 21,000,000 people volunteering to fight for him. Beginning in August 1964, Sukarno landed several thousand *kerilja*, guerrilla troops, on Malaya. The Malayan army and police, who in the 1950s had coped with indigenous guerrillas of Communist persuasion, quickly overcame the Indonesian invaders; but more important skirmishing took place along the northern border of Kalimantan. The British and their Commonwealth allies were forced to send troops, aircraft carriers, and other vessels to Singapore and Borneo, an expensive undertaking that had much to do with Britain's later decision to withdraw as soon as possible from all areas east of Suez.

During the early 1960s, Sukarno turned almost entirely away from the United States, which supported Britain on the Malaysian problem; and he grew cool to Russia, which similarly did not back his stand on the issue. He began to look toward Communist China, which held the more typically Asian view that Malaysia would simply be a British base from which opposition could be mounted against nationalistic movements in several countries. The relationship between Indonesia and China had been strained by the treatment of ethnic Chinese in the islands. In 1963 there were about 2,500,000 Chinese in Indonesia, roughly half of them in Java and Madura. The Hokkien were concentrated in eastern and central Java, west-coastal Sumatra, and the more easterly islands, with the Hakka in western Borneo, Bangka, and western Java including the Djakarta area. The Teochiu, who spoke Hokkien but were ethnically distinct and more given to farming, were scattered from east-coastal Sumatra through the Riaus to west-coastal Borneo, with a concentration at Pontianak. The Cantonese, on the average better capitalized than the other Chinese, and more inclined to be artisans, machine workers, or merchants, lived mostly in central and

347

eastern Java, southern and eastern Borneo, Bangka, and central Sumatra. Popularly, the Chinese were considered as forming two groups. One of these, the *Peranakan Tionghoa,* were native-born "children of the Indies." Before the twentieth century, Chinese women did not migrate to the islands, and the immigrant Chinese men took wives from the indigenous population. Thus, many *Peranakan* were of mixed ancestry, and had adopted Indonesian customs to a greater or lesser degree. The second group was called *Totok,* a word actually signifying "fullblood" but generally interpreted to mean foreign-born. Also included as *Totok* were those Chinese who adhered to the ways of the old country even though born in Indonesia. Wherever they went in Asia and other lands, the Chinese were inclined to remain somewhat aloof from the general populace, and to retain strong emotional ties with the ancestral home even though away from it for generations. These tendencies were least evident in Asian countries, for example Thailand, that had an indigenous elite; most evident in countries such as Indonesia where a European elite had deliberately fostered a pluralistic society. In the days of the Ethical Policy, the Dutch had even built separate primary schools for the *Peranakan,* keeping them away from the "inlanders"; and the *Totok* had operated their own, Chinese-language schools.

In some ways the *Peranakan* were more typically Chinese than the *Totok;* for in spite of their partly Indonesian background, the island-born Chinese had been isolated from many aspects of modern, Western culture, whereas most *Totok* were from Communist China, which had been trying to eradicate much of the older values. The Peking government had made overtures toward the *Peranakan,* some of whom visited mainland China; but being accustomed to cultural riches and a modicum of material wealth, they were appalled by the poverty, regimentation, drabness, and spiritual barrenness of their ancestral homeland. Nevertheless, only a minority of the *Peranakan* supported Chiang Kai-shek, who was widely regarded as a puppet of the United States and a Western imperialist bloc. This attitude was bolstered by the events of 1958, when arms and supplies reached the Sumatran and Sulawesian rebels from Taiwan (Formosa) where Chiang's faction was based.

Regardless of their attitude toward China's struggle, the Chinese of Indonesia found their position steadily worsening in the years after independence. By the terms of the Round Table Agreement of 1949, Indonesia-born Chinese automatically acquired Indonesian citizenship unless they formally rejected it by the end of 1951. Dual nationality was offered to them in 1955. Two years later, military commanders in eastern Indonesia closed the Chinese schools there. Beginning in 1959, effort was made to remove all Chinese from rural areas, confining them to the cities; and the removal was carried on by military force when such was necessary. The Peking government protested this harsh treatment. Some 390,000 Chinese opted for repatriation; but at that time Communist China was trying to maintain a cultural Great Wall about herself, and hastily segregated the comparatively affluent and enlightened repatriates, assigning most of them to state farms on Hainan Island. Repatriation was thus no welcome solution to the problem offered by an unpopular Chinese middle class in the islands. The Javanese *Peranakan*, beset by the army, some anti-Chinese bureaucrats, and Muslim competitors, placed themselves squarely behind Sukarno for protection; and it was only this position that saved them from being wiped out by the Indonesian armed forces around 1959 or 1960.

Peking had congratulated Sukarno on the Irian Barat affair, approved his Malaysian stand, and welcomed him royally when he visited. His foreign minister Subandrio made a trip to Communist China; and so did D. N. Aidit, who soon thereafter, in 1963, began to parrot the Peking line. By the end of 1964, Sukarno had recognized North Korea, North Viet Nam, and the National Liberation Front of South Viet Nam. He met in Shanghai with Chou En-lai, and in Djakarta with the Chinese foreign minister Ch'in Yi, who promised military aid against Malaysia. In New York, Subandrio met secretly with Indonesian diplomats and outlined a new strategy, intended to divide the British from the Americans and to eliminate all imperialist bases from southeastern Asia. The Peking government, itself not recognized by the United Nations, urged Sukarno to withdraw from that organization in protest of Malaysia's seating in the Security Council; and he did so. Not that he needed

349

much urging, for he already dreamed of founding a rival organization in which African, Asian, and Latin American problems would receive more consideration. Moving openly toward the left, toward the PKI and away from the army, he spoke more and more of *Nasakom*, an acronym derived from *Nasionalisme-Agama-Komunisme*, a "nationalism-religion-Communism" linkage that supposedly would revitalize Indonesian society. He took steps to establish *Conefo*, a "Conference of New Emerging Forces," and proclaimed a *Darsa Wasa* ("tenth anniversary" in Sanskrit-derived phraseology) celebration in Djakarta to mark that anniversary of the Bandung Afro-Asian Conference. Held in April 1965, the *Darsa Wasa* was attended by only 35 out of 60 invited nations, and only three heads of state showed up.

Over the protest of United States ambassador Howard Jones, and of diplomat Ellsworth Bunker (who had been told "to hell with your aid" because it had so many strings attached), Sukarno staged anti-American demonstrations, and plastered Djakarta with posters showing various Communist leaders smashing John Bull and Uncle Sam. Among the demonstrators was one of Sukarno's daughters, fifteen-year-old Rachmawati. By now Sukarno was in poor health, a circumstance that had not prevented him from taking three more wives. He was frequently troubled by kidney stones, an exceedingly painful malady, and once or twice he could barely finish a speech. Indonesian newspapers explained that at the inauguration of West Java's Djatiluhur hydroelectric and flood control dam, he had remarked that man now controlled the very elements; and for that sacrilege he had been afflicted with much pain, his people with floods, volcanic eruptions, and crop failures. On August 5, 1965, Sukarno collapsed on a speaking platform in Djakarta. Aidit rushed back from Peking with two specialists in acupuncture, a Chinese school of medicine that claims to effect cures by sticking needles in mysterious lines of force supposedly extending along the body.

The Communists had secretly set 1970 as the date for a complete takeover of Indonesia, and had planned to push Sukarno more and more down their path under cover of the Nasakom formula; but his apparent decline was one factor urging them to immediate action instead. A second factor was a rumor that the army might soon move against both Sukarno and the PKI; and a third was the American build-up in South Viet Nam in 1965, a show of force suggesting that the United States might become sufficiently resolute to oppose Communism firmly in southeastern Asia. Consequently, on September 30 and October 1, 1965, the PKI went into action, along with some radical left-wing politicians and some Communists who had infiltrated the army. Their plan called for the killing of seven top-ranking generals who stood in the way of Nasakom. One of the seven, Nasution, escaped over a wall into the garden of the Iraqi ambassador, but his five-year-old daughter was shot in the back. Nasution's escape came about because in the dark the attackers mistakenly seized his aide, Lieutenant Pierre Tendean, who resembled the general. Not so fortunate were generals Yani, Harjono, and Pandjaitan, all of whom were shot down in their own homes. Even less fortunate were generals Pariman, Suprapto, and Sutojo, for they were taken alive along with Tendean. The officers captured alive, and the bodies of the slain, were trucked to Lubang Buaja ("Crocodile Hole") near Halim airbase 15 miles south of Djakarta. Here they were turned over to the feminist Gerwani, the Indonesian Women's Movement, whose members had prepared themselves for the occasion by castrating and cutting up live cats, and by performing a nude rite called the "Dance of the Fragrant Flowers." The women beat the living men to a pulp with clubs and rifle butts, slashed and mutilated the bodies, gouged out the eyeballs, and threw the corpses into a well near the Lubang Buaja.

A comparatively unknown general, one whom the Communists had failed to consider, took dramatic action against the rebels. He was Suharto, who had coordinated the Irian Barat campaign, and who was now commander of Kostrad, the Strategic Forces. Assuming full command without consulting Sukarno, Suharto hid Nasution, alerted the navy and the civil police, tried unsuccessfully to reach the air force, and mobilized the army to put down the coup. For a time, however, he was slowed by uncertainty as to the nature of the plot and the role of Sukarno in the night's events.

The plot was broader and deeper than was at first realized, involving not only Djakarta but many other cities. In 1964, Aidit had established the highly secret Biro Chusus, the Special Bureau, and two of its agents, Sjam and Pono (aliases), had been in charge of the coup. The army had been infiltrated by Communists to an un-suspected degree; certain infantry, air force, and palace guard troops were regarded as sure allies in the take over. The Pemuda Rakjat, or People's Youth, and the feminist Gerwani were Commu-nist fronts. Air vice-marshal Omar Dhani, head of the air force, had been led to believe that he would replace Sukarno. Lieuten-ant-Colonel Heru Atmodjo, Dhani's assistant chief intelligence offi-cer, was involved, as well as Major Sujono, who directed paramili-tary training at Lubang Buaja. General Mustafa Sjarif Supardjo was a link between the Communists and their sympathizers in the military. Latief, who had become an infantry colonel in Djakarta, was one of the plotters; and Lieutenant-Colonel Untung, a para-trooper and commander of the Tjakrabirawa battalion, had led the assault. The president's palace, radio station, and telecommuni-cations center in Djakarta were to have been seized, and the coup publicly blamed on dissident army officers backed by the Ameri-can CIA. But of course these details of the conspiracy were re-vealed only with time, and on the morning of October 1 the situa-tion was clouded.

What of Sukarno? At 9:00 P.M. on the night of September 30 he had gone to Senayan, a Djakarta suburb, to address a group of technicians. Around 11:00 P.M. he went back to the Freedom Pal-ace, changed clothes, and drove to the Hotel Indonesia to join one of his wives, who was attending a wedding reception there. She was the Japanese Naoko Nemoto, introduced to the public as Ratna Sari Dewi, "Jewel Flower Goddess." He took her to her home at Slipi, another suburb, where he was awakened next morn-ing at 6:00 A.M. by one of his aides bringing news of the coup. At 6:30 he started for the palace but was advised by radio-telephone that plotters had occupied the radio station and three sides of Freedom Square, and had surrounded the palace. He went to the home of Haryati, another wife, who lived in Grogol, a Chinese sec-tion of Djakarta, where his aides found him and advised him to seek safety. The coup had not yet been put down, and at 7:30 A.M. Untung announced over the radio that his men had simply crushed an uprising of subversive generals who, backed by the CIA, had tried to do away with Bung Karno. Soon thereafter, Sukarno made for Halim. It was the plotters' base, but it was also where his Jet-Star airliner was kept in readiness. He remained at Halim for hours, talking with Dhani and Supardjo. Aidit and Sjam were hiding in a nearby house, and not far away the waters of a well near Lubang Buaja were stained with the blood of murdered and mutilated men. Around 2:30 P.M., Johannes Leimena, a deputy prime minister who was not pro-Communist, came to Halim at considerable personal risk, intending to tell Sukarno that Suharto was putting down the coup and would soon move against Halim.

In the meanwhile, the "September 30 Movement," as the plotters styled themselves, went on the air again to announce that a new Revolutionary Council of 45 men would now be the "source of all authority" in Indonesia. Mentioned were Untung as chairman, Supardjo as vice-chairman, Dhani, and Subandrio. Although a few people on the list were not pro-Communist and had been chosen without their knowledge, the roster revealed to Suharto the nature of the plot. He had been reluctant to shed blood if the coup had been engineered simply by misguided hotheads, but seeing that it was a broad-based Communist conspiracy, he sent into action his Kostrad forces, some loyal elements of the Djakarta garrison, the proud Siliwangi Division of West Java, and General Sarwo Edhy's paracommandos. Opposition in Djakarta melted away before him, and he deployed his men to attack Halim, but waited until he learned that Sukarno had left. Around 10:30 P.M. Sukarno departed for Bogor. Aidit and Sjam had escaped by plane to Djokjakarta, Supardjo to Bogor, Dhani to Madiun and then to Bogor, where he had been promised shelter by Sukarno. Suharto captured Halim during the night.

On the morning of October 3, the Communist newspaper *Harian Rakjat*, "People's Daily," in an editorial that had been written and printed a bit prematurely, hailed the September 30 Movement and depicted it cartoon-fashion as a great fist smashing an Indonesian general who wore U.S. dollar signs for epaulettes, and a cap initialed "CIA." Decreeing martial law, Suharto banned the paper. On October 3, Sukarno broadcast an announcement that he himself

353

was alive, well, and still in charge. Suharto went to Bogor for a conference, and was eventually named by Sukarno as Yani's successor to the post of chief of staff; but Sukarno continued to harbor Dhani, and later abetted Supardjo's temporary escape. On October 4 the seven bodies were recovered from the well near the Lubang Buaja, and there was widespread demand that the Communist party be banned. Sukarno refused, and did not attend the funeral of the murdered men; nor would the Chinese embassy fly its flag at half-mast to honor these dead.

In the coup, the Communists had taken over a good many cities besides Djakarta, but their grip on Semarang was broken in a day, on Djokjakarta in four days. In some towns the PKI held out for more than a week, and in parts of Surakarta until the end of October. Meanwhile, in Djakarta, the Ansor, a Muslim youth organization with army backing, burned the PKI headquarters to the ground, and splashed the city with painted slogans: *Sauté* Aidit! ("Fry Aidit!"). Ransacking the homes of Aidit and other Communists, the youths marched past the American embassy chanting, "Long live America!" Newspapers quickly announced that "CIA" stood for Chinese Intelligence Agency, and the September 30 Movement was given a name that could be acronymized to *Gestapu*. As the days went by, mobs sacked the headquarters of SOBSI and Pemuda Rakjat, demonstrated in front of the Chinese embassy, and attacked a Chinese university. Sukarno and Subandrio tried to quiet the rioters. Suharto ordered liquidation of the remnants of the Gestapu, and sent Edhy's paracommandos to purge the Communist-infiltrated battalions of Central Java. The PKI, realizing that it could no longer pretend innocence in the coup, armed itself and tried to take command of Central Java villages. Loyal army elements responded by creating People's Defense units made up chiefly of Muslim or nationalist youths with some military training. The Pemuda Rakjat rampaged through Central Java but was put down by paracommandos.

At the end of October 1965, the long-suffering country ran amuck. The word "amuck" is from the Malayan *amuk*, and there is nothing mysterious about it. Most Indonesians are exceptionally courteous, and inclined to bottle up resentments. One need not be a psychologist to understand that there is a limit to the number of tribulations and crushing disappointments that are tolerable without violent reaction. "To take arms against a sea of troubles and by opposing end them"—this is *amuk*, and it is known in all parts of the world. It is true that in Indonesia, several ethnic groups have been noteworthy for a willingness to condone *amuk* as a personal response to intolerable social pressures; but the uprising of 1965 was the inevitable consequence of a series of antecedent events in the islanders' history. The Indonesians had been exploited for centuries by the Dutch, virtually enslaved for a few years by the Japanese, at war with the British and the Dutch for another few, then riven by internal rebellion; and now the hard-won Republic was overtly threatened by the godless Communists and the Chinese. The statement has several times been published that the events of November and December 1965 came as a great surprise to everyone. This is not so. People who knew the Indonesians, and the torment they were undergoing, were predicting a bloody end to their patience as far back as early 1964, to be triggered by disappointment at Bung Karno's performance.

In these curious times, when some nations find it fashionable to coddle their subversives, the Indonesian approach to the Communist problem at least had the merit of simplicity. In eight weeks time, some 750,000 Communists, Chinese, and other unpopular types were shot, stabbed, speared, or hacked to death as the people took the law into their own hands. The figure 750,000 is tentative; some guesses run higher, some lower. Estimates are most reliable for Java and Bali, the combined figure for which is 350,000. Corpses packed the rivers like log-jams. The fishermen of Pekalongan, on the north coast of Java, threw away their catch because the fishes' stomachs were packed with human fingers, ears, and other hacked-off parts. In Surakarta the killing was done by certain anti-Communists with army backing. In most of West and Central Java it was done by the army itself. In most of East Java it was done by black-shirted Muslim youths, the Ansor killer squads. Devout Muslims killed unbelievers in the name of Allah. The Balinese killed with inconceivable fury, many of them blaming the 1963 eruption of Gunung Agung on the Communists' malign influence.

355

Throughout the islands, about 400,000 members of the Communist party, Chinese and indigenous, were exterminated. Also slaughtered were thousands of possibly non-Communist Chinese, and unpopular families whatever their ethnic origin or political affiliation. Indeed, whole villages were wiped out by night raiders, old scores were settled, feuds and vendettas pursued to a conclusion. Hatreds, the legacy of social injustice, had long accumulated, had developed increasing pressure like seething magma deep in the ground, and now exploded like Krakatoa.

The army also took 200,000 prisoners, the interrogation of which led to an unprecedentedly detailed exposé of Communist machinations. Aidit was killed, Untung captured, sentenced, and executed. Njono, Lukman, Njoto, Sakisman, Anwar Sanusi, Sudisman, Sjam, Rewang—all top-ranking Indonesian Communists—were either killed or captured. Subandrio, Dhani, and Supardjo were accused of complicity in the plot. The Communist party of Indonesia had been Asia's second largest, second only to China's; but by the end of 1965 it was nonexistent although there remained, of course, a scattering of underground operatives in hiding from the army.

Yet, Sukarno determined not to compromise with the generals, but to take full power again. Refusing to admit even a past error of judgment, he announced an intention to rebuild the PKI. He was his old self again, extolling Nasakom and daring the generals to depose him. The masses were spellbound as usual, but now there was another strong figure on the scene, Suharto; and they sensed that there would be a power struggle. Indonesian newspapers announced that Sukarno believed himself to be a reincarnation of Gadjah Mada, who had built the Madjapahit empire, and was protected by nine magical *kris*. (A *kris* is a wavy-bladed knife thought to derive magic power from its streaks of meteoritic iron, and to be able to talk, fly, swim, turn into a snake, or even beget human children.) To confront Sukarno's nine *kris*, the newspapers continued, Suharto had to obtain the mask of Gadjah Mada. Informed by a *dukun* (a soothsayer—no Indonesian politician would be without one) that the mask was in a temple at Blahbatuh on Bali, Suharto sent a jet plane to get it. The newspapers added that having sprin-

356

kled the mask with holy water, and offered it incense and flowers, Suharto became self-assured.

In some of the remoter provinces, hostilities were but gradually brought under control. In Kalimantan, the Dyaks were slaughtering Chinese as late as 1967, an ironic circumstance since it was the Communists who had organized the Dyaks into guerrilla bands and had armed them from Peking. But in Java and Sumatra, the *amuk* had fairly well run its course by the beginning of 1966. Sukarno maintained Subandrio, an alleged conspirator, on his staff and set him to repairing the Peking-Djakarta link. The army forced Subandrio's removal from the Armed Forces Operations Command and the Central Intelligence Bureau, although he remained a foreign minister and deputy prime minister. In January 1966, the KAMI, the Indonesian Students' Action Front originally formed by the army to combat Communist infiltration, demonstrated in Djakarta and Bandung against the badly deteriorated economic situation, and flaunted a few slogans attacking Sukarno personally but only on the issue of his polygyny. When Sukarno called a cabinet meeting in Bogor in mid-January, students mobbed the palace but were dispersed by armed guards. In February, Sukarno dismissed Nasution, abolished the armed forces staff he had headed, installed Dhani as minister for aircraft industry, appointed a new cabinet of 100 members, and confirmed Subandrio as first deputy prime minister and foreign minister. Suharto did not respond with direct action, but youth troops, 50,000 of them, stormed the Freedom Palace and the state secretariat building, disrupting traffic so that new cabinet members could not reach the palace to be sworn in. Then, by demonstrating more wildly and aggressively, the young people provoked the palace guards into opening fire; and a medical student, Arief Rachman Hakim, was killed. Now having a martyr, the youths whipped themselves up into a frenzy. Sukarno banned one of their organizations and closed the University of Indonesia. Calling themselves the "Generation of '66," and lumping Sukarno, Subandrio, and others as a "Generation of '45," the youths milled about, hung Subandrio in effigy, and ransacked the foreign ministry. Leftist students from Bung Karno University in Djakarta at-

357

tacked those from the University of Indonesia, and stormed the American embassy. Djakarta was in an uproar.

Sukarno called the leaders of nine major political parties to the Freedom Palace, gave them a blistering lecture, and made them sign a document deploring the activities of the anti-Communist students. Subandrio began rounding up pro-Sukarno army units and irregulars in preparation for an assault on the dissident youths, but Suharto forestalled further violence. Edhy's paratroopers, wearing no insignia or identifying berets, started to surround the palace, and the head of the palace guard reported to Sukarno that unidentified troops were closing in. Sukarno, Subandrio, and Chairul Saleh rushed out into the garden and departed in the presidential helicopter for Bogor. Suharto sent three generals to Bogor with an order for Sukarno to sign, giving Suharto full authority to take all measures deemed necessary to safeguard the people and the government. The generals also took a message from Suharto, to the effect that Bung Karno's personal safety could not be guaranteed without the signature. Sukarno signed, and Suharto had helicopters drop copies of the order while soldiers and students organized a parade. Sukarno returned to the Freedom Palace, which was guarded by Edhy's troops; and that same day, Suharto banned the PKI. Sukarno protested, accusing Suharto of having been behind the student uprising. Then, claiming to have relinquished no authority, the old revolutionary went back to Bogor. What a strange, slow drama was being enacted, revealing on the one hand the tact and caution of Suharto, on the other hand the awe in which Sukarno was still held.

The same three generals went back to Bogor to retrieve Sukarno, while Suharto's troops occupied the Istana Merdeka, as well as the radio and telecommunications center. With tank guns trained on the palace, Subandrio was arrested along with 14 left-wing cabinet members. A week later, Suharto announced a new, interim cabinet with Hamengku Buwono IX, Sultan of Djokjakarta, as first deputy prime minister in charge of economics, finance, and development, and with Adam Malik as foreign minister. Yet, concessions were made to Sukarno—he was legally "President for Life"—and some of his supporters were added to the cabinet. Confrontation with

Malaysia was already a dying issue, but Malik made plans to lay it to rest, and to restore friendly relations with the United States. In speech after speech, Sukarno undercut Malik's efforts, railing against the colonialism that he considered still to exist in southeastern Asia, even if called by some other name.

Trying to proceed in accordance with the constitution, Suharto summoned the MPRS, which was nominally the highest policymaking body in the land. It met in June, elected Nasution chairman, and listened to a rather pathetic speech from Sukarno, who said he would give up the presidency if desired and had no aim beyond service in the cause of freedom. The Congress ratified the transfer of power to Suharto, called for national elections inside of two years, proclaimed a neutralist foreign policy, announced an intention to rejoin the United Nations, outlawed the dissemination of all Communist propaganda, and intructed Suharto to form a new cabinet by next Independence Day. Sukarno would remain president, but not for life, and Suharto would be acting president if Sukarno were ill or absent from the country.

To all this Sukarno agreed, but he was not beaten yet. Even during his early years of imprisonment and exile by the Dutch, he had been able to maintain contact with the underground, for among his captors there had always been secret supporters ready to carry messages. And now a clandestine pro-Sukarno movement spread in parts of Java and Sumatra, while the few Communist leaders remaining at large began to distribute leaflets attacking Nasution and Suharto. Parliament responded by insisting that Sukarno speak no more of Nasakom, and by suggesting that he be called upon to explain his part in the September 30 Movement. Subandrio and Dhani, brought to trial and found guilty, shielded Sukarno, who claimed no foreknowledge of the plot; but some contrary evidence was adduced. Included in the evidence was an alleged copy of a letter from Aidit to Sukarno suggesting courses of action to be taken when the Communist coup got under way.

In February and March 1967, students demonstrated against Sukarno. As the weeks went by, it became evident that there was still a Communist underground in Java, gaining strength by taking a pro-Sukarno position and by utilizing certain religious cults as a

359

front. These cults had multiplied because the Indonesian masses, now having no single strong leader to adulate, turned to mystics for comfort; and the infiltration of "splinter" sects and cults is a part of Communist tactics. Astonishingly, the Communists were actually planning a coup in Bogor, but it was nipped in the bud. The most famous cult leader, Muljono, was killed by paracommandos, and his followers were rounded up. Under the name of Mbah Suro, Muljono had claimed to be a messiah whose coming was predicted in the twelfth century literature, and to be a reincarnation of a Madjapahit hero known as Suro. On a less rarefied plane he had been a PKI sympathizer if not member, and as a soothsayer he had given advice to Sukarno in the year following the September 30 Movement. The army dug up Mbah Suro's body three times to prove to cultists that he had not risen from the dead, but they remained unconvinced. Sukarno's wife, Hartini, was charged with having carried messages between her husband and the underground. She and another wife, Yurike, announced their intention of seeking divorce. Ratna Sari Dewi, meanwhile, had been sent back to Japan even though she was an expectant mother; for she had been accused of accepting kickbacks from Japanese firms involved with war reparations payments.

Isolated and attacked obliquely, Sukarno agreed in a series of meetings to relinquish all executive power in the interest of national unity. In the last act of the drama, Suharto announced that Sukarno's complicity in the September 30 Movement could not be demonstrated; that Sukarno would retain the title of president, but as a result of his failing health and certain practical considerations, would play no further active role in politics. Around this time, a Western journalist asked Nasution to supply a precise title for Sukarno. The chairman of the MPRS replied, "When an Indonesian meets a tiger, he calls it Grandfather; when he meets a crocodile, he calls it Scholar." A bungalow was built for the powerless Sukarno, where he lived in comparative seclusion. Occasionally he visited Djakarta quietly, and eventually he moved to the house he had occupied with Ratna Sari Dewi. In early 1969 he made a brief public appearance at the wedding of one of his daughters, but carefully followed security orders.

In June 1970, Sukarno was reported to be dying from kidney malfunction and high blood pressure. Fatmawati was prostrated with shock and grief. Ratna Sari Dewi was allowed to return briefly from Japan, bringing with her a baby daughter, Saritka Sari, whom Sukarno had never seen. Surrounded by seven of his children, on June 21, 1970, the 69-year-old revolutionary died. The body lay in state at Slipi, where tens of thousands of people filed by. Suharto ordered flags to be flown at half-mast for a week. Sukarno was not buried in Kalibata heroes' cemetery in Djakarta, but beside his mother in Blitar. Years before, he had said that he wanted none of his many titles carved on his tombstone, but only the words, "Here lies Soekarno, mouthpiece of the Indonesian people." And so it was done.

# CHAPTER IX

# THE NEW ORDER

GENERAL Suharto was born in 1921, the son of poor parents who lived on the outskirts of Djokjakarta. Culturally, he was more Javanese than the late Sukarno. From childhood, Suharto was exposed not only to animism and Islam, which blanket Java, but also to Hindu-Javanese thought, of which Djokjakarta had remained a center. His formal education was Western-style and in the Dutch language, but he also became a protegé of Raden Mas Darjatmo, who was a mystic in the old Hindu-Javanese tradition. Suharto joined the army when he was nineteen years old, near the end of Dutch colonial times. He pursued his military career through the period of Japanese occupation; and after the proclamation of independence, he served in Tentara Negara Indonesia, the Indonesian army that fought off the returning Dutch and their British allies. His rise through the ranks was rapid. As a TNI officer, he displayed exceptional military ability during the Dutch attack on Djokjakarta, and even briefly recaptured the city from the Dutch. In 1950 he helped put down the insurrection of Adiaziz in the South Moluccas, and later he coordinated the successful Indonesian campaign against the Dutch in Irian Barat.

Married, with one wife, Siti Hartinah, and six children, General Suharto lives modestly in an army villa in Djakarta. For a hobby he raises cage birds and tropical fishes. He has emerged as scrupulously honest, affable, quiet but firm, cautious, pragmatic. Among the problems that have confronted him and his staff are restoration of pleasant relations with Malaysia, the United Nations, and the United States; calming of the internal situation; and above all, improving the country's economic status.

As it happened, the Federation of Malaysia did not develop along expected lines, for Brunei never joined, and Singapore seceded in August 1965. Indonesia and Malaysia signed a treaty in August 1966, ending hostilities; and in September of that year Indonesia returned to the United Nations. The United States soon resumed economic aid. In early 1968, Adam Malik expressed Indonesia's intention to pursue an active, independent course in its foreign relations. He said that his country was openly and vigorously anti-Communist, valued the friendship of the United States, wanted to be friends with the Soviet Union, and was willing to be friends with Peking if that government would respect Indonesia's national sovereignty. The foreign policy goals of Indonesia, like those of the United States, included regional stability in Southeast Asia, better relations with Communist countries that desired such, and resistance to Communist "wars of liberation." Like many other diplomats in Southeast Asia and elsewhere, Malik felt that Communist insurgency, supported in part from outside, was the principal danger menacing the states of Southeast Asia, and he was fearful of the consequences if the United States failed to hold the line against Communism in South Viet Nam.

In October 1968, the MPRS elevated Suharto from acting president to president, with a five-year tenure.

In 1969, Moscow offered Indonesia $25,000,000 in aid for the completion of a steel mill, an atomic reactor, and a fertilizer factory, as well as for investment in fisheries and the mining of tin and bauxite. However, Moscow first wanted repayment of a huge sum, about $799,000,000 including interest, that had been sent to Sukarno for arms. Impoverished and now bitterly anti-Communist, Indonesia was in no mood or position to pay, and further discussion of the matter was postponed. Reluctantly, Moscow agreed to sell Indonesia some plane and ship parts, purchase from the Soviet Union being virtually a necessity since the planes and ships were mostly of Russian origin. Also in 1969, President Nixon visited Djakarta, the first United States president ever to do so. Nixon said that it was on the basis of common values and ideals, not of alliance or alignment, that the United States sought to cooperate with Indonesia; that a proud, independent, dynamic Indonesia could be a great influence for good in the modern world. He promised Suharto strong economic support, and offered to send him a piece of moon rock when American scientists had finished studying the specimens brought back from lunar exploration. President and Mrs. Nixon were warmly received in Indonesia, and there were no demonstrations.

For several years, America's aid to Suharto's government was nonmilitary, since economic considerations were paramount. However, in early 1970 Suharto visited Washington, and thereafter Indonesia began receiving increased military support from the United States. The Nixon administration asked Congress for $28,000,000 worth of military assistance to Indonesia in the fiscal year 1972, as compared with $18,000,000 the previous year and $5,800,000 the year before that. Even $28,000,000 is a small sum compared with the $1,000,000,000 pumped into Indonesia by the Soviet Union and Eastern Europe for arms and training during the period of 1960–1965. A greater part of the American military aid goes into the Indonesian army's civic action program of road building and related projects, although certain armed forces units are being upgraded and army interisland communications improved.

In 1970, a conference of twelve nations was held at Djakarta. Represented, in addition to Indonesia, were the Philippines, Malaysia, South Viet Nam, Cambodia, Thailand, Singapore, Laos, South Korea, and Japan, along with Australia and New Zealand. The conference called for the withdrawal of all foreign troops from Cambodia, and the sending of neutral observers to that country. In the United States, Suharto emphasized support for Cambodian neutrality, and Nixon expressed approval that Asian nations were taking steps of their own to solve Asian problems. Indonesia also went on record as disapproving the Soviet Union's 1968 invasion of Czechoslovakia.

The Suharto government has brought peace to Indonesia, a remarkable accomplishment in this land of conflict, revolt, coup, and counter-coup. Not that all ethnic or political groups are cooperating smoothly with each other, however. A problem still exists with the remaining Chinese of Indonesia, who control a disproportionately large segment of the economy. There is resentment toward this minority group, yet their economic skills are valuable. Potentially more dangerous are the Communists, who still plot and scheme beneath the cover of youth and party organizations, and of religious sects. In July 1970, Indonesian authorities in Djakarta smashed a Communist network which had been planning to revive the banned PKI. In the meanwhile, trials have continued of the Communists and their sympathizers taken in the massive round-up that followed the abortive Gestapu coup. In general, such trials have mostly involved important personages whose revelations open the way to further investigation and legal action; while lesser figures remain in exile on Buru on the Moluccas. Supardjo, recaptured in 1967, was executed in May 1970.

Outside Indonesia, there is some political maneuvering against Suharto. In later August 1970, he planned a trip to the Netherlands and West Germany; and at The Hague, a band of about 25 Indonesian rebels organized a violent demonstration intended to coincide with his visit. Christians from Ambon, they killed a Dutch policeman, took over the Indonesian embassy, and seized a group of hostages. Having drawn the desired attention, they surrendered. Claiming to represent 30,000 people who wanted an independent Republic of the South Moluccas, they named J. A. Manusama, a Rotterdam schoolteacher, as their "president." Suharto, learning of the demonstration, delayed his visit by a day, by which time the plotters were in jail. A few days later, in West Germany, Suharto's itinerary was curtailed because of danger from student groups demonstrating against his regime. In Tirana, Albania, the Communists sporadically issue a magazine called *Indonesian Tribune*. Devoted now to attacking the Suharto government, the magazine is distributed clandestinely in the islands.

366

One internal problem, facing but not peculiar to Indonesia, is that of population growth. By mid-1971 the country's population was estimated at 120,000,000, and that number was expected to double in just 20 years' time. Indonesian newspapers have cooperated in spreading birth-control information, and efforts continue to induce migration from overcrowded Java to sparsely settled parts of Sumatra and Kalimantan. Special considerations are given to foreign investors who set up operations in the out-islands.

The more advanced and politically dominant islands of Indonesia lie in the western and central parts of the country, and so it would be easy to dismiss the events of Irian Barat as of no great significance; but such dismissal would be short-sighted, for New Guinea has the obvious potentiality of becoming another "hot spot," with the people crying out single-mindedly for freedom, and the Communists fomenting disorder under the cover of nationalism and sectarianism. When that day comes, it is to be hoped that the posture of Indonesia and Australia is one that cannot readily be interpreted as colonialist. The Irian Barat referendum was held as planned, in August 1969. The few thousand literate Papuans and Melanesians were concentrated in former Dutch colonial towns where they had been indoctrinated with anti-Indonesian attitudes during the period 1949–1961. With perhaps 800,000 tribespeople scattered over Irian Barat's swamps, forests, and mountains, referendum by popular vote was out of the question, and so 1,025 tribal leaders were selected as speaking for the entire population. Pleased by gifts, awed by soldiery and some by a plane ride to Djakarta, these leaders (many of whom had never even visited a neighboring village for fear of sorcery) then assembled for *musjawarat,* Indonesian-style discussion leading to a consensus. The consensus was that Irian Barat should be annexed by Indonesia.

The referendum focused attention on a situation that had perturbed artists, anthropologists, and intellectuals generally: the wholesale burning of New Guinea art and craft work at the instigation of Christian missionaries. Missionary activity in the Southwest Pacific is a painful topic, for on the one hand it has involved many sincere and dedicated donors, but on the other hand it has involved all too many proselytizers who were misguided or even

367

despotic. The situation in Irian Barat is different from that which has existed farther west in Indonesia. In the western and central islands, the first Christian missionaries were Portuguese and Spanish Catholics. Although the Netherlands began as a Protestant nation, in modern times it has had a large Catholic population—its largest political party is the Catholic—and during colonial times there were both Catholic and Protestant missionaries in Indonesia proper, working among the non-Muslim minority. With considerable financial backing and the support of the colonial government, and trying hard to outshine the Muslims in modernizing the islanders, the Christians were able in many localities to obliterate major segments of the indigenous culture, both religious and secular. Their efforts were most successful among the Eastern Toradja and the Minahasa of Sulawesi, the Toba Batak of Sumatra, the Mentawai Islanders, the Ambonese and some other Moluccans, and the *Peranakan* Chinese. The Minahasans, many of whom became qualified for the civil service, were often cited as evidence that missionization could be salutary; and Christian Bataks, moving to Djakarta, have lately acquired a reputation for Western-style knowledgeability. Both Catholic and Protestant political parties have existed for decades in the islands. Although present-day Indonesia has only about 2,000,000 Catholics, Catholicism is well received there. Sukarno was favorably inclined toward it as a result of missionary kindnesses during his exile years, and today, Catholic clerics may even teach religion on government salary in any of the schools. Indonesian Protestants slightly outnumber Catholics.

But in recent decades the Christian missionary field has been invaded by so-called "splinter" sects which originated mostly in the United States. Of course, sectarianism is not peculiar to any time or country, but as it happened, the United States, proverbially a melting pot, received a variety of European immigrants who, together with their descendants, in many cases did not find adequate psychological support from the established creeds. Although sectarianism was rife in the United States in the last century, the year 1910 is generally selected as the approximate time at which American sects began to multiply and gain adherents, especially among alienated, culturally impoverished, urban members of the lower class. While a broad spectrum of religious views was advanced, the most popular sects tended to be fundamentalist, adventist, and evangelical. Their proponents, frowning upon the higher criticism, and taking religion to be incompatible with ratiocination, laid great emphasis upon literal acceptance of scriptural fables, the miracle stories which appeal to the emotions. Asserting that Jesus Christ will soon come again, the sectarians regarded themselves as the only people who will be "saved," such salvation being contingent upon promulgating the views of the sect and collecting money for it.

During Dutch colonial times, most of Netherlands New Guinea was not being developed but was classified as "closed territory" in which missionary activity was discouraged. But the Round Table Agreement of 1949, which freed the Netherlands East Indies, also called for a review of the status of Netherlands New Guinea. The Dutch soon opened and began to develop that area, possibly with the hope of reinforcing a claim to it. A world federation of fundamentalist churches had its headquarters in Amsterdam, a circumstance probably involved with the descent of sectarian missionaries upon the tribespeople. When western New Guinea passed to Indonesia in 1963, the Indonesians proper, true to the *Pantja Sila,* had no objections if Christian missionaries cared to work among pagan tribes, and perhaps did not grasp that the effect of such work might vary greatly with time, place, and denomination.

Concerned with emotional rather than intellectual matters, often hostile toward various ethnic groups with different beliefs, indifferent to or overtly disavowing allegiance to the state, and invoking constitutional or other guarantees of religious freedom, the sects are easily converted into a front for political subversives. Sometimes the sects have a very wide communications network and elaborate printing facilities, both of which encourage infiltration by subversives. Canada, Australia, New Zealand, the nations of eastern Europe, Malawi, and the United Arab Republic are among the countries that have regarded it as desirable to ban one or more of the sects, either for the duration of a war or indefinitely; while Britain, Greece, the United States, and Portugal at one time or another have probed or questioned certain of their activities. Hints have been multiplying that the Indonesian Communists, routed from so many hiding places by General Suharto's clean-up, now take refuge behind sects and schismatic religious groups generally, a likely circumstance in view of Communist tactics and sectarian vulnerability. But this is a matter to be elucidated with time; the immediate problem is the impact of sectarian teachings upon the people of Irian Barat.

A typical story is that of the Grand Valley of the Balim River, the remote "Shangri-la" whose existence was publicized during World War II (Chapter V). Soon after the Round Table Agreement, missionaries descended upon it. Between 1954 and 1962, a dozen mission stations, each with an airstrip, were opened in the country of the Western Ndani, from Grand Valley westward to Ilaga and north to the Swart River. One station was Catholic, the others representing fundamentalist sects. By 1958, the missionaries had a firm hold on the Ilaga people, who were encouraged to burn their weapons, headdresses, drums, armbands, pig tusks, necklaces, net-backs, penis sheaths, string skirts, woodcarvings, and other paraphernalia. Jabonep, a Papuan from North Balim, received three years' indoctrination at Ilaga, and was then turned loose to spread the gospel. As a convert he was more rabid than even his mentors. Hiking cross-country toward his birth-place, he urged the tribes to burn their sacred objects, promising that old women would become young again if baptized, and that baptism would confer physical immortality. Some missionaries, objecting to this doctrine, urged Jabonep's mentor to follow the Papuan and clarify his remarks. The Ilaga missionary then hiked through the Western Ndani country with a body of retainers, and at each village persuaded the tribespeople to burn their possessions. All through 1960 the burnings went on, different tribes having different ideas of what the cremations would accomplish. All thought that they would be rewarded with physical immortality and freedom from disease, but others expected to be transformed into white people. In February 1962, some missionaries used their prior knowledge of an eclipse to reinforce their position. At Bokondini the tribesmen spent the entire night before the eclipse in confessing their "sins," and would not look at the sky at all during the next day lest they be struck blind. In April 1962, an influenza epidemic spread from one of the mission stations, and many of the tribespeople died, the survivors carrying on both traditional and Christian rituals in the pitiful hope of halting the epidemic. In June, missionaries emphasized the great importance of Pentecost, and the arrival of that season touched off a new round of religious activity. Pupils went out to preach, giving such tearful sermons that some of the tribespeople considered an hysterical crying fit to be a necessary prelude to conversion.

Next, missionary attention was directed toward *jao* stones. These were smoothly polished fingering stones prized for the tactile sensation they would yield, and also used like money to settle debts. But since *jao* were made in two shapes symbolizing male and female, they were "evil" to the missionaries, who insisted that they be thrown into pits. Among the unfortunate tribespeople, the idea grew that all non-European items should be similarly discarded. The men tried to cut their hair in Western fashion. Previously, men and women had formed separate groups at gatherings, a traditional practice; but now man and wife sat beside each other as white people did. In-law avoidance was abandoned along with kinship usages that had no close Western counterpart. Marriage payments were given up, it being declared that brides were paid for by the blood of Christ. Exceptionally heart-rending were events at Karubaga in the center of the Western Ndani area. Here the people were led to believe that white skin was good, black skin bad and physically dirty. Chanting Bible verses, discarding most of their possessions, and washing many times daily with soap, the Karubagans expected to be transformed physically into white people at any moment. Also in 1962, a tribesman named Wingganggan, from Kuttime near Karubaga, felt the call to preach, announcing that he was guided by the spirit of his dead father and other departed relatives. He said that he often conversed with the paternal ghost, sometimes by radio. Wingganggan persuaded the vulnerable Karubagans to throw away their clothes and build new homes, assuring them that ancestral spirits would then stock the dwellings with steel axes, Western-style clothing, salt, and soap.

The pitiful story of the Western Ndani need not be pursued further. It is unusual only in that anthropologists, dispassionately studying culture contact, were in the area to record the events.

Also widespread in both Indonesian and Australian New Guinea are the so-called "cargo cults." These were noticed among the Melanesians at the beginning of World War I, when equipment and supplies were being stockpiled at various localities on the island, and multiplied during World War II when cargo ships and planes were unloading an endless stream of Western products. Unable to grasp the concept of factories, many of the tribes believe that the cargo is sent by Jesus, and will be delivered to them once they have discovered the formula for invoking his aid. In some areas it is believed that the white man maliciously diverts cargo intended by Jesus for the black man.

Christian missionaries are not the only ones who create sociological problems that will some day have to be resolved by other people. Islamic missionaries have been known to attach great importance to avoidance of the pig, an animal which in Irian Barat is utilized in connection with ceremonial life, social organization, subsistence, convivial feasts, payment of personal debts, tribal reparations that obviate warfare, ornamentation, and the manufacture of tools.

But, of course, the problems of Irian Barat will have to fester while those of Indonesia proper are being dealt with. Indonesia's greatest need, bolstering the economy, has been the chief concern of the Suharto government, which has accomplished much in this field. A team of economists, trained at the University of California and nicknamed the "Berkeley Mafia," was imported to guide the government in fiscal matters. The inflation rate, at 650 percent in 1965, was reduced to less than 25 percent by 1969, and less than 10 percent by 1971; and the currency was stabilized. Although rice is grown widely, an additional supply still must be imported; but the price of this grain has been brought down, and self-sufficiency in its production is anticipated by 1974. During the period 1970–1971, business journals mentioned Freeport Sulphur Company, Alcoa, Kennecott Copper Corporation, P. T. Caltex Pacific Indonesia, International Nickel Company of Canada, Ltd., and Kaiser Cement and Gypsum Corporation as among the firms investing in Indonesia. Reported backers included International Finance Corporation, Private Investment Corporation for Asia, Chemical International Finance Corporation, and Bamerical International Finance Corporation. Philippine logging companies, and Japanese conglomerates such as Mitsubishi Corporation, also have interests in the islands. By July 1971, foreign investors had spent about $400,000,000 in Indonesia, and had pledged investment of some $1,500,000,000, mostly in oil, rubber, timber, and minerals. In addition, the country receives $500,000,000 in foreign aid, about a third of it from the United States, another third from Japan. A formula has been worked out whereby Indonesia will repay her large foreign debts—totaling $4,000,000,000—over a 30-year period. General Suharto's renovation of the economy has been characterized as one of the great success stories of modern times. His regime has been designated Orba, an acronym of *ordo baru*, "new order."

Of course some groups and individuals have been restive under army domination. Certain politicians who had wanted faster action against Sukarno now want faster relaxation of military control, permitting new talent to take a hand in governmental affairs. However, Suharto's announced policy is a gradual relaxation of such control, and gradual conversion of the system of *musjawarat*, deliberation and consensus by the MPRS and Parliament, into a system of majority vote. The Muslims have clamored for more representation, especially since their large Masjumi party was banned for supporting the Padang government in its revolt. The conservative Muslim party, Nahdatul Ulama, has gained members, and in addition, Suharto has permitted the formation of a "modernist" Muslim party, the Partai Muslim Indonesia. Another source of Muslim dissatisfaction is the growing strength of Christianity as a result of missionary efforts well-financed from Western countries. Muslim-Christian tensions have been greatest in and near South Sulawesi, where in fact there have been armed clashes. Such outbreaks shocked the majority of Indonesians, who were taught religious tolerance by Bung Karno. As noted, Christianity's headway in Indonesia was among the culturally retarded; and in predominantly Christian parts of the republic, the populace differs from the Indonesian norm not only in religion but in cultural traditions generally. Toward the Moluccas, they may differ physically as well, there being a strong Alfur strain in this region. The watchfulness of the Suharto government limits Communist efforts to promote divisiveness among disaffected Christian groups, but something remains to be done in firmly uniting parts of central Indonesia with the rest of the republic.

Objections have been raised, especially by foreign investors, to graft and corruption. In 1970 Suharto pledged to attack corruption in high places, endorsed regulations that would prohibit government officials from accepting commissions proffered by businessmen, ordered such officials to report their total income, instructed the attorney-general to upgrade an anticorruption force, and submitted to Parliament a bill calling for the imprisonment or fining of those who accept kickbacks. Accordingly, abuses have been greatly reduced. In fairness, it should be noted that graft, corruption, nepotism, and related practices are concomitants of the merchant tradition wherever it exists. In the East, they are generally admitted to exist, whereas in the West they are likely to be legislated against but carried on clandestinely. Youth groups have protested corruption in Indonesia, but actually are looking for some role to play commensurate with the important one they assumed in the early days of the Suharto government. KAMI, a youth organization which once showed promise, collapsed into factional bickering on the death of Suwarto, a general who had done so much to encourage it.

But regardless of how impatient anyone may be to see further change, in broad historical view General Suharto has done a remarkably good and rapid job of rebuilding Indonesia, and has permitted as much of the democratic process as is feasible in this country which was not heir to a democratic tradition.

Indonesia's general elections, orginally planned for 1968, were rescheduled for July 3, 1971. Preparation for the election was firmly controlled by the army, giving rise to occasional cries of *intimidasi*, intimidation. Kopkamtib, the Command for the Restoration of Security and Order, was diverted from its principal task, that of ferreting out Communists, and put to supervising party rallies. About one-fourth of the would-be candidates were barred from running, mostly as a result of involvement with the Gestapu coup, Communist-front organizations, or the Padang rebellion. Nine political parties were recognized, from them coming candidates who would run against those of a government-supported coalition of army and functional groups. This is not to say, however, that the parties offered platforms differing markedly from that of the government; rather, the competition was for seats in the MPRS and the Dewan Perwakilan Rakjat (the Parliament). Of 920 members in the MPRS, a third are appointed by the government coalition, along with almost a quarter of the 480 Parliament members. General Suharto did little personal campaigning, and prohibited army personnel from voting. Russia sent good-will visitors to PNI candidates (among whom was Sukarno's son Guntur), and denounced the Suharto regime over Radio Moscow's Indonesian-language station.

As the time for the elections drew near, the government displayed its symbol on leaflets, banners, kites, buttons, and T-shirts: the silhouette of a *beringin*, a sacred fig tree resembling the banyan and the pipul. The portrayal is an ancient one, used thousands of years ago by the Harappans on their seals. Probably to the vanished Harappans, as surely to the modern Indonesians, the tree's sturdy trunk, umbrella-shaped crown, and cool shade symbolized not just physical protection but divine blessing. On Indonesian electioneering banners, the *beringin* was surrounded by a wreath of agricultural plant sheaves—a similar wreath adorns the President's Flag—and was accompanied by a motto, *Golongan Karna*. This motto, customarily acronymized to *Golkar*, is roughly translatable as "For the Sake of the Group" or "Because of the Group," the government coalition calling itself a group rather than a party.

On the appointed day 57,000,000 Indonesians went to the polls, where a majority of them punched the *Golkar* sign of the *beringin* on the ballot. This victory for the coalition was widely regarded as paving the way for accelerated political, social, and economic development over the next 25 years.

The irresistible rise of nationalistic sentiment, the emergence of Sukarno as a focus of this sentiment, the rigorous exploitation of the islands by the Dutch, the imprisonment and exile of Sukarno, the occupation of the country by the Japanese, the propounding of the *Pantja Sila*, Allied victory in World War II, the proclamation of Indonesian independence, war against the British and the Dutch in the name of freedom, Tan Malaka's uprising, the Round Table Conference, independence at last, the establishment of constitutional government, Darul Islam insurgency, the Padang rebellion, the acquisition of Irian Barat, political divisiveness and Sukarno's suppression of it, the decline of the economy, confrontation with Malaysia, the attempted Communist takeover, the *amuk*—what a kaleidoscopic series of episodes! And yet they have all taken place within the memory of many living Indonesians, along with extirpation of the Communists, the decline and death of Bung Karno, the emergence of General Suharto and army control, the easing of internal tensions, the resumption of cordial relations with the United Nations and the United States, the Irian Barat referendum, Suharto's attack on long-neglected economic problems, and the election victory of *Sekber Golkar*.

What next? The country has made clear its determination to force Indonesian culture upon the inhabitants of Irian Barat, although spokesmen for these people reported widespread resistance to it, and widespread belief that the referendum of 1969 was cynically rigged. In latter 1971, Operation Koteka went into action, from headquarters at Wamena in the middle Balim Valley. *Koteka* is the Ndani name for a penis-sheath, and the project aimed to put clothes on several hundred thousand uplanders, as well as involve them in a money economy and make them literate in Bahasa Indonesia. Of course civilization will come to these Irianese, and it could do so with minimal trauma if introduced gradually, under the guidance of cultural anthropologists. However, Operation Koteka was assigned to Colonel Bambang Sumitro, with a budget and timetable calling for completion of the project in two years. General Acub Zainal, military commander of Irian Barat, characterized the project as being "for humanity"; and the Christian missionaries of Irian Barat ostensibly approved it, there being little else they could do. No doubt the Indonesian army will dole out civilization with more sanity and compassion than would be expected of these missionaries; and so in one way, Sumitro's assignment represented a step forward.

But already there are beginning to emerge some New Guineans who are reminiscent of the young Sukarno—charismatic, patriotic, steeped in the mythologies that move the masses. A few other New Guineans are to some degree reminiscent of Hatta, patriotic, culturally sophisticated beyond the average. In Djajapura (which is Sukarnapura again renamed), a few hundred Irianese youths have formed the PBPM, an underground separatist movement whose initials stand for and call for a United Free Papuan State. The PBPM is not armed. Its members protest that the Irianese are economically, socially, and politically oppressed by the Indonesians proper; and hold that few Irianese, other than figurehead politicians such as Governor Frans Kasiepo, would proclaim themselves to be Indonesian. These members also draw attention to the scarcity of Irianese in the government and the commercial enterprises of Irian Barat. The PBPM is watched by General Ali Murtopo's OPSUS, the special operations intelligence unit which helped prod Indonesia toward the *Sekber Golkar* victory, and which is now working on several levels to bind the Irianese more closely to Indonesia. The PBPM recalls Sukarno's early PNI, which met clandestinely and was under surveillance. One supposes that behind sectarian, separatist, or other cover, there also lurk a few counterparts of Aidit, dedicated to the Communist philosophy, and poised to take all possible advantage of divisiveness. By ignoring the lessons of history, Indonesia has lit a time-bomb in its own backyard.

In 1971, the secretary of a United States sectarian alliance reported that West Kalimantan, East Kalimantan, the Toradja country and the Menado area of Sulawesi, Djakarta on Java, and the islands from Sumba to Timor were now ripe for further Christianization; and that at some localities the villagers had already been persuaded to "burn their fetishes." However, missionaries in central and western Indonesia are more easily watched than those in Irian Barat; and their impulses toward despotism will probably be curbed accordingly. For even the remoter regions are being opened to commerce, and hence to general scrutiny. Oil is flowing especially from the Sumatran fields, and Indonesia has be-

377

come the greatest oil-producing nation between the Middle East and the United States. On Kalimantan, foreign timber interests are felling the rainforest so rapidly as to bring protests from conservationists.

Indonesia is doing well in the field of international relations. The country had a pavilion at Expo '70 in Japan, adjoining the New Zealand entry near the center of the exposition. Indonesia has maintained pleasant relations with and received some encouragement from Australia, a nation anxious to avoid friction with its Asian neighbor. The Colombo Plan of 1950–1951, which at its inception seemed almost too informal to be useful, has permitted some Asians to be educated in Australia, and the result of such education will have far-reaching effects. Indonesian dealings with the Netherlands were smoothed to some degree in 1971, when Queen Juliana visited the islands she had once ruled. Later in that year, Indonesia demonstrated its neutralist position by abstaining when most other members of the United Nations voted to oust Nationalist China in favor of Red China.

In early 1972, after Nixon had visited Mao and Chou in Peking, Indonesians took rightful pride. For as a result of the new China-United States accord, an old phrase was suddenly spoken again: the Bandung conference. This had been Sukarno's conception, the First Afro-Asian Conference, held at Bandung, Java, in early 1955 (Chapter VIII). At that time, John Foster Dulles had rejected the five major principles put forth by the assembled delegates. Seventeen years later, Chou persuaded Nixon to accept them. As reiterated by Chou and Nixon, the principles urged each state to respect other states' sovereignty and territorial integrity, regardless of social systems; to refrain from aggression against other states; to refrain from interference in the internal affairs of other states; to admit equality and to work for mutual benefits; and to coexist peacefully with other states. On hearing the joint Chou-Nixon communique of 1972, many Indonesians wept, because Bung Karno had not lived to see this belated recognition of his efforts.

As 1973 opened, Indonesia was encouraging not just foreign investment but also tourism. Djakarta's Kemajoran airport had been remodeled; entry via Singapore or Malaysia was no longer prohib-

ited. Hotels, several of them luxury class, had been built or revitalized in Java, Bali, Sumatra, and Sulawesi. Tourist agencies, one of
them governmental, were offering package trips to points of interest; and in Djakarta, puritanical restrictions on night life had been
lifted. A remodeling of this city was in planning; and General Suharto had imported an American engineer to advise on matters of
street and highway accessibility, housing standards, water distribution, sewage disposal, and other problems. Suharto had lately visited several European capitals, including Brussels. There, he and
his foreign minister, Adam Malik, had conferred with Henry Kis-
singer. As a result of the conference, Indonesia would join Canada,
Poland, and Hungary in policing a ceasefire in Viet Nam.

And so in the years that have elapsed since the end of World
War II—very few years in the perspective of historical time—the
country of Indonesia has moved from a condition of enforced servi-
tude to one in which her attitudes and achievements could well
determine the course of events in Southeast Asia, and have worldwide repercussions.

> *Tuan Hadji memakai djubah*
> *Singgah sembahjang didalam lorong.*
> *Teluk tandjung lagi berubah*
> *Inikan pula dihati orang.*

> The honored Hadji in his vestments
> Stops in the middle of the road to make obeisance.
> Bays and capes are changing;
> How much more the heart of man.

379

CHAPTER X

# PANTUN OF THE PEOPLE

THE VERSE that concluded the preceding chapter was a Malayan *pantun*. A few more such verses seem ideal to conclude the book, for they reveal the Indonesian mentality in a way the unadorned facts of history can never do. The French *pantoum,* as popularized by Victor Hugo in his *Orientales,* takes its name from the Malayan, but not much else. The true *pantun Melaju* is a quatrain intended to be sung, sometimes to the accompaniment of musical instruments; but the plangency of the language, and the felicitous interweaving of ideas in a mere four lines, enable the *pantun* to stand as a poem. And this is the poetry of the people, for a *pantun* has no discoverable authorship, being handed down orally. While new, topical quatrains are heard, so are many old favorites, some perhaps centuries old. For example, in one *pantun* a humble man contrasts his lowly status with that of a Hindu who "bathes in oil" to the beating of a drum and the shrill wailing of the *serunai,* a Persian clarinet. It has been more than 500 years since a Hindu, anointing himself to the fanfare of drum and clarinet, was a living symbol of loftiness in any region where Malayan is spoken; and the verse may be as old as any writings in that language. Many of the old *pantun* have spread throughout the Malayan-speaking world, from Indonesia and Singapore into Malaysia.

In the usual *pantun*, the first pair of lines may describe a scene, an object, or an event; or may offer some general statement. The second pair describes an emotion, or an experience that arouses emotion; but just as the pairs of lines are linked by rhythm and end rhyme, so too are they linked by thought content, a parallel being drawn between the external or observable and the internal or emotional. The parallel may be obvious, or it may be quite subtle. Sometimes a point is made through contrast, as when the calm assurance of the praying Hadji is contrasted with the average man's uneasiness in a changing world. *Traduttori traditori,* the Italians say; and the usual Western translator of a *pantun* is indeed a traitor to its message, which even if understood is generally altered for the sake of meter and rhyme. As quatrains are presented here only to reveal the thinking of the Malayan-speaking people, they are here translated as literally as possible, without effort toward English versification.

The selections may begin with a comparatively simple *pantun* in which there is an obvious parallel between the first pair of lines and the second.

> *Dari mana punai melajang?*
> *Dari pada turun kepadi.*
> *Dari mana datang sajang?*
> *Dari mata turun kehati.*

> Whence come the pigeons soaring?
> From the swamp, descending to the rice stalks.
> Whence comes compassion?
> From the eye, descending to the heart.

The *punai* are fruit pigeons of the kind mentioned in Chapter III, and are a better symbol of compassion than might at first be realized. Colored mostly in shades of green, they are well-nigh invisible against their usual leafy background, but their beauty becomes

382

evident when they appear on the rice stalks where they find sustenance.

Like most forms of poetry, the *pantun* are often concerned with
love in its many aspects, and the next two verses need no explica-
tion beyond the comment that they are reminiscent of love poems
to be found in many other languages.

> *Tudjuh hari dalam hutan*
> *Air ta'minum nasi ta'makan.*
> *Sehari tiada pandang tuan*
> *Rasanja susut tubuh dibadan.*

> Seven days in the wilderness
> Drinking no water, eating nothing.
> One day without sight of you
> It seems as though my very being wastes away.

> *Permata djatuh didalam rumput*
> *Djatuh dirumput bergelang-gelang*
> *Kasih umpama embun diudjung rumput*
> *Datang matahari nistjaja hilang.*

> A jewel falls deep into the grass;
> Fallen in grass, it keeps on sparkling.
> Love's likeness: a dewdrop on the tip of a grass blade
> At sunrise, sure to vanish.

Some *pantun* include erotic imagery. The *kerengga* of the next
verse are the big, red, arboreal ants mentioned in Chapter III.

> *Kerengga didalam buluh*
> *Serahi berisi air mawar.*
> *Sampai hasrat didalam tuboh*
> *Tuan seorang djadi penawar.*

> Red ants inside the bamboo,
> A flask holding rosewater.

383

As long as there is desire in my body
One man serves as cure.

In the next selection, *bertjerai*, parting, usually refers to the separation or divorce of a married couple, and the verse has an emotional depth beyond the erotic.

*Asap api embun berderai*
*Tjatjak galah luan perahu.*
*Hadjat hati ta'hendak bertjerai*
*Kehendak Allah siapalah tahu.*

Smoke of fire, drip of dew
At the bow of the boat, the upright punt-pole thrust in.
A heartfelt wish: that we shall never part;
But who indeed knows Allah's will.

In the next quatrain, the two pairs of lines are more subtly linked.

*Lipat kain lipatlah badju*
*Mari 'ku lipat didalam puan.*
*Sukat air mendjadi batu*
*Baru saja lupakan tuan.*

Fold the skirt; oh, fold the blouse!
Come here, I'll tuck them inside the betel box.
When a barrelful of water turns to stone
Then will I forget you.

A betel box is rather a small container. The seemingly interminable folding of the doffed clothing is endearing while exasperating.

The *beruk* of the next *pantun* is the "coconut monkey" described in Chapter III. Although the adult often is ruffianly and scabrous of pelt, the baby is winsome and may splash about in a puddle as though bathing in an approved fashion.

*Anak beruk dikaju rindang*
*Turun mandi didalam paja.*
*Odoh buruk dimata orang*
*Tjantek manis dimata saja.*

The monkey's child in the leafy branches
Descends to bathe in a puddle.
Unattractive and shabby in the eyes of men
Pretty and sweet [you are] in my eyes.

Indonesians and other Malayan-speakers are fond of *perumpa-maan*, a general term (from *umpama*, likeness or similarity) that covers proverbs, mottos, familiar precepts, and figures of speech. The language is replete with them. *Ada gula, ada semut:* "where there is sugar, there are ants." *Diam ubi berisi, diam besi berkaret:* "silently the potato growing, silently the iron rusting." *Bergalah hilir, tertawa buaja:* "pole downstream and the crocodiles laugh." *Nasi sedap, gulai mentah:* "the rice just right, the curry half-done." In these and many other sayings the sentence is balanced, much like two short lines of verse. It is therefore not surprising that some *pantun* are didactic, suggesting expanded proverbs.

Padi muda djangan dilurut
Kalau dilurut petjah batang.
Hati muda djangan diturut
Kalau diturut salah datang.

Do not roughly brush the young rice plants;
If roughly brushed, the stems break.
Do not roughly command young hearts;
If [they are] roughly commanded, error appears.

In the next verse, the sound of the Malayan words is in keeping with their solemn meaning.

Sekotjak, mendua kotjak
Air segeluk saja tapiskan.
Tengah malam bangun mengutjap
Bantal dipeluk saja tangiskan.

A roiling, and then another;
With a dipper I filter the water.
In the middle of the night rising, praying,
Hugging the pillow, I weep.

*Kotjak* is the roiling of water, the stirring up of sediment, but figuratively it is mental turmoil. The dipper, *geluk*, today might be a tin cup, but originally it was a section of a coconut shell, a peasant's rude implement.

When a *pantun* is sung, a part of its charm comes from a pause at the end of the second line; what kind of parallel will the next two lines draw? The first two lines of the succeeding verse portray a common scene on a *perahu*, a sort of boat. Someone on the *perahu* has raised a brood of mynah birds, and has provided them with a perch in the deep shade. The fledglings, in the fashion of young birds generally, repeatedly stretch upward as far as they can, craning their necks, avidly presenting their toothless maws for food.

> *Anak tiung terdongak-dongak*
> *Terdongak-dongak dalam perahu.*
> *'Nak bertjium gigi rondak*
> *Malam-malam siapa 'kan tahu?*

> Mynah fledglings craning,
> Craning in the perahu's hold.
> Kiss the girl though her teeth are lacking;
> In the dark, who can tell?

The following verse has a brooding imagery. It may be recalled from Chapter III that the *kerbau*, the water-buffalo, easily becomes overheated, and at intervals must soak itself in water. A *kerbau* calf, tethered in full sun, would circle desperately until at last it would drop stunned, perhaps to die.

> *Tingi-tingi si matahari*
> *Anak kerbau mati tertambat.*
> *Sakian lama saja mentjari*
> *Baru sekali saja mendapat.*

> High, high the sun.
> The tethered calf dies.
> In the same way, after long seeking
> At last I have found.

In the old *pantun,* persons are often referred to not by any word that would identify their sex, but by noncommital expressions such as "this person" or "someone" or "young people." The procedure reflects the usages of everyday Malayan speech, but also increases the number of situations in which a *pantun* might be applicable, and may enable listeners of both sexes to find personal meaning in the verse. The following quatrain, a whimsical one, does not actually identify the sex of the wanderer or of the young people who are watched. The verse could therefore have several possible applications, of which the most likely one has been selected.

> *Djalan-djalan sepandjang djalan*
> *Singgah menjinggah dipagar orang.*
> *Pura-pura mentjari ajam*
> *Ekur mata dianak orang.*

> Wandering, wandering the length of the road
> Stopping here and there in people's yards.
> Pretending to look for a hen—
> And out the corner of his eye, peeking at the girls.

Western cliché has it that the East is mysterious, and that the Asians are inscrutable. Several streams of Asian culture—the Malayo-Polynesian, the Arabic, the Hindu-Buddhist, the Chinese—have become interwoven in Indonesia, but the country is not mysterious; it is just insufficiently studied. Nor are Indonesians inscrutable. On the contrary, they are as comprehensible as anyone else. A Klaten plowman toiling behind a bullock team to raise the rice that will feed his family, a tearful Denpasar mother bringing her baby to an army clinic for an anti-cholera injection, a Padang schoolchild counting the days until Ramadan (which also marks the start of vacation), a serious young student coping with an engineering text at Bandung, a Singaradja man enthusiastically betting his pittance on a fighting cock—these are people we can all understand. So are a Sentani Melanesian fingering his rosary to improve the fishing, an Asmat Papuan elder fingering his war-arrows as his tribal world collapses, a Bogor pedicab driver flaunting the *Golkar* symbol on his T-shirt, a "hard-hatted" Malay bringing in a new oil well in the swamps of the upper Siak, a muezzin calling the Bandjarmasin faithful to prayer as the sun rises over the Martapura River.

On Nias the islanders find something supernal in the great megaliths that dot the land. At Medan, dock workers from a dozen ethnic groups load coffee, tobacco, palm oil, and rubber; at Palembang they load oil and rubber. At Prapat, a Toba Batak says that ghosts walk by night in the house—now a guesthouse—where Bung Karno was once imprisoned by the Dutch. In a Djakarta restaurant, a *Peranakan* Chinese chef offers *ajam masak tuturuga,* braised chicken with coconut milk Minahasa style. At Pontianak, an official smilingly explains to an impatient Western visitor that *djam karet* means "an elastic hour." Komodo villagers, descendants of exiles, marvel that Dutch, British, Russian, and American scientists have all come to their remote little island to study its giant lizard. On Madura, a youth pampers a tawny bull which has won many races and will soon be entered in the bull-racing finals at Pamekasan. At any one of a dozen cities, a politician leans into a microphone while a crowd cheers or fidgets. At Borobudur, small groups of Buddhist pilgrims sit and contemplate the vast monument which was both built and abandoned by Indonesians, and is now restored. On the Pasar Minggu Road outside Djakarta, pedestrians jump aside as a sports convertible races past, driven by a scion of the wealthy; and back in the city, oldsters shake their heads in despair over adolescents who think they must dress, go long-haired, and generally behave like the delinquent types portrayed in movies from America. A diverse people the Indonesians, yes; but motivated in familiar ways.

Although the different islands have been differentially exposed to Malayo-Polynesian, Indian, Arabic, Chinese, and Western culture, with remarkable frequency the islanders have impressed visitors as similarly emphasizing courtesy and quietness under normal circumstances; as being similarly reserved, sensitive, understanding, tolerant, modest. The Republic's official motto, *Bhinneka Tunggal Ika*—"Unity in Diversity"—daily becomes more applicable with the spread of Bahasa Indonesia, the concomitant steep rise of the literacy rate, and the improvement of interisland communications generally, as well as the New Order's directiveness of policy and clear enunciation of aim. Of course many ethnic groups are still provincial, not yet able to expand their affection to encompass the entire nation; but all the Indonesian peoples, from Sabang to Merauke, from Lumbis to Dana, are alike in having deep affection for whatever part of the country they know and live upon.

> *Putjuk pauh delima batu*
> *Anak sembilang ditapak tangan.*
> *Sunggoh djauh negeri satu*
> *Hilang dimata dihati djangan.*

A sprout of wild mango, a ruby,
A baby catfish cupped in the hand.
From far away the native land is all one:
Lost from view, not to be lost from the heart.

# SELECTED

# REFERENCES

STUDIES ON OR IN Indonesia do not seem numerous when the country's size and complexity are taken into account. Indonesia's cultural and scientific riches have only been sampled, not mined. But in any event, the present introductory work is no place to compile more than a small fraction even of the existing literature. The references that follow include few brief journal articles, being nearly all limited to books or pamphlets. They are further limited to works in English; but it should be noted that many important studies on Indonesia have been published in the Dutch language.

## STUDIES ON SOUTHEAST
## ASIA GENERALLY

Agoncillo, T. A. et al. *The Far East and Australasia, 1970.* 2d ed. London, Europa Publications Ltd., 1971.

Albini, U., et al. (39 eds. and contributors). *The World and Its Peoples. Southeast Asia.* Vol. 1. *Malaysia, Indonesia, Philippines.* New York, Greystone Press, 1965.

Bastin, J., ed. *The Emergence of Modern Southeast Asia, 1511–1957.* Englewood Cliffs, N.J., Prentice-Hall, 1967.

Bone, Robert C. *Contemporary Southeast Asia.* New York, Random House, 1962.

Buchanan, K. *The Southeast Asian World: an Introductory Essay.* New York, Taplinger, 1967.

Cady, John F. *Thailand, Burma, Laos, and Cambodia.* Englewood Cliffs,

N.J., Prentice-Hall, 1966. [Contains material on early Indochinese kingdoms from which ancestral Indonesians emigrated.]

Clyde, P. H., and B. F. Beers. *The Far East: a History of the Western Impact and the Eastern Response: 1830–1970*. 5th ed. Englewood Cliffs, N.J., Prentice-Hall, 1971.

Crawford, J. *A Descriptive Dictionary of the Indian Islands and Adjacent Countries*. Kuala Lumpur, Oxford University Press, 1972.

Cressey, G. B. *Asia's Lands and Peoples*. 3d ed. New York, McGraw-Hill, 1963.

Dobby, E. H. G. *Southeast Asia*. London, London University Press, 1950.

*Fodor's Japan and East Asia*. New York, McKay, 1972. [A travel guide.]

Jones, P. H. M. (editor). *Golden Guide to South and East Asia*. 5th ed. Rutland, Vt., Tuttle, 1966.

Robequain, Charles. *Malaya, Indonesia, Borneo, and the Philippines*. London, Longmans, Green, 1954.

Tate, D. J. M. *The Making of Modern South-East Asia*. Vol. 1. *The European Conquest*. Kuala Lumpur, Oxford University Press, 1971.

## GENERAL ACCOUNTS OF INDONESIA

Atlantic Monthly Supplement. *Perspective of Indonesia*. New York, 1956.

Caldwell, M. *Indonesia*. Fair Lawn, N.J., Oxford University Press, 1968.

Fischer, Louis. *The Story of Indonesia*. London, Hamish Hamilton, 1959.

Grant, B. *Indonesia*. 2d ed. Zion, Ill., Melbourne University, through International Scholarly Book Service, 1968.

Hanna, Willard A. *Bung Karno's Indonesia*. Rev. ed. New York, American Universities Field Staff, 1961.

Legge, J. D. *Indonesia*. Englewood Cliffs, N.J., Prentice-Hall, 1965.

McVey, R. T., ed. *Indonesia*. Rev. ed. New Haven, Human Relations Area Files, 1967. [A major work, with minor revisions of the 1963 edition.]

Sundstrom, H. W. *Garuda: Introducing Indonesia*. Jericho, N.Y., Exposition Press, 1962.

Wallace, A. R. *The Malay Archipelago*. New York, Dover, 1962. [A reprint of the 1869 edition of this classic.]

## GEOLOGY AND BIOLOGY OF
## THE INDONESIAN REGION

Barrau, J., ed. *Plants and the Migrations of Pacific Peoples*. Symposium of the Tenth Pacific Science Congress. Honolulu, Bernice P. Bishop Museum, 1963.

Bemmelen, R. W. van. *The Geology of Indonesia*. 2 vols. The Hague, Martinus Nijhoff, 1949.

Brongersma, L. D. *The Animal World of Netherlands New Guinea*. Groningen, J. B. Wolters, 1958.

—— and G. F. Venema. *To the Mountains of the Stars*. Garden City, N.Y., Doubleday, 1963. [A readable account of the first expedition into the Star Mountains of Irian Barat.]

Fairchild, David. *Garden Islands of the Great East*. New York, Scribner's, 1943.

Honig, P., and F. Verdoorn, ed. *Science and Scientists in the Netherlands Indies*. New York, Board for the Netherlands Indies, 1945. [Also includes work in the social sciences.]

Neill, W. T. *The Geography of Life*. New York, Columbia University Press, 1969.

Richards, P. W. *The Tropical Rain Forest*. Cambridge, Cambridge University Press, 1952.

Ripley, S. D., and the editors of *Life*. *The Land and Wildlife of Tropical Asia*. New York, Time Inc., 1964.

Umbgrove, J. H. F. *Structural History of the East Indies*. Cambridge, Cambridge University Press, 1949.

## ARCHEOLOGY OF INDONESIA
## AND RELATED AREAS

Allchin, B., and R. Allchin. *The Birth of Indian Civilization*. Baltimore, Penguin, 1968.

Bernet Kempers, A. J. *Ancient Indonesian Art*. Amsterdam, C. P. J. van der Peet, 1959.

Bosch, F. D. K. *Selected Studies in Indonesian Archaeology*. The Hague, Martinus Nijhoff, 1961.

Groslier, B. *Indo-China*. Cleveland, Ohio, World Publishing Co., 1966.

Pigeau, T. G. Th. *Java in the 14th Century, a Study in Cultural History. The Nagara-Kertagama by Rakawi Prapanca of Majapahit, 1365 A. D.* 5 vols. New York, Humanities Press, 1960, 1963.

Piggott, S., ed. *The Dawn of Civilization: the First World Survey of Human Cultures in Early Times*. New York, McGraw-Hill, 1961. [Includes a chapter by Anthony Christie on early civilizations of Southeast Asia.]

Solheim, W. G. II. "Southeast Asia and the West," *Science*, Vol. 157, No. 3791, pp. 896–902. August 25, 1967.

—— "An Earlier Agricultural Revolution," *Scientific American*, April 1972, pp. 34–41.

Stutterheim, W. F. *Studies in Indonesian Archaeology*. The Hague, Martinus Nijhoff, 1956.

# SELECTED REFERENCES

## HISTORY OF INDONESIA

Bastin, John. *Native Policies of Sir Stamford Raffles in Java and Sumatra: an Economic Interpretation.* Fair Lawn, N.J., Oxford University Press, 1957.

Chatterji, B. R. *History of Indonesia, Early and Mediaeval.* 3d ed. Mystic, Conn., Lawrence Verry, 1967.

Day, Clive. *The Dutch in Java.* New York, Oxford University Press, 1966.

Forrest, T. *A Voyage to New Guinea and the Moluccas, 1774–1776.* Kuala Lumpur, Oxford University Press, 1970.

Miller, J. I. *The Spice Trade of the Roman Empire; 29 B.C. to A.D. 641.* New York, Oxford University Press, 1969.

Palmier, L. H. *Indonesia and the Dutch.* London, Oxford University Press, 1962.

Raffles, T. S. *A History of Java.* 2 vols. London, Black, Parbury, and Allen, 1817. [Also includes a description of Raffles' times in Indonesia.]

Reid, A. *The Contest for North Sumatra: Acheh, the Netherlands and Britain, 1858–1898.* Kuala Lumpur, Oxford University Press, 1970.

Schnitger, F. N. *Forgotten Kingdoms in Sumatra.* New York, Humanities Press, 1964.

Soedjatmoko. *An Approach to Indonesian History: Toward an Open Future.* Ithaca, N.Y., Cornell University, Modern Indonesia Project, Translation Series, 1960.

—— et al., eds. *Introduction to Indonesian Historiography.* Ithaca, N.Y., Cornell University Press, 1965.

Vlekke, B. H. M. *Nusantara: a History of Indonesia.* Rev. ed. Chicago, Quadrangle Press, 1960.

Zainu'Ddin, A. *A Short History of Indonesia.* New York, Praeger, 1970.

## HISTORY OF THE NETHERLANDS, INDIA, AND SOUTHEAST ASIA

Allen, R. *A Short Introduction to the History and Politics of Southeast Asia.* Fair Lawn, N.J., Oxford University Press, 1970.

Ariff, M. O. *The Philippines Claim to Sabah: Its Historical, Legal and Political Implications.* Kuala Lumpur, Oxford University Press, 1970.

Basham, A. L. *The Wonder that was India.* New York, Macmillan, 1954.

Bastin, J. and R. Roolvink. *Malayan and Indonesian Studies.* Fair Lawn, Oxford University Press, 1964.

Bingham, W., H. Conroy, and F. W. Iklé. *A History of Asia.* 2 vols. Boston, Allyn and Bacon, 1964, 1965.

# SELECTED REFERENCES

Boxer, C. R. *The Dutch Seaborne Empire, 1600–1800.* New York, Knopf, 1965.
Cohn, B. S. *India: the Social Anthropology of a Civilization.* Englewood Cliffs, N.J., Prentice-Hall, 1971.
Grattan, C. H. *The Southwest Pacific to 1900.* Ann Arbor, University of Michigan Press, 1960.
——. *The Southwest Pacific Since 1900.* Ann Arbor, University of Michigan Press, 1963.
Hall, D. G. E. *A History of South-east Asia.* London, Macmillan, 1955.
——, ed. *Historians of South East Asia.* London, Oxford University Press, 1961.
Marsden, W., ed. *The Travels of Marco Polo the Venetian.* Garden City, N.Y., Doubleday, 1948.
Penkala, M. *A Correlated History of the Far East: China, Korea, Japan.* Rutland, Vt., Tuttle, 1969. [Also includes cartographic and other material on Indonesia.]
Shaplen, H. *Time Out of Hand: Revolution and Reaction in Southeast Asia.* New York, Harper and Row, 1969.
Wilson, C. *The Dutch Republic and the Civilization of the Seventeenth Century.* New York, McGraw-Hill, 1968.

## SUKARNO, THE REVOLUTION, AND MODERN TIMES

Adams, C. *Sukarno: an Autobiography as Told to Cindy Adams.* New York, Bobbs-Merrill, 1965.
Alisjabana, T. *Indonesia: Social and Cultural Revolution.* Kuala Lumpur, Oxford University Press, 1966.
Bro, M. H. *Indonesia: Land of Challenge.* New York, Harper and Row, 1954.
Dekker, D. *Tanah Air Kita: Country and People of Indonesia.* New York, Lounz, 1951.
Douglas, S. A. *Political Socialization and Student Activism in Indonesia.* Urbana, University of Illinois Press, 1970.
Hughes, J. *Indonesian Upheaval.* New York, McKay, 1967.
Johnson, J. J., ed. *The Military in the Underdeveloped Areas.* Princeton, Princeton University Press, 1962.
Jones, H. P. *Indonesia: the Possible Dream.* New York, Harcourt Brace Jovanovich, 1971.
Kahin, G. M. *Nationalism and Revolution in Indonesia.* Ithaca, N.Y., Cornell University Press, 1952.
Kosut, H., ed. *Indonesia: the Sukarno Years.* New York, Facts on File, Interim History Series, 1967, 1970.

Kroef, J. M. van der. *Indonesia in the Modern World.* 2 vols. Bandung, Masa Baru, 1954, 1956.

Lasker, B. *Human Bondage in Southeast Asia.* Chapel Hill, University of North Carolina Press, 1950.

Lewis, R. *Indonesia: Troubled Paradise.* New York, McKay, 1962.

Mossman, J. *Rebels in Paradise: Indonesia's Civil War.* London, Jonathan Cape, 1961.

Multatuli [pseud. of E. Douwes Dekker]. *Max Havelaar: or the Coffee Auctions of the Dutch Trading Company.* London, British Book Centre, 1967. [A reprint of an influential classic.]

Nasution, A. H. *The Indonesian National Army.* Vol. 1. Crowell Collier and Macmillan, 1956.

——. *Fundamentals of Guerrilla Warfare.* New York, Praeger, 1965.

Ra'anan, U. R. I. *The U.S.S.R. Arms the Third World: Case Studies in Soviet Foreign Policy.* Cambridge, Mass., M.I.T. Press, 1969.

Sastroamidjojo, O. S. *The Indonesian Point of View.* New York, Lounz, 1963.

Shaplen, R. "A Reporter at Large: Indonesia." 3 pts. *The New Yorker,* May 17, May 24, May 31, 1969. [Good coverage of events involved with Sukarno's decline and General Suharto's emergence.]

Simon, S. W. *Broken Triangle: Peking, Djakarta, and the PKI.* Baltimore, Johns Hopkins Press, 1969.

Sjahrir. *Out of Exile.* New York, John Day Co., 1949. [This author is usually listed as Soetan Sjahrir, but *Soetan* is a title.]

Soekarno. *Toward Freedom and the Dignity of Man.* Djakarta, Department of Foreign Affairs, 1961. [This collection of speeches includes the announcement of the *Pantja Sila.*]

——. *Nationalism, Islam, and Marxism.* Ithaca, N.Y., Cornell Modern Indonesia Project, 1970.

Southall, I. *Indonesian Journey.* New York, International Publications Service, 1965.

Vittachi, T. *The Fall of Sukarno.* New York, Praeger, 1967.

Williams, M. *Five Journeys from Djakarata: Inside Sukarno's Indonesia.* New York, Morrow, 1965.

Woodman, D. *The Republic of Indonesia.* Chester Springs, Pa., Dufour, 1954.

## ETHNOLOGY OF INDONESIA
## AND NEARBY REGIONS

Bateson, G. and M. Mead. *Balinese Character: a Photographic Analysis.* New York, New York Academy of Sciences, 1942.

Belo, J. *Trance in Bali.* New York, Columbia University Press, 1960.

# SELECTED REFERENCES

——, ed. *Traditional Balinese Culture*. New York, Columbia University Press, 1970.

Cochrane, G. *Big Men and Cargo Cults*. Fair Lawn, N.J., Oxford University Press, 1970.

Covarrubias, M. *The Island of Bali*. New York, Knopf, 1956.

Cunningham, C. E. *The Postwar Migration of the Toba-Bataks to East Sumatra*. New Haven, Yale University, South East Asia Studies, 1958.

DuBois, C. *The People of Alor*. 2 vols. New York, Harper and Row, 1961.

Geertz, C. *The Social History of an Indonesian Town*. Cambridge, Mass., Massachusetts Institute of Technology, Center for International Studies, 1965.

Geertz, H. *The Javanese Family: a Study of Kinship and Socialization*. New York, Free Press, 1961.

Haar, B. Ter. *Adat Law in Indonesia*. New York, Institute for Pacific Relations, 1948.

Hanna, W. A. *The Magical-Mystical Syndrome in the Indonesian Mentality*. American Universities Field Staff, Reports Series, Southeast Asia, Vol. XV, No. 5, 1967.

Held, G. J. *The Papuas of Waropen*. The Hague, Martinus Nijhoff, 1957.

Koentjaraningrat. *Some Social-Anthropological Observations on Gotong Rojong Practices in Two Villages of Central Java*. Ithaca, Cornell University, Southeast Asia Program, 1961.

Lea, D. S. M. and P. G. Irwin. *New Guinea: the Territory and Its People*. 2d ed., Melbourne, Oxford University Press, 1972.

LeMay, R. *The Culture of South-east Asia: the Heritage of India*. New York, Humanities Press, 1954.

Matthiessen, P. *Under the Mountain Wall*. New York, Viking, 1962. [A popular account of tribal life in the Irian Barat uplands.]

Skinner, G. W., ed. *Local, Ethnic, and National Loyalties in Village Indonesia: a Symposium*. New Haven, Yale University, Southeast Asia Studies, 1959.

Snouck Hurgronje, C. *The Achehnese*. 2 vols. Leiden, E. J. Brill, 1906.

Stirling, M. W. *The Native Peoples of New Guinea*. Washington, D.C., Smithsonian Institution, War Background Studies, No. 9, 1943.

Vergouwen, J. C. *The Social Organization and Customary Law of the Toba-Batak of Northern Sumatra*. New York, Humanities Press, 1964.

Watson, J. B. *New Guinea: the Central Highlands*. Menasha, Wis., American Anthropological Association, Special Publication, Vol. 66, 1964.

Wertheim, W. F., et al., eds. *Bali: Studies in Life, Thought and Ritual*, 5. The Hague, W. van Hoeve, 1960.

Worsley, P. *The Trumpet Shall Sound: a Study of "Cargo" Cults in Melanesia*. New York, Schocken Books, 1967.

397

## SOCIOLOGICAL STUDIES ON INDONESIA

Barzine, M. Y., and S. I. Bruk. *Population of Indonesia, Malaya, and the Philippines*. Fair Lawn, N.J., Oxford University Press, 1966.

DuBois, C. *Social Forces in Southeast Asia*. Cambridge, Mass., Harvard University Press, 1959.

Jay, R. R. *Javanese Villagers: Social Relations in Rural Modjokuto*. Cambridge, Mass., M.I.T. Press, 1969.

Legge, J. D. *Central Authority and Regional Autonomy in Indonesia: A Case Study in Local Administration, 1950–60*. Ithaca, N.Y., Cornell University Press, 1961.

Liddle, R. W. *Ethnicity, Party, and National Integration: an Indonesian Case Study*. New Haven, Yale University Press, 1970.

Murdock, G. P., ed. *Social Structure in Southeast Asia*. New York, Quadrangle, Viking Fund Publications in Anthropology, 1960.

Nitissastro, W. *Population Trends in Indonesia. The Future*. Ithaca, N.Y., Cornell University Press, 1970.

Palmier, L. H. *Social Status and Power in Java*. London, Athlone Press, 1960.

Schrieke, B. *Indonesian Sociological Studies*. 2 vols. The Hague, W. van Hoeve, 1955, 1957.

Soemardjan, S. *Social Changes in Jogjakarta*. Ithaca, N.Y., Cornell University Press, 1962.

Vreede–De Stuers, C. *The Indonesian Woman: Struggles and Achievements*. The Hague, Mouton, 1960.

Wertheim, W. F. *Indonesian Society in Transition*. 2d ed. The Hague, W. van Hoeve, 1959.

## INDONESIAN POLITICS, GOVERNMENT, AND FOREIGN RELATIONS

Benda, H. J. *The Crescent and the Rising Sun: Indonesian Islam under the Japanese Occupation, 1942–1945*. The Hague, W. van Hoeve, 1958.

Bone, R. C., Jr. *The Dynamics of the Western New Guinea (Irian Barat) Problem*. Ithaca, N.Y., Cornell University, Modern Indonesia Project, Interim Report Series, 1958.

Brackman, A. C. *Communist Collapse in Indonesia*. New York, Norton, 1969.

Brecher, M. *The New States of Asia: a Political Analysis*. Fair Lawn, N.J., Oxford University Press, 1966.

Cockcroft, J. *Indonesia and Portuguese Timor*. San Francisco, Tri-Ocean, 1969.

# SELECTED REFERENCES

Dadian, L. Y. *Governmental Structures of Indonesia*. New York, Norton, 1969.

Day, C. *The Policy and the Administration of the Dutch in Java*. New York, Macmillan, 1904. [A liberal's view.]

Elsbree, W. H. *Japan's Role in Southeast Asian Nationalist Movements, 1940–45*. Cambridge, Mass., Harvard University Press, 1953.

Feith, H. and L. Castles. *Indonesian Political Thinking, 1945–1965*. Ithaca, N.Y., Cornell University Press, 1970.

Gordon, B. K. *The Dimensions of Conflict in Southeast Asia*. Englewood Cliffs, N.J., Prentice-Hall, 1966.

Kahin, G. M. *Governments and Politics of Southeast Asia*. Ithaca, N.Y., Cornell University Press, 1959.

——, ed. *Major Governments in Asia*. Ithaca, N.Y., Cornell University Press, 1958.

Mezerik, A. G., ed. *The Malaysia-Indonesia Conflict, 1965*. New York, International Review Service, 1965.

Mintz, J. *Mohammed, Marx, and Marhaen: the Roots of Indonesian Socialism*. New York, Praeger, 1965.

Pye, L. W. *Southeast Asia's Political Systems*. Englewood Cliffs, N.J., Prentice-Hall, 1967.

Taylor, A. M. *Indonesian Independence and the United Nations*. Ithaca, N.Y., Cornell University Press, 1960.

Toland, J. *The Rising Sun: the Decline and Fall of the Japanese Empire, 1936–1945*. 2 vols. New York, Random House, 1971.

Tumakaka, J. K. and others. *The Indonesian Concept of Guided Democracy, a Collection*. New York, Crowell Collier and Macmillan, 1959.

Vandenbosch, A. *The Dutch East Indies: Its Government, Problems, and Politics*. Berkeley, University of California Press, 1942.

## ECONOMICS OF INDONESIA

Allen, G. C., and A. G. Donnithorne. *Western Enterprise in Indonesia and Malaya*. New York, Macmillan, 1957.

Biro Pusat Statistik (Central Bureau of Statistics). *Statistical Pocketbook of Indonesia*. Djakarta, issued annually.

Braake, A. L. Ter. *Mining in the Netherlands Indies*. New York, Institute of Pacific Relations, Netherlands and Netherlands Indies Council, 1944.

Dewey, A. *Peasant Marketing in Java*. Glencoe, Ill., Free Press, 1962.

Furnivall, J. S. *Netherlands India: a Study of Plural Economy*. New York, Cambridge University Press, 1967. [Reprint of a 1939 work.]

Galenson, W., ed. *Labor in Developing Economies*. Berkeley, University of California Press, 1962.

Geertz, C. *Peddlers and Princes: Social Development and Economic*

*Change in Two Indonesian Towns.* Chicago, University of Chicago Press, 1963.

Higgins, B. H. *Indonesia's Economic Stabilization and Development.* New York, Institute of Pacific Relations, 1957.

—— and J. Higgins. *Indonesia: the Crisis of the Millstone.* New York, Van Nostrand Reinhold, 1963.

Johnson, R. J., M. Sadli, and Subroto, eds. *Readings in Business Administration and Economics.* Djakarta, University of Indonesia, Faculty of Economics, 1961.

Myrdal, G. *Asian Drama: an Inquiry into the Poverty of Nations.* New York, Pantheon, 1968.

Ormeling, F. J. *The Timor Problem: a Geographical Interpretation of an Underdeveloped Island.* Groningen, J. B. Wolters, 1956.

Panglaykim, J. and H. W. Arndt. *The Indonesian Economy: Facing a New Era?* Rotterdam, Rotterdam University Press, 1966.

Simkin, C. G. F. *The Traditional Trade of Asia.* Fair Lawn, N.J., Oxford University Press, 1969.

Tedjasukmana, I. *The Political Character of the Indonesian Trade Union Movement.* Ithaca, N.Y., Cornell University, Modern Indonesia Project, 1959.

Thomas, K. D. and J. Panglaykim. *Indonesian Exports: Performance and Prospects, 1950–70.* Rotterdam, Rotterdam University Press, 1967.

United States Economic Survey Team. *Indonesian Perspectives and Proposals for United States Economic Aid: Report to the President of the United States.* New Haven, Yale University, Southeast Asia Studies, 1960.

Wit, D. *Indonesian Labor: a Management Survey.* Washington, D.C., Governmental Affairs Institute, International Studies, Foreign Labor Practices Series, 1961.

Wolters, O. *Early Indonesian Commerce.* Ithaca, N.Y., Cornell University Press, 1966.

## THE CHINESE MINORITY

## OF INDONESIA

Blythe, W. *The Impact of Chinese Secret Societies in Malaya: a Historical Study.* Fair Lawn, N.J., Oxford University Press, 1969. [These societies flourish in Indonesia and many other countries.]

Cator, W. J. *The Economic Position of the Chinese in the Netherlands Indies.* Oxford, Blackwell and Mott, 1936.

Muaja, A. J. *The Chinese Problem in Indonesia.* Djakarta, New Nusantara, 1958.

Williams, L. E. *Overseas Chinese Nationalism: The Genesis of the Pan-*

*Chinese Movement in Indonesia, 1900–1916.* Glencoe, Ill., Free Press, 1960.

Willmott, D. E. *The Chinese of Semarang: a Changing Minority Community in Indonesia.* Ithaca, N.Y., Cornell University Press, 1960.

——. *The National Status of the Chinese in Indonesia.* Ithaca, N.Y., Cornell University, Modern Indonesia Project, 1961.

## AGRICULTURE AND HUSBANDRY IN THE INDONESIAN REGION

Bauer, P. T. *The Rubber Industry: a Study in Competition and Monopoly.* Cambridge, Mass., Harvard University Press, 1948.

Geertz, C. *Agricultural Involution: the Processes of Ecological Change in Indonesia.* Berkeley, University of California Press, 1963.

Grest, H. D. *Rice.* 2d ed. London, Longmans, Green, 1955.

Isaac, E. *Geography of Domestication.* Englewood Cliffs, N.J., Prentice-Hall, 1970.

Mears, L. A. *Rice Marketing in the Republic of Indonesia.* Djakarta, P. T. Pembangunan, 1961.

Pelzer, K. J. *Pioneer Settlement in the Asiatic Tropics: Studies in Land Utilization and Agricultural Colonization in Southeastern Asia.* New York, Institute of Pacific Relations and American Geographical Society, 1945.

Spencer, J. E. *Shifting Cultivation in Southeastern Asia.* Berkeley, University of California Publications in Geography, Vol. 19, 1966.

Terra, G. J. A. *Farm Systems in South-east Asia.* Netherlands Journal of Agricultural Science, Vol. 6, 1958.

## RELIGIONS IN OR AFFECTING INDONESIA

Andreae, T. *Mohammed: the Man and His Faith.* Rev. ed. New York, Barnes and Noble, 1955.

Bouquet, A. C. *Hinduism.* New York, Hutchinson University Library, 1966.

Conze, E. *Buddhism: Its Essence and Development.* New York, Harper and Row, 1959.

Eliot, C. *Hinduism and Buddhism: an Historical Sketch.* 3 vols. New York, Barnes and Noble, 1921.

Geertz, C. *The Religion of Java.* Glencoe, Ill., Free Press, 1960.

Holt, P. M., A. K. S. Lambton, and B. Lewis, eds. *The Cambridge History of Islam.* New York, Cambridge University Press, 1971.

Ions, V. *Indian Mythology.* London, Paul Hamlyn, 1967.

Landon, K. P. *Crossroads of Religion.* Chicago, University of Chicago Press, 1969.

# SELECTED REFERENCES

Morgan, K. W. *The Religion of the Hindus Interpreted by Hindus.* New York, Ronald Press, 1953.

Natsir, M. *Some Observations Concerning the Role of Islam in National and International Affairs.* Ithaca, N.Y., Cornell University, Southeast Asia Program, Data Paper No. 6, 1954.

Renou, L. *The Nature of Hinduism.* New York, Walker and Co., 1962.

Wilson, B. *Religious Sects: a Sociological Study.* New York, McGraw-Hill, 1970.

## THE REPRESENTATIONAL AND PERFORMING ARTS OF INDONESIA

Auboyer, J. and R. Goepper. *The Oriental World.* New York, McGraw-Hill, 1967. [Includes much on religious art.]

Brandon, J. R. *On Thrones of Gold: Three Javanese Shadow Plays.* Cambridge, Mass., Harvard University Press, 1967.

Crandall, R. W. et al., eds. *Encyclopedia of World Art.* 10 vols. London, McGraw-Hill, 1959–1968. [See, especially, entries by R. Heine-Geldern on Indonesian and New Guinean art and culture.]

Fraser, D., comp. *The Many Faces of Primitive Art.* Englewood Cliffs, N.J., Prentice-Hall, 1966. [Includes a chapter by R. Heine-Geldern on tribal art styles of Southeast Asia, and one by F. Speiser on art styles in the Pacific.]

Holt, C. *Dance Quest in Celebes.* Paris, Les Archives Internationales de la Dance, 1939.

*Indonesian Art.* New York, Asia Institute, 1948. [Well-illustrated catalogue of a loan exhibition from the Royal Indies Institute of Amsterdam to the Albright Art Gallery of Buffalo.]

Lentz, D. A. *The Gamelan Music of Java and Bali.* Lincoln, Nebr., University of Nebraska Press, 1968.

Ulbricht, H. *Wayang Purwa: Shadows of the Past.* Kuala Lumpur, Oxford University Press, 1970.

Wagner, F. A. *The Art of Indonesia.* New York, Crown, 1959.

Zarina, X. *Classic Dances of the Orient.* New York, Crown, 1967.

Zoete, B. de and W. Spies. *Dance and Drama in Bali.* New York, Harper and Brothers, 1939.

## LITERATURE AND LANGUAGES OF INDONESIA

Ali, A. *The Flaming Earth: Poems from Indonesia.* Karachi, Friends of the Indonesian People Society, 1949. [One of the first substantial, English-language anthologies of modern Indonesian verse.]

# SELECTED REFERENCES

Clark, S. J. and E. Siahaan. *Structure Drill in Indonesian.* Rutland, Vt., Tuttle, 1970.

Danosoegondo, P. *Bahasa Indonesia for Beginners. Book 1, Book 2.* Sydney, Sydney University Press, 1966, 1969.

Dykstra, R. R., ed., and J. C. Riedhorst, tr. *A Malay Dictionary. Malay-English, English-Malay.* "Southwest Pacific Area," Office of the Assistant Chief of Staff, G-2 (Sydney, A. H. Pettifer), 1944. [A practical work. Malayan or Indonesian dictionaries are diverse in their coverage.]

Echols, J. M., ed. *Indonesian Writing in Translation.* Ithaca, N.Y., Cornell University, Modern Indonesia Project, Translation Series, 1956. [Many of the included works suffered in translation.]

—— and H. Shadily. *Indonesian-English Dictionary.* Ithaca, N.Y., Cornell University Press, 1963.

Horne, E. *Beginning Javanese.* New Haven, Yale University Press, 1961.

——, Kustiani, and Koentjaraningrat. *Intermediate Javanese.* New Haven, Yale University Press, 1963.

Jaspan, M. *Folk Literature of South Sumatra.* Zion, Ill., Australian National University Press through International Scholarly Book Service, 1964.

Kramer, A. L. N., Sr. *Van Goor's Concise Indonesian Dictionary. English-Indonesian, Indonesian-English.* Rutland, Vt., Tuttle, 1966.

Pino, E. and T. Witterman. *Indonesian-English and English-Indonesian Dictionary.* 2 vols. 4th ed. New York, Heinman, 1966.

Raffel, B., ed. *Anthology of Modern Indonesian Poetry.* Berkeley, University of California Press, 1964.

Sarumpaet, J. P. and J. A. C. Mackie. *Introduction to Bahasa Indonesia.* New York, Melbourne University Press through Cambridge University Press, 1966.

Wigmore, L., ed. *Span: An Adventure in Asian and Australian Writing.* Melbourne, F. W. Cheshire, 1958.

Winstedt, R. A. *A History of Classical Malay Literature.* Fair Lawn, N.J., Oxford University Press, 1970.


## INDONESIAN BIBLIOGRAPHEES

Coolhaas, W. Ph. *A Critical Survey of Studies on Dutch Colonial History.* The Hague, Martinus Nijhoff, 1960.

Fürer-Haimendorf, E. von, ed. *An Anthropological Bibliography of South Asia.* 2 vols. New York, Humanities Press, 1958.

Irikura, J. K. *Southeast Asia: Selected Annotated Bibliography of Japanese Publications.* New Haven, Human Relations Area Files, 1968.

Kennedy, R. *Bibliography of Indonesian Peoples and Cultures.* New

Haven, Human Relations Area Files, 1955. [Edition revised by T. W. Maretzki and H. T. Fischer.]

Pilling, A. R. *Aborigine Culture History: A Survey of Publications 1954–1957.* Detroit, Wayne State University Press, 1962. [Contains material on New Guinea.]

Postmus, S. and others. *Nutrition Bibliography of Indonesia.* Honolulu, University of Hawaii Press, 1955.

## RECORDINGS OF INDONESIAN MUSIC
## AND SPEECH

It should be noted that album jackets, and brochures accompanying albums of Indonesian music, often contain inaccuracies in their descriptions of musical styles, selections, and instruments.

*Golden Rain; Balinese Gamelan Music, Ketjak: the Ramayana Monkey Chant.* Nonesuch, Explorer Series.

*Indonesia.* Ethnic Folkways Library. [Selections from Java, Sumatra, Bali, and Malaya.]

*Indonesian.* Cleveland, World Publishing Co. [A language manual and records.]

*Jasmine Isle: Javanese Gamelan Music.* Nonesuch, Explorer Series.

*Music for the Balinese Shadow Play: Gender Wayang from Teges Kanyinan, Pliatan, Bali.* Nonesuch, Explorer Series.

*Music from the Morning of the World: the Balinese Gamelan.* Nonesuch, Explorer Series.

*Music of Indonesia.* Folkways. [Selections from Sulawesi, Ambon, Bali, Java, and Sumatra.]

*Music of the Orient.* Decca. [Includes selections from Java and Bali.]

*World library of Folk and Primitive Music.* Vol. VII. *Music of Indonesia.* Columbia Records.

# INDEX

# INDEX

Cults, religious, 359 f.
Culture system, see Cultivation system
Currents, oceanic, 149
Cycads, 48

Daendels, Hermann, 287
Dampier, William, 2
Darjatmo, Raden Mas, 363
*Darsa Wasa*, 350
Darul Islam, 7, 333, 338, 340, 343, 346
Darwin, Charles, 168 f.
Deer family, 93
Deforestation of Indonesia, 44 ff.
Deities, Aryan, 228 f.
Dekker, E. D. (Multatuli), 292
Dekker, E. F. E. D. (Setiabudi), 297 f.
Demak, 252, 266
Denpasar, 7
Depression, Great, 307 f.
Derris, 63
Deutero-Malays, 210
Dewan Nasional, 339
Dewan Perwakilan Rakjat, 375
Dewey, Thomas E., 333
Dhani, Omar, 352, 356, 359
*Dharma*, 230
Dhole, 86
Diemen, A. van, 279 f.
Digul River, 17, 21
Dingo, 174
Diponegoro, 291
Dipterocarps, 62
Djakarta, 7, 379
Djambi Province, 6 f.
Djawa Hohokai, 319
Djojohadikusumo, S., 341
Djokjakarta, 20
Djuanda, 339 f.
Dog family, 86
Dogbane family, 58
Domestic animals, 90 ff.
Domestic plants, 53 f., 56 f., 64 ff.
Dong-son culture, 197, 216 ff.
Dravidians, 226 ff.
Drums, bronze, 217 f.
Duality, mystic, 205
Dubois, Eugène, 169 f.
Ducks, 134
*Dukun*, 356
Dulles, John Foster, 34, 341, 378
Dutch Period in Indonesia, 271 ff.
Dvipantara, 237 f.
Dwellings of New Guinea, 192 f.

Earthquakes, 29 f.
East India Company, see Vereenigde Oost-Indische Compagnie

East Java Province, 6 f.
East Kalimantan Province, 6
East Nusa Tenggara Province, 6
Eightfold Path, 234
Eijkman, Christiaan, 90 f.
Eisenhower, Dwight D., 344 f.
Edhy, General Sarwo, 353 f., 358
Elephants, 87 f.
Elapids, 122 f.
Elevations in Indonesia, 12 ff.
Endangered species of Indonesia, 124 f., 161 f.
Epiphytes, 38, 48, 52, 60
Equatorial Countercurrent, 149
Ethical Policy, 296
Expo '70, 378

Fakiran Rakjat, 309
Fatmawati, 316 f., 360
Faunal regions, 78 f.
Feminists in Indonesia, 334 ff.
Ferns of Indonesia, 48
Fertile Crescent, 226
Figs, 58, 375
Fishes, aquarium, from Indonesia 143 f.; brackish-water, 145 f. freshwater, 141 ff.
Fish poisons, see Piscicides
Flint industries, early, 170 f.
Floral regions, 47 f.
Flores, 11
Flores Sea, 8
Fly River, 17
Forced delivery system, 283
Forest: cloud, 40; monsoon, 39 f.; montane, 41; moss, 41; subalpine, 41; submontane, 41; swamp peat, 40 f.; see also Rainforest
Four Noble Truths, 234
Freberg, Bob, 328
Freedom Palace, see Istana Merdeka
Frogs of Indonesia, 137 f.
Fu-nan, 221

Gadjah Mada, 246
Gama Gama, 10
Ganesa, 88, 196
Gapi, 313
Gas, natural, in Indonesia, 23
Geckos, 117 f.
Gedeh, 27, 282
*Gender wajang*, xii
Generation of '45, 339
Generation of '66, 357
Geology of Indonesia, 8 ff.
Gerakan Wanita Indonesia, see Gerwani
Gerindo, 313, 327
Gerwani, 336 f., 351 f.

# INDEX

Plateaus of Indonesia, 13
Pleistocene Period, 58, 142, 172
Plural society, 286
Poegoeh, 300
Political parties, 312 f., 327, 344; *see also* individual entries
Polo, Marco, 1, 4, 8, 24, 248, 251
Polygyny, 336
Pool, Thomas, 283
Pope, Allen, 341
Population growth in Indonesia, 367
Ports, principal, 28
Portuguese loan-words: in English, 259 f.; in Malayan, 268 ff.
Portuguese Period in Indonesia, 4, 68 f., 258 ff.
Poso, 18
Possum family, 102
Pottery, *see* Ceramics
Prawiranegara, Sjafruddin, 341
Preanger region, 282 f.
*Prijaji,* 254
Primates, 95 ff.
Proclamation of Indonesian Independence, 321 f.
Proto-Malays, 210
Provinces of Indonesia, 5 ff.; *see also* individual entries
*Pudjangga Baru,* 315 f.
Puntjak Mandala, 14
Punjak Pass, 27
Puntjak Sukarno, 15
Puputan, battle of, 297
Putera, 313, 319
Pythons, 120 f.

Quraish, 248
Quinine, *see* Cinchona

Rachmawati, 350
Raffles, Thomas Stamford, 288 ff.
Rafflesia, 61
Rainfall in Indonesia, 30 ff.
Rainforest, tropical, 22, 37 ff.
Rajendra Choladeva I, 245
Rakata, *see* Krakatau
Ram fighting, 91
Ramie, 73
Rantekombola, 12
Ratna Sari Dewi, 352, 360
Rats, Old World, family, 98
Rattan, 51 f.
Reefs, coral, 15 f., 153 ff., 164
*Renville* agreement, 330
Republic of Indonesia, formation, 333
Republic of the United States of Indonesia, 332
Reserpine, 58
Revolutionary government, 341

Rhinoceros family, 88 f.
Riau Archipelago, 1
Riau Province, 6 f.
Rice, 56 f.
*Rigveda, see* Vedas
*Rijsttafel,* 57
*Rimba,* 40
Rindjani, 12
Rivers of Indonesia, 17 f.
Rocks: igneous, 16 f.; metamorphic, 16; sedimentary, 15 f.
Roem-Royen agreement, 332
Roman Empire, contact with Indonesia, 221 f.
*Romusha,* 312, 319
Roosevelt, Eleanor, 334
Round Table Conference, 332, 369
Rubber production in Indonesia, 25, 71 f.
Rumpf, G. E., 150 f.
Rupiah, decline of in 1960s, 346

Sabah, 3, 34, 346
Sago, 50
Sahul Shelf, 8 f.
Sailendra Dynasty, 243 f.
Sajap Kiri, 330
Salak, 282
Saleh, Chairul, 321, 339
Salim, Hadji Agus, 7, 298, 333
Salt, 24, 191 f.
*Samaveda, see* Vedas
Samosir, 10
Sandjaja, 243
Sanskrit, 228; loan-words in Malayan 240 ff.
*Santri,* 254 f.
Sarawak, 346
Sarekat Dagang Islam, 298
Sarekat Islam, 298 ff.
Sarekat Rakjat, 305
Sarinah, 297
Saritka Sari, 361
Sartono, 305
Sastroamidjojo, Ali, 305
Sato, Kenryo, 317
Schouten van Hoorn, William, 283
Scorpions, 126
Sculpture, Greek-influenced, 231
Scythians, 236
Sea-snakes, 151 f.
Sea-turtles, 162
Sects, Christian, 368 ff., 377
*Sedjara,* xi
*Sekber Golkar,* 375 f.
Selat Melaka, 222, 265 f.
Selat Sunda, 265 f.
*Semak,* 40
Semeru, 12

# INDEX

Tambora, 19
Tanah Merah, 21, 307
Tangkuban Perahu, 10, 282
Tan Malaka, 328
Tapa cloth, 58 f.
Tapir, 89 f.
Taro, 54 f.
Tasman, Abel, 283
Tea, 71
Teak, 61 f.
Tempe, 18
Temperatures in Indonesia, 26 f.
Tendean, Pierre, 351
Tengger, 10
Tentara Negara Indonesia, 363
Thailand, prehistory of, 218, 226, 239
Thamrin, Md. Husni, 309 f.
Tiger, 84
Timberline of Indonesian Mountains, 41
Timbers of Indonesia, 61 f.
Time zones of Indonesia, 2 f.
Timor, 4, 11 f.
Tin in Indonesia, 7, 23
Tjakrabirawa battallion, 352
Tjibodas, 27, 74
Tjokroaminoto, Hadji Oemar Said, 298 ff.
Toba, Lake, 10 f.
Tobacco, 68 f., 190, 270
Tojo, Premier, 317
Tomistoma, 135
*Totok*, 348
Tourism in Indonesia, 378 f.
Trade, premodern, 82 f., 107 f., 211, 222 f., 237, 250
Treaty of Tordesillas, 264
Treefrogs, 60, 138 f.
Trepang, 155
Tribal organization in New Guinea, 201 ff.
Tri Koro Darmo, 301
Trimurti, 228
*Tripitaka*, 234
Truman, Harry S, 326
Turtles of Indonesia, 134 f.
Tuwuti, 18
Typhoons, 29

United Free Papuan State, 377
United Nations, 326, 337
United Nations Committee for Indonesia, 331

Untung, 352, 356
Upanishads, 229
Utjap Mulu, 12
*Utusan Hindia,* 302

Vaishyas, 231
Vandenbosch, Johannes, 291
Vardhamana, 232
*Varna,* 230
Varuna, 229
Vaz de Torres, Luis, 284
Vedanta, 232
Vedas, 228 f.
Vereenigde Oost-Indische Compagnie, 70, 276 ff.
Viet Nam, 177, 209, 212, 216, 219, 279, 379
Village Act of 1906, 294
Vipers: pit, 116 f.; true, 116
Vishnu, 230
Volcanos, 9 f.
Volksraad, 307, 312

*Wajang kulit,* xii, 30
Wallace, Alfred Russel, 9 f., 15, 79, 128 f., 168 f., 269
Warfare, intertribal, 205 ff.
Water buffalo, *see* Kerbau
Westerling Affair, 329
Westerling, "Turko", 329
West Irian Province, 6 f.
West Java Province, 6 f.
West Kalimantan Province, 6 f.
West Nusa Tenggara Province, 6 f.
West Sumatra Province, 6 f.
Whales, 161 f.
Widjaja, 246
Wilhelm (mountain), 13
Wilhelmina (mountain), 13
Wilopo, 33 f.
Winganggan, 371
World War I, effect on Indonesia, 300
World War II: events of in Indonesia, 310 ff.; Netherlands in, 323

*Yajurveda:* see Vedas
Yamin, Muhammad, 304
Yani, General, 351
Yavadvipa, 237
Young Java, 301
Yurik, 360

Zeehandelaar, Stella, 336